The Future of Batterer Programs

The Northeastern Series on Gender, Crime, and Law
    Editor: Claire Renzetti

For a complete list of books available in this series, please visit www.upne.com

Reassessing
Evidence-
Based
Practice

The Future of
Batterer Programs

Edward W. Gondolf

Northeastern University Press | BOSTON

Northeastern University Press

An imprint of University Press of New England

www.upne.com

© 2012 Northeastern University

All rights reserved

Manufactured in the United States of America

Designed by Kathy Kimball

Typeset in Minion by Integrated Publishing Solutions

University Press of New England is a member of the Green
Press Initiative. The paper used in this book meets their
minimum requirement for recycled paper.

For permission to reproduce any of the material in this
book, contact Permissions, University Press of New
England, One Court Street, Suite 250, Lebanon NH 03766;
or visit www.upne.com

Library of Congress Cataloging-in-Publication Data

Gondolf, Edward W., 1948–

The future of batterer programs : reassessing evidence-based
practice / Edward W. Gondolf.

p. cm.—(The Northeastern series on gender, crime, and law)

Includes bibliographical references and index.

ISBN 978-1-55553-769-2 (cloth : alk. paper)—

ISBN 978-1-55553-770-8 (pbk. : alk. paper)—

ISBN 978-1-55553-771-5 (ebook)

1. Wife abuse—United States—Prevention.   2. Abusive men—
Rehabilitation—United States.   3. Victims of family violence—
Services for—United States.   I. Title.

HV6626.2.G664 2012

362.82'925250973—dc23   2011042525

5 4 3 2 1

To my parents,

with appreciation

for their loving example

and enduring support

Contents

II. The New Psychology of Batterers

III. The System Matters

Preface

A Disconcerting Appeal to Evidence-Based Practice

A woman who had been battered by her former husband recently contacted me about batterer programs. The court case against her former husband had been dismissed after he had undergone six weeks of individual therapy with a social worker. The woman was concerned about what appeared to her to be a short-term and insufficient treatment for her husband's previous violence. She also was fearful because of her husband's continued threats and harassment after he had completed treatment. For instance, when returning their child from a visit with him, the husband said, "I'm going to get you for all of this!"

The woman's husband had sought treatment from the social worker rather than participating in the established batterer program ordered by the judge. The batterer program was four to six months of weekly group sessions, following an orientation and intake meeting. Like most such programs, it included reports to the court, links to the local battered women's program, and referrals to other services as needed. The woman gave me the social worker's letter to the judge indicating the details of a different approach.

The social worker's treatment consisted of three meetings for individual assessment, the last of which included the man's current woman friend. These meetings were followed by three individual therapy sessions addressing the man's psychological issues. The letter to the judge pointed out that the social worker was employing an "evidence-based approach" substantiated by research. According to the letter, the research on conventional batterer programs suggested that the programs were not very effective, and the social worker as a licensed professional had the training to evaluate and treat the former husband effectively. The judge had taken the letter at face value and closed the case.

Claims and Counterclaims

This one case reflects what is going on through much of the country. There are claims that batterer programs are simply not effective and, furthermore, are ideologically rooted in an outmoded feminist paradigm—a perspective that sees men's acting out of a sense of entitlement or control over women as an extension of sexism in society and gendered roles in relationships. As a result, many specialized programs for domestic violence offenders are being questioned, replaced, or supplemented by alternatives. In some jurisdictions, court referrals to the established programs have dropped substantially. In others, mental health or alcohol treatment programs are dealing with the offenders. At the same time, there are counterclaims that batterer programs are making an important contribution to the work against domestic violence and are headed in the right direction. From this point of view, many of the alternatives have diverted attention to the batterers' psychological well-being and away from victim's safety.

This contention is fueled, at least in part, by the call for evidence-based practice—programs and treatment shown to be appropriate and effective in addressing the problem of concern. What has become a movement cuts across medical, psychological, and criminal justice fields and expects treatment and intervention of all sorts to be justified by research. Increasingly, referrals, funding, and certification are being tied to this sort of justification and documentation. The aim is not only to ensure that programs are efficient and effective. It is also to weed out programs that might be based on pet theories, an entrenched philosophy, isolated observations, anecdotal evidence, or a political agenda.

There is no doubt that a lot has been learned from working with batterers over the years and from the spate of research that has examined batterers and batterer programs. At face value, experimental evaluations of batterer programs suggest that they may not be very effective, compared to simply putting offenders on probation. As critics of batterer programs also note, much of the recent research points to psychological deficits in male batterers and provocations from complicit partners that warrant a different approach. However, research in the broader criminal justice field, and other approaches to program evaluation, offer support for the established batterer programs and the direction they are heading.

In sum, the future of batterer programs as we know them is unclear, thanks in part to the increasing calls for evidence-based practice. The options for programs and treatment are becoming more diverse—some might say the field is now in disarray. A more positive view might be that batterer programs are continuing to evolve along their original guidelines of safety for victims and accountability for perpetrators. There has been an increased development and use of risk assessment, efforts to better engage men, supplemental treatment and referrals, oversight with the court and probation, and case management or follow-up. These developments are likely to make conventional batterer programs more effective and may be the way forward.

In light of all of this, should the social worker's letter mentioned above have been enough for the judge? Do the social worker's claims represent the future of programming for batterers? What does the research evidence really say about established programs, as well as the alternatives being posed? And what is the role of practitioners in that "say"? To what degree might we rely on their experience and observations to sort things out?

Do Programs Work?

My own answers to these questions have been taking shape over the last several years. Admittedly they have been pushed and pulled by a variety of influences. My involvement with batterer programs since their emergence in the late 1970s, and with treatment centers for juvenile delinquents prior to that, offers a grounded perspective on the programs' operations. Additionally, my own research on batterer programs and their context over three decades has produced a vast amount of evidence to consider. The recent backlash against batterer programs, or stereotypes of them, has prompted me to reexamine all of the above.

As a result, I've found myself looking over my own and others' evidence like a detective of sorts, seeking the illusive evidence-based practice of batterer programs. Overall, I've found a much broader debate about what evidence is essential, how that evidence should be interpreted, and how it should be applied. It's a debate that extends well beyond batterer programs, but it may be more acute or complicated with regard to such programs: Batterer programs tend to be community-based rather than highly professionalized, and part of a broader system of interventions rather than free-standing treatment. Therefore, they tend to be more difficult to characterize and investigate.

What launched the reporting in this book were a few major findings from my search for answers. First, the handful of experimental evaluations suggesting that batterer programs are relatively ineffective didn't fit the results of the research that I'd been involved in over the years. Our more complex analyses revealed that the programs had at least a moderate effect, and that the program's context had an impact on the outcome. Second, I found counterevidence and qualifications both to the research being used to promote alternatives to batterer programs and to the assumptions associated with those alternatives. For instance, psychodynamic treatment or couples counseling appear to have limited application to violent offenders in general. Third, criminal justice research appears to reinforce the fundamentals of batterer intervention that the critics of batterer programs attribute primarily to feminists. For example, the research supporting cognitive-behavioral approaches with offenders in general, the effect of the accountability of drug courts, the development of risk management with violent offenders, and the widespread endorsement of coordinated responses, all lend support to the direction of established batterer programs.

The debate and confusion over batterer programs may, therefore, illustrate some of the problems associated with the growing movement toward evidence-based practice. Evidence-based practice is vital to sorting out inefficient and ineffective interventions across the criminal justice system. It is also increasingly being used to direct funds during the current financial crisis facing local and state governments. But the misuse of evidence can be disruptive and detrimental to program development. Overemphasis on tentative findings, highly selective use of studies, and quoting one or two studies to make a point can be very misleading. And the yearning for some decisive directives, especially amid disagreement and uncertainty, can push us toward an overly simple answer. In this sense, the book becomes a case study of evidence-based practice itself.

The biggest contention is over the biomedical model of evaluation represented in the gold standard of experimental designs. The difficulty in implementing these sorts of studies and interpreting them has raised questions from those who see the need for a broader perspective on treatment programs and social intervention in general. The alternative, however, is not merely less rigorous research and more descriptive arguments—or "antiscience," as some critics call it. There are ever-more-sophisticated designs, measures, and analytical approaches to program evaluation that represent programs in their contexts. This sort of research tends to focus not just on what works but also on how to improve it, in contrast to experimental evaluations that simply identify a measure of effect. Experimental designs still have an important role to play, and batterer programs need to pay more attention to the challenges that research raises—but in conjunction with the results of other research and the programs' own experience.

Response to Potential Critics

To some critics, these sorts of arguments may appear to be justification for maintaining the status quo. In the book, I do recognize essential principles forged in long-standing batterer programming and reinforced in criminal justice research and practices. I also identify the evolution of batterer programs that builds on these principles with ongoing modifications and innovations. Ultimately, I find that some well-worn ideals about intervention beg for better implementation, rather than being faulted for short-sightedness or viewed as the basis of program failure.

A further charge might be that the book is itself "anti-science" or against evidence-based practice. In fact, my aim is to apply the standards of science to the claims about batterer programming and the evidence behind those claims. A more critical look at the research shows that much of it is relatively weak by scientific standards, and that more developed research from other fields often provides further clarification. In other words, my intention in the book is to broaden the discussion of what evidence-based practice is—to push it further, not undo it. It is more accurate at this juncture to view evidence-based practice not as a decisive verdict on batterer programs, but as a continuing interchange between research from a variety of fields, perspectives, and methods, on the one hand, and practitioner experience, observation, and practicality, on the other hand.

One other clarification: the book is not meant as an unconditional endorsement of existing batterer programs or practitioners in the field of domestic violence. There are admittedly entrenched positions among them, as well as among some researchers, that warrant reexamination and revision. Most important of all is the need for more research savvy among practitioners. That of course may be difficult to develop amid the demands of everyday practice, funding cutbacks, and clients' immediate crises. However, it seems increasingly necessary in order to participate in the process of evidence-base practice and to prevent its misuse and imposition from outside the field. Certainly more could be done to make a critical review of research available to practitioners—and efforts in this area are being made through conferences, newsletters, and Internet sites. More could also be done to involve practitioners in the formulation, interpretation, and application of the needed evidence. Implicit in the book, therefore, is a call for more interaction between practitioners and researchers—and a process that grounds and broadens evidence-based practice.

The book offers an admittedly ambitious overview of batterer program issues, the controversy surrounding them, and the research associated with their effectiveness. This is perhaps its greatest strength—and its greatest weakness. It is a strength in that the book puts the question of batterer programs and their effectiveness in a much broader context and, in the process, promotes a "system perspective" of intervention. I also introduce evidence from other fields and compare studies on alternative approaches.

But the ambitious overview is a weakness because many topics necessarily receive short shrift. Full articles and books are available on any one subject, such as attachment disorder or risk assessment, each of which are summarized here in few pages. The book is also clearly not a manual that prescribes detailed procedures for choosing a particular kind of staff training or risk assessment tool. It attempts to illustrate the nature and extent of the debate over program effectiveness and pose some means to resolve, or at least chart, it. Moreover, stepping back to view the big picture does shed a different light on much of the more narrowly focused evidence. It also highlights an evolution of batterer intervention that appears to be on the right track overall.

The Future of Batterer Programs

Introduction

Where Are Batterer Programs Headed?

Batterer intervention programs are at a critical juncture. Despite their central role in addressing domestic violence over the last thirty years, their effectiveness in stopping men's violence toward and abuse of their female partners is increasingly questioned. A handful of experimental program evaluations show that participation in a batterer program has little or no effect, compared to being only on probation. The call for evidence-based practice, therefore, leaves batterer programs vulnerable to criticism and dismissal. The door has been swung open for clinical psychologists, in particular, to explore and promote a variety of other approaches to battering. Some of them claim that batterer programming in its current form needs to be augmented or replaced with a more sophisticated approach. Specifically, identifying and treating a variety of psychological issues, and even different types or categories of offenders, may be the wave of the future.

In addition, many battered women's advocates have long been suspicious of batterer programs. From their point of view, the kind of batterer program that consists of short-term weekly discussion groups is not enough to offset society's reinforcement of abuse and violence against women. Most batterers appear to be very resistant to change and, in fact, don't have sufficient reason to change. As a result, many battered women's advocates call instead for more accountability, supervision, and containment of batterers—and more protection, resources, and support services for battered women. From this point of view, the future should include heightened court oversight and more extensive probation supervision for the batterers, and additional protections and resources for battered women. Supervised child visitation and enforced protection orders are likely to help these women more than batterer programs.

The range of responses may reflect a time-honored tension in the criminal justice system between punishment and treatment. We still face this tension when dealing with drug addicts and sex offenders. Are sex offenders, for instance, sick and in need of help, or are they hardened perpetrators who need to be contained? Some current and potential victims would like them to be removed from society or at least watched intently. But clinicians would argue for confidentiality in order to build trust, engage their clients, and conduct therapy.

However, the dichotomy may be a false one given the innovation of therapeutic jurisprudence and the problem-solving courts that accompany it. There is an increasing integration of the punitive side—what is often referred to as accountability—with treatments for behavioral problems. Accountability has been the backdrop of batterer programs, leading to what some would call "coerced treatment." Most of the program participants are referred by the courts, supervised by probation officers, and subject to further sanctions for noncompliance. Similarly, drug and alcohol offenses are increasingly addressed in specialty drug courts that mix accountability and treatment. The courts refer offenders to treatment and impose further sanctions, such as jailing and fines, if the offender fails to comply with the required treatment. This is surely a stick-and-carrot approach.

Improving what has been developed over the last twenty or thirty years would seem to make the most sense, but it is not immediately clear how to proceed along these lines. Batterer programs represent an ever-expanding array of approaches, formats, and linkages. Some programs appear more like group therapy, in which men explore their psychological problems and personality issues. Others are more instructional, developing interpersonal skills or exposing beliefs and attitudes related to abuse. Some programs conduct extensive individual assessments, while others rely primarily on observations of the men in the group sessions and feedback from the men's partners.

The variations go even further. The training and experience of program staff, for instance, range from clinical psychologists with doctorates to reformed batterers. Programs may use video clips, homework assignments, visual aids, and role- playing. The ideal length for a program is itself a major issue. Courts in some jurisdictions require as little as three months of weekly sessions, while others— for instance, in California—require a year's worth of sessions for domestic violence offenders. Some programs vary in length according to the severity and history of the offender's violence, or in response to a risk assessment indicating the likelihood of more severe violence.

A Snapshot of Batterer Programs Today

The variations in program approach, session format, counselor styles, staff training, referral procedures, court oversight, participant characteristics, emerging innovations, and community collaborations all make it hard to put batterer programs in one bag. They are also very much still in progress, rather than fixed entities. Yet the prevailing batterer programs admittedly have some basic commonalities. Most of the participants are men referred by courts or probation officers to weekly group sessions that last about two hours. In each session, one or two staff members lead a discussion among six to twenty men (generally ten to fifteen) about the men's abusive behavior. Some programs are more didactic in approach, and others are more process-oriented, but most follow what might be termed a gender-based, cognitive-behavioral approach (or at least include some elements of that). In other words, the programs usually focus on exposing the thought patterns related to abuse and violence, restructuring those patterns, and developing alternative behaviors. Beliefs and attitudes associated with a distorted sense of masculinity are often explored and questioned in the process.

Increasingly, batterer programs are also assessing participants for alcohol abuse and psychological problems that may result in additional referrals to treatment in-house or through another agency. There is an increasing attention within programs to other therapeutic issues, such as past trauma, depression, and other psychological problems. Program staff members generally report compliance with program requirements to the court, and further sanctions are often imposed for noncompliance. Most programs also have some association with battered women's services, to gain the woman's point of view and help the men's partners obtain the services they need.

The Purpose and Content of the Book

The main argument of this book is that, within the trends above, a progressive evolution of batterer intervention continues that warrants acknowledgment and affirmation. The point is less to find out what works best than it is to make what we already have work better. A set of parameters is emerging that provides direction for more effective and efficient implementation. One example might be that of risk assessment. From the inception of batterer programs in the late 1970s, there has been a fundamental concern with victim safety. Battered women advocates at the time came up with their own lethality checklist, based on their observations and experience. The scaling, procedures, and administration of such checklists were underdeveloped, but the idea of identifying particularly violent men—those likely to be beyond the reach of a batterer program—persists. There is now a spate of risk assessment instruments and approaches bolstered by reliability and validity tests. But the limitations of these instruments have also heightened the need for risk management—a kind of ongoing assessment and monitoring of cases.

Do Programs Really Not Work?

What might seem an obvious assertion on the surface—that batterer programs continue to evolve—may not appear that way among individuals working in the criminal justice field or evaluating the effectiveness of such programs. The mantra of the day is that "batterer programs don't work," or don't work very well. As a result, some states are questioning batterer program standards and guidelines. Judges have reportedly cut back on referrals to batterer programs, and some funding agencies have reduced financial support. The variety of innovations and alternatives, ranging from couples counseling to brain scans, might suggest a field scrambling to find a new way—or simply in disarray.

My efforts to respond to this apparent uncertainty about batterer programs are the focus of this book. A critical review of the research from a broader perspective raises several main points. The first main point of the book is that the evidence-based practice movement of the day warrants some caution, more practitioner input, and a broader perspective. The movement has turned to experimental evaluations to help sort out and substantiate programming in many fields. Increasingly, program development and policy decisions hinge on research results. But without practitioner input and acknowledgement of study limitations, the research can easily turn into a series of misleading sound bites. There are generally qualifications and limitations of the research, and often counterevidence and different perspectives, to be weighed. The "doesn't work" sound bites alone can therefore leave programs susceptible to redirection against practitioners' intentions, and also leave courts and victims confused as to what to do. In my view, a more substantial dialogue between practitioners and researchers is essential—one that would turn evidence-based practice into an interactive process rather than what seems to some practitioners as a decree from on high.

The second point: The claim that batterer programs "don't work" is arguably based on the narrow perspective embodied in four experimental evaluations that have been conducted of batterer programs. The evaluations are compromised by shortcomings in their implementation, and their results have been overgeneralized. More complex evaluations indicate a program effect beyond the deterrence incurred by arrests and court oversight, and a perspective on batterer programs in the context of the criminal justice system brings a more meaningful interpretation to program evaluations. Further research also has demonstrated the existence of a group of batterers who warrant enhanced supervision, containment, and treatment.

The New Psychology of Batterers

Third, the book raises some cautions regarding the burgeoning "new psychology" that is being applied to batterer intervention. Much of it springs from the current catchphrase that "one size *doesn't* fit all" and that much of the violence is rooted in psychopathology or neurobiology. There may be different types of batterers based on their psychological tendencies and behavioral histories, as well as men at different stages of development and receptivity, or readiness to change. My intention here is not to debunk the possibility of helpful innovations and insights, but to point out that many of them are themselves insufficiently substantiated in terms of evidence-based practice. A recent issue of an academic journal, for instance, was devoted to the contradictory research on the readiness-to-change theory, and research in the alcohol field continues to raise questions about tailoring programming to that particular construct. At the same time, these efforts represent a greater effort to appreciate the array of problems that men bring to batterer programs and to more fully engage men in a process of change and healing—and thus reduce the programs' dropout rates.

Fourth, there is some compelling support for the idea that a substantial portion of violent perpetrators share certain characteristics—or commonalities—that are most appropriately addressed by the prevailing cognitive-behavioral approaches for men who batter. A long line of theory and research in the criminal justice field, for instance, provides evidence of the thought process of neutralization—how we justify or excuse violent behavior—and of the social reinforcement or "opportunities" for such behavior. The popularity of cognitive-behavioral approaches for many kinds of criminal offenses rests on the role of "cognitive scripts," which are the assumptions one carries about how the world works or should work. Evaluations of drug and alcohol treatments, as well as other criminal justice programs, have similarly shown that cognitive-behavioral approaches are at least as effective as, or more effective than, other approaches.

Fifth, a main challenge facing batterer intervention is the subgroup of chronically violent men who are largely unresponsive to batterer programming. Program evaluations suggest that batterer intervention contributes to the eventual cessation of violence for the vast majority of men referred to batterer programs, and the reduction of other forms of abuse over time. One size appears to fit most. At the same time, there are men who assault their partners again early in the program and do so repeatedly after the program ends. These men are the ones who give batterer programs a bad name and lead to horror stories that stigmatize batterers. Not surprisingly, these men tend to have long histories of violence and criminality, along with severe psychological and addiction problems. However, they do not fit into a category or type that can be identified from a police lineup. Doing more to identify and contain such men, as well as providing additional support and protective measures for their partners, would substantially improve outcomes.

A Coordinated Response for High-Risk Men

Sixth, a coordinated response throughout the criminal justice system is needed to develop a valid risk assessment of participants in batterer programs and ongoing case management of high-risk men—those with the potential for continuing to perpetrate severe violence after the program. In order to obtain sufficient and valid information to make such an assessment, input from a variety of sources is needed. The criminal justice system has records that identify men's criminal history, and battered women's advocates are in a position to obtain the victims' accounts of the men's behavior. Probation officers may also have information on the men's additional needs and program compliance, and batterer program staff members can offer observations of the men's behavior and reports of problems. Records from mental health or addiction treatment may also contribute to the formulation of a valid assessment. Once some determination of risk and danger is made, the same sources are needed to develop a response to the case. A variety of options may be orchestrated to bring about greater containment of the man and more protection for the woman.

A seventh and final point: One of the main challenges facing the field is how to develop and sustain the coordination among the community agencies and services in order to achieve this sort of assessment and management. More basically, how do we build linkages between batterer programs and the criminal justice system that reinforce men's compliance to a batterer program and ensure additional treatments when needed? Studies of coordinated responses suggest that they fall far short of the ideal for a variety of reasons. Although they have certainly increased the connections and communications among community services, domestic violence councils haven't wholly closed the gaps. Protocols and policies need to be monitored and revised continually, and procedural details specified and refined. Some centralized and quasi-independent authority ultimately needs to oversee the information flow and coordination among agency heads, and case managers can help to identify and resolve problems at the ground level. Ideally, a different mind-set of one unifying policy for domestic violence cases, rather than merely linked components, would be achieved.

In sum, I echo a closing assertion of my previous book, *Batterer Intervention Systems*, devoted to a multisite evaluation of batterer intervention: the system matters (Gondolf 2002a). But I go further in discussing the emerging innovations within batterer programs and their possible contribution to improving program outcomes and community safety overall. In the process, I attempt to mark the direction of the field amid vigorous debate and outright confusion. Many new ideas are being explored, which is helping to invigorate the field as well as cause conflict. In many ways the assumptions and lessons of the past offer some guideposts for the future. For instance, a coordinated community response was an ideal long before its recent sweep through the criminal justice field in general. In fact, the development of batterer programs was, at least in part, an outgrowth of victim advocates' training and working with the courts to coordinate intervention. Something other than jailing was needed for the influx of offenders that resulted from these efforts.

Reporting and Research

This book is a form of reporting as well as a review and critique of research. It's capped, admittedly, with my own efforts to make meaning of what I've observed and done. I draw on my participation in a 100 or more academic meetings and practitioner conferences devoted specifically to batterer intervention. My presentations, follow-up questions, and informal discussions with practitioners have partly shaped the overview that follows. Interestingly, there is no comprehensive survey or catalog of batterer programs and their approaches to draw on.

As a researcher, I'm the first to admit that these sorts of impressions are unsystematic and subjective, but they do help to ground the research interpretations and amplify the issues that are at the heart of the book. The more technical aspects of the research I leave to the study reports and academic reviews, striving instead for the big picture as well as a peak behind it. That is, the book considers the debates and controversies that surround the research and its interpretations, along with an overview of the mosaic of studies related to batterer intervention. There are, however, details in the later chapters that may be tedious to some, but given the claims and counterclaims being made, a thorough critique seems warranted.

The book mainly examines batterer research in light of the push for evidence-based practice throughout the criminal justice field. In the process, it exposes the impositions and misuses of evidence-based practice in social services and illustrates the potential consequences for batterer programs. The future of batterer programs may be shaped by the experimental program evaluations underlying evidence-based practice, but other research on batterer programs and related criminal justice studies suggests a different direction. The book's objective, therefore, is to promote a broader picture of batterer intervention beyond the narrow version of evidence-based practice. The prevailing biomedical model used to establish much of the so-called evidence is shown to be inadequate for the systemic nature of domestic violence intervention.

Critics of batterer programs have argued that the approaches and policies were dominated by practitioners' narrow observations, personal philosophies, and political ideologies. The policies, the critics claim, were imposed by feminist activists and battered women's advocates drawing on ideology rather than research. Many of the practitioners' assumptions, approaches, and practices admittedly warrant substantiation and documentation. But a substantial portion of practitioners argue that the pendulum has now swung too far the other way. Abstract and narrowly focused research is being used to dictate programming and policy through evidence-based practice and the recommendations that emerge from it. The result is a misrepresentation of batterer programs and increasing difficulty in getting funding and court referrals.

The reality is much more complex than either of these two views suggests. The state standards and guidelines developed in most states during the 1980s and 1990s typically include some review of the research literature that supports the current programs. That literature may have been selective or overridden by more recent studies, but several state committees at least considered a great deal of the past research in formulating standards. Much of the recent research has been developed by researchers who are familiar with practice themselves. However, there are some clear camps of researchers whose specialties, orientations, or agendas lead them to different emphases and recommendations. Consequently, there is much to sort through beyond one position or another. This book represents one such effort to do so.

The Audience

The book attempts to address a number of key questions that should concern a broad audience of researchers and practitioners: What are batterer programs like at this point? Are these programs effective? What is the best program approach? Should treatment vary for different kinds of batterers? How do we improve batterer program outcomes? What should the next big step be for intervention? As suggested above, the book offers some new and perhaps unexpected answers. In fact, each chapter addresses one of these questions in the order above. However, this book speaks most directly to researchers and policymakers. In the context of today's evidence-based practice movement, it attempts to extend the scope of the evidence and the recommendations based on it. The book also extends the critique of prevailing studies that has been slighted in their recommendations.

I hope the book will also serve as a resource for practitioners, especially directors and staff of batterer programs. It will give them an overview of the issues and debates heightened by the call for evidence-based practice. A full sense of the research landscape is needed to address the increasing questions addressed to programs. The information in the book might also assist practitioners in sorting through the diversity of approaches and innovations swirling about. In sum, the bigger picture presented here offers at least some parameters to guide a program in its development—as well as its survival.

Additionally, the book reinforces the role of the courts, probation, and other services in making batterer programs more successful and extending the impact of intervention overall. Judges, probation officers, and prosecutors, for instance, are essential in establishing the accountability that increases compliance with programs and improves outcomes. They also have a part in directing noncompliant batterers to further services and helping to contain them as needed. In a sense, they are an extension of the batterer programs, and the information in this book attempts to highlight that fact.

The book is meant, most of all, to be supportive of battered women's advocates and services that have been the driving force of the field. Specialization over the years has separated the development of batterer programs from their roots in these services. The overview here, then, should aid in assessing the batterer programs and promoting the linkages with women's services that the programs need to improve intervention. In fact, the book recommends a coordinated community response that is centered on battered women's advocacy and services. On a more basic level, the main points of the book might help women's service providers to better inform battered women of what to expect from batterer programs. The information can reinforce decisions regarding a woman's well-being and safety.

There is one additional message that book has to offer this range of practitioners. The implementation of many known fundamentals is weak in most jurisdictions—and perhaps overwrought in a few. For instance, many jurisdictions do not follow up with program dropouts. Ultimately, to improve batterer programs the system of which they are a part needs to function better. Making that happen requires the collaboration of all the players involved in intervention. The concluding chapter lays out how to get this done, as well as why it is important to do so.

To accommodate the wide range of readers who may be drawn to this book, the contents are arranged for selective reading and for reading on various levels. The chapters are written to stand alone, with pertinent material from other chapters repeated as necessary. Therefore, a reader who is drawn to one issue in particular can go directly to the chapter that addresses that topic. Also, the ending section in each chapter offers a summary of the research and issues presented in detail within that chapter. Some practitioners may choose to skip the more technical sections, such as the ones on meta-analysis and statistical modeling in chapter 2, and go to the summary section for an overview. Readers interested in more details can not only go to the heart of each chapter, but can also explore the extensive footnotes and references. In this way, the book is intended to serve as a resource for a variety of related topics and issues confronting the field—and for the diversity of researchers and practitioners working in it.

I | SORTING OUT
BATTERER PROGRAMS

1 | The Uncertain State of Batterer Programs

A Diversity of Views

The Need to Sort Out Programming

We tend to talk about batterer programs as a distinct form of intervention. The term conjures up the familiar image of men in a group talking about their problems for a few hours each week. A counselor or group leader explores with the men why they do what they do to their partners and teaches the men how to stop their hurtful behavior. The court has usually sent the men to the group—few come voluntarily—as a punishment for their domestic violence offenses. Ideally, the men finish a certain number of group sessions and stop their abuse and violent behavior. Like going to treatment for any other personal or interpersonal problem, the men appear to get treatment that addresses the underlying issues and leads to a cure. At least, that is the general impression that most members of the public have of these programs: you have a problem and you get it fixed.

There is, of course, much more to it. A closer look reveals that batterer programs vary considerably in format, duration, approach, and collaborations. As mentioned in the introduction, some require many more sessions than others; some are more didactic than oriented toward discussion; some take place in a classroom, and others in a living room; and so on. In addition, many innovations have been proposed to make the programs more effective—everything from special homework assignments to brain scans. A persistent tension between rehabilitation efforts and accountability draw some programs more in one direction or another. The greatest rumblings of the day, however, emerge from fundamental differences over treatment approach, particularly whether domestic violence should be recast as mutual combat between men and women rather than a combination of male domination and female subjection.

Batterer programs still, for the most part, employ a gender-based, cognitive-behavioral approach and rely heavily on linkages, especially with the courts and probation. The fact that programs have aspects of both treatment and education, and of both accountability and punishment, make them an unwieldy enterprise—or at least one that doesn't fit neatly into familiar service models. A lot of programs have made curriculum changes or introduced innovations to better engage participants and reduce dropout, but many of the basics persist. The question remains, however, whether the programs are effective in all of their efforts, and whether any of the program developments add to their impact. Do the programs need to go further, or in a different direction entirely?

The first half of this chapter attempts to summarize the current state of batterer programs, drawing largely on the author's involvement in practitioner and academic conferences, several research projects, and discussions with colleagues. At least a couple of program surveys help to confirm the major impressions that come from this experience (Labriola, Rempel, O'Sullivan, & Frank, 2007; Price & Rosenbaum, 2009). The result is at least a tentative picture of where we are, and what the main issues appear to be. There are some fundamental commonalities among the prevailing programs, but also some inherent tensions and outside concerns that challenge them. Amid these challenges, and the variations they bring, is what appears to be an ongoing evolution from the basic format and approach.

The latter half of the chapter considers the prospects of evidence-based practice for identifying or substantiating the way forward. It is difficult to conduct evaluations—especially the preferred experimental ones—of social programs, and also to apply the research results directly to practice. We see from the criticisms and cautions that the so-called evidence can easily be misused, although it can also be beneficial. Practitioners, therefore, need to assume a more active role in responding to the evidence and shaping the evidence-based practice movement that is upon us. Otherwise, misleading bottom lines may rule the day. The implicit evolution may also be obscured or ignored.

Perspectives from Program Directors

In recent years, I've conducted an informal survey of directors of long-standing batterer programs. The range of responses reflects some shift in program emphasis and also exposes the disparities and sense of unease about where such programs are headed. A program director for one of the first programs in the country lamented that batterer programs are likely to be subsumed by mental health clinics in the not-too-distant future. Another director saw programs diversifying their services and orientations in a way that would turn batterer programs into multiservice centers. Others have talked about the new wave of assessment and diagnosis being used to direct men to additional treatments. Another program director highlighted the expanding support of men's partners and the work done on the men's relationships, as well as their personal problems. There has also been discussion about deepening the counseling to heal the hurts from men's own trauma, economic hardships, and broken families.

Two colleagues who work primarily with African American and Latino men think the future of batterer programs lies in moving beyond the heavily punitive approach that has dominated the field. Along with others, they promote more compassionate services for the men. Batterer programs could do more to engage men—that is, help them get more involved in the process of change and desire to change. In the view of these colleagues, the heart of a batterer program is about its staff members' relationships with the men, forming a kind of partnership or "alliance," as it is called in psychotherapy circles. This comes from appreciating where the men are coming from, valuing the efforts they make to participate in the program, and respecting them as individuals. In fact, engagement is likely to result from helping men to reevaluate a life dominated by abuse, violence, and a lack of community support and opportunity. Moreover, some softening in approach may be warranted to offset the men's negative reactions to what they perceive as the heavy hand of the criminal justice system.

In contrast, other program directors, whom I respect equally, question the softening of batterer programs as a distraction from the real issues. One director in this group maintains that, in order for batterer programs to be effective, they must do more to contain domestic violence offenders. Court oversight, sanctions for noncompliance, probation supervision, and jail time for severe and repeated assaults all need to be heightened.[1] In his view, the roles of batterer programs are to educate men about the consequences of their behavior and promote community oversight of that behavior.

One leader in the field has devoted her efforts to refining protocols, procedures, and policies among components of the criminal justice system—for example, police, judges, prosecutors, victim advocates, and probation officers—in order to ensure and maximize a consistent and decisive response to domestic violence offenders. According to her, batterer programs are a part of this process. They are where men learn to take responsibility for their behavior and find ways to change it. Along these lines, another long-time director urges batterer programs to more broadly orchestrate a change of community norms and attitudes. Men in her program are helped, educated, and motivated to become agents of change, as well as positive examples to other men. The program emphasis, in this case, is more on prevention and social change than on "fixing" individual men.

A Range of Innovations

The range of innovations and considerations were evident in the smorgasbord of program sessions at a recent national conference on batterer programs. Sessions addressed issues familiar to batterer intervention historically: men's identity (authentic masculinity, male entitlement, power and control, fatherhood) and accountability (enhanced probation, court collaboration and oversight, mediation and restorative justice, child visitation supervision). There were also sessions on the long-acknowledged special issues of alcohol abuse and cultural differences. However, the vast majority of the sessions focused on psychological issues, assessment, and counseling techniques.

The psychological issues were represented in sessions on the relationship of trauma, psychopathology, neurobiology, and attachment disorders to violence, and how those problems might be identified and treated. The array of sessions on counseling techniques included engagement methods, compassionate responses, motivational interviewing, treating neurobiological conditions, individualizing curricula, promoting personal transformation, building apology skills, and preventing relapses. The assessment sessions explored differentiating batterer types: career criminals, psychopathic clients, those ready to change and high-risk offenders.

The diversity of topics reflects a growing sophistication in batterer programming, but it also suggests a diffusion of approach from the focus of the founding programs (see Aldarondo & Mederos, 2002; Caesar & Hamberger, 1989).[2] The attention is increasingly on the psychology of violent men and treatment for them. The earlier programming conformed more to an educational or didactic approach that was fundamentally cognitive and behavioral in nature. The focus of many founding programs remains on the thought patterns associated with abuse and violence, the gendered beliefs that reinforce those patterns, and the skills that help interrupt abusive behavior.

In part, the new approaches are a reaction to the "one size fits all" appearance of educational-based programming. Or are they merely an expansion of the established programming, with more attention to the compounding problems that domestic violence offenders bring with them? If so, how does the mix of ideas fit together? Are we, as one program director forecasted, moving toward a mental health model that assesses and diagnoses the men's problems and prescribes treatment for them accordingly? Or are we supplementing the core cognitive-behavioral fundamentals with additional treatments as needed?

The theme of the conference was aptly "bridging perspectives," suggesting the need to bring some unification in approach or essentials. The question remains how we should integrate, combine, and manage these various aspects of batterer programs. Do some approaches or additions compete with or counter others? Are some more essential than others? What approaches, or combination of approaches, substantially improve outcomes? Ideally, research will be able to answer such questions. In nearly all the conference sessions, the presenters appealed to various studies to support a particular approach and invoked their own observations and experience to elaborate on it. But the research on the array of topics is ultimately limited and in many cases inconclusive, as I discuss in part 2 of this book.

An Apparent Standoff

It would be helpful if there were an evidence-based model to assess all of the innovations and resolve all of the controversies. However, it is difficult to isolate the effect of one innovation opposed to another and also account for the interactive effect—or synergy—of several aspects working together. Maybe an underlying factor is at work—such as an increased effort to respond to men more fully, make them resolve to change, and hold them to that resolution. Is improving outcomes a matter of continuing what has been done in the past, only more systematically and thoroughly? Is any improvement attributable to the increased complexity of programs, and the expanded assessment and diversified treatment in them? Or is it pointing to a change of direction represented by new ideas, new emphases, and new approaches?

These sorts of questions, at the same time, are blunted by the experience of many advocates for battered women who continue to look at batterer programs with caution and even suspicion. The views of the director of one of the largest women's centers and shelters in the Southeast reflect the founding perspective of the battered women's movement and current sociocultural studies of violent behavior: "Batterers do what they do because it works. They don't have much motivation to change, because they are not really held accountable in the community at large. In their worldview, they believe that they are entitled to use violence in order to control their partners. They mostly get what they want using violence, so what is the motivation to change?" The director concludes: "These men do not see themselves as criminals. They see their behavior as justifiable for a multitude of reasons, like she was 'talking to the wrong person' or 'showed up late.'" This women's center director advocates for better protection, support, and resources for battered women, and more action from the community against abusive men: "Why don't employers fire batterers? Why don't neighbors and family members hold the man accountable?" (See Tift, 1993, for more on this perspective.)

At another extreme is a faction of clinicians and researchers who argue that our current batterer programs have failed miserably because of their initial premise, which the critics denounce as simplistic and ideological (Babcock, Canady, Graham, & Schart, 2007; D. Dutton, 2010; D. Dutton & Corvo, 2006; Hamel, 2010; Mills, 2006; Straus, 2010). They believe that a gender-based analysis of domestic violence is blind to the fact that women are as violent as men. Multiple factors underlie domestic violence, including personality disorders and couples' interactions. The response to domestic violence, therefore, needs to be lifted out of the criminal justice system and addressed primarily through psychotherapy and couples counseling, according to these critics.

Interestingly, both views—the gendered and the gender-neutral—draw little support from the current state of evaluations of batterer programs. As I elaborate in the next chapter, one faction draws heavily on the handful of experimental evaluations of conventional batterer programs that show little or no effect from attending a batterer program (Babcock, Green, Webb, & Graham, 2004; Feder & Wilson, 2005). Meanwhile, the other points out that there is little experimental research testing the recommended alternative interventions for domestic violence. As a result, we have a standoff approaching that of Republicans and Democrats in the political arena, with no apparent settlement ahead (see Muno, 2008).

The Evolution of Batterer Programs

At recent conferences of practitioners in the area of domestic violence, I've made it a point to ask the audience for a show of hands on questions about the state of batterer programs. Are the programs generally factionalized, with a diversity of approaches and settings? Are they in the midst of a major overhaul or paradigm shift? Or are they best characterized as evolving from a set of fundamentals by accommodating some innovations along the way? Audiences are consistently split across the three options I pose. It could be that there is some of each going on simultaneously, or that the extent of each varies for different communities or regions. But the consensus underneath the raised hands is that a transition is underway. Our interpretation of where programs are now is likely to shape their trajectory for the future.

The *diversification* view—that batterer programs are splintered by a variety of innovations—licenses multiple program approaches, with little standardization or core philosophy. Admittedly there is an array of program approaches, as shown in the program overviews in the volume *Programs for Men Who Batter: Intervention and Prevention Strategies in a Diverse Society*, edited by Etiony Aldarondo and Fernando Mederos (2002). As the title suggests, some programs have tailored their approach to the cultural differences of Latinos or African Americans. Others have revised their approach to better accommodate men with alcohol or psychological problems.

The concern is that unbridled diversification could cause some programs to spin off on tangents, as well as leading others to break helpful new ground. There are also signs of different factions emerging and competing within batterer intervention: those practitioners who support and promote more of a mental health model of treatment, those who put a heavy emphasis on supervision and accountability, and those who stick more to the founding gender-based, cognitive-behavioral approach.

The view that batterer programs are in the midst of a major *overhaul* has explicit implications of its own: batterer programs need to be replaced with a totally new approach. The claim is that the existing programs directed toward victim safety and perpetrator accountability are ineffective and ill-conceived. The most vocal critic, Donald Dutton, has laid out a scathing indictment in his *Rethinking Domestic Violence* (2007), and several academic articles (see, for example, D. Dutton, 2008, 2010; D. Dutton & Corvo, 2006). He denounces batterer programs for being locked in feminist ideology and unresponsive to the realities exposed by research. Batterer programs need to be freed from the criminal justice system, so the argument goes, and conform to a mental health approach that responds to the distinctive psychopathology of batterers. Those in Dutton's camp argue that batterer programs also need to take a gender-neutral approach that recognizes women as being just as violent as men, and to work with a man and his female partner together as a couple.

Although this position represents the extreme, there are certainly elements of it filtering through the field. There is increased programmatic support for women who have been violent toward their male partners; batterer programs are increasingly addressing the mental health needs of participants; and a number of programs include a substantial portion of "voluntary" participants from outside the criminal justice system. However, most of these changes are less a paradigm shift and more an accommodation of a broader clientele.

An *evolution* of batterer programs is more likely to build on founding assumptions and principles. Rather than develop tangents or replacements, innovations are being integrated into existing program approaches. We already see screening for parenting problems, mental health needs, alcohol abuse, and dangerousness that sends men to additional treatment or intensifies their work in a batterer program. There are programs that incorporate special sessions on alcohol abuse or parenting, while others refer men to supplemental treatment or special sessions devoted to those areas. This sort of evolution continues to use arrest and court oversight to direct men into, and keep them in, batterer programs; it maintains the focus on safety and accountability, and group sessions remain based largely on cognitive-behavior techniques.

Fernando Mederos writes of the evolution of batterer programs as a progressive one, broadening the approach rather than replacing it: "It is possible to integrate a deep practical commitment to accountability and victim safety with a supportive perspective that is culturally competent and multifaceted, recognizing that men encounter multiple and diverse challenges in the change process" (2002, p. 22). Admittedly this implies a less restrictive framework than suggested in some of the earlier program standards and guidelines, which prescribe curricula and procedures. It points to a more holistic approach that addresses obstacles to change such as racial discrimination, economic disadvantage, and traumatic experiences. This version of evolution also proposes a more expansive view that includes preventive and early intervention programs tailored to the community needs and culture. Batterer programming might be incorporated within fatherhood education, substance abuse treatment, and job training. In this way, knowledge about domestic violence, and how to stop it, would be conveyed beyond the confines of batterer programs.

Gender Assumptions

Male Violence against Women

An underlying set of assumptions shapes the current state of batterer programs to varying degrees. At its core is the belief that domestic violence is perpetuated primarily by men against women. The gender assumptions are, however, less predominant today than they were during the time when batterer programs began. Twenty years ago, programs were differentiating themselves from less informed mental health programs and confronting a criminal justice system still slighting reports of domestic violence (Mederos, 2002; Thorne-Finch, 1992). With cross-training from battered women's advocates and other experts, this neglect is less of an issue, albeit still a concern.

For some programs, a strict gender analysis is still very much in the forefront (see, for example, Adams & Cayouette, 2002; Pence, 2002; Sinclair, 1989, 2002). Sometimes the gender assumptions are openly discussed as "first principles" that direct practice and policy. More generally, they are in the background as a broad framework for innovations and adaptations (Mederos, 2002). Most state standards and guidelines for batterer programs begin with a list of these assumptions under the title of "philosophy," "principles," or "rationale" but tend to expand into broader practical concerns that range from assessment to court collaboration (Bennett & Piet, 1999).

The gender assumptions are familiar to most people who are in contact with the domestic violence field—in part because they were the impetus for intervention work beginning in the late 1970s. Behind the abuse is men's need for power and control—that is, getting their way and being in charge (Thorne-Finch, 1992). Beliefs about how the world should operate—at least, one's immediate world—create high expectations for one's partner. These expectations are decisively imposed on others, or cause frustration when they are not met. Men have plenty of reinforcement for these expectations, and aggression to enact them. They learn them from the examples of their fathers, their peers, and television and movie characters, as well as from watching or playing sports, and military experience. This interpretation is often referred to as a social learning or socialization model of behavior (Bandura, 1973).

A feminist analysis goes further, to point out the structural and organizational aspects of society that amount to a patriarchy in which men dominate women (Thorne-Finch, 1992). A more complex psychological tendency toward misogyny—a deep-seated hatred or disregard for the feminine—enforces this structure as well as reflects it. The "F word" (feminism, in this case), and the extent of its analysis, is uttered less in batterer programs in today's altered society. However, feminism's broader concern with social justice and focus on women's safety persists, with much substantiating sociological and gender role research. The point here is that violence against women is a social problem as well as a personal one.

The feminist movement of the late 1970s did much to expose the injustices that women faced in society and in the home, and also the shortcomings of community agencies like police, criminal courts, social services, and health care in their response to women's special challenges and problems (see Schechter, 1982). There was a need for institutional reform at the community level as well as for social change more broadly. Reflecting this viewpoint, many batterer program guidelines promote linkages with community agencies to monitor and contain men's behavior. They encourage educating the community at large about the need for and possibilities of social change. This social problem orientation is also behind guidelines that define domestic violence as more than merely a dysfunctional couple, an anger problem, a psychological disorder, or alcohol-induced behavior. The violence, according to this point of view, is fundamentally a learned behavior and ultimately a choice that can be unlearned, as social learning and rational choice theory would have it (Bandura, 1973; Cornish & Clarke, 1986; Gelles, 1983). Thus, gender-based, cognitive-behavioral techniques and approaches permeate much of the work.

Answering the Claims of Gender Neutrality

Critics from the outset have attacked this set of gendered assumptions as "ideological," "doctrinaire," and "unsubstantiated" (see, for example, D. Dutton, 2010; D. Dutton & Corvo, 2006; Straus, 2010). They draw primarily on general population surveys—especially the National Family Violence Survey, which uses the controversial Conflict Tactics Scales, to show that men and women are physically aggressive to about the same degree (Archer, 2002; Straus, Gelles, & Steinmetz, 1980; Moffitt. Caspi, Rutter, & Silva, 2001). They also point to the fact that women are increasingly arrested for domestic violence along with their male partners. The inference is that women are as violent as men, and violence is seen to be ultimately a two-way street (McNeely & Robinson-Simpson, 1987; Mills, 2006). Drawing on a variety of studies examining the factors associated with violence, the "mutual combat" proponents also point to multiple causes for domestic violence (D. Dutton & Corvo, 2006). Their emphasis is more on the immediate alcohol, mental health, and couple dynamics, rather than on male beliefs about power and control. As mentioned above, the treatment approaches should therefore include women and men together, and should particularly address the psychological and addiction problems of both partners.

Most practitioners and researchers involved in the domestic violence field are already well aware of the debate (see Muno, 2008). But suffice it to say that there is disagreement, first of all, over the methods used in the general population studies, and over different results from victimization and crime surveys (Catalano, 2007; Tjaden & Thoennes, 2000). The central concern is that the focus on tactics in Conflict Tactics Scales measurement de-contextualizes aggression and violence—it doesn't sufficiently account for the differences in strength, intent, force, and impact (Holtzworth-Munroe, 2005; Saltzman, 2004; Saunders, 2002; Schwartz, 2000). A woman's push generally doesn't equal a man's.

The scales also don't sufficiently capture the "constellation of abuse" that surrounds individual tactics or events (Dobash & Dobash, 2000). Even what appears to be mutual combat may, on closer inspection, turn out to be experienced by the woman as further intimidation and coercion (Stark, 2007). One more limitation is that the results of the general population surveys do not apply to the cases that dominate the courts and social services (Johnson, 2008). The violence in those cases tends to be more severe and extensive. In addition, men's violence outweighs women's resistance and self-defense, and coercion and control of women are more likely the result than mutual combat.

The gender-based batterer interventions are, moreover, not without theoretical and practical support from the criminal justice and related treatment fields (for a summary, see Gondolf, 2007a). The prevailing treatment approaches for violent offenders are predominantly cognitive-behavioral—that is, they focus on exposing and restructuring the underlying beliefs, expectations, and attitudes associated with the behavior of concern, in this case the offender's violence and abuse. There is also a general acceptance that much of today's interpersonal violence is often linked to an inflated sense of self that compensates for low self-esteem or even self-loathing (Baumeister, 2001; Baumeister, Smart, & Boden, 1996). Social reinforcement in gang subcultures, crime-ridden neighborhoods, or greed and expedience help to further prop up such behavior.

Safety and Accountability as Guideposts

Safety First

If there is a credo extending from the gender assumptions, it is this: male batterers should be held accountable, and their female victims should be made safe. Victim safety and perpetrator accountability are of course a fundamental principle of criminal justice in general. However, they have been reemphasized for domestic violence cases because of the history of the field. In the early 1980s, police were more likely to issue a reprimand to a batterer rather than make an arrest, courts tended to put men who were arrested on "open probation,"[3] and judges did little to sanction men who did not comply with referrals to batterer programs. Many advocates for battered women, echoing the broader victims' rights movement of the day, felt that men generally got away with domestic violence, which put women further at risk (L. Walker, 1989).

How, then, are safety and accountability to be extended through batterer programs? The concern about safety has led to the priority of interrupting and suppressing men's abuse and violent behavior. Although this seems like an obvious objective, it is not clear how best to achieve it. Most batterer programs emphasize behavioral change through an assemblage of cognitive-behavioral techniques and skills borrowed from other fields, as a batterer program survey verifies (Price & Rosenbaum, 2009).[4] The focus is on helping men avoid violent behavior, not necessarily feeling better about themselves. Many batterer programs have also maintained a relationship with battered women's services in order to get feedback about women's safety—in general and in regard to specific cases. Increasingly, programs are conducting some variation of risk assessment to more effectively respond to dangerous offenders and to intensify safety planning for the men's partners. In sum, the safety concern puts the focus on the woman's well-being rather than the man's.

The Role of Accountability

"Accountability" has become a buzzword by itself. For batterer intervention, it refers to prompting batterers to take responsibility for their behavior and ensuring that there are consequences if they don't. There is something fundamentally therapeutic in helping clients realize that their behavior is something that they initiate and ultimately can control—or at least largely influence (C. Rogers, 1992). This is particularly relevant in cases of addiction and violence, where blame, justification, and excuses often typify the client's outlook: "Such and such made me do it." First the individual must "own" the problem, in order to address it. The ownership can be empowering or motivating if it enables one to do something about one's behavior problems. If a problem is all another person's fault, there's much less that the client can do about it.

The other part of accountability is that offenders face further consequences if they fail to comply with court referral to a batterer program, or if they continue to abuse their partners or their children. Punishment in the form of increased penalties, supervision, or containment is imposed for noncompliance. The rationale for this aspect of accountability comes from the underlying notion of deterrence that permeates the criminal justice system, and the desistance theory that accompanies it (see, for example, Maruna, 2001, 2006; McNeill, 2006). Consequences alone can make certain behaviors seem too costly.

The heavy fines and loss of license, for example, aim to do that for drunk driving. Additionally, consequences can serve as a motivator to make more substantial change. When a doctor tells a man he may die from smoking, he is more inclined to seek ways to quit smoking.

In other words, treatment can be enhanced by a bit of coercion—the carrot and the stick can complement one another. Evaluations of drug courts, in particular, have reinforced this notion (D. Wilson, Mitchell, & MacKenzie, 2006). They show that treatment coupled with consequences increases the likelihood that a person will seek and continue treatment. A broader secondary effect may come from accountability, as well. The certainty of consequences also sends a message to the community at large that men can and must change—an effect that is considered to be "general deterrence."[5] It is a message that can help offset the rationalization that abuse and violence are no big deal, something that is tolerated or is a private matter. In this way, the accountability contributes to a change in social norms, as drunk-driving penalties have done with drinking.

The Inherent Tensions Facing Batterer Programs

Punishment versus Therapy

As straightforward and familiar as the above-mentioned guideposts might appear, they contribute to several tensions that permeate batterer programs. The most basic is the ongoing tension between punitive consequences for abuse and rehabilitation efforts to prevent future abuse.[6] Some programs fall on one end of the spectrum or the other, either emphasizing stricter supervision, containment, and sanctions for offenders, or pushing for expanded and more intensive treatment of the variety of ills besetting offenders. Most programs try to strike some balance between rehabilitation efforts and warranted sanctions. Finding that balance is the key. Too close a linkage with the criminal justice system may heighten participants' resistance to education and counseling, and also make it difficult for program staff to establish and maintain the rapport that facilitates change. For instance, several experts in the field urge that we pay more attention to therapeutic alliance and engagement with program participants as a means of improving outcomes (C. Murphy & Maiuro, 2008; C. Murphy & Ting, 2010). When accountability predominates, men may think that their disclosures of abuse or noncompliance with the program could lead to further consequences. As a result, they are more likely to withhold information and try to "game" the staff—that is, tell them what they want to hear (Heckert & Gondolf, 2000a).

On the other hand, since the beginning of batterer programs, many women's advocates have worried about the tendency to soothe and cajole men. In the process, programs might individualize problems in a way that diffuses responsibility and rationalizes some of the men's behavior. The "problem" becomes a man's alcohol abuse, stressors in his life, or a psychological disorder, rather than threats to the woman's safety and well-being. Of course, addressing those factors in the man's life might, in some cases, help reduce his abuse and thus result in greater safety for the woman. The debate lingers as to what degree that is so, as I will explore further in a later chapter.

These sorts of tensions are doubtless exacerbated by the professionalization of the field. Batterer programs emerged largely as a community-based service rather than a highly professionalized one. As professional psychologists and social workers have increasingly been drawn to the field, not only is more attention being paid to men's psychological and social needs, but also staff allegiance to program formats or goals has lessened. Increasingly, program staff members are bound to the ethics and standards of their own professional training and associations, and less so to directives and guidelines from battered women's advocates and domestic violence coalitions. Some staff members of more "professionalized" programs also believe that they know more about how to stop men's abuse than do advocates who deal primarily with battered women (many of whom do not have male partners in a batterer program). As some studies suggest, participants in batterer programs tend to be a different population than those who have partners who have been in women's shelters (see, for example, Gondolf, 1998b). Advocates, on the other hand, believe that some program staff members are manipulated by program participants, and unwittingly sympathize and ultimately collude with them in a way that heightens the danger for women.

Broadening Concerns

The underlying perception of domestic violence as a social problem poses an additional tension—one between social change and service delivery. To what degree can program participants be motivated to challenge other men in the community about their abuse and violence, and to what extent should a batterer program devote its time and resources to community education and social change? Some programs are heavily invested in cross-training, institutional reform, and community education, as a recent program survey documents (Price & Rosenbaum, 2009). Service delivery to batterers is still important in these programs, but more as a means to the broader goal. Other programs struggle to keep up with the demands of service delivery. Just having enough staff to cover the court referrals is all that most programs can afford. The practical concern of dealing with dropouts, participants' payments, and staff competence can be almost all-consuming. Also, the effort to maintain accountability requires some collaboration with the courts or probation offices, and with that comes another layer of resources and staffing beyond operating program sessions. In the end, service delivery usually trumps social change.

Despite the clear objective of stopping abuse, batterer programs have become a nexus for a host of other related issues as well. Inevitably, a substantial portion of the program participants have children who are affected either by witnessing their father's abuse or by being victims of it themselves. Batterer programs are increasingly developing special curricula for parenting in response to the concerns about children (Bancroft & Silverman, 2002; Edleson & Williams, 2007). Marital rape and other forms of forced sex often accompany an abusive relationship and are receiving more explicit discussion, as is sexuality in general. Then there are the persistent questions about women who are also violent toward men. Nearly every batterer program in the country regularly faces claims that "It was all her fault," "She started it," or "My wife is the one who needs to be in a batterer program, not me."

Some of these claims are exaggerations that serve as further denial or justification of the man's violence. As discussed above, some women are indeed aggressive or violent, but usually in self-defense or retaliation. As most people in the field continue to assert, it is hard to equate the woman's behavior to the man's, given the physical impact of the man's violence and the coercion that generally accompanies the cases that make it to court. Nonetheless, reckoning with the increase in dual arrests that accompany the accusations of male batterers is an issue that continues to challenge the safety and accountability guideposts. I return to this issue several times later in the book, but our focus here is on men's programs and the overwhelming majority of arrestees who are male.

The Search for Standards

Another ongoing tension lies in the effort to establish a "standard of care" similar to what we see in other treatment and service fields. In an effort to keep batterer programs focused on their fundamental objective, nearly all states (forty-five as of January 2008) have developed specific guidelines or standards for batterer programs (BISCMI, 2008). Sometimes standards or guidelines are warranted for quality control and consumer assurance, perhaps so victims know what treatment their batterers are getting, but program standards themselves have become a matter of controversy (Maiuro & Eberle, 2008). They do vary substantially. Some are extremely detailed in terms of staffing, training, curriculum, and linkages to women's services and the courts. Others present broader parameters and considerations. Some standards are tied to funding and technical assistance; compliance with others make programs eligible for referrals. Some standards are voluntary guidelines; others are mandated policies. The underlying issue is what should be included in the standards or guidelines, and who should determine and enforce them.

With diversity of programming and staffing on the rise, are current standards and guidelines too imposing, or not restrictive enough? Do they allow for too much deviation from fundamental assumptions, or have they become too doctrinaire and even authoritarian? The uncertain answers to these sorts of questions have been further muddied by the mounting suspicion that batterer programs in their current form don't work. By implication, the standards and guidelines that direct programming are also discredited; the conclusion that follows is that other approaches and formats—from couples counseling to psychiatric care—need to be tried. There is also a new-found faith that research will set the correct course, and any standards must promote evidence-based practices, as the next chapter discusses.

In the meantime, even with standards in place, competition among programs festers in some cities. One program might emphasize treatment of substance abuse along with domestic violence; another may be more psychologically oriented. Some programs may be longer and more expensive, others shorter and less costly. Domestic violence offenders are sometimes able to shop around for the best or easiest deal, and the least expensive and cumbersome program. Accountability may be undermined in the process. In response, some courts have reverted to assigning batterers to one of the available programs on a rotating basis, to the program nearest the batterer's residence, or to the program with a specialty that matches the batterer's apparent needs, such as alcohol treatment.

Inevitably program staff, particularly directors, feel some pride in their program. Staff members, of course, need to feel some confidence and belief in what they are doing. Being a true believer helps to convey enthusiasm to program participants and makes it easier to persuade them that behavioral change is possible (Frank & Frank, 1993). The downside is not only the loopholes that the competition gives batterers, but also programs' becoming highly critical of one another, less responsive to coalition building, and promoting themselves rather than listening to others. Yet there is an underlying view that some form of competition is healthy for any field—just how much and in what form are the issues. Ultimately, some sort of coordination and cooperation at all levels, as recommended throughout this book, is essential.

A Big Job, Few Resources

Batterer programs are faced with an ongoing shortage of resources needed to address the immense task they face: to undo a deeply rooted personal and social problem. On the one hand, they have difficult and often intractable participants to corral and engage. According to the multisite study I led (Gondolf, 1999a), as much as half of the men have been arrested before, a substantial portion have psychological or alcohol problems, and a third or more are likely to be underemployed or unemployed. Many of the participants are in the programs because other services and agencies, including the criminal justice system, previously failed to fully address their problems.

On the other hand, most batterer programs collaborate with a criminal justice system and other social services that have their own agendas, perspectives, and limitations. The program might want to work on community and social change efforts as well. Yet the funding for most batterer programs depends largely on participants' fees, which are meager as a result of a low-income clientele. State and local correction departments would be a logical source for further funding, but most of these potential sources are facing cutbacks themselves. And the state funds from the federal Violence Against Women Act are generally earmarked for women's services, which sorely need them.

Program directors say that it is unfair to charge batterer programs with such a difficult and vast mission without providing the required resources. The programs are then judged to be ineffective, not doing everything they aspire to, or not doing it as thoroughly as intended. There may be a self-fulfilling prophecy at work here: a long-standing suspicion of batterer programs may undermine them, intentionally or not. It is true, as suggested above, that batterer programs have been the stepchild of the battered women's movement and the services and organizations it initiated. Funds and support have been devoted primarily to the protection and well-being of battered women—a crucial objective. There is also the question, laced with the tensions discussed above, of whether batterer programs may be wandering from the guideposts of victim safety and perpetrator accountability—and therefore undeserving of additional funding from the Violence Against Women Act allocations.

In the final analysis, batterer programs do have to reconcile their extensive scope and financial limitations. Somehow most programs across the country have been able to keep going and keep developing. In the process, there is an evolution whose direction may be hard to identify precisely, but some underlying parameters do seem to be ordering and directing the general trajectory. As batterer programs were emerging in the mid-1980s, my initial book, *Men Who Batter: An Integrated Approach to Stopping Wife Abuse* (Gondolf, 1985), identified two coexisting perspectives on batterer intervention: social action and social service. These may help to further summarize the tensions and diversity that beset such programs even today.

The social action perspective reflects a broader sociological viewpoint that sees domestic violence as a social problem reinforced by societal organization, socialization, and interpersonal dynamics. Social problems like domestic violence could be explained by a variety of theories including rational choice and social learning, as mentioned in this chapter. The feminist perspective brought further insights into the place of gender roles and power dynamics in the subjection of women and violence against women in general. From a social service perspective, cognitive-behavioral techniques were also being developed to address the violence of returning Vietnam veterans and the anger and aggression of many people at the time. Batterer programs began to adopt some of those techniques to help end the violence of men coming to their programs and promote change in their individual behavior.

My impression was that these perspectives were being integrated and could complement one another in the course of group dynamics. I attempted to summarize this point: "Social services can serve as an arena where social action principles are taught and refined, as well as where hurting individuals are helped" (Gondolf, 1985, p. 11). A possible integration has been promoted since then in many textbooks for social work practice and community psychology (see, for example, Aldarondo, 2007). It is also taking place in many batterer programs today.

One director of a statewide coalition of battered women's services more recently offered a similar observation. She saw the battered women's services as juggling the mission to help, protect, and serve battered women with the need to reform institutions like the criminal justice system. The women's services also needed to train staff at other community services agencies, educate the public about domestic violence, lobby for funding and support, and sustain change in the larger society. She felt that there was a hybrid kind of social service agency being forged in the process—one that went beyond delivery of services. The services were, in fact, invigorated and heighted by the larger ideals, and the ideals were grounded and informed by the services. Perhaps batterer programs, in finding their way forward, are doing something similar. If so, this makes programs harder to categorize and evaluate in simplistic terms, even though there is an increasing demand to do just that.

The Evidence-Based Practice Movement

New Criteria for Supporting Programs

Many in the domestic violence field are looking to evidence-based practice in order to determine the future of batterer programs, or at least help sort out their direction (see, for example, Corvo, Dutton, & Chen, 2008). These days, medical treatments that are part of criminal interventions are expected to justify their approaches with outcome evaluations that demonstrate their effectiveness. New approaches are being built around scientific research that shows promise. On the surface, this emphasis on documentation makes good sense. We practitioners should be held accountable for the effectiveness of our treatments and interventions to the people they are intended to serve, and to the communities that look to them for help. Private funders, insurance companies, and the tax-paying public, as well as the individuals paying for services, want to know if their dollars are being well spent.

Moreover, evidence-based practice can help referee between diverse approaches in a field, and even resolve controversy. It adds documentation to claims girded with biases and assumptions, and cries "foul" to those programs that don't measure up. As mentioned above, some state and local policymakers are already appealing to evidence-based practice to revise batterer program standards and guidelines. Funders are also turning to the bottom line of evidence-based practice to give or cut funding to batterer programs. And courts and social services are considering evidence-based practice as a criterion for referrals to batterer programs. Without evidence of effectiveness, they are inclined to divert domestic violence offenders to open probation, mental health services, or alcohol treatment. In sum, evidence-based practice has significant implications for funding, program guidelines, and referral.

There is no doubt that we are entering an age of evidence-based practice. A quick online search of research articles from the last decade produced over 1,000 with "evidence-based practice" in the title, and another 2,000 articles have the term in their abstract or key words. President Obama has endorsed the idea in his repeated promises that science will return to policymaking, and that the government will support what works, according to science. The popularity, philosophy, or longevity of a program is no longer enough to ensure its funding or acceptance. Government program cuts are already being made under a credo of pragmatism. For instance, the state of Washington has an affiliated research center that assesses for the legislature the evidence base of social services and criminal justice programs.

The current evidence-based practice movement emerged in the 1990s in the medical field, where it had a clear mission to improve treatment and bring more consistency to practice (Gilgun, 2005). Were patients receiving the best, most current medical attention—not only for their sake, but also for the sake of the insurance companies paying for it? Physicians were obviously educated at different times and under different philosophies—and could be beholden to their own theories and, in some cases, outdated practices. They might have been exposed to different information during their practice as well, to say nothing of persuasion from manufacturers of drugs and medical devices. The introduction of evidence-based practice was a way to help standardize approaches and invigorate medical practice.

Science seeks to isolate causal relationships with greater certainty. The pertinent causal questions in the medical field are: What contributes to certain symptoms or a disease, and what treatment most effectively cures that disease? To answer such questions, we need to achieve methodological precision, control, and objectivity. The ideal way to achieve this is experimental research in which subjects are randomly assigned to various treatment options, including little or no treatment. Known as randomized clinical trials, these experimental evaluations of treatments or programs have become the gold standard for evidence-based practice (see, for example, Boruch, 1997; Boruch, Snyder, & De-Moya, 2000; Dunford, 2000a; Sherman, 2009). Such trials form the basis of the tests for new medications reviewed by the Food and Drug Administration. Used to determine which medications can be marketed in the United States, the method is relied on to keep the public safe from harmful or ineffective drug treatments.

A recent book by R. Barker Bausell, the former research director of the Complementary and Alternative Medicine Specialized Research Center (funded by the National Institutes of Health), demonstrates the importance of experimental evaluations in the medical field. According to *Snake Oil Science: The Truth about Complementary and Alternative Medicine* (Bausell, 2007), nearly one-third of Americans report relying on alternative medical treatments for their healthcare. Yet Bausell, a biostatistician, makes the case that controlled experimental research exposes the vast array of these treatments as ineffective—and not evidence-based practice. He shows how the many studies that appear to support everything from acupuncture to prayer are flawed. Not only do they employ weak research designs, but they are also naïve to validity issues.[7]

The Misuses of Evidence-Based Practice

An Implicit Hierarchy

Despite its potential contributions, evidence-based practice is meeting with some objections and controversy in a variety of fields. A host of recent academic articles in fields from healthcare to social work have pointed out misuses of evidence-based practice that may be confusing practice rather than helping it (see, for example, Gilgun, 2005; Holmes, Murray, Perron, & Rali, 2006; Mullen, Bledsoe, & Bellamy, 2008; Norcross, Beutler, & Levant, 2006; Pollio, 2006; Ramey & Grubb, 2009; Reed & Eisman, 2006; Shlonsky & Gibbs, 2004; Thyer, 2004). The main concern is that evidence-based practice is increasingly being used as a bottom line rather than as a process. That is, research findings are being reduced to a seemingly categorical statement about what works. However, the yes-no dichotomy—thumbs up or thumbs down—betrays the complexity, nuance, and qualifications of research. Any one study is part of a much broader, ongoing discourse (as researchers politely call it) among a variety of studies and findings. One, two, or even three studies do not the truth make. According to the critics of the evidence-based movement, what we have at best are some suggestions rather than a final ruling.

The more severe critics fear an autocratic hierarchy of experimental researchers dictating policy (or at least influencing it heavily) to marginalized practitioners (Holmes, Murray, Perron, & Rali, 2006; Pollio, 2006; Ramey & Grubb, 2009). Evidence-based practice has perhaps inadvertently set up a new class of research experts who issue what are supposedly more objective and reliable truths than those of practitioners immersed in day-to-day crises. In an effort to be objective, researchers may become detached so as not to overidentify with a program or policy that they are evaluating. This detachment leaves some practitioners feeling further on the outside of the research results.

Researchers become problem solvers because of their value-free science, but with an authority that sometimes exaggerates their results. "The cognitive elite become the political elite," as the sociologists Peter Berger and Hansfield Kellner (1981) complain. The authors go on to warn about the "scientification" of daily life, in which decisions are increasingly dictated on the appearance of a value-free research that is actually value-laden in its applications. According to Berger and Kellner, the narrow focus of research "fails to expose the deeper issues facing society and disrupting our lives, and ultimately to change our view or consciousness in a way that truly makes a difference" (p. 127). Our problem solving is reduced to tweaking and tinkering within the larger sociopolitical order that breeds the problems.

This is admittedly a more radical critique, but it has some relevance—particularly to the domestic violence field. The movement against domestic violence was founded on a broader intent of social change aligned with the women's movement (Lehrner & Allen, 2009; Schechter, 1982). Violence against women was seen as an extension of the patriarchal structure of society that ultimately needed to be exposed and addressed. In this view, evidence-based practice not only neglects this sort of critique, but it also helps to reinforce and perpetuate its concerns. The deeper injustices associated with domestic violence are nudged out of the analysis and end up slighted in the interventions (Tift, 1993).

The Neglect of Other Knowledge

Much has been written about the need for collaboration between researchers and practitioners, and about the contribution that practitioners can make to the research process (Edleson & Bible, 2001; Gondolf, Yllo, & Campbell, 1997; Kilpatrick Resick, & Williams, 2001; J. Campbell, Dienemann, Kub, Wurmser, & Loy, 1999; L. Williams, 2004). This contribution ranges from helping to recruit subjects to interpreting findings. At the same time, many practitioners and their programs are not "research ready"—they don't have the time or training to participate directly in the development, interpretation, and application of program evaluation. As a result, they are left out of the process by default—or at least feel left out.

Furthermore, other sources of knowledge are often excluded from the consideration of evidence-based practice. In a reputable European healthcare journal, a group of health science academics liken the evidence-based movement to "a dominant ideology that comes to exclude alternative forms of knowledge, therefore acting as a *fascist* structure" (Holmes, Murray, Perron, & Rali, 2006, p. 181). This postmodern critique may bring the accusation to its extreme. It is true, nonetheless, that the positivist preference for experimental evaluation has contributed to the dismissal of other research designs as less rigorous (see, for example, Feder & Boruch, 2000; Sherman, 2009).[8] For instance, clinical observations, action or participatory research, social constructionist analysis, feminist methodologies, and naturalistic longitudinal designs tend to be omitted from meta-analyses and research reviews of evidence-based practice (see, for example, Feder & Wilson, 2005). Yet a combination of methods is increasingly being recommended to more fully assess the complexity of interventions (Government Accountability Office, 2009; Vijayendra & Woolcock, 2003).

In some cases, nonexperimental studies can arguably preempt experimental studies that are compromised by the implementation problems so many of them encounter (Angrist, 2006; Heckman & Smith, 1995). In particular, it is often not possible in the real world to randomly assign subjects to one treatment or intervention instead of another, which is a prerequisite of experimental evaluations. In a Broward, Florida, experimental evaluation of a batterer program, defense attorneys initially objected to having their clients sent to treatment as opposed to a nontreatment control group (Feder, Jolin, Feyerherm, 2000). Battered women, judges, or probation officers overrode or changed the random assignment for a treatment placement in as much as 30 percent of the eligible cases in a Brooklyn experiment (Davis, Taylor, & Maxwell, 2000).[9] Consequently, quasi-experimental studies or qualitative formative evaluations, which include all potential subjects, may offer a better sense of the operation and usefulness of certain batterer programs, as researchers of psychotherapy, alcohol treatment, and medical procedures have argued (see Persons & Silberschatz, 1998; Gillgan, Sanson-Fisher, & Shakeshaft, 2010; Grapow, von Wattenwyl, Guller, Beyersdorf, & Zerkowski, 2006).

This swirl of criticisms and concerns about the shortcomings of evidence-based practice raise ethical concerns among the critics (Ramey & Grubb, 2009). Bottom-line interpretations of research may be misleading or incomplete and thus prematurely change or disrupt programs. The implication for the domestic violence field is that current estimates of evidence-based practice may not be enough by themselves to evaluate the effectiveness of batterer programs or to identify the best direction for their future. Yet in some places, these evaluations are already imposing consequences that may not be fully justified.

Research Findings versus the Real-World Context

Translating Research into Practice

Another issue besetting evidence-based practice is the difficulty of translating it directly into practice. A recent article from the mental health field summarizes the difficulties in applying evidence-based practice to real-life situations in clinical practice. The authors preface their list of problems in this way: "These arguments are creditably well-aired in the psychology and mental health literature" (Ramey & Grubb, 2009, p. 76). Evidence-based practice does not necessarily translate into effectiveness in clinical practice (Franklin & Hopson, 2007; Westen, Stirman, & DeRubeis, 2006), and it is not clear whether the use of manuals would improve outcomes (Addis, Cardemil, Duncan, & Miller, 2006). (Most experimental evaluations and clinical trials expect the experimental treatment to follow a manual of procedures in order to ensure the integrity of what is being tested. Clinical practice, however, tends to be much more flexible and eclectic.) Additionally, evidence-based practice has done poorly with people from nondominant cultures and minority groups in general. It has frequently been difficult to implement with special populations and has been less effective with them as well (Norcross, Beutler, & Levant, 2006; Sue, Zane, Levant, Silverstein, Brown, & Olkin, 2006).

Heather Ramey and Sarah Grubb go on to explore the underlying tension between research and clinical orientations. As mentioned above, scientific research seeks to establish a focused and parsimonious causal explanation for outcomes—and, thus, to heighten internal validity. It imposes a systematic and regimented methodology that strives for precision, control, and objectivity. Research also moves toward generalizations drawn from a variety of subjects. Clinicians, on the other hand, give priority to clients' preferences, focus on the social context as well as the individual characteristics, and respond differently to marginalized clients, including those from ethnic and racial minority groups. In sum, there are different mind-sets at work, a fact clearly stated by an audience member at a recent domestic violence conference: "Researchers don't know what the heck they are doing. Their studies just aren't relevant or real to us—let alone understandable. I see them primarily as parasites on those of us doing the frontline work."

Although this statement may appear unduly harsh, it reflects the fact that many practitioners have experienced what they consider to be counterintuitive (or just plain wrong) research results. Some past research has fed debate and controversy—and caused confusion among practitioners. The contested National Family Violence Surveys, for instance, suggested that women are as violent as men (Straus, Gelles, & Steinmetz, 1980; see also Straus, 2010); the noted Minneapolis police study of the 1980s and its replications seemed to disagree on the impacts of arrest (Sherman, 1992; Garner & Maxwell, 2000); and the experimental evaluations of batterer intervention programs indicate little or no effects, while nonexperimental evaluations reach the opposite conclusion (Gondolf, 2004a). A more recent project, a multisite evaluation of judicial oversight of domestic violence cases, produced mixed results that run counter to the experience of the practitioners involved in the study (Visher, Harrell, & Yahner, 2008).[10]

The Practitioner Perspective

Negative comments about researchers may also be influenced by practitioners' day-to-day challenges of limited resources and staffing, inconsistencies in court referral and oversight, and administrative shortcomings and limitations. Many practitioners are frustrated with what they have to endure to do their work, yet they persist in the belief that they are doing some good. They observe changes in program participants, receive positive feedback from the men's families, and experience useful impacts on other agencies and services that research too often fails to capture. In sum, these practitioners feel shortchanged.

In my research efforts with many different practitioners, I've encountered a persistent gap between research and practice perspectives. Practitioners tend to think in global terms—that is, they consider broader, multifaceted, and entangled relationships. In addition, they are sensitive to a variety of idiosyncrasies, exceptions, and contingencies among their program participants. Yet because of the need to act, they often must fit complex situations into a category. In order to get things done, program staff tend to sort the world into boxes—clients who are antisocial or depressive, receptive or unreceptive, and dangerous or not dangerous.

As a researcher, I find myself trying to focus on one or two key questions that narrow the complexity of domestic violence intervention into a manageable set of straightforward relationships: for instance, the association of offenders' prior arrests and alcohol use with their completion of a program for batterers. You might say that I start with imposed categories and move toward probabilities and generalizations. Ideally, research can expose patterns within complexity that are overlooked by practitioners. It might also show the limitations of a practitioner's categorizations—that is, sorting out clients solely on the basis of general impressions and experienced judgments.

The application of evidence-based practice is ultimately left in the hands of practitioners in their day-to-day reality (Lipsky, 1983). As suggested in articles about evidence-based practice, so-called judgment-based practice may be more the de facto rule (Pollio, 2006). That is, practitioners may be informed about the evidence-based practice established by research, but they are left to apply it as they see fit in their encounters with clients. In the process, the burden of interpretation and application is shifted overwhelmingly to the practitioners. Deliberately or not, judgment-based practice of this sort may be more the norm for reasons I elaborate below. In brief, most practitioners do what they deem to be most effective, appropriate, and feasible.

The Importance of Program Context

Program Circumstances

The most resounding criticism of evidence-based practice is its failure to sufficiently account for context—at least in its overextended application (Smyth, 2010; Smyth & Schorr, 2009). Batterer program evaluations, for instance, need to be interpreted in light of the program's relationship to the courts, linkage to other services, oversight of program dropouts, and its area's unemployment rate and other demographics—any or all of which could be influencing program outcomes (Gondolf, 2002a; Gondolf & Jones, 2001). In other words, we don't necessarily know the degree to which most evaluation results represent the effect of the program, as opposed to that of its context. As I discuss further in the next chapter, what appears as a lack of effect could be related to the high dropout rates associated with a lack of court oversight, or to the court's assigning highly difficult criminal cases into a program.

A second issue of context has to do with external validity, or the degree to which a study's results can be applied to other settings. The differences across program contexts are certainly evident in our multisite evaluation of batterer intervention (Gondolf, 1999b). Program participants in one city were subject to periodic court review and immediate sanctions for noncompliance; in another city, probation officers were responsible for bringing noncompliant participants back to court. The former approach contributed to a swift and certain response, and the latter to only occasional and long-delayed consequences. One city had an abundance of therapists available to serve as batterer program staff; another recruited primarily former educators and social workers.

Moreover, by the time most program evaluations are completed, the programs have adopted innovations, their context has shifted, and staff has changed. They are not necessarily the same programs that were studied. Program practitioners whom I have interviewed confirm that their programs are constantly evolving, adapting, and improving. The diversity of programming across the country and even within jurisdictions makes it even more difficult to apply evidence-based practice findings to a specific program. There are regional, cultural, state, and local differences surrounding the programs as well (Gondolf, 2004b). As a result, many practitioners dismiss the available program evaluations: "They just don't apply to our program."[11]

Political Influences

There is another, even broader, context that receives little explicit attention but is being mentioned in the academic debates over evidence-based practice (see, for example, Holmes, Murray, Perron, & Rali, 2006; Ramey & Grubb, 2009). Social science research is especially susceptible to political and societal trends over time. Some of this influence, of course, lies in the research dollars that flow largely from government agencies. The requirements and topics that determine what research gets funded are generally derived by a select group of experts who identify the needs of the field, coupled with public concerns pushed by various advocates and politicians. A recent example is the shifting of criminal justice funds and research from street crime to terrorism prevention in response to the 2001 attack on the Pentagon and New York's World Trade Center. Experts, politicians, and advocates pushed the new agenda forward, much as they did in the early 1990s in the case of the Violence Against Women Act.

One more relevant shift has been the turn from a strong emphasis on collaborative evaluations for domestic violence programs in the early 1990s, toward a more detached and ideally more objective research posture in the latter half of that decade. This shift is seen in the great weight placed on experimental evaluations by the turn of the century. Recently I questioned a staff member at a federal funding agency about the increased emphasis on experimental evaluations. In reply, the staff member pointed to the Government Accountability Office: "It wants to know 'what works' and, ultimately, what programming warrants financial support in the future."

Agencies that fund research, therefore, increasingly expect their funded research to be relevant, have an impact, and contribute to policy. Grant solicitations commonly ask applicants to assert practical implications along with their research findings. In order to get funding and contribute to the field, the researchers oblige. But in the process, we researchers may overstate our case, or be guided by our own agendas. Of course, we want our theories and expectations to be validated, and our science to impress our colleagues. We are trained to suspend our particular perspective and set aside our personal biases and hopes. Research colleagues with different perspectives, the peer review process in journals, and the eventual judgment of the overall scientific community provide a set of checks and balances. But competing schools of thought, tribes of interest, or outright factions do persist. Various batterer program researchers, as mentioned above, argue very forcefully for the development of engagement strategies, more accountability and oversight, or a turn toward couples or individual counseling—all based on their respective interpretation of research findings.

A concrete illustration of the potential influence of the broader political and economic context on experimental evaluations is the mounting critique of clinical trials for medications (Abramson, 2004; Angell, 2004; Chafetz, 2005). Several books, ranging from the superscientific to the polemical, have exposed the pharmaceutical companies' distortion of medication research. The most relevant here is Marcia Angell's (2004) detailed examination of the clinical trial research, too much of which has been financed by pharmaceutical companies seeking evidence that will get their drugs approved for use and distribution. In making her claims, Angell draws on her twenty-year experience as the editor in chief of the *New England Journal of Medicine*. She gives accounts of studies with negative outcomes that were suppressed, biased sampling that was encouraged, and other methodological problems that were ignored. Despite the checks and balances of scientific committees and peer reviews, research results often end up distorted.

The Impact of Context on Subject Selection

The political context of research can have an impact on more subtle aspects of research design. According to a recent article in the *American Journal of Psychiatry* (Wisniewski et al., 2009), the drug manufacturer generally gets to decide who is accepted as a subject in the study. In major clinical trials of antidepressant medication, patients with milder forms of depression have typically been excluded, which affects the results. The excluded group is less likely to respond to a placebo, making the experimental drug look less effective by comparison. Patients with chronic depression are also generally excluded. They are less likely to respond to the drug and make it look ineffective, and they are more likely to show side effects.

This inclusion-exclusion bias raises major questions about whether the research results can be generalized to most people, as well as about the detrimental impacts it may have on the most severe cases. As I will discuss in more detail below, these observations about what is called subject-inclusion criteria have been largely neglected in the evaluations of batterer programs. The evaluations tend to include the vast array of arrested offenders, ranging from those with extensive criminal records to those with no past arrests. Yet many men with criminal records have not been responsive to a variety of previous interventions and are unlikely to be responsive to batterer programming either (see Puffett & Gavin, 2004). The characteristics of the samples also vary widely depending on police, court, referral, and screening practices—and community demographics (Gondolf, 1999b). This variation alone may affect not only the outcomes but also the application of the findings, as was demonstrated in the replications of the police-arrest experiment originally done in Minneapolis (Sherman, 1992). The replications produced different results in other cities with different populations (Garner & Maxwell, 2000).

The implications of the medical evidence-based practice for the domestic violence field are admittedly not direct. Clinical trials in the medical field are much easier to implement and control. Also, the clinical trials of medications have been used to promote the use of various medications, whereas the experimental evaluations of batterer programs have been used to denounce them. The funds for the batterer program research, moreover, come primarily from government agencies that have greater checks and balances on them and wider advisory and review teams. As mentioned, some interest groups have criticized domestic violence research in general as being too influenced by battered women's advocates (see, for example, D. Dutton, 2010), while others see it as dominated by positivist social scientists (see, for example, R. Campbell & Wasco, 2000). In either case, the agendas set by agencies, and the criteria they support, have an impact on what kind of research gets done, how it is interpreted, and what gets attention.

Whose Evidence, Whose Interpretation?

Competing Interests

The fact is that most research is highly qualified and subject to interpretation, even if this is not acknowledged. The possible limitations and shortcomings span issues from sample characteristics to measurement approaches. All of the following need to be considered: the process from the selection of the research design to the implementation of that design, the unique characteristics of the sample as related to the categorical nature of the outcomes, and the variables selected for the analysis that will lead to the significance level of the coefficients. The researchers are left to weigh the results against other studies, other explanations, and other circumstances—in essence, to make a judgment call.

Years ago, a sociology textbook, *Sociology Reinterpreted* (Berger & Kellner, 1981), proclaimed that the role of the social scientist was to determine what *is*, rather than what *ought to be*. The authors were referring to what has come to be called pure versus applied science. In the later, we invoke assumptions, values, and biases, to connect the dots, so to speak. In the former, we simply present the dots. The question is, whose values are to be considered in the interpretation and application of the research? In this light, the bottom line of evidence-based practice is much more open-ended—and also subject to external politics. It is subject to the values and biases needed to apply raw findings.

On the surface, research efforts strive to depoliticize policy decisions with ostensibly unbiased—or, at least, less biased—information. Vying factions, agendas, and motives come into play in the interpretation and application of results (for a discussion of an example of this in the domestic violence field, see Dragiewicz, 2011). There is also the context of competing interests. As a recent article in the policy oriented *National Journal* reported, the domestic violence field is itself marked by two factions: what the article termed the "family conflict" proponents and the "violence against women" proponents, who draw on different studies and interpretations to support their views (Muno, 2008). Although that dichotomy may be overly simplistic, some very different interests are at work. Father's rights groups, for instance, have been influential in promoting the family-conflict orientation, while battered women's services have endorsed the violence-against-women orientation.

The Effect of Bias

A recent book on the deep divide in many policy debates in our country cites a Stanford University study to illustrate the role of biases in interpreting research: "The students were shown the same two studies: one suggested that executions have a deterrent effect that reduces subsequent murders, and the other doubted that. Whatever their stance, the students found the study that supported their position to be well-conducted and persuasive and the other one to be profoundly flawed . . . Students on each side accepted the evidence that conformed to their original views while rejecting the contrary evidence—and so afterward students on both sides were more passionate and confident than ever of their views" (quoted in Kristof, 2008, p. 1). The impact of our biases on evidence-based practice may, therefore, depend a great deal on how restrained we are from inserting our own views into the debate and how willing we are to hear the views of others.

The same book, *True Enough: Learning to Live in a Post-Fact Society*, by Farhad

Manjoo (2008), raises another issue regarding the interpretation of research. Besides selective interpretations of the same research articles, we tend to emphasize articles that support our point of view. As Manjoo illustrates, we seek out information that reinforces our prejudices. One study presented listeners with static-filled recordings of speeches that they believed were to be judged on their persuasive power. The listeners could push a button to reduce the static and make the recording easier to understand. When smokers heard a speech connecting tobacco with cancer, they didn't try to improve the recording's clarity to hear the message more fully. But they did tend to push the button for speeches espousing no link between smoking and cancer. Nonsmokers tended to do the exact opposite.

This sort of selectivity is evident among those researchers who support the view that domestic violence is predominantly perpetrated by men and those who view it as perpetrated nearly equally by men and women (see Muno, 2008). Either group can easily select from competing studies to support their views. How, then, do we sort which study is the most valid or viable? We can keep researching, weigh the limitations of the studies, broaden the context, and consider the experience of practitioners. The critics argue that the researchers themselves need to be more forthright in acknowledging the limitations of their work and alternative interpretations of it. But if they did that, they would end up stepping back from the applications and implications expected by their funders, and sought by practitioners and policymakers. The ideal may be an open dialogue and debate across perspectives rather than "talking past each other," as Ramey and Grubb (2009) interpret the situation in the mental health field. "What is lacking in the evidence-based practice and mental health literature is an open dialogue and debate with other perspectives" (p. 76).

Integrating Research and Practice

Practitioner Input

The academics writing about the misuses of evidence-based practice do not all dismiss such practice (see, for example, Mullen, Bledsoe, & Bellamy, 2008; Pollio, 2006; Shlonsky & Gibbs, 2004). They are ultimately trying to improve it. In essence, they propose changing from a top-down direction from academics to practitioners to a democratized interaction between the two groups (Pollio, 2006). Evidence-based practice was initially developed to help integrate innovations into physicians' practice (Evidence-Based Medicine Working Group, 1992; for a summary, see Gilgun, 2005). It was clearly meant to be a process, in which medical practitioners raised issues to researchers, researchers developed information, practitioners responded to what the researchers found, and new research was formulated in reply to their response. Evidence-based practice has lost much of that process as it has been extended to other fields. Although there may be, as I have suggested above, political pressures behind this shift, there are also some practical concerns. "Critical consumers" of the research are needed to activate and continue the process. Practitioners need to have the incentive, training, and opportunity to interact with and respond to researchers—to give them feedback. With the heavy workloads and crisis-driven schedules of most practitioners, this sort of research readiness is difficult to achieve and maintain.

Numerous scholars of social work have proposed—and outlined steps toward—the sort of research readiness that would enable more practitioners to be involved in the process of evidence-based practice (Gilgun, 2005; Mullen, Bledsoe, & Bellamy, 2008; Pollio, 2006). In turn, researchers also would benefit from greater "practice wisdom" in order to appreciate the outlook and experience of those affected by their research. There are a number of proposals to address this need in batterer program evaluation and research. The 2009 national conference on batterer intervention adopted the theme of bridging perspectives in order to encourage an open exchange between researchers and practitioners. An online network of practitioners is actively discussing the misuses of evidence-based practice directed at batterer programs and ways to respond. One federal agency, together with a regional nonprofit organization, convened a seminar of researchers and practitioners to frankly debate the evidence-based practice research and its application to batterer intervention (BISCMI, 2009).

Program directors and coalitions have developed workshops on addressing the limits of existing evidence-based practice research, interpreting batterer program evaluations, and presenting research to community referral sources. Finally, proposal solicitations are being developed for research to be initiated by programs, which would enable individual programs to develop their own documentation and evaluations. And federal agencies have issued proposal solicitations for long-term research-practitioner collaborations for criminal justice interventions, beyond the more superficial cooperative agreements that accompany many program evaluations and research studies.

Structural Integration

The ideal of integrating practitioner experience into program and policy decisions has precedent in much of the medical field. During my affiliation with the

Psychiatric Institute and Clinic at the University of Pittsburgh Medical Center, I encountered several structural ways of ensuring practitioner participation that served as a check on the issuing of directives based on evidence-based research alone. The center's clinical research generally involves extensive collaboration between researchers and practitioners in designing, conducting, and interpreting the studies. The resulting teams cut across disciplines, including medical researchers, biostatisticians, physicians, and nursing staff. Ideally, they also include patient advocates. Admittedly, these sorts of teams are made possible, in part, as a result of much larger grant funding than is generally made available in the criminal justice field.

In many training hospitals, consensus panels are also established for new innovations and treatments. A variety of researchers and practitioners, along with administrators and advocates, convene to discuss reviews of the research, practitioners' experience, and administrative issues. There is some wrangling to sort out what might be the best practice, based on a number of criteria. "Best practice" is increasingly used in a variety of ways that may be synonymous with "evidence-based practice." But it also suggests a systematic sorting through of researchers' and practitioners' recommendations, and an emerging consensus around certain practices. (For an example in the domestic violence field, see Beaupre, 2006.)

We also see a standard of care being developed by a variety of sources, including representatives from insurance companies that ultimately pay for the care. The standard is not necessarily evidence-based or best practice, but more often than not, it is negotiated with the stakeholders who are affected by the treatment or care. The domestic violence field has a parallel in the development of state standards and guidelines for batterer programs. Some academics argue, however, that they have relied too much on practitioners and advocates rather than on research (see, for example, Maiuro, Hagar, Lin, & Olson, 2001). Others would say that we need to weigh more critically the evaluation research already in existence. What does it really say—and not say—given the issues surrounding evidence-based practice? The next chapter reviews in detail the available evaluations of batterer programs, and what they do and do not imply for practice.

2 | The Debate about Program Effectiveness

The "Doesn't Work" Chant

The Evidence-Based Claims

If we look to current evidence-based practice for the state and direction of batterer programs, the answer might seem clear and confused at the same time. "Batterer programs don't work" has become somewhat of a chant among some researchers in the field. Numerous academic articles declare that batterer programs are ineffective, according to a handful of experimental batterer program evaluations (Babcock, Canady, Graham, & Schart, 2007; Corvo, Dutton, & Chen, 2008; D. Dutton, 2010). These evaluations show little or no treatment effect when batterer program participants are compared to those in a control group. Given the movement toward evidence-based practice and its experimental gold standard, most researchers consider these results to be a sufficient verdict.

Researchers from the Center for Court Innovation make the point as they summarize their own study on batterer intervention in New York City: "Programs using popular education and/or cognitive-behavioral models do not reduce future domestic violence—as confirmed in this and other previous experimental studies" (Labriola, 2005; see also Labriola, Rempel, & Davis, 2005). The "doesn't work" claim has been incorporated into the evidence-based practice rubric as well. An article titled "Toward Evidence-Based Practice with Domestic Violence Perpetrators" concludes: "The current best evidence clearly does not support investing substantial public funds in the continuation, let alone the mandating, of the standard domestic violence program model" (Corvo, Dutton, & Chen, 2008, p. 125). An earlier article in a popular magazine spread the word to the public, using even more emphatic language: "Batterer programs simply aren't working. They are failing . . . Domestic violence is the only field where you can fail for 25 years and wind up being considered an expert" (Raab, 2000, p. 245).

These assertions do not in themselves tell us much else about batterer programs. The experimental evaluations imply that batterer intervention, as we know it, should become extinct, or at least be replaced with another approach. But they don't answer two crucial questions: "*Why* exactly don't batterer programs appear to work?" "*Where* should the field be headed?" We are left with only cuts in funding, referrals, and support for batterer programs in scattered cities and states. Unfortunately, there are several recent examples of this.

In response to the experimental evaluation in New York City, the Deputy Chief Administrative Judge of New York State issued a memo to the courts: "Given these findings, it is worth reiterating that batterer intervention programs should not be relied upon to change offender's behavior" (Kluger, 2005, p. 1). The court referrals to batterer programs continue to decrease as a result. Batterer programs are reporting that judges are increasingly hesitant to refer domestic violence offenders to batterer programs. Some judges claim that the fees that programs charge the men are a hardship. Why should they pay if the programs aren't making a difference?

A city official in a northwestern state called me to ask for an opinion about a recent decision of his county commissioners. They were planning to cut the budgeted allocation for batterer programs because of the academic articles that asserted programs had little or no effect. Referrals to batterer programs may also be declining because of the increased availability of other options. In another example, a member of a state committee reviewing batterer program standards sent me an e-mail message to check on the committee's pending recommendation. Because there was no research supporting the effectiveness of conventional batterer programs, the revised standards would permit the courts to refer domestic violence offenders to a variety of options. These would include individual counseling, couples counseling, and mental health treatment, instead of just batterer programs. The clinicians in charge of each option would determine the length and specifics of the treatment. These impacts of the "doesn't work" view suggest the potential decline and even disappearance of conventional batterer programs in the future.

Alternatives to "Don't Work" Programs

The alternative to a program that "doesn't work" is to do something else. The immediate alternative is leaving offenders on probation without batterer programming. The drawback here is that probation supervision naturally varies substantially in intensity and in consequences for probation violations. In a study in Seattle, only about 30 percent of the men who violated probation were returned to court, and only a small portion of them received further sanctions (Babcock & Steiner, 1999). In another city, the wait to get a hearing for a violation of domestic violence probation was between three and six months (Gondolf, 1999b). Yet some cities have developed specialized supervision for batterers by probation officers with expertise in domestic violence, involving weekly check-ins instead of monthly or sporadic ones.

In any case, some battered women's advocates remain concerned that merely being on probation sends a message that men can get away with violence toward women—or at least get off easy (Stark 2007, p. 72). The other readily available option is jail time, which certainly is appropriate and even necessary for severely and chronically violent men. Jailing itself does offer a battered woman an immediate reprieve from abuse, but there are instances of harassment and threats from a jailed partner. Moreover, a few preliminary studies show that women may be at an increased risk of violence when the man is released, compared to women whose partners are sent to a batterers program (see, for example, Babcock & Steiner, 1999).

The "doesn't work" chant has also served as a launchpad for a variety of batterer program innovations. Rather than opt out of batterer programs altogether, the idea is to tweak them. A stack of academic articles start by asserting that according to "the evidence," batterer programs are ineffective, and therefore some innovation is warranted. These articles then propose an innovation based on the authors' studies of batterer characteristics and intervention techniques. The topics are familiar to most people in the field, and some are recycled from other problem areas like substance abuse: differential typologies, readiness to change, impulsivity and hostility, racial and ethnic differences, and so on. For instance, one proposal is to divide batterers into types and assign men to groups that address the issues that affect each type, such as dysphoric versus narcissistic tendencies (Holtzworth-Munroe & Meehan, 2004).

A variety of different counseling and treatment approaches have been put forth as well, including motivational interviewing, therapeutic alliance, and dialectical therapy. (These innovations are discussed in the next two chapters.) Although there is preliminary evidence that many of these innovations may have a contribution to make, there is yet no gold-standard evidence that any of them are more effective overall with batterers than current programs. Experimental evaluations of the innovations have generally not been done. The few existing ones show negligible effects or mixed results (Levesque, Driskell, & Prochaska, 2008; Murphy & Maiuro, 2008; C. Murphy & Ting, 2010).

As suggested in the opening chapter, a third alternative—and a vigorously promoted one—has been basically to scrap batterer intervention entirely and recast it as a gender-neutral problem of dysfunctional and pathological couples (D. Dutton, 1998; Corvo, Dutton, & Chen, 2008; Hamel, 2005; Mills, 2006). In other words, women are aggressive and violent and need treatment as much as men do, and underlying personality and impulse disorders are of primary concern in treating both men and women. The recommendation here is to lift batterer intervention out of the criminal justice system and into the family counseling and mental health arenas. The faction promoting this approach draws primarily on surveys of couples' conflict in society at large, in contrast to the research with so-called clinical samples behind the innovations mentioned above. Those surveys with the Conflict Tactics Scales have repeatedly indicated aggressive and violent tactics are used by women at nearly the same rate as by men (see Straus, 2010). The survey results have been replicated across countries and age groups, including in a recent international study of college students (Straus, 2004).

There is a rationale for some sort of criminal justice intervention that focuses primarily on men's violence against women. It goes beyond ideology or philosophy but is grounded in intervention research that appears to support gender asymmetry, especially in court-related samples. A couple of contributions, however, do emerge from the gender-symmetry claims. One is the recommendation for expanded attention to women who resort to physical force, and the development of programs, protocols, and curricula to help them change their behavior (Hamberger & Potente, 1994; Larance, 2006; S. Miller & Meloy, 2006; Swan & Snow, 2006). The reasons for working with women separately from their partners rather than in mixed groups or couples counseling are enumerated in the next chapter, along with the implications of another proposal from the gender-symmetry proponents. The results of research examining the psychological issues of violent men are reflected in some of the innovations for batterer programs mentioned above.

A more critical review of the program evaluations and considerations of alternative approaches opens the door on a different view: one that recognizes the contributions of batterer programs and supports their evolution. As I discuss in this chapter, the few experimental evaluations of batterer programs are compromised by several methodological, conceptual, and implementation problems. Statistical modeling with nonexperimental data, moreover, indicates that batterer programs have at least a modest effect. Broader reviews of the research recommend supplements to resolve the programs' problems and systemwide coordination, rather than undoing or replacing the programs. Finally, practitioners are increasingly questioning the interpretation and application of available program evaluations and pressing for a fuller discussion of research findings and research tailored to program realities.

Experimental Evaluations

Experiments as the Gold Standard

At the heart of the debate over the effectiveness of batterer programs is a series of experimental evaluations that have drawn a great deal of attention. In 1996, the National Academy of Sciences concluded in *Understanding Violence against Women* that "randomized, controlled outcome studies are needed to identify the program and community features that account for the effectiveness of legal or social service interventions with various groups of offenders" (Crowell & Burgess, 1996, p.140). Articles in a special 2000 issue of the prominent journal *Crime and Delinquency* promoted experimental evaluations as essential for policy decisions in the criminal justice field in general, dismissing most other evaluations as not sufficiently rigorous science (Boruch, Snyder, & DeMoya, 2000; Dunford, 2000a). Specifically, the outcomes of quasi-experiments comparing batterer program completers with program dropouts (or offenders not required to participate in the program) were likely to be influenced by the variation in characteristics across the comparison samples.[1] Random assignment was the most certain way of achieving comparable samples and getting a result that could be attributed to the treatment.

These endorsements, along with a demand to resolve the long-standing concerns about the effectiveness and usefulness of batterer programs, contributed to the federal funding of several experimental evaluations of batterer programs. The four most recent and cited experimental evaluations have produced, at face value, rather discouraging results (Davis, Taylor, & Maxwell, 2000; Feder & Dugan, 2002; Dunford, 2000a; Labriola, Rempel, & Davis, 2008).[2] According to those studies, abusive men randomly assigned to a batterer program have outcomes similar to men in a control group receiving no batterer program treatment. But the results are actually more nuanced than that. For instance, one study found a small but significant improvement in subsequent arrests (Davis, Taylor, & Maxwell, 2000), and one meta-analysis of program evaluations identified a small but significant effect overall (Babcock, Green, & Robie, 2004). But there was apparently no more than a negligible effect on subsequent assaults based on women's reports, despite the low response rates (Feder & Wilson, 2005).

Experiments face an array of implementation challenges in the criminal justice system. There is widespread concern about sample override (when a judge or victim's advocate changes the random assignment) and attrition (when the subjects disregard their assignment or drop out of a program). Other problems include the effects of subgroups, insufficient treatment monitoring, compensating treatments in the control group, intention-to-treat versus treatment-received effects, simplistic outcome measures, and low or biased follow-up response, according to domestic violence researchers (Dobash & Dobash, 2000; Mears, 2003; Gondolf, 2001; Saunders, 2008) and evaluators in the criminal justice field in general (Cordray, 2000; Goldkamp, 2008; Berk, 2005; Weisburd, Lum, & Yang, 2003). Although researchers promote efforts to negotiate the array of challenges facing criminal justice experiments (see, for example, Berk, 2005; Cissner & Farole, 2009; Davis & Taylor, 1999), even the experts acknowledge that experimental designs too often end up being the "bronze standard" rather than the gold (Berk, 2005, p. 416).

The fundamental contributor to this "bronzing" is the difficulty of achieving a random assignment given subjects who opt out of a study, practitioners who override assignments, and agencies that directly oppose or undermine assignments (Berk, 2005; Dobash & Dobash, 2000; Goldkamp, 2008; Hollin, 2008). Consequently, it is important to weigh these issues in assessing the handful of experimental evaluations of batterer programs. As several researchers reviewing these evaluations have pointed out, the bottom line of these experiments needs to be qualified. I would add that they also need to be augmented with findings from alternative approaches, especially statistical modeling of treatment actually received (Aldarondo, 2002, 2010; Gondolf, 2001; C. Murphy & Ting, 2010; Saunders, 2008).

The Groundbreaking Batterer Program Experiments

The San Diego Navy Experiment (Dunford, 2000b) might be considered the most controlled and extensive of the available batterer program experiments. The military setting enabled the successful recruitment of a large sample of domestic violence cases ($N = 861$) and a high response rate from the victims (75 percent throughout the follow-up period). Furthermore, the study served more as a clinical trial in comparing a newly established batterer treatment to several other options besides a nontreatment control group: a couples counseling group and intensive monitoring of the offender with no other treatment provided. The trade-off here was between the successful implementation of the experimental conditions (what is often referred to as experimental integrity) and the ability to generalize findings to the civilian population. In the world at large, the high degree of oversight, sanctions, and directives to the subjects are not possible. Not only were military officers able to monitor their soldiers' behavior every day, but the military could also impose severe sanctions. It could end a man's employment and all the benefits that included, such as housing, discounts for food, income, and status. This sort of leverage simply does not exist in a civilian community.

Two other evaluations, funded by the National Institute of Justice (NIJ), were conducted at about the same time in Brooklyn, New York, and Broward County, Florida. These have received substantial attention, in part because they were in familiar community settings with established batterer programs. They have also been highlighted in special NIJ reports, distributed to court personnel and practitioners online and through direct mailings (see, for example, Jackson, Feder, Forde, Davis, Maxwell, & Taylor, 2003). The Brooklyn Experiment (Davis, Taylor, & Maxwell, 2000) used random assignment to forty hours of batterer programming over twenty-six weeks as the treatment ($n = 129$) and forty hours of community service as the control group ($n = 186$) for men convicted of misdemeanor offenses against an intimate partner. Later in the study, the researchers had to switch the assignments to either an eight-week intensive program ($n = 61$), or an equivalent amount of time doing community service, such as clearing vacant lots or painting senior citizen centers.

The Broward Experiment (Feder & Dugan, 2002) included convicted batterers who were randomly assigned to a probation-only control group or to both probation and a six-month court-mandated psycho-education program for batterers that lasted twenty-six weeks ($N = 404$). In this and the previous study, the researchers conducted follow-up interviews with the men's female partners six and twelve months after sentencing, and men's attitudes were also measured on a self-administered scale. Probation and arrest records were used to supplement the low response rate of the women (30 percent at six months). They became the primary evidence of the study's outcome.

A more recent experiment in domestic violence courts in the Bronx, New York (Labriola, Rempel & Davis, 2005, 2008), added some complexity to the results of the previous two NIJ experiments. Domestic violence offenders were randomly assigned to a batterer program, plus monthly court monitoring, or to only graduated monitoring ($N = 420$). The men reported to the court for a review of their compliance with the order to attend the batterer program, avoid contact with their partner, and pay required fees. This design resulted in four options: batterer program plus monthly judicial monitoring, batterer program plus graduated monitoring, monthly monitoring only, and graduated monitoring only. The study found that neither the batterer program nor the court monitoring produced a reduction in subsequent arrests or victims' reports to the researchers of violence. The authors have acknowledged as limitations of the study its small sample size (approximately 100 men in each of the four options), poor implementation of the judicial oversight, typical program dropout rates (30 percent), the low response rate of the men's female partners (25 percent), and judges' exclusion of some potential subjects (14 percent).[3]

Implementation Problems

As the studies themselves acknowledge, implementation problems arose throughout. The extent and details of these problems, however, are not readily available in the published reports of the research findings. Some of the experimental reports do present limitations that lessen their impact and application (see, for example, Dunford, 2000b; Labriola, Rempel, & Davis, 2008). Implementation problems and the limitations they imply have been more fully discussed in several reviews of the research (Aldarondo, 2002, 2010; Gondolf, 2001; C. Murphy & Ting, 2010; Saunders, 2008). The details of which particular implementation issues apply to each of the batterer program evaluations, and the qualifications they raise, are discussed in these articles.

The main highlights include court override of random assignments, design and procedural revisions during a study, low response rates for follow-up interviews, high program dropout rates, controversy in the courts over random assignments, and exceptional community or institutional context (for example, military oversight or lax court oversight). As mentioned above, these problems are not unusual in experimental evaluations and are openly discussed in several reviews of criminal justice evaluations in general (Davis & Taylor, 1999; Berk, 2005). The proponents of the experimental designs argue that, even with their limitations, the experiments offer a more accurate indication of program effectiveness than any of the alternative quasi-experimental designs (Dunford, 2000a). The question remains, however, how to interpret, apply, and use the results amid the challenges of implementation.

The difficulties in implementing the intended experimental conditions are noted in the introduction to the NIJ booklet summarizing the Broward and Brooklyn evaluations: "In both studies, response rates were low, many people dropped out of the program, and victims could not be found for subsequent interviews. The tests used to measure batterers' attitudes toward domestic violence and their likelihood to engage in future abuse were of questionable validity. In the Brooklyn study, random assignment was overridden to a significant extent, which makes it difficult to attribute effects exclusively to the program" (Jackson, Feder, Forde, Davis, Maxwell, & Taylor, 2003, p. iii). It is not therefore clear whether the programs failed or the experiments were sufficiently flawed as to misrepresent the actual outcomes. As the NIJ summary acknowledges in its conclusion, the program operation (such as intake screening and referral, staff training and experience, and treatment integrity) or the program context (such as court procedures, probation oversight, and community services available to men and women) may contribute to the apparent lack of effect.

An independent review of the studies, which remains supportive of such experiments overall, cites some additional shortcomings of the batterer evaluations: "Careful review of these experimental studies further indicates that they fall short in important ways . . . most notably in not demonstrating treatment adherence and therapist competence, providing inadequate specification of interventions, having low partner contact rates, and/or having high levels of attrition from the treatment and research protocols" (Eckhardt, Murphy, Black, & Suhr, 2006, p. 379). A research summary for judges concludes: "Despite a large number of studies with much speculation, treatment programs for offenders remain underevaluated. One of the biggest problems with this sentencing option is compliance, which remains the responsibility of the courts or probation officers" (Worden, 2000, p. 12).

Conceptual Issues

These criticisms about lack of compliance and court oversight point to another familiar challenge to experimental designs. The question of the "intention to treat," as opposed to "treatment received" (sometimes referred to as dose-response), is intensified in the batterer program evaluations because of especially high dropout rates.[4] The men randomly assigned to a batterer program do not necessarily receive the intended treatment. Yet dropouts are included in the experimental or program group, and their outcomes are likely to counterbalance those of the men who did not drop out. This effect is especially the case in the experimental evaluations of batterer programs with dropout rates as high as

70 percent—a level far above the 30 percent to 40 percent at other sites (see, for example, Feder & Dugan, 2002).

The more relevant policy issue then becomes what is the outcome for the men who actually do receive the intended treatment. As discussed in the previous chapter, determining this outcome essentially requires a quasi-experimental design that includes statistical techniques to simulate comparison groups that did or did not receive treatment (more on some of these techniques appears below). Interestingly, the researchers in the Broward evaluation did compute a regression equation to test for a program effect based on attendance. The equation included background factors—such as age, education, employment, and relationship status—to control for possible differences between those who attended a few sessions and those who attended most or all of the sessions. An effect did appear, but the small sample size of program attenders limited the number of background variables that could be used and their statistical significance (Feder & Forde, 2000).

The major conceptual challenge to the experimental designs for studies of batterer programs, however, is the impact of the programs' context (Hohmann & Shear, 2002). To what degree does the biomedical model of treatment fit an intervention that is rooted in a broader set of components? Batterer programs in general tend to be enmeshed in a system that includes arrest, court action, victim services, probation supervision, and other community services. In fact, all of the following have been shown to influence the characteristics of the men in batterer programs and the containment of the men who drop out or are diverted from programs: screening procedures, orientation sessions, risk assessment, case management, noncompliance policies, victim contact, custody supervision, competing programs, and specialized protocols. In one study (Gondolf, 2000c), court review alone reduced the percentage of men who never went to the assigned program ("no shows") from 30 percent to 5 percent, and maintained a completion rate of 70 percent for men who did enroll in the three-month program. Overall the percentage of court referrals who completed the program rose from 48 percent to 65 percent following the implementation of a monthly court review. Conforming to the drug-court model (K. Burke, 2010), the court received compliance reports periodically, and evidence of noncompliance resulted in further sanctions from the court.

From the founding of batterer programs, victims' advocates have worked for a "coordinated community response" of which batterer programs were merely a component (Pence, 1989; Pence & Shepard, 1999). So a broader question is the degree to which the effect of batterer programs can be isolated from the coordinated response. Some of the failure attributed to a program may be the result of a system that fails to sufficiently sort out chronic offenders, increase sanctions or intensify treatment for dropouts, or offer sufficient supports and services for the men's partners. In some settings, a batterer program is viewed as a kind of monitoring and sorting device that identifies men who need further services, supervision, or containment—and a source of additional feedback for their partners.

These sorts of contextual considerations are receiving fuller attention throughout the evaluation field, as discussed more fully in chapter 6. Moreover, the scope of concern reaches beyond the intervention system itself. A recent opinion piece in *The Chronicle of Philanthropy* points to the community and cultural context as important factors to weigh: "What's more, [experimental] studies obscure the role of systemic forces, such as public-housing availability, child-welfare policy, anti-poverty benefits requirements, and other social services, on [sic] the way people live. They also seek to minimize, not build on, the role of cultural context and local knowledge that might help a program succeed [or fail], making experimental-design evaluation less useful" (Smyth, 2010).

Several solutions have been developed for the contextual concerns posed by experimental designs. The most obvious, but the most costly and difficult to achieve, is a multisite experiment that tests program and control options at a variety of locations. Multisite studies have been done of treatments for depression (Elkin, Shea, & Watkins, 1989) and alcohol abuse (Project MATCH Research Group, 1997) with results that overturned some of the conclusions drawn from single-site evaluations. In the domestic violence field, no such multisite experiment exists or is even on the horizon.[5] We are left instead to compare existing single-site experiments across their locations, comparisons that are limited because of different sample characteristics, follow-up measures, and study procedures. Even if the experiments were more similar, comparisons would still fail to account for the intention-to-treat problem, which might vary in degree across locations. Dropout rates are likely to be affected by differences in court oversight, participant screening, and program policies.

Several other approaches are available in the field of program evaluation—all with trade-offs of their own. Multiple methods are increasingly being used to help represent the broader intervention and its context (Bowen, Brown, & Gilchrist, 2002; R. Campbell & Wasco, 2000; Cross, Dickmann, Newman-Gonchar, & Fagan, 2009; Government Accountability Office, 2009). Direct observations of programs and court and probation procedures, open-ended interviews with staff and community leaders, and field studies of programs, their intervention system, and the surrounding communities have been recommended. Although determining what effect is attributable to the batterer program remains problematic, descriptive information about the context can help qualify and interpret a program's outcomes. The multisite study I led used some of these additional methods to explore the program context and collected some specific information on community resources and services (Gondolf & Jones, 2001). The question of program effect was addressed in statistical modeling discussed below.

There are increasing recommendations for system-analysis in the evaluation field (for example, Smyth & Schorr, 2009). Systems analysis is, of course, a broad term but is commonly used in business management to represent the operations of an entire corporation and its component parts (Weiner, 1990). It is also increasingly a perspective brought to public health projects considered to be an "open system" interacting with a variety of other service agencies, informal networks, and the community at large. The field of community psychology has also promoted systems thinking as a way to understand and improve interventions. A recent special issue of the *American Journal of Community Psychology* was devoted entirely to the topic (Kelly, 2007). Textbooks, such as *Fourth Generation Evaluation* (Guba & Lincoln, 1989), are now also available to help design a systems approach to program evaluations.

In the domestic violence field, this approach is reflected in the system audits developed by the founders of the touted Duluth model as means of monitoring a coordinated community response (Sadusky, Martinson, Lizdas, & McGee, 2010). Although the audit identifies intermediate outcomes in terms of "service delivery" (for example, 911 calls, police arrests, court referrals, program dropouts, and noncompliance sanctions), it does not calculate a specific outcome attributable to the batterer program. The three-city quasi-experimental evaluation of the Judicial Oversight Demonstration project comes closest to a system evaluation (Visher, Harrell, & Yahner, 2008). It examines the outcomes in terms of victims' reports and subsequent arrests of an enhanced intervention system compared to less developed systems. It speculates on the effect of the batterer programs on the overall outcome, but it concedes that the effect of the individual components is not detectable—nor is their intent. The study is discussed in chapter 6, along with several other evaluations of intervention systems.

Implementation Back Stories

The implementation challenges discussed thus far are openly acknowledged across fields and disciplines. However, another level of concern about implementation is generally not fully acknowledged or discussed. This has to do with the "uncontrollable events" that researchers inevitably encounter in the messiness of social services and interventions—the barriers, resistance, obstacles, and breakdowns that arise unexpectedly and that require negotiations and modifications. They comprise the proverbial back stories of experimental evaluations that further qualify a study as well as often revise it. This is another way of saying that experimental studies are usually not as neat and tidy as they appear. The intent of "rigor" in a study's design may not be rigor in practice—and more is left to interpretation than meets the eye.

Most of the published articles reporting on experimental evaluations of batterer programs do not substantially discuss the implementation back story and the qualifications it raises for the findings. Yet domestic violence intervention admittedly includes a complexity of contextual factors—including questions of victim access and safety, issues regarding researcher-practitioner collaboration, and the overriding priorities of the criminal justice system—that make evaluation research particularly challenging (Mears, 2003). However, a couple of articles do recount the challenges of implementing evaluations of domestic violence interventions, and their implications for future research (Feder, Jolin, & Feyerherm, 2000; Visher, Newmark, & Harrell, 2008).

Lynette Feder and her associates (2000) reviewed the challenges they faced in conducting the Broward, Florida, experiment with a batterer intervention program, and also a Portland, Oregon, experiment with an arrest and prosecution partnership in domestic violence cases. The Broward experiment exposed familiar problems of resistance from agencies, staff turnover, and shifts in agency support despite initial agreements. All of these problems were compounded by growing opposition from the prosecutors, who objected to the random assignments and used court action to block the study. This opposition increased the resistance from other parties involved in the study, created a hostile environment in the courtroom, lowered the morale of the research staff, and resulted in staff turnover. As a result, the researchers had to recruit and train new staff, convene regular meetings to address morale, and reeducate agencies about the merits of the experiment. To the researchers' credit, the experiment was completed, although not without questions about the effects of the "hostile environment" and procedural adjustments on the results (Dobash & Dobash, 2000; Gondolf, 2001; Saunders, 2008). The authors raise the need for a major public relations effort to counter suspicion and resistance to experiments in general. Even with that, "some things are beyond one's control" (Feder, Jolin, & Feyerherm, 2000, p. 391).

My colleagues and I encountered several of these "beyond control" situations in our recent efforts at experimental evaluations of batterer program innovations. The first were in our evaluation of culturally focused batterer counseling (Gondolf, 2007a). This study randomly assigned African American men to one of three batterer program options: a conventional mixed-race group, a conventional group consisting only of African Americans, and a culturally focused group of all African Americans (N = 501). The random assignment process was relatively successful, in a large part because the batterer program made the assignments. It operated multiple groups and had routinely assigned men to groups at its own discretion, following an intake and orientation session.

Despite the relatively positive ratings of the culturally focused counselor by the group participants and a group monitor, the training consultant felt that the counselor was not conducting the sessions in an ideal way. The consultant also complained about a conflict with the female program director who oversaw the other group programs. Additionally, tension existed between the culturally focused counselor and the program director and other staff members. These people admittedly resisted changes that the innovation brought to established procedures and operation. As a result, the culturally focused counseling was more of an appendage to the existing program than a fully integrated part of it. As in the case of many clinical trials, the experimental treatment did not have the support and longevity that the other more-established approaches received.

These sorts of problems and others are presented as qualifications to our findings in our reports and articles. Nonetheless, the bottom line that the experimental group—the culturally focused counseling—had little or no effect has been emphasized by some reviewers who respect the gold standard of experimental design. Other reviewers, however, highlight the broader, racially charged context of the court-based programs with predominantly African American participants. As a result, they question the implementation and implications of the study, and others like it (Potter, 2007).

Despite the challenges in the previous experiment, I was emboldened by the successful random assignment and track record at the research site to embark on another, more ambitious experiment (Gondolf, 2009a, 2009b). Our research team developed an experimental evaluation of what we termed "supplemental mental health treatment"—referral of batterer program participants who screened "positive" for mental health problems. This treatment was to be in addition to attending the required batterer program under a court mandate for a domestic violence offense. The experimental group was to be a random sample of the "positive" men who were informed that the evaluation and any prescribed treatment were part of the court requirement: the control group was to be the men who screened positive but were not referred to the additional mental health treatment ($N = 479$).[6]

Six months of planning established a streamlined referral protocol and agency support. Yet the experimental design soon fell apart. For one thing, the compliance to the mental health treatment was minimal due to breakdowns in the referral system. Some men were not properly notified about the supplemental mental health treatment at program intake, the sending of the verification forms was inconsistent, the batterer program office forgot to notify the court liaisons of referral noncompliance, and some of the judges chose to accept completion of batterer program alone as sufficient.

The undoing of the random assignment was, however, largely due to "uncontrollable events," rather than outright resistance. Shortly before the research was scheduled to begin, the human subjects committee overseeing the mental health clinic withdrew its approval, largely based on the consent procedures for the female partner interviews. After that initial delay, the prosecutor announced that his office could no longer support the experiment because of a high-profile murder: A batterer program dropout had stalked and shot his wife while she was attending a church service.

Additionally, turnover of key personnel effected the study implementation. The batterer program's executive director was fired for embezzling program funds and committing medical insurance fraud. The administrator of the clinic left for a few months due to illness, and her temporary replacement was not sufficiently versed in or committed to the project. The prosecutor in charge of the domestic violence court was promoted, and his replacement was unfamiliar with our project and allowed men not to comply with mental health treatment. Last but not least, the court administrator who had assisted us for many years was dismissed during a citywide reorganization of the courts.

This laundry list of staff turnover and organizational complications raises the question of whether we had been lucky in our past studies. The narrow focus of our culturally focused counseling experiment, and of another study of counseling sessions on parenting, contributed to the successful random assignment in those cases. The assignments were within existing programs rather than to other agencies and in collaboration with them. Moreover, the "naturalistic" nonexperimental design of our multisite evaluation of batterer intervention systems avoided the kind of implementation problems that occurred in imposing innovations on established practice and amid ingrained procedures.

I published a separate article about the lessons learned in the two problematic experiments—including my efforts to negotiate the implementation problems and the adjustments we made to address them (Gondolf, 2010). Interestingly, the most important findings in both the culturally focused and mental health studies were those related to implementation. The former study exposed the need to develop programmatic supports and "cultural competence" within an established batterer program. The latter helped to identify a variety of coordination needs, competing priorities, and the importance of case management to improve referral compliance and impact. Despite the negligible effect revealed in the salvaged quasi-experimental study, the participating practitioners ended up very supportive of the supplemental mental health treatment and eager to continue a revised version.

The point of these back stories is to illustrate that there is usually much more to batterer program experiments than meets the eye. Also, they show that implementation faces obstacles beyond anticipating challenges to random assignments. There is a whole set of problems that can significantly alter the setting and have an impact on the results, as well as on the intended design of a study. According to a recent review of experimental evaluations, these kinds of implementation problems are widespread, yet discussion of them is conspicuously lacking (Durlak & Dupree, 2008).[7] The systematic review and meta-analysis examined the impact of implementation problems on 500 quantitative evaluations of adolescent health programs, such as those focused on mental health, drug use, violence, and bullying. It identified a "powerful impact" of implementation on outcomes. Specifically, the effect size is substantially higher "when programs are carefully implemented free of serious implementation problems" (p. 340).

The questions for batterer program evaluations, then, become what sort of impact did the variety of implementation problems—in both the front story and the back story—have on the outcomes, and what alternative information might they have exposed? Moreover, do alternative approaches to evaluation, which avoid such problems, produce more or less valid results? With these sorts of questions, it would seem premature to make policy or program decisions based primarily on the available experiments—or at least without weighing more of the possible implementation problems and their likely impacts.

Meta-Analyses and Effect Sizes

Meta-analysis is an increasingly popular tool for summarizing program evaluations and filtering out the less rigorous studies. Many researchers and policymakers believe that this statistical procedure produces an emphatic and understandable verdict on program effectiveness (Durlak & Lipsey, 1991).[8] It offers a standardized measure of effect size for a combination of single-site evaluations of both quasi-experimental and experimental design (Cohen's d, with the value of 0 to 1, is the most commonly used). Meta-analysis "pools" or combines separate study samples into one large sample, which is particularly helpful given the relatively small single-site samples with low response rates that are typical with batterer program studies. The results represent a summary of all the evaluations that are included and may also detect variations across program sites and approaches, and research designs and methods.[9]

Over the last decade, there have been three meta-analyses of batterer program evaluations, which differ slightly in the evaluations they include (Babcock, Green, & Robie, 2004; Feder & Wilson, 2005; Smedslund, Dalsbø, Steiro, Winsvold, & Clench-Aas, 2007).[10] The two more recent ones have drawn the most attention since they include the current experimental evaluations. The 2004 meta-analysis led by Julia Babcock selected fifteen of the most methodologically sound batterer program evaluations and included three of the experimental evaluations discussed above (Babcock, Green, & Robie, 2004). Similar to the other meta-analyses, this one found only a small effect size for batterer programs overall. Effect sizes (computed with Cohen's d statistic) were 0.10 for the experimental designs ($n = 8$ effects), 0.41 for the quasi-experimental evaluations, and 0.24 for all of the studies combined ($N = 20$ effects; confidence interval = 0.15–0.33) based on women's reports. The results basically confirm that the experimental studies, taken together, show a minimal effect.

The subsequent meta-analytic review by Lynette Feder and David Wilson (2005) covered ten studies: four randomized experimental designs (one more than the previous meta-analysis) and six "rigorous" quasi-experimental designs (equivalence for the quasi-control group was established using statistical controls or matching procedures). Official arrest reports suggested a small but positive decrease of repeat violence in the experimental designs. The mean effect size was 0.26, which translates into a reduction in recidivism from 20 percent to 13 percent. However, victim reports, which are generally considered to provide a more valid indication of ongoing abuse, indicated that the mean effect size for the experimental designs was near zero. The authors concluded that batterer programs appear to be ineffective and questioned their current use overall—or at least until further randomized experiments show otherwise.

Interestingly, the authors of the former meta-analysis (Babcock, Green, & Robie, 2004) raise some cautions echoed by meta-analytic researchers in general. They acknowledge the variability in the quality of the evaluations, con-founding effects of the criminal justice system, and moderate effects of several programs lost in the averaging. Two programs, moreover, produced effect sizes of 0.70, and three others had effect sizes in the 0.40–0.50 range. The authors con-clude, therefore, with the cautionary note: "One of the greatest concerns when conducting a meta-analysis is the ease at which the 'bottom-line' is recalled and the extensive caveats for caution are forgotten or ignored" (p. 1046).

A 2007 meta-analysis from the Cochrane Collaboration[11] questions any "doesn't work" interpretation of the previous meta-analyses more explicitly (Smedslund, Dalsbø, Steiro, Winsvold, & Clench-Aas, 2007): "The method-ological quality of the included studies was generally low . . . The research evi-dence is insufficient to draw conclusions about the effectiveness of cognitive-behavioral interventions for spouse abusers . . . We simply do not know whether the interventions help, whether they have no effect, or whether they are harm-ful" (p. 18). An earlier analysis funded by the Centers for Disease Control and Prevention used a broader inclusion criteria of fifty intervention and preven-tion programs and reached a conclusion similar to the more selective Cochrane Collaboration: "The diversity of data, coupled with the relatively small number of studies that met the inclusion criteria for the evidence-based review, pre-cluded a rigorous, quantitative synthesis of the findings" (Morrison, Lindquist, Hawkins, O'Neil, Nesius, & Mathew, 2003, p. 4).[12]

The meta-analysis of the Cochrane Collaboration may carry some extra weight, due to the collaboration's reputation for compiling reviews of biomedi-cal experimental evaluations to guide medical practice in particular. Following the established Cochrane approach, Geir Smedslund and colleagues conducted an exhaustive search of the literature on batterer programs and made indepen-dent ratings of the studies based on strict criteria (Smedslund, Dalsbø, Steiro, Winsvold, & Clench-Aas, 2007). Six randomized controlled experiments of batterer programs were accepted for the analysis, using a relative risk measure and confidence intervals (a different quantitative procedure than the previous meta-analyses).

Even with further evaluations there may still be cautions and contexts to weigh in interpreting and applying effect sizes. An article summarizing re-search and policy for child services concludes: "In a brilliant essay, Jacob Cohen (1990) reflected on the statistical lessons he has learned and offered the follow-ing advice: 'Finally, I have learned that there is no royal road to statistical indi-cation, that the informed judgment of the investigator is the crucial element in the interpretation of the data, and that things take time.' Let us use our best judgment when we bring research to bear on policy questions—and, when we do, let us take the time to evaluate effect sizes in context" (McCartney & Rosenthal, 2000, p. 179). Statisticians have raised additional concerns with the bottom line use of meta-analyses (for example, J. Cohen, 1994; A. Jones & Scharfstein, 2001; Mann, 1990; Loughran & Mulvey, 2010).

The debate over effect sizes—how to interpret them and how useful they are—extends to other treatment areas as well. Several meta-analyses of research on sexual offender treatment show a similar range of effects when subsequent arrests are included as an outcome, but negligible effect sizes based on experiments with victimization outcomes (Marshall & McGuire, 2003). A comparison of effect sizes across criminal justice interventions suggests that some treatments work better than others and that treatment works better than deterrence only. The authors of this comparison suggest, however, that the variation is probably the result of the differences in samples and the problematic and resistant participants in some studies. Interestingly, effect sizes for voluntary psychotherapy tend to be much higher (0.32–0.44), but surprisingly low for established medical practices such as aspirin to reduce heart attacks (0.03) and chemotherapy for breast cancer (0.08). Prominent researchers consequently propose the use of a more complex indicator of effect—namely, "harm reduction" (Marshall & McGuire, 2003, p. 660; see also Marlatt, 2002). Such an indicator would include the degree, impact, frequency, and change of the violence over time, rather than a simple "yes" or "no" about the commission of subsequent offenses.

Additionally, if we use aggregate effect sizes, we may miss the more important questions for program and policy development. That is, with which men does a program work, and why? Most clinicians and practitioners will claim that their efforts clearly affect some individuals more than others: there is a "heterogeneity of treatment," therefore, that needs to be considered. Two prominent researchers, reviewing the "naïve" uses and misuses of effect sizes in the *Handbook of Quantitative Criminology*, emphasize this point: "Our position is that failure to consider the effects of heterogeneity of treatment may rob us of many opportunities to be more useful than we currently are to policy makers. The question may be posed as to whether something 'works' or not, but there are multiple ways that we can provide an answer that illuminates under what conditions and how it works best" (Loughran & Mulvey, 2010, p. 180). As I discuss in chapter 5, it is the men who do not respond to batterer programs, and who fall through the intervention system as a whole, who are increasingly the focus of research and policy.

Statistical Modeling

Instrumental Variable and Propensity Score Analyses

An entirely different way to address the conceptual and implementation issues associated with experimental program evaluations is statistical modeling—specifically the use of instrumental variable analysis and propensity score analysis. The goal of both analytic approaches is to simulate experimental conditions by controlling for potential differences in subject characteristics across the comparison groups, such as program completers versus dropouts. That is, the analyses attempt to balance two nonequivalent groups on measured subject characteristics in order to produce a more accurate estimate of the effects of a treatment. The two analytical procedures use two different statistical techniques to do so.

Instrumental variable analysis uses "instruments," or equations, as variables to isolate the effects of a predictor on the outcome, such as committing another assault (Angrist, 2006; Angrist, Imbens, & Rubins, 1996; Heckman, 1997). For instance, an equation for program dropout, built with the characteristics associated with dropout, is entered into the overall equation for program outcome. The dropout equation takes the place of using the simple dichotomous variable of dropout versus completion. This is an important step when the subject characteristics used to control for the comparison group differences are associated with both the program completion and re-assault—that is, program completion by itself is "endogenous" (it comes from within the control variables for program outcome) rather than "exogenous" (it is independent of other control or predictor variables).[13] In other words, simply using a list of singular background variables as controls in a conventional regression predicting outcome is "naïve," according to statisticians (see Angrist, Imbens, & Rubins, 1996; Heckman, 1997).

Instrumental variable analysis also enables the use of equations to control for the influence of the program's context—such as court referral, compliance monitoring, and police arrest rates—on the outcome. An equation of the context variables is entered as an "instrumental" variable into the overall equation predicting the program outcome. This sort of influence is typically unaccounted for in experimental designs. Finally, the instrumental approach uses what is called an "error term" to help account for unobserved variables, such as subjects' level of motivation. These variables may otherwise differ across the comparison groups and influence the outcome.

Propensity score analysis deals with the likely difference between two comparison groups—known as selection bias—in a different way (Luellen, Shadish, & Clark, 2005; Rosenbaum & Rubin, 1983). It computes the probability (or "propensity") that a subject will end up in one group as opposed to the other. That probability is then used to weigh or adjust the outcomes that might otherwise be influenced by the "bias" of one group over the other. This approach can also be used to identify the probable outcomes for different subgroups (those with different propensities). In contrast, experimental designs produce an average outcome for each comparison group, such as 40 percent of the control group, but 30 percent of the treatment group, committed new assaults.

These two methods have been used extensively in education, agriculture, public health, delinquency, and economics (Angrist, 2006; Kelejian, 1971; Rosenbaum and Rubin, 1983). Criminal justice researchers have also begun to use them in order to approximate equivalent comparison groups (Apel, Bushway, Brame, Haviland, Nagin, & Paternoster, 2007; Apel, Bushway, Paternoster, Brame, & Sweeten, 2008; Foster, Wiley-Exley, & Bickman, 2009; Loughran & Mulvey, 2010). These researchers also recommend using propensity score and instrumental variable analyses to offset the implementation problems encountered in experimental evaluations and to address more specifically the policy questions at hand.

In their landmark paper, James Heckman and Jeffrey Smith ground these recommendations with theoretical and statistical examples of the experimental limitations. They conclude: "This paper has assessed the commonly made arguments concerning experimental methods of social program evaluation. While experiments can eliminate the potential for selection bias to affect mean-impact estimates, we find that the existing literature overstates many of the other arguments in their favor. There is a sizeable divergence between the theoretical capabilities of evaluations based on random assignment and the practical results of such evaluations. Moreover, experimental advocates ignore promising developments in the theory and practice of non-experimental evaluations" (1995, pp. 108–109).

Unfortunately, the results of statistical modeling as such are not incorporated in meta-analysis except as a quasi-experimental study with unbalanced completer and noncompleter groups. In addition, evaluations that use statistical modeling are often mistakenly dismissed as merely quasi-experiments or nonexperimental studies of less scientific rigor. It is important to note that statistical modeling is much more than that, and its proponents argue that it can in fact be a better representation of outcomes than many experimental efforts (Angrist, 2006: Heckman, 1997). Admittedly, most researchers continue to hold that experiments are preferred and should be pursued, and their results heeded.

The Advantages of Statistical Modeling

Statistical modeling does answer the "intention to treat" problem of experimental evaluations, as well as many of their broader implementation problems. As previously discussed, experiments do not account for the subjects who drop out of the experimental or treatment group, resulting in the average effect on those *intended* for treatment and not necessarily on those who actually *receive* it.[14] Experiments in the criminal justice field tend, therefore, to test a "diluted treatment," so to speak (Gartin, 1995). The statistical modeling simulates equivalent comparison groups of those who actually receive treatment and those who do not. These approaches also address other conceptual problems encountered in experiments. As explained above, instrumental variable analysis is able to control for contextual factors through the creation of instrumental variables, and propensity score analysis is able to identify the effects on subgroups rather than just the average effect on subjects overall.

Furthermore, statistical modeling alleviates the implementation problems associated with conducting experiments in the courts and represents a more realistic picture of program operation. It does not require a program that is artificially imposed, as in the Navy's experimental batterer program evaluation, nor is it disruptive to the court procedures, as in the Broward experiment. Overrides of random assignments—either by a judge, advocate, attorney, or subject—are virtually eliminated. Additionally, "treatment migration," seen when subjects switch to another option after their initial assignment, is curtailed. These approaches also alleviate the hidden background stories of negotiations, resistance, and interference that often accompany experimental implementation. More fundamentally, they circumvent the ethical and cost issues posed by experiments (Dobash & Dobash, 2000).

The Drawbacks of Statistical Modeling

The major drawbacks of these approaches are that they require large sample sizes and extensive data on background characteristics. Experimental studies are not as concerned with subjects' characteristics because the random assignment balances out the experimental and control groups, and these studies don't need especially large sample sizes to discern differences between the groups. Moreover, instrumental variables that are truly exogenous and sufficient are difficult to establish, and weak ones can produce unstable results. (There are statistical tests to examine this problem and estimate its extent.)

The other stock criticism of statistical models is that they inevitably fall short of equivalent comparison groups. There are always subject characteristics that are unaccounted for and likely to influence the outcome. Although random assignment is designed to correct for that problem, the equivalence of comparison groups is still uncertain. Random assignment merely increases the probability of equivalence, although the increase can be substantial when the random assignment is faithfully implemented. Another major complaint is that the statistical models artificially create a misleading comparison group. The nontreated or partially treated men are drawn from the program participants and, after being exposed to various levels of treatment, drop out for one or more of a large number of reasons. Not surprisingly, proponents of statistical modeling have responses to these sorts of criticisms as well as counterclaims against experimental design (Heckman, 1997; Heckman & Smith, 1995; Staiger & Stock, 1997).

We acknowledged, for instance, that the results of our instrumental variable analysis should be viewed with caution (A. Jones & Gondolf, 2002). Based on exhaustive tests, our so-called instruments may not be fully independent or exogenous. However, Alison Snow Jones, the statistician leading the analyses, defends the results as superior to existing approaches and rejects outright dismissal of the instruments as misguided (A. Jones, 2010). Critics, she points out, would do better to heed a subsequent recommendation in the analysis report: "The selection bias that can result from 1) failure to complete and 2) failure to enroll, in combination with 3) the problem of sample attrition could compromise results from even the best designed randomized study" (A. Jones & Gondolf, 2002, p. 94). (The "selection bias" is the difference between the quasi-control or comparison sample and the experimental or treatment sample that makes them hard to compare.) As previously discussed, these have been major drawbacks in the previous experimental evaluations of batterer programs. Jones concludes: "In sum, the Jones et al. (2004) and Jones and Gondolf (2002) papers represent very sound examples of the correct application of the propensity score matching and IV methods to non-experimental data (i.e., data that were not randomized)" (A. Jones, 2010).

Statistical Modeling with a Multisite Evaluation

As described elsewhere (Gondolf, 2002a), our multisite evaluation used a naturalistic quasi-experimental—some would say nonexperimental—design to investigate the outcomes associated with batterer intervention. With their variations in approach, system, and region, the four program sites provided some instructive contrasts in themselves. The large sample size across the sites, the high response rate in the follow-up part of the study, and the extensive and complex database of batterer characteristics and outcomes enabled us to apply statistical modeling to our evaluations in a way that had not previously been achieved. In addition, our research team observed the procedures and operation of the system components and monitored events, issues, and culture in each community. This included collecting some data on fundamental influences affecting program performance, such as program referral and dismissal, police arrest patterns, and the availability of services.

In our instrumental variable analysis of program effect, court referral, program cost, program length, and compliance monitoring formed the context "instrument" for program completion. Those individual variables have all been shown to influence whether a participant completes or drops out of a program (Daly & Pelowski, 2000). Moreover, these variables external to the batterer program varied across the research sites and thus affected programs differently. The court response at the Pittsburgh site, for instance, was the most swift and certain and resulted in substantially more men complying with the court referral. The Denver-based program, on the other hand, received a greater percentage of voluntary referrals from outside the court system, and thus more men were likely to drop out because of the lack of accountability.[15] The instrumental variable for the re-assault outcome was based on the probability of arrest, the availability of women's domestic violence services, and local unemployment rates. These contextual variables are related primarily to program outcome, according to at least a few prior studies (for example, A. Jones & Gondolf, 2001). Although far from comprehensive, the re-assault instrument offered a control for the variation in program sites that helped differentiate the re-assault outcome from the program dropout predictor with which it is otherwise interrelated.

The major finding from the instrumental variable and propensity score analyses was that completing at least three months of a program of weekly batterer sessions reduced the probability of re-assault during a fifteen-month follow-up period by approximately 50 percent (Gondolf & Jones, 2001; A. Jones, D'Agostino, Gondolf, & Heckert, 2004). More specifically, the instrumental variable analysis produced a range of from 44 percent to 64 percent, based on two separate specifications or analytical procedures.[16] That is, the batterer programs had at least a "moderate" effect in reducing subsequent assaults, according to statisticians (Kazdin, 1994). In our follow-up with 480 women, these percentages imply that if all their partners had completed the programs, 86 women rather than 155 would have been re-assaulted.[17] These numbers are especially impressive given some of the qualifications that surround them. The sample of program participants includes a high portion of problematic men with criminal histories, alcohol abuse, psychological problems, low incomes, and limited education, as well as inconsistency in court oversight and supplemental treatments.

Additionally, the results could be considered conservative, since most men in the noncompletion comparison group received some treatment rather than none.[18] The moderate program effect is, moreover, supported by a series of related studies with other quantitative and qualitative variables from the multisite evaluation. Separate studies showed (1) little deterrent effect from perceived sanctions, as opposed to a program effect (Heckert & Gondolf, 2000b); (2) men's and women's attribution of change to the programs; (3) men's use of avoidance techniques learned in the programs (Gondolf, 2000a); and (4) recommendations of the program from both men and women (Gondolf & White, 2000).

Our propensity score analysis with the same data offers a means of further verifying the instrumental variable analysis and also producing more detail about the outcome. After adjusting the comparison groups of program completers and noncompleters with propensity scores, program completion reduced the probability of committing a subsequent assault during the fifteen-month follow-up period by nearly 50 percent for the men ordered to attend the program by the court, and 33 percent for the overall sample which included "voluntary" referrals. (The higher reduction in subsequent assaults among the court-ordered batterers who complete a program is substantially related to the coercive reinforcement of the courts, as I discuss further in chapter 6.)

The propensity score results also indicate that the program effect was greatest among those men at the highest risk of dropping out, and lowest among men with severe psychological problems. The greater effect for the dropout-prone men suggests that improved program completion may yield substantial benefit in terms of reductions in subsequent assaults. In other words, keeping batterers in a program is an important goal for batterer intervention. The low program effect associated with severe psychological problems suggests the need for screening for such problems and providing supplemental psychological services.

These latter findings give a very different picture than the average outcomes derived from experimental evaluations and point to differential effects that have implications for the intervention system as a whole, as well as individual programs. Moreover, program completion in general reduces the probability of re-assault by an amount that is of practical importance (a conservative 50 percent for men ordered to participate by the court). In light of the relatively low cost of batterer treatment programs (A. Jones, 2000), this effect appears more than sufficient to support the continued funding and referral to such programs.

Conclusion: Making Sense of It All

Are Batterer Programs Effective or Not?

Our overall point is that there are contrasting findings from alternative approaches that have been neglected in the focus on experimental evaluation. Experimental results and meta-analyses suggest that batterer programs have little or no effect. Yet sophisticated statistical modeling indicates otherwise. Both approaches, as I have tried to show, have their limitations and trade-offs. The remaining question is: Do the results of the statistical modeling, with the possibility of some remaining bias in the comparison groups, trump the results of poorly implemented experiments that address only the intention to treat? One approach may be more accurate than another, but that is hard to assess at this state of the research. Which set of limitations is greater is currently a judgment call.

Perhaps the two sets of findings supplement one another. Arguably, the experiments suggest that simply sending men to a batterer program is not sufficient in itself, and the statistical modeling indicates that some men warrant an enhanced intervention of some sort. That might include simply prompting more men to actually receive the program treatment through court oversight or a motivational orientation, or more intensive batterer programming and supplemental treatments for problems like alcohol abuse. In any case, the number of experiments and statistical models is relatively small compared to those conducted with alcohol treatment, sex offenders, and other violent criminals. A review of those results in the "what works" literature offers generic evidence about programming to add to the mix for batterers.

What is clear now is that we should avoid making any bottom-line assertion about the effectiveness of batterer programs. Despite the pressures for evidence-based practice, the programs' effect in general remains a matter of debate among researchers. It would seem that the discourse needs to be broadened rather than narrowed. In a later chapter, I make the case that complementary research not only tilts toward the findings of the statistical modeling, but also points to innovations that would improve the overall outcome of batterer programs.

Both the instrumental variable and propensity score analyses reveal the existence of a subgroup of unresponsive batterers who appear to account for the experimental lack of effect. Although a substantial portion of men do appear to be affected by the programs, a portion warrants more or additional treatment. Who are these men, and what should be done with them? Is it simply a matter of replacing or modifying the batterer treatment, broadening and tightening the intervention system as a whole, or some combination of both approaches? These sorts of questions go well beyond the superficial response that batterer programs "don't work."

Systematic Reviews of the Evaluation Research

A Narrow Positivist View

There are numerous published reviews of batterer program evaluations that attempt to sort through the studies and issues mentioned above. The information they include, the interpretations they draw, and the recommendations they pose vary dramatically. Some reviews are from a strict "positivist" view, which takes at face value what appear to be the most scientific findings. Positivism sees authentic knowledge as based on research that is objective, systematic, verifiable, and empirical—in other words, rigorous science. The result is a narrower sense of evidence-based practice, derived from evaluations that emulate experimental conditions. The focus in regard to batterer programs is, therefore, almost exclusively on the bottom-line outcome of the experimental batterer program evaluations and the meta-analyses that accompany them (for example, D. Dutton & Corvo, 2006; Corvo, Dutton, & Chen, 2008; Feder & Wilson, 2005).

As mentioned, the experimental outcomes show little or no effect. These lead to recommendations that point in two directions: one, increasing accountability or containment of offenders, adding community service or enhancing supervision, and often increasing prevention efforts in the community at large; and, two, replacing batterer programs with psychotherapeutic treatments and couples counseling. The overall implication seems to be that if batterer programs "don't work," it makes sense to revert to fundamental criminal justice interventions without such programs or overhaul the programs entirely.

This orientation also reinforces the views of those who see batterer programs more as a vehicle to social change than as treatment for individuals. At a roundtable discussion convened by the Center for Court Innovation in New York City, a select group of researchers and practitioners considered the role that intervention plays in resetting social norms as well as in containing men who batter their female partners. The summary noted one participant's complaint: "Conducting 'research on what makes people change behavior leaves us with defining domestic violence as a behavior that can be treated and for which we can look to therapy' . . . Instead the challenge for us is to think, 'How do you do massive social change?'" (Turgeon, 2008, p. 345). Similarly, men's programs like Men Stopping Violence in Atlanta promote a community-accountability model. Their broader aim is to "disrupt the traditions of abuse and dominance" that sustain violence against women at the individual, familial, local, national, and global levels (U. Douglas, Bathrick, & Perry, 2008, p. 247). The program in this sense is a base from which to engage men and institutions from the larger community in challenging the social messages underlying abuse.

In one sense, these recommendations echo the "just say 'no'" campaign against drug use of the 1980s. The idea of sending clear messages and organizing to change norms, of course, is part of the equation—and a part that has been neglected in addressing most social problems. A panel at the American Society of Criminology a few years ago reached the same conclusion about the impact of the Violence Against Women Act the 1990s (Boba & Lilley, 2009; Gelles, Ellliott, Ford, Holtzworth-Munroe, & Gondolf, 2002). The researchers agreed that more effort and funding needed to be devoted to the prevention of domestic violence, as opposed to the investments already being made in the criminal justice interventions with crisis cases.

But one might argue that there needs to be further investment in both prevention and intervention, and that intervention needs to be more than putting men on intensive probation, in community service, or in jail. The limited effectiveness of these approaches in stopping men's violence has been suggested by a few nonexperimental outcome studies (see Babcock & Steiner, 1999). More important, the series of outcome studies on drug courts show that coupling treatment with court supervision can improve the results (D. Wilson, Mitchell, & MacKenzie, 2006). Recent studies also suggest that even apparently intractable men, specifically those with psychopathic tendencies, may be responsive to treatment (Skeem, 2008; Skeem, Monahan, & Mulvey, 2002; Skeem, Plaschek, & Manchak, 2009). The treatment itself can help reinforce a message of change to individual men and the community at large. Ideally, our response to social problems should occur on multiple levels—micro (the individual crisis), meso (the neighborhood), and macro (the society).

The "What Works" Approach
There is another form of positivist research review that offers a broader perspective on program effectiveness, and that in the process evokes some support

for the conventional batterer program approach. It is the "what works" literature that considers a variety of program approaches and interventions in a particular field, and looks for common themes or principles associated with effectiveness. "What works" was launched in the criminal justice field in a famous 1974 article about prison reform by the American sociologist Robert Martinson. He made a sobering deduction from available research: "Nothing works!" The conclusion initially sent a jolt through rehabilitation efforts and funding cuts followed. A debate also followed, over what critics considered a "socially constructed" policy position. Like the debate with regard to evidence-based practice today, the critics called for researchers to "qualify their findings and temper their conclusions" (Sarre, 2001, p. 45).

In more recent years, "what works" studies have resulted in more positive assessment of the possibilities of rehabilitation. Several professional associations, including one devoted to community corrections and another focused on drug courts, have issued official statements on "what works" based on research reviews. Most of these cover the breadth of research on various interventions to ascertain features or components that contribute to a reduction in recidivism. They vary, however, in the substantiation for their recommendations, interpretation of the research, and number of studies that are considered behind a claim. We do not yet have a set standard for "what works"—and such a standard will probably be very hard to establish.

One of the more recent extensive reviews of criminal justice interventions, *What Works in Corrections* (Mackenzie, 2006), puts forth a few basic conclusions about what contributes to effective outcomes. It considers a wide range of research: systematic research reviews, meta-analyses, simulation studies, and program evaluations scored for their scientific rigor on everything from boot camps to drug courts, and from sex offender treatment to prisoner work programs. (The scoring is based on a standard developed by the University of Maryland in an extensive project on "what works.") The author concludes: "First, a cognitive transformation must occur within the individual. Second, the individual's environment must provide the opportunity for a bond or tie to form ... The individual-level change occurs first and is required before ties can be formed with social institutions" (p. 337). The author recommends treatments with a cognitive-behavioral orientation to further this individual preparedness. Interestingly, supervised probation, work release, vocational training, and life-skills programs are not in themselves particularly effective without this treatment component. Intensified supervision programs by themselves don't appear to significantly reduce recidivism, according to the research review. However, such supervision coupled with treatment does tend to show an effect.

This broad "what works" review leads to the speculation that it is not the increased control from supervision that is effective, but rather the increased treatment or rehabilitation compliance that the supervision promotes. Applying this to domestic violence intervention, it would seem that a combination of batterer programs, with their cognitive-behavioral emphasis, and accountability measures (along with further supervision that might accompany that) would make sense. Also, either accountability or treatment alone is less likely to be effective in reducing recidivism. It may be that the more narrow reviews of the batterer program evaluations miss this connection and may consequently have reached short-sighted conclusions.

The Gender-Neutral Agenda

The most emphatic "don't work" reviews draw from research largely outside of batterer program evaluations to make their claim and assert their agenda (D. Dutton & Corvo, 2006). They go further from the "what works" consideration of related program and intervention research, to the population beyond the intervention. As I have argued elsewhere (Gondolf, 2007a), the mainstay of their position is drawn from the "extraneous" community-based surveys using the Conflict Tactics Scales (Acher, 2002; Moffitt, Caspi, Rutter, & Silva, 2001; Straus, 1999). On the surface, the controversial findings of these surveys suggest that women are as violent as men. As discussed in chapter 1, there are many questions about this interpretation, including the methodological debate over equating the tactics of men and women; the surveys' absence of context, dynamics, and impact of events; and men's and women's different experience of violence (DeKeseredy, 2000; Dobash & Dobash, 2004; Holtzworth-Munroe, 2005; Saltzman, 2004; Saunders, 2002; Schwartz, 2000; for a full summary of the issues, see Belknap & Melton, 2005). Nor does the gender-neutral interpretation account for the coercion that women disproportionately face in these relationships. Evan Stark (2007) documents this concern in the case studies of his lengthy book, *Coercive Control: How Men Entrap Women in Personal Life*, as do Mary Ann Dutton and Lisa Goodman (2005) in their measure of coercion across a variety of samples of men and women.

Moreover, the counterevidence from other surveys and analyses undercut the "tactics" results. For instance, victimization surveys using other approaches of questioning and measurement produce very different results, with women being the primary victim of men's violence (Bachman, 2000; Bureau of Justice Statistics, 2004; Tjaden & Thoennes, 2000). Analyses of community samples versus clinical samples (that is, court cases, batterer program participants, battered women's services) also point to very different types of violence across the two sets of samples. The less severe "situational couples violence" tends to predominate in the community samples and the more severe "intimate terrorism" perpetrated primarily by men prevails in clinical samples (Johnson, 2008).[19] Our analyses of the tactics of the batterer program participants and their female partners adds support for the latter findings (Gondolf, in press).[20]

There is also a backdrop of opposing perspectives and agendas that one newspaper article characterized as the "family violence" versus "violence against women" (Muno, 2008). Admittedly the "family violence" adherents oppose what they consider to be "feminist ideology" (D. Dutton, 2010; D. Dutton & Corvo, 2006; Straus, 2010). The "violence against women" proponents consider this sort of dismissal to be a backlash against academics, practitioners, and activists who disagree (J. Crowley, 2009; Dragiewicz, 2011; DeKeseredy & Dragiewicz, 2007; DeKeseredy & Schwartz, 2003). While the "family violence" faction has organized itself into a highly vocal and visible group, the debate it represents has been around since the emergence of the battered women's movement in the early 1980s (McNeely & Robinson-Simpson, 1987).[21]

The landmark book summarizing the initial National Survey of Family Violence, *Behind Closed Doors: Violence in the American Family* (Straus, Gelles, & Steinmetz, 1980), exposed the physical pushes and shoves, hits and kicks, and outright beatings among couples. With it came a concern about husband beating by women, but also an unclear sense of the extent and nature of women's unprovoked attacks against men and the mutual combat identified in the book. A 1988 article (McNeely & Robinson-Simpson, 1987) and a series of letters to the editor of the professional journal *Social Work* (Singer, Darling, Jackson, & Gondolf, 1988) laid out the now-familiar retort. The letters were responding to a publication in *Social Work* that asserted domestic violence was a two-way street and calling battered women's services into question.

As Dan Saunders concluded over two decades ago, the authors "may have led social workers further from the truth by failing to mention important limitations of the research they cite, ignoring evidence that counters the research, and relying heavily on conjecture, opinion, and anecdotal evidence. Existing evidence shows that women are abused to a greater extent than men and thus our priorities for services and legislation have been placed properly. Especially disturbing is that the conclusions made by the authors may be used to block services for battered women, deny them their rights, and suggest types of intervention that may increase their risk of victimization" (1988, p. 179).

These counterarguments continue to this day, with at least ten academic articles published in the most recent decade (see Belknap & Melton, 2005). It is clear in the articles that there are legitimate conceptual, methodological, and interpretative issues with the "two-way street" claims that are far from resolution or dismissal.[22]

Improving Batterer Programs

A third group of reviews of the batterer program evaluations goes well beyond the narrow positivist stance. They weigh experiments, quasi-experimental studies, and statistical modeling, while acknowledging the limitations of all these approaches in assessing programs' effectiveness (for example, Saunders, 2008). The broader reviews tend to reach a more encouraging conclusion about batterer programs. They present a range of judgments from "cautionary outcomes" to a "modest effect." For instance, in the book he co-edited on batterer programs, Etiony Aldarondo provides an overview of arrest and protection order research, as well as batterer program evaluations: "The data show that each level of intervention is making modest and important contributions to stop and reduce violent behavior" (2002, p. 16). However, in the most recent systematic review focusing on batterer program evaluations, Chris Murphy and Laura Ting acknowledge that "valid debates remain as to the relative value of experimental versus naturalistic evaluation designs, the utility of complex statistical modeling of program effects, which studies and effect sizes should be included in meta-analytic reviews, and how to interpret findings in light of widespread methodological problems such as high subject attrition, systematic violation of random assignment, and inadequate documentation of intervention adherence" (C. Murphy & Ting, 2010, p. 40).

The predominant verdict is that batterer programs show promise but warrant improvement. There are separate promotions of personal favorites, such as motivational interviewing (C. Murphy & Ting, 2010), specialized treatments for different types of batterers (Saunders, 2008), and parenting training (Edleson, 2008). As I discuss in the next chapter, these approaches, while promising, have themselves yet to be tested in experimental outcome evaluations, and some show negligible impacts overall. However, this set of reviews unanimously supports the addition of substance abuse treatment, culturally sensitive counseling, risk assessment, and case management—most of which are ready being added to varying degrees. And the reviews conclude that batterer programs need to be more closely coordinated with the courts, the rest of the criminal justice system, and other community services. Saunders elaborates: "The integration of abuser, survivor, and criminal justice interventions within each community may provide the key to the most effective interventions" (2008, p. 166). "Batterer programs cannot operate in a vacuum," concludes Edleson (2008, p. 18) in his review of the research.

In sum, reviews of the batterer program evaluations have pointed to program extinction as well as evolution. A narrow focus on experimental evaluations, and the meta-analyses that accompany them, lend support to replacing or disbanding batterer programs as ineffective. There is a vocal faction that reaches beyond the program evaluations to community surveys to make their case for psychotherapy and couples counseling, in contrast to stricter positivists who revert to the basics of criminal justice controls and containment. In essence, we have a minimalist interpretation that accepts only what has been supported by experiments and is thus left with deterrence. This interpretation opens the door as well to extraneous descriptive research outside of batterer intervention to argue for a new direction, such as studies of batterers' psychological characteristics and of types of batterers.

Reviewers who take a broader and more critical view of the research, along the lines I have outlined in this chapter, recommend supplements and modifications to batterer programs to improve them. Most of these recommendations are already being implemented to varying degrees across the country. They reinforce rather than revamp existing programs. Moreover, the recommendations from these reviewers situate batterer programs as part of a larger system of intervention. Substance abuse treatment, risk assessment, and case management, as our research team set forth, are really about extending programming beyond the weekly batterer group sessions. They foster and enhance a coordinated community response. The issue for evaluation, in this light, becomes the effectiveness of such coordination, and the batterer programs' contribution to the overall response.

Practitioners' Response

Initial Indifference

Practitioners are in the midst of an escalating, but relatively ad hoc, response of their own—one that has moved from indifference to initiative. As recently as 2008, only a small portion of practitioner audiences at several batterer intervention conferences knew of the experimental evaluations in the field. Less than 5 percent at one meeting indicated they had heard of them.[23] Yet a bulletin from the National Institute of Justice summarizing two of the experiments had been distributed widely via the institute's website and mailings to practitioners (Jackson, Feder, Forde, Davis, Maxwell, & Taylor, 2003). In the last several years, criminal justice personnel in particular have become increasingly aware of the bottom line of these experiments. The experimental results are having an impact on batterer programs in at least selected jurisdictions.

We can only speculate about the reasons for the slow response from practitioners to the experimental evaluations that have drawn so much attention in academic and policy circles. As mentioned in chapter 1, the tension between practitioners and research permeates the criminal justice field in general. A recent published roundtable discussion on court innovations noted a "cultural suspicion of anything academic" (Berman, 2008, p. 99), despite the need for decision making based on data and self-reflection. The pressure for practitioners to live in the moment adds to the tension in a practical way. Crises order the practitioner's day and tend to preclude long-term planning, according to the panel. As a result, "there is almost a complete disconnect between practice and the parallel universe of research" (p. 103). One could argue that this sort of tension has been particularly acute in the domestic violence field.

Many practitioners feel that prominent studies, especially the national surveys using the Conflict Tactics Scales (Straus, 1979), have been used to counter the efforts to establish and promote domestic violence services. Others feel that the evaluation research is not particularly relevant or applicable to their work. They claim it generally fails to capture the complex and broad outcomes to which programs aspire. At least a few directors of batterer programs have written pointed critiques of the narrow focus of evaluations and their failure to consider community impacts (Carlin, 2001; R. Crowley, 2001). Probably the most likely explanation is that most program staff members are preoccupied with sustaining their respective programs amid all sorts of practical demands, not to mention financial shortfalls. With the experimental evaluations and demands for evidence-based practice having discernible impacts, staff members are becoming more informed through a series of practitioner conferences and online discussion groups. They also have created a website containing information that questions the bottom-line interpretation of the batterer program experiments.[24]

One group of about twenty program directors met at two practitioner conferences to consider their own response to the research.[25] They listed contributions attributed to batterer programs that went far beyond the available research. The list confirms a broader perspective of outcomes, as well as a broader view of the role and usefulness of batterer programs. The group mentioned what might be considered secondary impacts of the conventional outcomes of reduced abuse among participants. They cited the deterrent and educational impacts, arguing that batterer programs send a message to the community at large that men need to and can change, and a message to survivors that their male partners are the ones who have a problem. The directors say that the programs have also helped to promote institutional reform in the criminal justice system and among many community services. That is, the programs' presence has not only drawn referrals but also helped to draw attention to domestic violence and the need to respond specifically to it. Many of the directors claim, for instance, that their programs have increased awareness of battering and skills for working with batterers in substance abuse, mental health, and children's services.

Batterer programs have some very practical and direct impacts on domestic violence cases themselves. They serve as a resource for many women who want to stay with their partners, provide oversight and monitoring of men arrested for domestic violence, and supply information about batterers that can help decision makers like judges, probation officers, and child welfare workers. The programs have also promoted interactions and coordination across the criminal justice system and service agencies around domestic violence cases. Finally, amid the fiscal constraints of the day, they offer a cost-effective option to over-crowded and ineffective jails.

Practitioners' Initiatives

A number of trends have brought practitioners more directly into the research discourse and debate. One trend is the increased expectation that practitioners will be not just advisors on a particular program evaluation, but also joint conceptualizers and interpreters of the research. For instance, judges, probation officers, battered women's advocates, and batterer program staff members met in November 2009 to challenge researchers' interpretations of the influential Judicial Oversight Demonstration project (BISCMI, 2009). The published findings suggested that making community response more coordinated and including batterer programs within that response do not substantially improve outcomes (Visher, Harrell, & Yahner, 2008). A series of audio conferences, conducted through the Muskie School of Public Service at the University of Southern Maine, has also promoted this sort of expanded discussion. At least a few researchers tempered their published claims of program ineffectiveness when teamed with the practitioner discussants in these ninety-minute broadcasts (BWJP, 2008).

A second trend is a more informal effort to develop practitioner-led evaluations to help document and develop the complexities of their work. The concern here is that the prevailing batterer program evaluations do not represent the more developed programming and intervention systems in the field, nor do they take into account the full range of the programs' impacts and contributions (such as the programs' role in assessing risk or sending noncompliant men back to the courts). The Respect agency in the United Kingdom, for instance, has launched an evaluation project of its community-based network of programs. A project manager and advisory committee from Respect are working with a group of university researchers that Respect recruited in a competitive solicitation of its own.[26]

A related matter, discussed in some of the critiques of evidence-based practice, is the need to develop research readiness among practitioners (McCrystal & Wilson, 2009; Pollio, 2006; Shlonsky & Gibbs, 2004). In order for practitioners to respond more meaningfully to research findings and develop documentation of their own, they need training workshops and technical assistance regarding the basics of program evaluation. Such workshops might offer a fuller discussion of the limitations and shortcomings of research, along with the contribution of scientific inquiry to program and policy development. The national conference "Bridging Perspectives: Intervening with Men Who Batter" in May 2009 included a few sessions with this intent (Debonnaire, 2009; Nitsch & Garvin, 2009).

These trends represent an expansion of the current conception of evidence-based practice to include broader feedback from practitioners, more discussion of interpretations, and a diversity of methods and designs. The 1990 origins of evidence-based practice in the medical field included and promoted just such features (Gilgun, 2005). It is clear, however, that these efforts need further resources and leadership to sustain them. The Batterer Intervention Services Coalition of Michigan and the Domestic Abuse Project of Minneapolis will apparently continue to hold specialized batterer program conferences in the near future. Getting information and technical assistance to the programs that need it the most, and that often lack the funds to send staff members to such meetings, is still a major issue for the field. But information does seem to be trickling down. And the attendees at future meetings are likely to show a new awareness of and a proactive response to the existing research. This possibility bodes well for the prospect that evidence-based practice will revert to the feedback loop it was initially intended to be (Gilgun, 2005).

II | THE NEW PSYCHOLOGY OF BATTERERS

3 | The Cognitive-Behavioral and Psychodynamic Divide

Which Counseling Approach?

A Variety of Alternatives

The second most frequently asked question about batterer programs—after how effective are they—is what counseling, education, or therapeutic approach works best. Like the first question, the second has a variety of competing answers, but in this case there is even less substantive evidence to draw on. Practitioners have favorite approaches based on a variety of reasons that range from their own training, pet theories, personal agendas, and underlying philosophies to supportive studies and clinical observation. Some of the approaches are competing and even mutually exclusive; others overlap and reinforce each other. So it seems hard to identify the best approach among so many. There are various criteria for what is most appropriate, justified, sensible, substantiated, or effective. There have been few attempts, however, to compare outcomes directly, and we do not have clear information about the nature and extent of the approaches actually in use. However, the Duluth program, founded in the late 1980s in Duluth, Minnesota, is probably the best known program approach and has been the most influential over the years.

A survey of 276 batterer programs found that "representatives from about half of the responding programs on a web-based questionnaire reported using some variation of the Duluth approach" (Price & Rosenbaum, 2009, p. 761). A quarter of the respondents considered their programs to be "therapeutic," a term that suggests a more psychodynamic approach compared to the strict cognitive-behavioral or psycho-educational approach associated with Duluth. (Only 7 percent of the respondents checked "pro-feminist" on the inventory of approaches.)[1] The apparent popularity of the Duluth approach may be largely attributable to support for that approach in the majority of state standards for batterer programs, as well as its early inception. It also combines concerns of battered women's advocates with basic cognitive-behavioral aspects. As I discuss below in this chapter, some critics nonetheless dismiss the Duluth program as ineffective, ideological, and simplistic (for example, Babcock, Canady, Graham, & Schart, 2007; D. Dutton & Corvo, 2006). Given the questions about effectiveness, several approaches are in fact vying to replace the predominant gender-based, cognitive-behavioral approach.

A flood of alternatives are available. The range of manuals for batterer programs, for instance, has grown exponentially in the last ten years or so. Here is just a brief list of program approaches represented in published books and articles for batterer programs. First are the approaches that emphasize batterers' thought patterns: cognitive-behavioral (Hamberger, 2002), skill-building (Wexler, 2006), strengths-based (Lehmann & Simmons, 2009), solution-oriented (Lee, Sebold, & Uken, 2003), anger management (Kassinove & Tafrate, 2002), anti-sexist (Bancroft, 2003; Russel, 1995), consciousness-raising (Paymar, 2000; Kivel, 1998), and narrative therapy programming (Jenkins, 1990; Augusta-Scott & Dankwort, 2002). Next are the approaches that focus on the emotional aspect of men's abuse: psychodynamic treatment (D. Dutton, 1998), dialectical behavioral therapy (Fruzzetti, 2000), compassion workshops (Stosny, 1995), and trauma rehabilitation (Briere & Scott, 2006).[2]

In addition, several published workbooks are in circulation (for example, Fall & Howard, 2004; Gondolf, 2000e; Sonkin & Durphy, 1997), along with manuals from established batterer programs like Emerge, Alternatives to Domestic Abuse, Manalive, Amend, Men Stopping Violence, Domestic Abuse Project, Domestic Abuse Intervention Program (the Duluth program), and several others (see Aldarondo & Mederos, 2002). All of these programs, and most of the manual authors, offer training for their approaches, as well.

There appear to be some common themes running through the approaches. The cognitive-behavioral approaches focus on the thought partners associated with abuse and violence and the operation of the behavior of concern. They typically include exposing and acknowledging the behavior, taking responsibility for it, identifying alternative behaviors, and restructuring thoughts, beliefs, and attitudes. These more present-oriented approaches include the thought-control and interpersonal techniques of mainstream cognitive-behavioral therapy illustrated in anger management and solution-oriented approaches. They vary from the broader social-political considerations of the gender-based consciousness-raising of the Duluth program and narrative therapies.

Another theme is the more emotive approaches that center on the psychological tensions, fears, hurts, and pains that tend to be unconscious or barely conscious elements of behavior. These approaches tend to be more psychodynamic in orientation; they explore past experiences, parental relationships, and latent fears and inadequacies. A recent interest along these lines has been in the treatment of attachment disorders, brain trauma, borderline personality disorder, and couples dynamics. These themes and the approaches associated with them may overlap and complement one another, or apply to some men more than others. They also reflect the different orientations in psychological theory that emphasize the rational or cognitive as opposed to the emotive and unconscious aspects.

As a group, the extensive array of guidebooks, workbooks, manuals, and training sessions represent a clinical conviction that battering men can change their behavior and a commitment to furthering that change. They offer, in a sense, a counter to the victim advocates and program evaluations that suggest they "don't work." In fact, some proponents boast impressive success based on participant testimonials and limited follow-up (for example, Stosny, 1995). The implication is that, based on clinical observation, experience in other fields, and batterer research, something does work—at least for some men. From the standards of evidence-based practice, however, the support for one approach over another is arguably slim. The evidence against cognitive-behavioral approaches is also questionable, as discussed in the previous chapter. The ideal would be to have randomized clinical trials—experimental evaluations—comparing the different approaches head-to-head. This sort of evaluation, however, is unlikely given the concerns about cost, implementation, and the time it takes to do such an evaluation. Ultimately, several different trials would be needed to account for the diversity of approaches and formats. And we would still be left with many of the criticisms of experimental evaluation discussed in the previous chapters.

The Impetus of the Array

Where do all these treatment approaches, and the idea that men can be "treated" or counseled out of domestic violence, come from? They appear to spring from a "new psychology." However, the search for a magic elixir has long been at the center of American psychology. As sociological texts speculate, our society's emphasis on the individual as the autonomous agent of behavior is perhaps our greatest strength but also a major challenge (for example, Conrad, 2007; Ellis & DeKeseredy, 1996). We tend to focus on finding "the loose screw" inside the individual, in what might be termed a medical perspective or disease model.

There is no doubt that many of the men who are sent to batterer programs have conscious or unconscious demons. Much of the counseling and educational work with men who batter their female partners has been an attempt to unseat those demons. The ideal result is a man restored, or freed to be less hurtful toward others. As discussed in previous chapters, many battered women's advocates over the years have doubted the possibility of this happening, and have called instead for more protection for women and better containment of the men. Their horror stories of relentlessly violent and abusive men support this view, along with the "revolving door" that many court officials call the flow of repeat offenders.

The claims drawn from experimental evaluations that batterer programs "don't work" have reinforced and in some instances propelled the case for alternative treatments and approaches. If we could just find a treatment better suited for batterers, or better match batterers to appropriate treatments, program outcomes might be substantially improved. This understandable view—to find a better way—has drawn new possibilities from developments in psychology and psychiatry. There have definitely been advances in therapeutic techniques, like those derived from psychodynamic approaches for attachment disorders and from neuroscience for brain damage and aggression. These reinforce the long-standing assumption that a better assessment of a batterer's psychological issues, problems, and conflicts can lead to a more individualized course of treatment.

This line of thinking has been heightened with regard to domestic violence through the mounting research on batterers. A recent study of research articles published about domestic violence demonstrated the existence of a burst of research on batterers' characteristics and the risk factors associated with violence (Jordan, 2009). The vast majority of articles were authored by psychologists and focused on the psychological problems of the men.[3] These problems are in turn associated with violence and considered to be underlying causes or contributors to the violence. Most of the articles concluded with implications for treatment and intervention that address batterer etiology.

The study of articles questions the source of the trend as well as its impact. Is the field being narrowed or even preempted by the advent of clinical psychology, or is it being expanded and advanced? The perspectives of social workers, sociologists, anthropologists, and criminologists tend to emphasize the social context of an individual's battering. Moreover, battered women's advocates have viewed intervention as fundamentally about social, community, and institutional change, rather than individual treatment and services (Lehrner & Allen, 2009).

The Masculine Paradox

Many of the program approaches represent the "old psychology"—or the tried and true version, depending on one's perspective. These are those approaches based substantially on social learning theory (Bandura, 1973). The founding programs, such as Duluth, Emerge, and Amend, helped develop and launch the prevailing set of assumptions. That is, men are taught through socialization about the expediency and normality of violence and about their supposed right to get what they want from women. They see subjection and abuse of women in their own homes growing up, hear it endorsed in some churches, watch it in films and television programs, follow it in sports and the military, and so on. Underlying this socialization is the social structure that endorses and promotes male dominance and privilege in what we've come to call the patriarchy. As one academic author wrote early on: "Men abuse women because they can"—that is, in a largely male-dominated society, they get away with it, for the most part (Gelles, 1983, p.157).

Although the social landscape continues to change, with women in greater positions of authority and men's subjection of women being challenged, the vestiges of patriarchy remain conspicuous. Sociologists point to the explosion of pornography, furiously violent video games, male initiations such as those in the Tailhook incident of 1991, the continuing appeal of slasher or splat movies, the misogynist gangster rap on MTV, the international trafficking of female sex workers, and the allegations of rape against high-profile athletes. Some have argued that the adverse social influence on men today may be more through supermasculine subcultures in college fraternities, sports teams, groups of drinking buddies, and street gangs (for example, Schwartz & Nogrady, 1996). The rash of male politicians, sports stars, and television celebrities involved in serial sexual affairs adds to this impression. It further illustrates the relationship of subcultures, as well as powerful status, to a sense of entitlement and the abuses that go with that.

Various theories on the psychology of masculinity have elaborated and refined these basic assumptions (Levant & Pollack, 1995). Many of them have been explored and promoted in what has been referred to as the men's movement (Clatterbaugh, 1997; Messner, 1997) and men's studies (for example, Bowker, 1998).[4] In a psychodynamic sense, many men develop an underlying fear of intimacy caused by their upbringing and become hypermasculine to compensate for a sense of inadequacy. Absent or overbearing fathers have left some men feeling unworthy or unsure of themselves. They turn to the masculine images around them for a sense of identity and worthiness (Ackerman, 1993). They may also be rebelling from an overbearing mother and exaggerate their masculinity to individuate themselves—that is, to establish themselves as distinct individuals.

The notion of hypermasculinity points to a persistent quandary in criminology: the extent to which aggression reflects an inflated sense of self in the form of entitlement or narcissistic tendencies, or a core fear and doubt that reflects low self-esteem and even self-hatred (Baumeister, Bushman, & Campbell, 2000; Ostrowsky, 2010; J. Walker & Bright, 2009). There is an obvious integration of what on the surface appears contradictory. The bravado and aggression that spill over into violence toward women may be a compensation for underlying insecurities and needs. The directors of Amend, one of the original batterer programs, summarize this gendered social and psychological view in the field: "We recognize that to a large extent, violence and abuse are learned behaviors that are in fact reinforced by our society. Indeed, we live in a patriarchal society that reinforces male privilege. This patriarchal system strains males to act out without remorse, to view issues in terms of black and white, and to value physical strength and ridicule weakness . . . The lack of conflict resolution skills combined with violence as the primary experience in the family of origin, in addition to the trauma experienced, make violence an easy choice—the only choice a perpetrator may think he has in response to frustration, stress, grief, and feelings of inadequacy" (Pettit & Smith, 2002, p. 5).

There is a somewhat paradoxical underside to the patriarchal society that provides men with a sense of privilege and entitlement. Some of the past gender analyses have pointed to the hardships of a man's world (for example, Ferrell, 1974; Fasteau, 1981; Fine, 1988). Holding things in, acting tough, and being in charge have immediate payoffs but also hurt men psychologically, wear them down physically, and put them in a competitive and defensive mode that undercuts their social support. Men also put themselves in a position of greater risks that lead to injury and harm. As a result, men are more likely to suffer heart disease, alcoholism, and death. They suffer more trauma in combat, work accidents, and car wrecks than women do. There is another layer of hurts. The male pecking order leaves more men losers than winners (Faludi, 1999). Resentment over losing can easily turn into outbursts at home, among friends, or against competitors. Too often a man's identity is tied up with his job, his toys, and his sports. If those are lost, so is he.

This man's world exposes, in sum, a contradictory image in which many men act out of frustration, hurt, and pain rather than deliberately or sadistically out of control and power (Katz, 2006; Richetin & Richardson, 2008).[5] In this view, men appear as victims themselves who need care and healing. Many men, however, do behave like monsters wielding unchecked power to get and keep their way: "My way or the highway!" Conceivably, such a man may be asserting control toward others in order to feel more in control himself, or at least to feel like a man in his household if not in the rest of the world. Or he may be just extending the expectations and rules of his man's world to his home, and especially toward his woman.

The recent profiles of soldiers on leave from Iraq vividly illustrate these sorts of tendencies (Aronson, 2005; Edge & Buchanan, 2010). Many of these men have difficulty readjusting to family life back in the United States. Not only does the military train the men to be aggressive in ways that spill over into the men's relationships at home, but many returning soldiers also suffer from psychological problems related to traumatic incidents, battle fatigue, and their lowly status as "grunts." Just as the demands and training of combat don't fit the home front, some lessons of the workplace, streets, and sports world may not be appropriate for personal relationships.

The New Psychology

The so-called new psychology, focusing more on men's individual psychological problems, raises objections to the established gender-based, cognitive-behavioral approaches. The concern is that batterer programs focus too much on the socialized beliefs about gender that men in general bring into the group. The critics call this a single-factor or cultural-deterministic view. The causes of domestic violence are complicated and have multiple underlying factors. As Linda Mills puts it: "Our solutions need to expand theoretically and academically, but also in terms of whom we bring to the table in terms of the recovery effort. We need to recognize the causes of domestic violence are not only exclusively related to what people believe and what people believe about women" (quoted in P. Cohen, 2010). Each man has a history of his own, a unique makeup, and special circumstances that need to be assessed and taken into consideration.

The foundational gender-based approaches spotlight commonalities that may predispose a man to objectify and abuse women, but they fail to explain why a particular individual is violent and another is not. Why, for instance, does one brother abuse his female partner, while another is largely supportive and respectful? More specifically, why did Tiger Woods betray his wife with multiple affairs, while Phil Mickelson, another famous golfer, remain so true to his ailing wife?

The new psychology highlights the distinctive individual factors and couple dynamics that contribute to violence. It purports to provide a multifactor view beyond the single factor that its proponents ascribe to the prevailing gender-based analysis. Donald Dutton concludes his critique of batterer programs: "Psycho-educational interventions, currently in use as the court-mandated outcome of arrest for spouse assault, are misdirected, focusing on 'male privilege' and 'acceptance of violence' . . . Most importantly, we need to stop thinking of the problem in superficial and overly broad 'gender analysis' terms, and then proceed with the recognition and treatment of the psychology of intimate personal violence in its deeper individual and interpersonal forms" (2008, p. 140–141).

The new psychology considers more immediate or direct influences, such as personality type, psychological syndromes and disorders, trauma history, motivation (or treatment readiness), and relationship issues. These sorts of influences differ with an individual's upbringing and experiences, as well as with a genetic predisposition that may have inclined an individual to perceive and react in certain ways. For instance, there is increasing concern that many repeat offenders may have suffered early abuse or neglect that affected their brain development. As a result, they tend to react impulsively to threatening circumstances rather than thinking things through.

Research does show some correlation between these sorts of individual problems or issues and the severity and extent of violence (for a summary, see Cellini, 2004; Mitchell & Beech, 2011). However, the relationship between specific treatments of psychological problems and improved outcomes is not so clear. In fact, there is little evidence as yet that alternative treatment approaches to address an array of individual problems are any more effective than the prevailing gender-based, cognitive-behavioral approach (Butler, Chapman, Forman, & Beck, 2006; Leichsenring & Leibing, 2003; Landenberger & Lipsey, 2005). Program participants may have enough in common as a result of their exposure to similar social influences, or the cognitive approach may be sufficiently effective across the range of individual problems. As I elaborate later in this chapter, the question of treatment approach may be more about how we stop violence, rather than why a person is violent. The how and why are not necessarily the same. A crude analogy might be that high-priced speeding tickets do slow down the majority of drivers, regardless of their reasons for speeding. But of course a subgroup of drivers speed despite the ticketing.

This points us to another potential contribution of the new psychology. Why do a substantial portion of participants in conventional batterer programs drop out and commit new offenses? Program studies show that 30 percent to 65 percent of enrollees don't complete the programs, depending on program length and court reinforcement (Daly & Pelowski, 2000). Another 5 percent to 40 percent never show up for a batterer program following a court mandate. The new psychology, and the alternative treatments it suggests, could help improve the outcomes for this apparently problematic group of men. Research in the alcohol and drug field, for instance, has identified a subgroup of patients who drop out of treatment and relapse regardless of the treatment approach (Hubbard, Marsden, Rachal, Harwood, Cavanaugh, & Ginzburg, 1989; Project MATCH Research Group, 1997). That subgroup has generally been considered to have a dual diagnosis: they are not only addicted to alcohol or drugs, but they are also affected by another psychiatric disorder that warrants specialized or extended treatment.

Program completion might also be improved by an even more basic aspect of the new psychology. Many of the alternative approaches are likely to engage men more directly by seeing them as individuals. Rather than confronting the men as "bad guys" or coming across to the batterers as anti-men, much of the new psychology considers the men to also be victims of sorts. As the disease model of alcoholism suggests, alcoholism is a disease rather than an issue of immoral or failed character. Some of its proponents consider such an approach to be more compassionate, more respectful, and more accommodating (for example, D. Dutton & Corvo, 2006; Stosny, 1995). As a result of it, they argue, men feel less threatened, become less resistant, and turn out to be more responsive.

However, the founding gendered psychology doesn't necessarily neglect the men's individual needs or issues, as is illustrated in the discussion of specific approaches below. Programs like Emerge, Amend, the Domestic Abuse Project, and Menergy have integrated psychological assessments and treatments into their program, while maintaining aspects of a gendered cognitive-behavioral approach. Such programs would also argue that they do attempt to involve men in the process of change in a variety of ways. That may include individual intake sessions, motivational interviewing, and furthering individual accountability. The interaction of men in these groups and their realization that they are not alone in their problems contribute to their engagement. Nonetheless, the new psychology and the programs coming from it do amount to a shift in emphasis.

Sorting It Out

As illustrated below in this chapter, the assumptions about psychological treatments are based largely on rather weak predictive studies and very preliminary evaluation research. Substantial clinical trials or experimental evaluations have yet to be conducted. The main justifications for the new psychology are the insights it brings to individual behavior, and the claim that conventional batterer programs "don't work." The logical conclusion is that the reason such programs don't work is because they are not treating the right problem or problems. A different diagnosis leads to a different prescription, so to speak.

There are few challenges to this stance, however. One is that the research doesn't necessarily show that batterer programs "don't work," as explained in the previous chapter. Second, the evidence is weak that some other approach is substantially more effective with offenders ordered by the court to participate in a program. Third, as the defenders of the gender-based, cognitive-behavioral approaches argue, the prevailing approach may be addressing more of men's individual problems than critics acknowledge. Fourth, it is not yet clear which of the several aspects of the new psychology deserves the most attention. The new psychology could be considered to be a variety of competing theories and treatments, or an array to draw from in an eclectic way.

The future of batterer programs may lie in sorting out whether the new psychology—or psychologies—represents a paradigm shift, as some argue (R. Stuart, 2005). The idea behind a paradigm shift to more psychologically focused treatments is based largely on two assumptions. One is a somewhat stereotypic view that psychological issues of men are largely neglected in the conventional batterer programs. Such issues may even be aggravated by the shaming effect of the gender-based approaches that, some clinicians believe, accuse and blame men (Wexler, 2010). Most batterer programs, including the Duluth program, would counter that they are responsive to the men's psychological needs in the course of their screening and group observations.

Arguably, the masculine psychology incorporated in many batterer programs does recognize men's internal conflicts, fears, hurts, and pains. It admittedly tends to analyze them in a social context and attend to the cognitive reinforcements for those problems. As far back as the early 1980s, anti-sexist batterer programs devoted whole sessions on men's self-care and compounding problems (see Gondolf, 1985). Since then, programs increasingly screen for mental health problems and addictions—or, in some cases, the court arranges for individual assessments along these lines (Gondolf, 2009a).

The alternative view, promoted in this book, is that the new psychology augments or supplements the existing programs. It may expose issues accounting for the subgroup of men unresponsive to batterer programming, as well as reinforce the efforts to more fully engage men in the process of change. The new psychology also renews the efforts to further help and heal men, beyond simply changing or redirecting their behavior.

There is a vestige of resistance to the new psychology that must be acknowledged. Accommodating batterers' psychological needs seems, to some domestic violence practitioners, a tall order—one that requires many resources and may be counterproductive in the long run. The concern is that psychological treatment can too easily become a distraction from the primary objective of improving women's safety. Moreover, the new psychology may indulge men's self-pity, narcissistic tendencies, and justifications for their behavior. It may weaken the motivating message that men must and can change. The gender-based approaches provide at least some counterbalance to a consuming new psychology, and direct men's attention to women's needs rather than just their own.

A further claim might be that a gender-based approach offers an integration of the social and individual, or at least the potential for that. The clinical psychologist Etiony Aldarondo has published a popular edited volume, *Advancing Social Justice through Clinical Practice* (2007) that documents this sort of integration. However, sufficient articulation of this sort of integration has yet to emerge, let alone be established. The spate of new approaches may be evidence that proponents of batterer programs need to explain their approach and develop it further—especially how it integrates meeting personal needs and social issues.

The remainder of this chapter sorts through the major psychological conceptions and treatments that counter cognitive-behavioral approaches. The intention is to weigh the evidence supporting them, the practical issues that each raises, and the contributions they offer the field. Overall, there is no doubt that the new psychology raises awareness of the individual differences of the men in batterer programs. In the next chapter, I review further programmatic innovations that identify and accommodate men's differences in an effort to engage batterers more fully in treatment. The assumption there is that men are more likely to participate and respond to treatment if their individual differences are recognized and considered.

The new psychology definitely exposes the complications, problems, and issues that many men bring with them to treatment. Whether these sorts of problems are causal or compounding is an open question that reaches far beyond the domestic violence field. It may also lead away from the fundamental issue of what to do—which treatment approach to use. The debate over effectiveness leaves the question of causality unanswered. The proponents of the new psychology make points that deserve attention and ultimately some accommodation, but the call to supplant established programs may not be justified.

Attachment Theory Lacks Outcome Evidence

The Basics of Attachment

The Abusive Personality and Attachment

The call to address men's emotional needs is probably most notably presented in Donald Dutton's portrayal of "the abusive personality" in his book of the same name (1998). The book, along with several articles elaborating the conception and its implication for treatment, explicitly challenges the gender-based, cognitive-behavioral approach, especially in the form of the Duluth program. Dutton's compelling arguments are built primarily on attachment theory that crystallized in the 1970s to explain particularly the aggression of children from troubled homes (Bowlby, 1969). According to this approach, a central component of abuse and violence is the attachment style of batterers, generally related to borderline personality disorder or dependent tendencies.

Attachment theory has become increasingly popular in psychotherapy as a means of organizing a variety of personality traits, emotional problems, and interaction patterns into a theoretical framework (see Sonkin & Dutton, 2003). It helps, in turn, to guide and direct psychodynamic treatment toward a more effective and longer-lasting outcome, according to its supporters. Several published articles articulate the theory as it applies to adult men who batter and advocate psychodynamic treatment approaches to address their battering (Bartholomew & Allison, 2006; Fonagy, 1999; Gormley, 2005; Mayseless, 1991; Sonkin & Dutton, 2003; Stosny, 1995; West & George, 1999). The theory is obviously well established.

At its heart, attachment theory helps to explain "the seemingly irrational outbursts that accompany real or imaged separation" (Sonkin & Dutton, 2003, p. 106). Childhood trauma—including detached parenting, neglect, and child abuse—creates a fear of loss or abandonment. The individual reacts with anger, despair, or detachment in response to separation or fear of it. In adulthood, these emotions are expressed toward one's partner, who is perceived as leaving, flirting, or less than fully loyal or attentive. Dutton and colleagues show that batterers may be distinguished by an especially insecure or fearful attachment style that is related to high levels of anxiety and anger (Dutton, Saunders, Starzomski, & Bartholomew, 1994). Severe dysfunction, moreover, makes for an attachment disorder that is usually associated with either borderline or dependent personality disorders.[6]

Attachment theory has several specific implications for treatment (Bowlby,

1988). It implies the need for a safe place or secure base to explore thoughts and feelings, and alleviate the distrust, anxiety, and fear associated with attachment issues. The patient needs to explore the attachment in current relationships and also with the therapist. He or she also needs to consider early childhood experiences, the attachment issues they gave rise to, and their role in current relationships. Finally, therapy should help the patient find a safe way to regulate his or her fear, anxiety, and anger, which flare up especially in relationships. Attention to the unconscious and conscious feelings, and their childhood roots, places this approach squarely in the psychodynamic realm (Levy & Orlans, 1998). (Some other more "here and now" therapies have been developed to address attachment issues as well.) Steven Stosny incorporated many of these ideas into his "compassion workshop" manual of 1995. His approach specifically addresses the attachment issues of men who abused their partners and the childhood experiences behind them.

Dan Sonkin and Donald Dutton (2003) go further in identifying the variations of insecure attachment in batterers, which they relate to three batterer "types," discussed in the next chapter. Avoidant, preoccupied, disorganized, and fearful attachment styles are all defense mechanisms for coping with the underlying anxiety associated with attachment disorders. The therapist needs to take these variations into account and therefore assess for them at the outset. At least two self-report assessment instruments have been established for these purposes, along with guidelines for clinical interviewing. In this approach, the alliance or relationship with the therapist becomes a crucial element of the treatment, as does the exploration of emotions and hurts that encumber them. Gendered beliefs and attitudes become less relevant in the process, and could be considered a diversion from the deeper emotional regulation that needs to be done.

In many cases, the childhood attachment issues are a reaction to the mothering that a man receives, and they turn into an unconscious resentment of women in adulthood. But the woman hating here is related more to the man's mother than to the masculine socialization and cultural attitudes. The gender-based, cognitive-behavioral approaches not only focus on the latter but also attend to the here and now—the current behavior of concern—rather than the past. The proponents of attachment theory attribute the ineffectiveness of batterer programs, suggested in experimental evaluations, to the failure of conventional batterer programs to treat attachment. The attachment approach also belies the apparent "one size fits all" view implied in the relatively undifferentiated cognitive-behavioral approach.

Attachment as a Batterer Characteristic

The claims for attachment treatment rest primarily on studies of batterer characteristics, rather than treatment outcomes. Considering the promotion of this approach, it is somewhat surprising that there is only one controlled evaluation of a psychodynamic approach with batterers, and that involved only a small group of men (Saunders, 1996). That study comparing psychodynamic and gender-based, cognitive-behavioral groups offered some support with limitations (Saunders, 1996), as discussed in the next chapter. Moreover, other outcome studies compare psychodynamic and cognitive-behavioral approaches with personality disorders associated with attachment issues and show no difference in outcomes (Leichsenring & Leibing, 2003; Perry, 2004). The main support for treating attachment issues in domestic violence cases comes instead from a few studies comparing small groups of batterer program participants (or violent men recruited from the general population) with a group of nonviolent men. The authors of these studies generally report that their findings are limited by small sample sizes, uncontrolled comparison groups, and noncausal associations (in other words, the relationship of the attachment to the violence is not clear).

The cited studies use mainly "dependency" measures (for example, how dependent one person is on another for emotional reinforcement); one study uses the Adult Attachment Inventory. For instance, John Kesner and colleagues found variables related to attachment to be significant predictors of domestic violence in a mixed sample of ninety-four participants in a batterers program and mental health clinic. Those who had been violent were more likely to have had an uncaring mother and lower self-esteem. However, the authors note that "cautions should be exercised in drawing conclusions from this data" (Kesner, Julian, & McHenry, 1997, p. 225).

Another set of comparison studies revealed contradictory findings, using interpersonal dependency as an indicator for insecure attachment (Buttell, Muldoon, & Carney, 2005). The first compared 105 men in a batterer program to 25 nonviolent men and found no significant differences. A second study by the same researchers compared two other groups of batterers ($n = 158$) and nonviolent men ($n = 25$) and did find a significant difference in the dependency scores. However, there was a wide range of dependency among the batterers, suggesting that "dependency issues only related to a subset of the sample" (p. 216). The researchers concluded that "more research is needed" to address the "confusion" (p. 213).

A more complex comparison between distressed, nonviolent couples ($n = 13$) and couples experiencing domestic violence ($n = 23$) used the Adult Attachment Interview and found the husbands in the second group were more likely to be classified as having insecure attachment (Babcock, Jacobson, Gottman, & Yerington, 2000). These results reflect those of an earlier comparison of subjects who were also drawn from the general population. On average, violent men (n = 24) had higher scores on measures of dependency and self-esteem than did distressed, nonviolent (n = 24) and happy, nonviolent men (n = 24) (C. Murphy, Meyer, & O'Leary, 1994).

Additionally, Dutton and colleagues make an indirect inference from the re-arrest outcomes of a quasi-experimental program evaluation: based on a previous study using the Millon Clinical Multiaxial Inventory (MCMI-III; see Millon, 1994), they suggest that men with avoidant or antisocial tendencies and borderline personality disorder are more likely to be re-arrested (Dutton, Bodnarchuk, Kropp, Hart, & Ogloff 1997). The researchers compared the re-arrests of men who completed the program (n = 158) with those of dropouts (n = 167) for an average of five years and up to eleven years after treatment. The number of re-arrests was highest for some extreme subgroups. Dutton and colleagues had previously found an association between results of an attachment questionnaire and reports from the wives on an abuse inventory at program intake (Dutton, Saunders, Starzomski, & Bartholomew, 1994). (The previous study was based on 120 men in a batterers program and a demographically matched sample of 40 men from the community.) The researchers therefore inferred that the subgroups with high arrests rates may be the men with attachment issues.

Attachment theory does offer useful insights into relationship dynamics and violent behaviors and has been instructively applied to abused children and battered women, as well as batterers (Henderson, Bartholomew, & Dutton, 1997). However, a recent review of the research literature on attachment theory in general provides a cautionary conclusion that reflects the even fewer studies on attachment and domestic violence: "It is incumbent on researchers and clinicians to recognize the serious limitations of the knowledge base for attachment theory" (Bolen, 2000, p. 147). The most we can say is that batterers may be more likely to show some tendencies associated with attachment issues, but many batterers do not. Still in question is whether these tendencies amount to a distinctive personality that warrants specialized treatment.

Similarities to the Addictive Personality

Several parallels can be drawn between the abusive personality in the domestic violence field and the addictive personality in alcohol treatment (Nakken,

1996). There is a similar indication of an association between attachment and addiction, and also questions about the evidence for a specialized treatment approach. The addictive personality is a constellation of personality traits and behavioral tendencies that include many of the same as those in the abusive personality: low self-esteem, fear of abandonment, anxiety, and shame that can be traced back to childhood experiences (Lang, 1983). Its proponents also urge that this personality construct needs to be considered in developing new and more effective treatments. One important implication of the addictive personality is that it implies that willpower—exerted in cognitive restructuring, social support, and behavioral alternatives—is not enough. Deeper therapy is needed. However, research support for these assertions is limited. According to the British psychiatrist Ciaran Mulholland, "modern, well-organized studies do not support a role for personality in addiction. Most of the theories outlined above are not well supported by scientific evidence" (2005). The strongest critic of the field, Staunton Peele (1998), goes further to dismiss the addictive personality as a myth.

The construct is debated because of the gender differences in addiction patterns and behavior, the distorting effect of the alcohol use, and inconclusive treatment outcomes. In other words, why do men generally drink and behave differently when intoxicated than women do, if an addictive personality is central? Is the addictive personality a predisposing factor or a result of the addiction? Researchers continue to explore different treatment approaches, and particularly the mechanisms associated with substance abuse. The association of personality tendencies with addiction does not fully explain why some people are addicted and others with similar personalities are not. There is also a mix of protective factors or resiliency in proscriptive or longitudinal studies that suggests the importance of situational variables over time and an elusive personality structure (for example, Vaillant, 1995).

Cautions about Applying Neuroscience

The Case for "Brain Science"

Attachment theory has neurobiological implications as well. Childhood trauma is thought to affect brain development, which in turn affects the personality tendencies associated with attachment issues. "Disrupted and anxious attachment not only leads to emotional and social problems, but also results in biochemical consequences in the developing brain. Infants raised without loving touch and security have abnormally high levels of stress hormones, which can impair the growth and development of their brains and bodies," explains one pair of clinical experts on treating attachment issues (Levy & Orlans, 1998; p. 27). Neuroscience, sometimes called neurobiology or "brain science," is increasingly being used to help explain a variety of intractable behaviors, especially those that appear impulsive and beyond rational direction. It is drawing increasing attention from researchers in the addiction field. In particular, it offers support for the view that batterers get caught in fits of anger and appear to just "snap" at times.

Neuroscience has received a great deal of publicity recently through a special television series (Rose, 2009) and newspaper features of all sorts. It is touted as the new frontier of behavioral research, which may answer some perplexing questions about mental disturbances and crime in general. In fact, a National Academy of Sciences review of criminal justice research posited that biomedical research, especially studies of the brain, may help to explain why so many criminals appear unresponsive and resistant to rehabilitation and change (Reiss & Roth, 1993). The implication is that our current social interventions, including batterer programs, largely fail because they do not address the underlying debilitation of the brain and its functioning. Violence in this light may be more a disease rather than a character defect. Biology is playing a determining role.

Neuroscience has been most vividly represented in the brain imaging studies that show different parts of the brain "lighting up" in certain circumstances more in normal individuals than in violent ones. The frontal lobe, responsible for reasoning, tends to appear less active in the violent subjects. The theory is that individuals who have been traumatized during childhood—abused or neglected—suffer brain damage of sorts. That is, the areas of reasoning in the brain do not fully develop, and consequently the thinking that would resist or redirect impulses is impaired. As a result, the individual becomes quick to anger and act impulsively. Medication for the brain dysfunction is therefore recommended, instead of cognitive-oriented counseling. The latter appeals to thought processes that may not be fully functional.

An interesting side note is that brain scans themselves are, according to the experts, subject to interpretation (Ezzell, 2000; Wahlund & Kristiansson, 2009). The scans actually suppress lower levels of lighting up throughout the brain in order to force the dramatic highlights that appear in the displayed brain scans. It may be an over interpretation, then, to suppose that some parts are working and others are not. There is also a question about inferences of association and causality. Debate continues over the extent to which one area of the brain determines certain behaviors, and the extent to which complex brain activity and meditating stimuli are at work. In other words, we are still a long way from learning much about prescribing treatments based on brain scans, although they admittedly reinforce an important research path toward an understanding of how the brain works.

One relevant application of the current theories of brain development appears in the studies on the intermittent explosive disorder (IED). As the name suggests, IED is characterized by outbursts of temper and violence that occur in response to minimal provocation. In people with this disorder, a low level of activity appears in the cognitive and reasoning part of the brain, which checks impulsive reactions. Researchers have identified the high prevalence of IED underlying many of the violent outbursts in our society—from road rage to school shootings (Kessler, Coccaro, Fava, Jaeger, Jin, & Walters, 2006). They estimate that at least a third of domestic violence perpetrators, or those we frequently refer to as batterers, is likely to suffer from this disorder (Kotulak, 2006). If this is the case, then batterers should be referred to psychiatric care, and their violent outbursts treated more as a medical problem—along the lines of hypertension and diabetes. To what extent, then, should we blame the brain for violent behavior and treat it in the course of intervention? Cognitive-behavioral approaches typical of most batterer programs essentially prompt men to take responsibility for their behavior and, in the process, invoke free will in men's choosing not to act violently toward others. However, men with IED are thought to have a diminished capacity to make such choices and thus to benefit from such programs.

Limitations and Concerns

There are concerns that the rising popularity of neuroscience may lead to its premature application to criminal interventions. The potential misuse and overuse come with the tendency to draw conclusions based on reducing complex, nuanced, and qualified research to an oversimplified bottom line (Eastman & Campbell, 2006; Garland & Frankel, 2004; Zeki & Goodenough, 2006). Most neuroscience researchers themselves caution against this. One recent review of the applications of neuroscience concludes: "Neuroscience is increasingly identifying associations between biology and violence that appear to offer courts evidence relevant to criminal responsibility . . . However, there is a mismatch between questions that the courts and society wish answered and those that neuroscience is capable of answering. This poses a risk to the proper exercise of justice and to civil liberties" (Eastman & Campbell, 2006, p. 311). A recent edited volume on the topic of neuroscience and the law similarly questions using the implications of neuroscience in legal decision making (Garland & Frankel, 2004). It cautions that the law assumes that individuals are responsible for their actions and are capable of learning and abiding by the rules of society. The assumption that an individual is not capable of these behaviors requires a stronger body of evidence than is currently available in neuroscience.

Researchers themselves point out several limitations (Goldberg, 2005). How the brain works and translates into "mind" are still mysteries. The association between brain activity and violent behavior is just that—an association, and not necessarily a cause. Moreover, the effectiveness of brain-related treatments is still uncertain. Most researchers, including those promoting IED, still acknowledge a role for cognitive-behavioral group counseling (Goldberg, 2005). Therefore, the research does not indicate replacing current batterer counseling and education, but raises additional considerations and supplemental treatment for extreme cases. In fact, proponents of IED acknowledge that conventional cognitive-behavioral approaches can assist and reinforce behavioral changes initiated under medication. Brain scientists concede that the brain itself is malleable—having plasticity—and therefore is still subject to development or change through the stimuli of interaction (Rose, 2009).[7]

Questions for Batterer Intervention Programs

The more basic issues are the extent of brain-related problems like IED among domestic violence offenders, and the need for medically oriented treatments. Should most batterers first go through an extensive assessment for such disorders and brain problems? Should batterer treatment be delivered in medical settings or clinics that may recommend counseling as a supplement to medical treatment for violence? Or is it sufficient to keep batterer programs in the community, with the possibility of additional referrals for men with extreme behavioral problems?

The answers lie partly in the numbers of men who might be identified as having brain-related impairments that warrant medical treatment in addition to, or instead of, batterer counseling or education. The assertion that as many as one-third of batterers may be acting out of IED seems high in light of our batterer research. In our court-mandated samples, our research showed very little evidence of symptoms associated with IED. According to the Millon Clinical Multiaxial Inventory (MCMI-III) administered to 864 batterers in our multisite study, less than 10 percent of the men evidenced symptoms of impulsive, posttraumatic stress, or borderline personality disorders (Gondolf, 1999c). Our research team found similar results using the Brief Symptoms Inventory in a subsequent study with nearly 1,000 men in Pittsburgh (Gondolf, 2009a). Moreover, approximately two-thirds of the men who screened positive on the inventory for psychological distress, and who received a clinical evaluation at a major teaching hospital, were diagnosed with an adjustment disorder requiring no further treatment. Only 5 percent of the evaluated men received a diagnosis related to impulse control. An additional study of the women's descriptions of violent incidents produced very few cases in which the pattern of violent events could be characterized by independent outbursts or explosions of rage (Gondolf & Beeman, 2003).

A practical issue is the resistance of batterers to comply with psychiatric or neurological evaluation and treatment ordered by courts. The men's resistance to such referrals appears to be very high in our studies, and the ability and willingness of psychiatric clinics to supervise compliance seems low (Gondolf, 2009a). Only 23 percent of the men who were ordered to mental health treatment were actually evaluated; 15 percent were advised to receive treatment; and 8 percent attended a treatment session. Just 6 percent of the voluntary referrals ever sought an evaluation. This low compliance rate, even under the court-mandated stipulations, suggests that sending men directly to mental health treatment for evaluation may not be practical. Batterer programs typically provide case supervision and violence education, which have much higher compliance rates. As noted in the previous chapter, over two-thirds of the men in our multisite evaluation of batterer interventions completed a minimum of three months of weekly sessions (A. Jones, D'Agostino, Gondolf, & Heckert, 2004; Gondolf & Jones, 2001).

In sum, courts should be cautious about applying the implications of neuroscientific research at this stage. Another article examining the advances of neuroscience concludes: "From the legal and research perspective, available findings [regarding neuroscience] must be viewed as preliminary at best, and caution must be exercised so the information is not inappropriately applied from general findings to a specific case" (Cellini, 2004, p. 3). Thus, it makes sense for now to continue to refer men to batterer programs and reinforce their compliance with this programming through supervision and sanctions, as has been shown in the "drug court" model (Gondolf, 2000c). Batterer intervention programs obviously need to send men with problems of explosive rage, depression, and alcohol abuse for additional evaluation and treatment. These sorts of problems are associated with the men who tend to drop out of batterer programs, regardless of their approach. Once again, the challenge appears to be how to keep such men in any kind of treatment and engage them in a process of change. In other words, how do we more effectively contain them and protect their potential victims?

Cognitive-Behavioral Approaches

The Case for a Gender-Based, Cognitive-Behavioral Approach

Application to Violence

The gender-based, cognitive-behavioral approaches are based on the belief that men's violence is primarily a learned behavior and can be unlearned, as social learning theory suggests (Bandura, 1973). According to related rational choice theory, men choose to act in certain ways in response to emotions and external circumstances (Cornish & Clarke, 1986). However predisposed in terms of personality characteristics or psychological problems, the mechanics, so to speak, of going from the predisposition to an action is a cognitive or thinking process. It is not just automatic or uncontrollable, even though outbursts may seem so at times. The violence is, as one expert in batterer programs puts it, more the result of "abusive thinking" than of an abusive personality (Bancroft, 2003, p. 3). Becoming more aware or conscious of the thinking behind the acts helps the violent person avoid, interrupt, or redirect them.

Our thinking patterns, or cognitive schema, are largely the result of socialization: we learn what to expect, think, and do from family, friends, institutions, media, and society at large. Our sense of self is wrapped up in the beliefs and attitudes we derive from these influences. That is where the gender aspect comes in. The beliefs that help to set our expectations for ourselves and others substantially reflect the messages we get about how to be a man or a woman. These are messages that are substantially reinforced by our male-dominated society, and the structures and interactions we experience daily in that society. In this process, men tend to learn not only how to mistreat women and view them as sex objects, but also how to settle conflict and disagreement with force.

A need for power and control, which most batterer programs work to address, sums up this outcome. Several clinical studies, in fact, have observed and documented cognitive scripts associated with power and control (Catlett, Toews, & Walilko, 2010; Henning & Holdford, 2006; Hamberger & Lohr, 1997), and similar cultural messages socialized in young boys (Kindlon & Thompson,

2000; Pollack, 1998). Admittedly, men frequently view themselves as victims (and they may well be, at work, in a bar, or in their home of origin). Their response to their perceived victimization is often a self-justified overreaction to regain a sense of power, status, or what they call respect (for an extensive social commentary on the issue and its impact, see Faludi, 1999).

As the expectations for how women and men should behave become more rigid, men's behavior is likely to be more demanding and imposing—and ultimately abusive. Inflated or distorted expectations based on men's belief systems may also lead to frustration. As such expectations become unrealistic and unattainable, they can't be met by the man or his partner. The resulting emotions are expressed in the form of a burst of anger or efforts to impose compliance with the expectations. Those outbursts can appear expressive or instrumental—or both. The man can end up angrily trying to "fix" the situation with abusive force. There is also a preventative or enforcing tendency to put down and control others in a way that fulfills expectations and avoids upsetting the apple cart. From this point of view, it is the man's misguided beliefs that are at issue.

A commonplace definition of cognitive-behavioral theory gets to its essence: "The cognitive-behavioral theory holds that one's own unrealistic beliefs are directly responsible for generating dysfunctional emotions and their resultant behaviors . . . , and that we humans can be rid of such emotions and their effects by dismantling the beliefs that give them life."[8] Exposing and addressing the expectations, and the beliefs that support them, are therefore essential parts of cognitive-behavioral treatment. Such treatment tends to focus on the thoughts related to the behavior of concern—abuse and violence, in the case of batterer programs. The exposure and discussion of beliefs and attitudes, however, usually lead to consideration of where they came from and their legitimacy. Experiences with one's parents and peers—and what we learn as children about how to think and behave—end up on the table. This is part of the broader process of cognitive restructuring that is associated with cognitive-behavioral treatments.

The Impact of Male Culture

As previously mentioned, the gender-based cognitive-behavioral programs assume that the underlying beliefs to be addressed are rooted in the male culture that promote aggression in men. At least two lines of research illustrate the operation and impact of that culture and the need to address it in treatment. One consists of several books by psychiatrists, psychologists, and researchers who have explored the development of aggression, bullying, and violence in boys

(Garbarino, 1999; Kindlon & Thompson, 2000; Pollack, 1998). In the process, they have revived the concern about a negative male culture that contributes to the violence. The consensus of these experts is that social messages, interactions, images, and roles pressed on boys today warrant our primary attention. Ultimately, our best intervention is to help boys and young men recognize and counter the socialization and social pressures that result in aggression and violence. One of the best-selling workbooks for dealing with boys' problems starts with "uncovering the myths" of the "'boy code" (Pollack & Cushman, 2001, p. xix). The authors discuss such topics as keeping a stiff upper lip, being tough or looking like a sissy, the idea of sex as a conquest, and not giving in or really listening. The implication is that we need to address these same topics in adult men. In fact, that is what is done in many men's programs, as shown in the guidebook *Men's Work: How to Stop the Violence That Tears Our Lives Apart* (Kivel, 1998).

The impacts of the underlying masculine culture and the socialization that accompanies it have also been documented in broader social studies. In their groundbreaking book, *Culture of Honor*, Richard Nisbet and Dov Cohen (1996) investigate the role of honor in the high murder rates in southern states. They conducted ethnographical and social history research, as well as laboratory experiments, to demonstrate the existence of a code of honor from the perspective of what they call cultural psychology. They consistently found that honor—protecting one's sense of manhood and reputation—was associated with aggression and violence. Honor was explanatory even when they controlled for individual temperament, history of slavery in a region, poverty, and climate. In other words, the honor effect cut across personality profiles and social class. The violence reflected a "concern with blows to reputation or status—with violation to personal honor—and the tactical belief that violence is an appropriate response to such an affront" (p. 2). The authors also show that public policy and the legal system historically viewed a murder as justifiable homicide if it was in response to a personal affront. This leniency further reinforced the tendency to defend one's honor with violence.

According to the authors, young men are socialized into this code through the expectations of their family, friends, and the society around them: "The young men of the South were prepared for these violent activities by a socialization process designed to make them physically courageous and ferocious in defense of their reputations" (Nisbet & Cohen, 1996, p. 107). From an early age, boys were taught to think much of their own honor and to be active in its defense. Honor in this society meant pride in masculine courage, physical strength, and warrior virtue. Male children were trained to defend their sense of honor without a moment's hesitation. Men were expected to take a stand and not back down, or be considered not much of a man. This unwillingness to accept insults is typical of other codes of honor throughout history, from the knightly traditions of medieval Europe to the modern military era. It is also acutely evident in the code of the street that prevails in inner-city gangs, and in the honor killings in South America and India. But the code of honor described here is one less based on false virtue and more on self-preservation. Young men feel a need to take care of themselves amid increasing competition and dwindling resources—as well as limited status.

These sorts of findings and their interpretation lend some obvious support to the attention in many batterer programs to male socialization and beliefs about manhood. Nisbet and Cohen state: "From this perspective, intervention programs that show individuals that they are living in a state of pluralistic ignorance with regard to disapproval of nonviolent behavior, or programs that teach ways to get community respect without resort to violence, seem more likely to succeed" (1996, p. 94). A cognitive-behavioral approach that addresses gender beliefs and attitudes would seem to make sense.

Continued Wide Use

The stock criticism of cognitive-behavioral approaches is that they do not go far enough in dealing with personal problems. They appear to advocate positive thinking or raw willpower, rather than the emotional exploration and wrangling of most psychotherapy. According to their critics, cognitive-behavioral approaches focus too much on the here and now and neglect the childhood experiences that form batterers' personalities and the underlying unconscious needs, wants, and fears. A preoccupation with behavioral change may distract programs from the more fundamental need to heal psychic wounds, with the result that matters only get worse. One of the historical contentions is that cognitive-behavioral approaches too often produce a quick fix with short-term gains but long-term losses.

Regardless of these concerns, cognitive-behavioral approaches have gained wide support across a variety of fields. And regardless of the merits of the causal theory of behavior, cognitive-behavioral approaches appear to capture how to interrupt, desist, or redirect behavior. They have been adapted to everything from smoking, overeating, depression, addiction, and borderline personality disorders to interpersonal violence and sexual assault (for example, Marshall, Anderson, & Fernandez, 1999). Across these problems, controlled evaluations suggest that cognitive-behavioral approaches are for the most part as effective or more effective as comparison approaches (for example, Butler, Chapman, Forman, & Beck, 2006; Marshall & Pithers, 1994; D. Wilson, Bouffard, & Mac-Kenzie, 2005). Brief cognitive-behavioral therapies, for instance, are purportedly based on evidence that longer-term process-oriented treatments are not necessarily more effective than shorter-term approaches (Dewan, Steenbarger, & Greenberg, 2004; see, for example, Marshall & Serran, 2000). Alcohol treatment has, accordingly, been drastically overhauled from the standard twenty-one-day residential treatment of the past to the seven-day outpatient treatments of the present that largely follow cognitive-behavioral principles.

Individuals with various personality tendencies and psychiatric disorders also appear to benefit from cognitive-behavioral approaches, according to some personality theories and outcome studies (Butler, Chapman, Forman, & Beck, 2006). Admittedly, some individuals with thought disturbances, severe psychiatric problems, or neurological problems are not responsive and can suffer further as a result under this approach. But clinicians and researchers have recommended that even individuals with IED should receive a highly structured form of cognitive-behavioral treatment along with medication (Kessler et al., 2006).

Research Support

What we broadly characterize as the gender-based, cognitive-behavioral approach draws on several experimental evaluations and meta-analyses that support the approach with a variety of criminal offenders (for example, Lipsey, Chapman, & Landenberger, 2001; Polaschek, Wilson, Townsend, & Daley, 2005; D. Wilson, Bouffard, & MacKenzie, 2005). That is, there is substantial generic evidence to support batterer programs. However, research on the impact of batterers' characteristics on program outcomes is comparatively weak, as discussed in the previous section. The more psychologically disturbed and more severely violent men are more likely to drop out of batterer programs and assault their partners again, but it is not clear that any treatment approach will substantially improve those outcomes. In fact, cognitive-behavioral approaches appear as appropriate and effective as other treatment approaches, if not more so.

The case can in fact be made that a structured cognitive-behavioral approach is appropriate for the vast majority of the men ordered by courts to attend batterer programs. As my colleagues and I have said in our research articles on the issue (Gondolf, 1999c; White & Gondolf, 2000), one size appears to fit most—despite the popular outcry against "one size fits all" programs and for a variety of tailored alternatives. As mentioned above, most of the men in our multisite evaluation eventually stopped their violence following the batterers program. At the thirty-month follow-up, 80 percent of the men had not physically abused their initial or new female partners in the previous year, according to their partners' reports (72 percent response rate, n = 618 of 864) (Gondolf, 2000d). Four years after program intake, 90 percent of the men had not abused their partners in the previous year.

Moreover, cognitive-behavioral approaches are generally prescribed for individuals with narcissistic and antisocial tendencies (for example, Choca & Van Denburg, 1997), and the majority of men in our studies show either or both of these tendencies, according to MCMI-III results (White & Gondolf, 2000). Even with subclinical or depressive profiles, the scores on the narcissistic subscale tended to be elevated. In other words, these tendencies were evident in most of the men, even if they appeared to be more of a borderline personality disorder or depressive type. This finding reflects the results of a research review on violent offenders in general, which concluded that inflated expectations, self-righteousness, and threatened egotism characterize the vast majority of these men (Baumeister, Smart, & Boden, 1996). Clinical texts recommend highly structured and didactic approaches—advice that conforms to the principles of cognitive-behavioral therapy—for men with these sorts of profiles (Choca & Van Denburg, 1997; Craig, 1995).

This approach has also been developed to effectively address other personality disorders. A meta-analysis of 250 psychodynamic and cognitive-behavioral treatment outcomes found both approaches to be effective in treating other personality disorders (Leichsenring & Leibing, 2003; Perry, 2004). A review of sixteen meta-analyses on treatment outcomes of cognitive-behavioral approaches similarly found "support for the efficacy of cognitive-behavioral therapy for a wide range of psychiatric disorders" (Butler, Chapman, Forman, & Beck, 2006, p. 17). Even so, only 15 percent of the batterer program participants in our multisite study show evidence of severe personality dysfunction, and over half indicated low personality dysfunction—that is, at a subclinical level, not warranting specialized psychological treatment (White & Gondolf, 2000).

Most important, several research reviews and meta-analyses in the criminal justice field assert that cognitive-behavioral approaches are effective with violent criminals and criminal populations in general (for example, Landenberger & Lipsey, 2005; Lipsey, Chapman, & Landenberger, 2001; Pearson, Lipton, Cleland, & Yee, 2002; Polaschek, Wilson, Townsend, & Daley, 2005; Wilson, Bouffard, & MacKenzie, 2005). The most recent meta-analysis echoes the conclusion of others: "The evidence summarized in this article supports the claim that cognitive-behavioral treatment techniques are effective at reducing criminal behaviors among convicted offenders" (Wilson, Bouffard, & MacKenzie, 2005, p. 198). Moreover, different variations and generic forms of cognitive-behavioral treatment seem to be equally effective, according to further meta-analyses of high-quality controlled evaluations (Landenberger & Lipsey, 2005, $N = 58$; Wilson, Bouffard, & MacKenzie, 2005, $N = 20$).

The previous chapter discussed what could be considered the specific evidence of the success of cognitive-behavioral approaches with batterers, in addition to the generic evidence presented above. The results of our multisite study that used complex statistical modeling showed a moderate reduction in subsequent assaults that was attributable to participation in the batterer programs (Gondolf & Jones, 2001; Jones, D'Agostino, Gondolf, & Heckert, 2004). Additionally, the vast majority of men's partners endorse these programs, attribute the men's change to the batterer programs, and feel safer as a result (Gondolf & White, 2000).

Practical Advantages

Even if psychodynamic approaches have equivalent or slightly better outcomes with some batterers, several practical considerations give an edge to gender-based, cognitive-behavioral approaches. According to its proponents, cognitive-behavioral treatment presents a clear and decisive message of personal responsibility and change. It can be helpful in breaking through the projections, excuses, and justifications associated with violent men, which make them resistant to treatment. It also reduces the tangents and avoidance that too easily emerge in less structured approaches.

As a result, the cognitive-behavior approach appears more compatible with criminal justice expectations. Court officials and probation officers are most concerned about the assaultive behavior that led to the batterer's arrest, and they want assurance that the crime itself is being explicitly addressed. Unless there is a diagnosis of a severe psychiatric disorder, other forms of therapy may seem to be a mental health "cop out" from the crime, as some victims' advocates have claimed (Bancroft, 2003). It could also be argued that the cognitive-behavioral approach is easier to implement. Many of its essentials have been converted into workbook or manual format, which require less intensive training and clinical supervision than psychodynamic therapy would.[9]

Another practical issue is that of getting men into psychotherapy in the first place, especially treatment using psychodynamic approaches that require deeper insight and self-disclosure. Men in general are famously resistant to such treatment for a variety reasons, related mostly to masculine self-image and socialized habits of interaction. It is estimated that less than a third of psychotherapy patients are men, and many of them are in treatment only because someone insisted on it (Wexler, 2010). Of course the men coming to treatment through the courts tend to be even more resistant, as the high no-show and dropout rates across interventions with criminals suggest. In response to men's resistance, several books specifically address how to involve and engage men in psychotherapy (for example, Engler-Carlson & Stevens, 2006; Wexler, 2009).

One expert on psychotherapy explains men's resistance to it this way: "There is a mismatch between the relational style of many men and the touch-feely atmosphere of most counseling and psychotherapy . . . Too often therapists—both male and female—try to massage men into being more like women in the ways they express themselves and experience their emotions. A major disincentive, even with men who know they need help, is the very idea of sitting in a room, talking out loud about all this touchy-feely stuff; it creeps them out" (Wexler, 2010, p. 23). Proponents of cognitive-behavioral approaches consequently see them as a better fit for criminal offenders in particular. Cognitive-behavior approaches tend to come across as less "touchy-feely" and more about the practical steps to stopping dangerous behavior. The criminologist Edward Latessa summarizes the point: "Talk therapy doesn't work because the primary needs are skill-based. Offenders need to practice and rehearse ways of handling a situation" (quoted in Yeung, 2010, p. 30)

The most important advantage of cognitive-behavioral approaches is their appeal to victims' rights groups, specifically to battered women's advocates. These approaches, as mentioned, are distinguished by their focus on the behavior of concern—in this case, the men's abuse of and violence against women. With all the controversy surrounding batterer programs, their victims at least want reassurance that the programs are explicitly and directly addressing men's violence, rather than allowing the men to focus on their personal problems. The victims generally want their abusive partners to be held accountable for their behavior and not to blame their violence on women or personal issues. The research on so-called brief therapies, associated with the cognitive-behavioral approach, also suggest quicker results at least in the short term (Dewan, Steenbarger, & Greenberg, 2004; Kim, 2008). That is, many victims are likely to see some relief or interruption of abuse more quickly than with other approaches, although this has yet to be established in research on batterer programs' outcomes.

Moreover, the victims' perspective is a central concern of most of the gender-based, cognitive-behavioral approaches. Victims' advocates have raised concerns over the implications of pathological and brain-based explanations for domestic violence (for example, Bancroft, 2003). These explanations appear to displace the responsibility for the violence from the individual, and reinforce batterers' tendency to project blame and accountability. Batterers frequently play out this displacement of responsibility in their presentation of violent incidents (Catlett, Toews, & Walilko, 2010; Henning & Holdford, 2006). They describe themselves as losing control or "snapping," to make the violence appear accidental or to minimize a constellation of abuses. Without corroborating information carefully gathered from victims, what appears to be IED may actually be a form of narcissistic or antisocial manipulation. The gender-based, cognitive-behavioral approaches at least acknowledge this tendency and attempt to keep the focus on the women's safety. Such programs are less about making a man feel better about himself, and more about doing what it takes to stop his abuse and violence. The cognitive-behavioral assumption is that the two are not necessarily tightly connected. One review of the treatment of violent psychiatric patients notes: "Echoing the claims of cognitive-behavioral proponents, psychiatric researchers remind us that assessments of the propensity for violence are fundamentally different from the process of reducing it" (Kraemer, Kazdin, Offord, Kessler, Jensen, & Kupfer, 1997, p. 342).

Overall, cognitive-behavioral approaches are promoted as being more compatible with criminal justice intervention and more efficient to implement—and at least as effective as other approaches.

Contributions of the Duluth Program

A Popular and Widespread Program

The Duluth Batterer Program, as it is popularly known, probably best represents the fundamentals of the gender-based, cognitive-behavioral approach that has dominated the domestic violence field. It is the best known among batterer programs, and the main target of the criticism directed at mainstream batterer programs in general (see D. Dutton & Corvo, 2006). In 2007, the Duluth program, formally titled the Domestic Abuse Intervention Program, was being used in all fifty states and seventeen foreign countries (Pheifer, 2010). It is specifically recommended in a quarter of the state standards for batterer programs, and elements of it appear in almost all standards and guidelines. The

Duluth Power and Control Wheel, for instance, is a staple across a variety of programs.

The popularity of the program rests on its grounded and common-sense aspects. For example, the Duluth program—like many other gender-based, cognitive-behavioral approaches—attempts to bridge several practical concerns. It was developed in large part as a response to the male batterers flooding the courts following the criminalization of domestic violence in the 1980s. Misdemeanor charges and overcrowded jails left many of the men on open probation with little supervision. The mental health and family counseling programs of that time not only were inappropriate referral sources for the resistant men but also had been shown, in at least a few studies, to be clueless about domestic violence (for example, Harway & Hansen, 1993). The Duluth program offered the courts a reliable referral that was sensitive to the concerns of victims and battered women's advocates.

At the same time, the Duluth program remains essentially a cognitive-behavioral approach, as it explains on its webpage (www.duluth-model.org). The Cochrane Collaboration's meta-analysis of batterer programs also classifies Duluth as cognitive-behavioral (Smedslund, Dalsbø, Steiro, Winsvold, & Clench-Aas, 2007). Another meta-analysis concedes at least a substantial overlap between the Duluth program and those identified as cognitive-behavioral programs (Babcock, Green, & Robie, 2004). The Duluth program definitely pays attention to the conscious thought processes of its participants—that is its cognitive dimension. The gendered beliefs that it explores, along with the justifications and minimizations confronted in the Power and Control Wheel, could be considered the cognitive scripts that are generally addressed in cognitive-behavioral approaches.

The behavioral dimension of the program lies in its explicit attention to the range of actions men take toward their partners. Not only does the program expose the specific behaviors that need to be acknowledged and stopped, but it also promotes and develops alternative behaviors that are nonviolent and more respectful of the men's partners. The fundamentals converge into what is a largely accepted practice with violent offenders, sex offenders, and addicted patients (for example, Landenberger & Lipsey, 2005; Wilson, Bouffard, & MacKenzie, 2005).

Fundamental Concepts

The Power and Control Wheel

Part of the appeal of the Duluth program is its basis in the experiences of battered women. As Ellen Pence, one of its founders, recalls, she and a few of her colleagues sat down with what today we would call focus groups of battered women. Together they explored what the women's relationships with their partners were like beyond the events that brought the partners to court (Pence, 2002). The stories that the women told and the impacts of their partners' behaviors began to converge. What emerged was a picture of control in which the violent events were a small, albeit punishing, part. Out of this came the Power and Control Wheel, which identified the specifics of intimidation, threats, emotional abuse, economic abuse, male privilege, using children, and minimizing and blaming—as well as physical and sexual violence. The accompanying Equality Wheel illustrates the positive antidote to the controlling behaviors of the first wheel: negotiation, nonthreatening behavior, respect, trust and support, honesty and accountability, responsible parenting, shared responsibility, and economic partnership (Pence & Paymar, 2003).

The two wheels have become a teaching tool in their own right throughout the field. In a very concrete and accessible diagram, the wheels expose the dynamics of an abusive relationship and their impact, and what the man can do about it. They also offer a way to confront denial, expose behavior, and prompt acknowledgement of the man's problems—in therapeutic terms, the first step toward behavior change. But the program goes further, with vignettes that illustrate the behaviors on the wheels and logs of the men's actions and intentions during the week. Pence writes: "Men do many, many things everyday automatically—things that they never stop and think about—that are also abusive, violent, and controlling" (Pence, 2002, p. 24). The logs help the men become more aware of what they are doing, start to monitor their thoughts and behavior, and ultimately make better choices about how they should live.

The Dialogical Format

The Duluth founders also explored how to engage potentially resistant and defiant men, as well as those who might appear emotionally charged and penitent. The dialogical format, based on the educational theories and practice of Paulo Freire (2000), was adopted as an innovative means of working with the mostly lower-income and working-class men. Freire's methods were developed primarily with poor Brazilian farmers who were faced with a sense of subjection and resignation. The Duluth founders observe that many of the batterers similarly felt put upon by society and stuck in their masculine roles. The aim is to raise their awareness of the capacity to change against overwhelming impositions of external forces and internal beliefs, doubts, and fears.

Graham Barnes, a former Duluth program director and currently a research specialist at the Battered Women's Justice Project, summarizes the group experience this way: "Even though men recognize that they are all so different in their life circumstances, they see how their common experience of being raised has gotten in the way of what they want. Most of us want to be loved, cared for, and to feel like we belong to a family—a family that cares about us, appreciates us. Yet the things we learned in growing up have stopped us from feeling that love and connection and closeness. We are often feeling alone, untrusting, untrusted and bitter" (personal communication, May 2, 2010).

Through guided exchanges, recognition of common themes, and prompting examples or vignettes, the men are moved toward self-examination and reflection. In current terms, they became more self-aware and mindful. Rather than just learning techniques to interrupt violence, the Duluth approach also helps men strategize about alternative behaviors, based on a shift in outlook. In response to the vignettes, for instance, the men role-play ways they might respond, such as discussing an issue, expressing their feelings, and clarifying the problems. Ideally they also develop some empathy for what their partner has felt and experienced. In the process, the men can become conscious of their partners' and their own humanity.

Barnes describes this difficult part: "The groups help men to see what we need to do to make things right. For that brief time we're in a group together—even with many men not wanting to be there but still feeling that common pain—we are figuring out how we can make some changes for the better. Then we leave the room, go out the door, and all the world is working against what the group gave us. We don't want to come back to the group because we're already going blind again, because the sexist world we live in doesn't reinforce what we experience in the group. Groups can be hard for men to be in, they confront us with our own shortfalls and the challenges before us, but we need that. It's part of a bigger process of change at work" (personal communication, May 2, 2010).

Distinguishing Aspects

A Women-Centered Focus

The Duluth program has been routinely cast as a feminist vestige of the battered women's movement—to both its credit and its discredit (Caesar & Hamberger, 1989; Aldarondo & Mederos, 2002). The inherent feminism lies in part with the program's grounding in the experience of battered women. It is in this sense women-centered or -focused. The courts—however inconsistently—are victim-focused, as well, in their intent of bringing protection to the victim and retribution to the perpetrator of a crime. An offender who ends up in jail, on probation, or in a treatment program (for example, drunk driving classes) is there primarily to make the situation better for potential victims, not necessarily for himself.

The Duluth program also prompts a power analysis of men's relationships that reflects the critical theory associated with feminism. In examining why and how men do what they do, the advantages it brings them, and the disadvantages it causes others, all come to the surface. Ellen Pence points out: "We see battering behavior as a logical outcome in a society that until recent years openly gave men entitlement to women's servitude and authorized them to use violence in order to maintain their place of privilege—while simultaneously seeing men who do so as brutes" (2002, p. 10). Much of the writing and discussion in the domestic violence field has, of course, revolved around the role of gender, masculinity, male socialization, misogyny, and patriarchy as aspects that predispose men to violence toward women. These social constructs shape underlying attitudes and beliefs about oneself, others, and relationships that need to be addressed in the course of change, according to the feminist point of view.

Community Organizing

As most practitioners in the field are well aware, there is another essential component to the Duluth program that is too often slighted in its replication. The Duluth program and curriculum were designed as part of a larger coordinated community response (Shepard & Pence, 1999). It was to be one component of a system that also included arrests, court action, probation supervision, victim supports, additional social services, and further sanction for noncompliance. These components were intended to bring not only personal assistance to the victims of domestic violence, but also accountability in the sense of expectations, requirements, and consequences for the perpetrators.

What has become the Duluth model is more than a medical approach in which treatment is delivered to the batterer; rather, it is a systemic approach of both stick and carrot. To this end, much of the work and impact of the Duluth program has been in collaboration with other agencies and services in the community, particularly women's and children's programs. The shared trainings, protocols, and linkages contribute to institutional reform and intervention enhancement that arguably make the difference in batterer program outcomes (Gondolf, 2002a). This is a topic that we explore further in chapter 6.

Overwrought Replication

As mentioned previously, a vocal and organized faction of clinicians and researchers has dismissed the Duluth program as merely educational, ideological, and simplistic (for example, Hame1, 2010; Babcock, Canady, Graham, & Schart, 2007; D. Dutton & Corvo, 2006). Some have gone as far to denounce it as brainwashing, shaming, and anti-male. There are admittedly misuses and abuses of the Duluth program—as there are of other approaches and therapies—that may warrant criticisms of this sort. Some staff in its many imitators are not sufficiently trained, skilled, or supervised to administer the Duluth program as it was designed. Their own assumptions and personal agendas may go unchecked, or they simply may not have the skills to facilitate group discussion. Unfortunately, we have no measure of the skill and quality levels of programs' staffing, and state standards for batterer programs have varying staff requirements and generally loose quality controls.

One of the biggest drawbacks, according to Graham Barnes, is that the implementation of the Duluth program has sometimes been "too rigid, too overwrought, and too combative. Some group leaders feel like they need to drag men to nonviolence" (personal communication, May 2, 2010). As Barnes explains, this rigidity is not the intent of the Duluth program, nor is it representative of Duluth's dialogical approach: "We are thinking adults asking deep questions about who we are, and how we can make things right with our family. Once a facilitator team understands the themes, and can come at them from several different angles, and practices using the log, then we can relax a bit and have looser discussions with the men to see where they might need to go with their own learning" (ibid.).[10]

The Gender Debate

The opposition's overarching concern is that women's violence toward men is neglected in the Duluth program and batterer programs in general. Suffice it to say that women's use of force against their male partners is acknowledged and being addressed through programs for women (Larance, 2006; Swan & Snow, 2006), and training that is sponsored by the Duluth Domestic Abuse Intervention Program and others. As has been pointed out above, research (for example, Gondolf, in press) shows the vast majority of court cases do fit what Michael Johnson (2008) has identified as "intimate terrorism." The women's aggression in these cases is largely in self-defense, reaction, or desperation in response to men's power and control over them. It tends to be minor in comparison to the violence and abuse perpetrated on them by their male partners.

There is also a therapeutic rationale for dealing with women separately from their male partners, and for using different approaches. Women's violence is more likely to be rooted in past victimization and trauma, and women are more likely to openly disclose their partner's abuse in a group separate from their partners, free of potential reprisals (Swan & Snow, 2006). And most important, as many battered women's advocates argue, the women are more likely to be safer in all-women groups where they can speak freely without their partners getting angry and taking it out on them later. The prevailing treatment approach in the addiction field that separates primary substance users into programs like Alcohol Anonymous, and family members into Al-Anon, might be an example of this consideration.

Too Confrontational?

Duluth counseling is criticized especially for being confrontational and shame-based (D. Dutton & Corvo, 2006). Almost all batterer programs are implicitly, if not explicitly, confrontational in nature, because they begin with the premise that certain behaviors and attitudes are wrong and need to be changed. This approach obviously contrasts with nondirective or reflective therapies that encourage the client to discover or realize his needs and solutions, and that rely heavily on what is known as a therapeutic relationship to help the client do so. Confrontation, from a cognitive-behavioral point of view, is a fundamental step in countering denial or resistance, and exposing the behavior in need of change. Cognitive-behavioral approaches to alcohol treatment, for example, famously confront the alcoholic in a family intervention in order to break down denial. The question about confrontation, then, is not *should* it be done, but *how* it should be done. If the confrontation is antagonistic, hostile, or accusatory, it certainly can be detrimental or counterproductive. However, most experienced counselors confront batterers in a more subtle and encouraging manner, while still exposing and redirecting the rationalizations that reinforce abuse.

The concept of shame is a more complex issue (Gilligan, 2003). There is some concern that shame about one's behavior turns inward and undercuts one's sense of worth. A man can be left feeling that he can't change and doesn't deserve anything better. At the same time, many violent people—especially those with antisocial and narcissistic tendencies—do not feel much guilt or personal responsibility for their violent or abusive behavior. Instead they are likely to project blame onto other individuals or external circumstances. Ideally, we want these men to feel some guilt for what they have done. According to cognitive-behavioral proponents, guilt can help in accepting responsibility for one's behavior, and accepting responsibility is a step toward exerting some change in behavior or attitudes (for example, Hamberger, 1997, 2002; McGuire, 2006; Polaschek, Wilson, Townsend, & Daley, 2006). As long as a man asserts that his behavior is somebody else's doing, he has little—or at least, much less—influence over it. Scolding or condemning individuals in a way that could lead to shame is not what the Duluth program promotes. However, confronting men's abusive behavior in a calculated way does have some justification.

Anger Treatment

Critics of Duluth counseling also objects to Duluth's position on anger and anger management. The Duluth program focuses on beliefs and attitudes associated with violent behavior, rather than primarily on the anger often associated with violent events. The causal role of anger in violence and the usefulness of treating anger as a way to stop violence remain issues beyond the domestic violence field. An article in *U.S. News & World Report*, for instance, indicated that the limited research on anger management showed little impact on recidivism, and a Department of Justice report criticized the courts for using anger management as a panacea for violence (Koerner, 1999). An extensive review of the research on anger and violent offenders concludes that anger management programs may in fact be counterproductive with overcontrolled violent offenders as well as with outright antisocial ones (Davey, Day, & Howells, 2005).

Admittedly, several studies show a higher prevalence of hostility or anger among men who used violence against their partners compared to nonviolent men (Norlander & Eckhardt, 2005; Schumacher, Feldbau-Kohn, Slep, & Heyman, 2001). However, other studies challenge the assumption that violence against women is primarily anger-based. For example, Wagdy Loza and Amel Loza-Fanous (1999a) used nine psychological tests to assess 252 prisoners incarcerated for violent crimes and reviewed their criminal records. The researchers found no significant difference between the prisoners' past violence and their measures of anger or risk for future violence. Although anger management techniques may be included in conventional batterer programs, these researchers conclude that anger management programs do not appear to be sufficient in themselves (Loza & Loza-Fanous, 1999b).

Furthermore, a more recent assessment of anger in 190 batterer program participants showed a relatively low portion of men with high levels of anger (Eckhardt, Samper, & Murphy, 2008). The findings were based on clustered scores from the State-Trait Anger Expression Inventory. The authors concluded that "the majority of partner abusive men do not present with anger-related disturbances" (p. 1600). They do note that the extreme anger of at least a portion of men may warrant special attention or additional treatments, but anger management programs that focus exclusively or primarily on anger are likely to be insufficient to deal with that level of problem.

The Duluth program acknowledges that some men warrant more intensive therapy for psychological problems than it is equipped to provide by itself. Its emphasis on a coordinated community response encourages referrals and collaboration with other treatment services to meet special needs of program participants. A program description states: "Once at the program, it may be decided that a particular offender needs a special type of rehabilitation (e.g., treatment for alcoholism) in which case a separate plan is worked out between the men's program coordinator and the probation officer" (Pence, 2002, p. 10). (More details on screening and referral are in the current Duluth program manual [Pence & Paymar, 2003].)The assumption of the Duluth program, however, is that the curriculum and group process are essential to stopping violence—that mental health or addiction treatment alone is generally insufficient. The social reinforcement of men's violence and abuse of women, and the justifications and rationalization that facilitate such behavior, require much more.

Supportive Research

The popular slogan confronting the Duluth program and batterer programs in general is that "one size does *not* fit all." The implication is that batterer programs, and particularly Duluth, are ineffective with the diversity of batterers that are mandated by the courts to attend programs. As discussed above, our research team inferred from our multisite evaluation that "one size fits most" (Gondolf, 2002a). The vast majority of men in the Duluth-oriented programs in our study did eventually stop their violence for an extended part of the four-year follow-up period. A subgroup of men did repeatedly assault their partners during the follow-up; they were more likely to have psychological problems, according to a mental health inventory (Gondolf & White, 2001). However, neither these men nor the sample at large had any distinguishing profile (White & Gondolf, 2000). In fact, over 60 percent of the men appeared "normal" in that they had subclinical scores on the subscales of the inventory.

Most notable was the commonalities across the psychological profiles of the men in our batterer program research. The majority of men showed elevations on the narcissism and/or antisocial subscales, regardless of the other subscale results (White & Gondolf, 2000). These elevations reflect the concerns that batterers tend to have an inflated sense of self or sense of entitlement that inflates their expectations, demands, and blame of others. It is these commonalities that programs like Duluth specifically address and that probably account for our finding that "one size fits most." Along with other points, the commonalities among the men also challenge the call for specialized and individualized therapy for batterers. This is not to overlook the ongoing evolution of batterer programs and the innovations in engaging resistant men through motivational or culturally specific counseling. Duluth itself has been a pioneer in adapting its program to Native American men, a version called "Mending the Sacred Hoop" (Gilberg et al., 2003).

The Duluth program offers a bedrock of fundamentals to assess the claims and counterclaims of the day. The grounded and experiential basis of the program, and its sociological as well as cognitive dimensions, make it a bridge among perspectives. It appears as efficient and practical amid the financial constraints facing human services in general. Perhaps most important is the vision behind the Duluth program. It is intended to be both a part and a facilitator of a larger process of community building. Pence once said to a group of practitioners: "Why are we here, really? Why do we persist in this work? It has much to do with our yearning for social justice—and for a better and safer community" (Gondolf, 2010, p. 1002). This ideal sets the Duluth program apart from many of the more psychological programs vying for attention.

Conclusion: Challenging the Divide

The Contentious Backdrop

The new psychology of batterers is surely having a reinforcing impact on batterer programming. This is not so much because it is something new, but because it increasingly is being used to address a long-standing tension within batterer programs. As mentioned at the outset of this book, batterer programs have struggled to balance the desire to help and heal men with the need to protect and support women. The two ends, of course, are not necessarily mutually exclusive, but they are also not necessarily the same. Early advocates of battered women voiced concern about programs' colluding with violent men, and batterer program staff members' not staying focused on stopping the violence. These issues are of course not limited to the domestic violence field. In fact, they are debated throughout the criminal justice system. Victim's rights activists have frequently challenged the coddling of criminals: To what degree does an offender warrant rehabilitation over punishment or containment? Have we become too soft on crime, with all the attention we give the criminal? Is any treatment warranted and worthwhile?

These sorts of questions have been intensified with regard to batterer programs in part because of the well-organized advocates of battered women, along with the widespread extent and impact of battering. The increasing entry of clinical psychologists into the treatment of batterers also adds the counterpoint of psychotherapy and its scientific knowledge base. The rapid expansion and popularity of clinical psychology graduate programs, the professionalization and organization of the mental health field, and the insurance and compensation structure of psychotherapy add a substantial weight to the psychological emphasis in the domestic violence field. As mentioned above, scholarly publications on batterers are dominated by the psychological perspective and further substantiate the emphasis on the hurts and needs of batterers. In some sense, there is a political tussle in process over which perspective, emphasis, or paradigm should dominate the field. That is, the differences in emphasis have become politicized.

On another level, a difference in perspective across disciplines undergirds what appears at times to be a battle among various camps. Clinical psychology, as I have discussed, generally focuses on the psychopathology underlying the violence and on therapies tailored to the batterer's psychological needs (for example, D. Dutton, 1998). Social workers in the field have promoted an ecological framework of battering that considers not only individual needs, but also the community and social influences that shape behavior (for example, Edleson & Tolman, 1992). The work of criminologists, in contrast, tends to substantiate the role of deterrence through accountability, and desistence through behavioral change and case management (for example, Bledsoe, Bibhuti, & Barbee, 2006; Labriola, Rempel, O'Sullivan, & Frank, 2007). It's not that these perspectives can't complement one another, or that each is more applicable than others in some cases. But the vested interests and concerns of one camp sometimes seem threatened by those of another. Defending these interests contributes to an intensification of perspective, like Republicans refusing to compromise with Democrats, or one religious sect damning another. The treatment divide, of course, has been further complicated by the issue of gender. To what degree is battering a product of a troubled mind or a sexist society? Is the predisposition for domestic violence primarily in personality or society?

When I recently tried to discuss some of these issues with a colleague, he threw up his hands and said, "Welcome to the cultural wars." His point was that the disagreements over the role of gender had become reified positions bolstered by self-contained assumptions, social agendas, and perceived adversaries. Dogmatic and ideological factions on all sides drowned out the voices of those in the middle. A legitimate caution needs to be considered, however. That is, how do established batterer programs avoid being usurped by the new psychology alone, and how do entrenched programs accommodate some of the psychological insights regarding batterers? Understandably, some advocates dig in their heels against what they perceive as an increasing onslaught of psychological treatments for men who have criminally attacked, abused, and injured women and children.

Evidence-Based Answers

Our review of the research evidence suggests a murky picture. Despite what proponents assert of one approach or another, much of the research they use to support their position is selective, preliminary, or inconclusive. Admittedly, that is often the nature of research. As argued in previous chapters, methodological limitations and conceptual qualifications are involved in most social science studies—to greater or lesser degrees—and the findings are subject to interpretation and discussion. Yet the practitioners of the world need and want a bottom line, and direct answers to their questions about how to proceed. The resistance to a psychotherapy takeover or to an overly diversified approach has less to do with ideology, antipathy toward science, or the early days of activism. There are evidence-based arguments to prop up different perspectives and positions, including those considered feminist or ideological. What we don't have, in terms of evidence-based practice, are multisite clinical trials or experimental evaluations that would point to one or more "winners." But the debate that continues to swirl around the multisite clinical trials in the fields of alcohol abuse and mental health suggests that such evaluations would not bring a definitive answer either. As I outlined in the earlier chapter on evidence-based practice, program practitioners, victims' advocates, court officials, service providers, and researchers need to weigh all the options together.

To my mind, the new psychology is invigorating aspects of intervention that have been neglected or underdeveloped in some programs. It has generally helped to soften the overarching stereotype of all batterers as monstrous villains, and the view that deterrent or punitive measures alone will suppress their behavior. The challenge is applying some of the insights without overly pitying violent men and diverting attention from the safety and well-being of their victims. The new psychology has, at a minimum, focused greater attention on the compounding problems of batterers that are undeniably associated with dropping out of programs and committing new assaults. It strengthens the call throughout the field for fuller engagement of men—getting them more involved in the program, and more committed to change. One obvious reason for this call has been the dropout rates of programs—as high as 70 percent. (Of course, high dropout rates are not entirely attributable to the programs.) Another is the need to make programs more effective, and have more of an impact on a wider range of men.

With ardent arguments for a variety of approaches, but with tenuous or competing evidence behind them, how is this engagement best to be achieved? The cognitive-behavioral essentials of most programs appear justified and warranted with the majority of court-referred batterers. That approach has been shown to be as effective as, or more effective than, other approaches with violent or addicted offenders, as well as depressive patients. Clearly some batterer program participants warrant more attention. Depending on referral resources and staff training, programs are either screening men and referring them to supplemental treatment, treating men with psychological problems in a separate group, or developing specialized behavioral health programs for domestic violence. Most programs also continue to develop intake, orientation, or motivational sessions to increase participant buy-in. Although uneven, this direction is probably more than sufficient. The major issue at hand is what to do with the men who are outright resistant, unresponsive, and dangerous, regardless of the program's approach.

In sum, the debate over program approach is significant but may be overwrought. The dichotomy between psychodynamic and cognitive-behavioral approaches may be a false or unnecessary one. The cognitive-behavioral approach still has generic evidence and conceptual support in its favor. However, incorporating treatment for the special needs of batterers within this approach may assist in reducing dropout and re-assault rates. Referrals for supplemental treatment can help to meet those needs, while keeping the focus on behavioral change in the batterer program groups. The point is to send a consistent motivating and deterring message that men can and must stop their violence.

There is clearly a subgroup of men who appear to be unresponsive to batterer programs, regardless of the approach or the type of batterer. The new psychology of batterers does not identify these men or offer a treatment that would necessarily improve the outcomes overall. In our research, the most dangerous of these men dropped out of other programs and resisted psychotherapy or mental health treatment. As elaborated further in later chapters, more engagement and healing of men are certainly warranted, but the more far-reaching evolution of batterer programs is toward risk management of the problematic and unresponsive batterers. The program approach that best supports and complements this sort of effort may be the most effective in the long run. The gender-based, cognitive-behavioral approach, at least according to the evidence laid out here, is a suitable candidate in this regard. At least it is one that cannot be readily dismissed, as its critics attempt to do. It is a basis to build on, rather than something to overturn and replace.

4 | The Many Efforts to Categorize Batterers

Not All the Same

Men who batter their female partners are not all the same. At least, this has become a truism in the field. At conferences and in articles, the opposition to "one size fits all" approaches is cited to justify diverse and tailored treatments for batterers (for example, Corvo, Dutton, & Chen, 2008; Holtzworth-Munroe & Meehan, 2004; Levesque, Driskell, & Prochaska, 2008; Stith Rosen, McCollum, & Thomsen, 2004). This raises a direct challenge to what is referred to as the "one size fits most" approach of the gender-based, cognitive-behavioral programs. These programs are accused of neglecting and even rejecting differences among batterers that warrant special attention. According to the critics, not only do their program outcomes suffer, but the poor fit may further aggravate many men. According to the critics, the "one size fits most" programs are unresponsive to the diversification of batterers because they are built on a single-cause theory of violence—namely, sexism in society (for example, Babcock, Canady, Graham, & Schart, 2007; D. Dutton & Corvo, 2006; Mills, 2009). As discussed more fully in this chapter, the causality assumptions of the gender-based programs are more complex than that, and the question of how to interrupt and stop violence may not follow directly from cause or etiology (Kraemer, Kazdin, Offord, Kessler, Jensen, & Kupfer, 1997).

However, there is no doubt that the men coming to batterer programs do differ obviously from each other in terms of the pattern of their violence, their motivation to change, their interaction with partners, and their race and ethnicity. The practical question is whether these differences constitute measurable and discrete categories that are also predictive of outcomes. That is, can we put our finger on a distinct and diagnostic type, or do we have instead a set of tendencies or dimensions that vary across time and situation? The second and most important question for batterer programs is whether the types matter. Can they be practically and consistently discerned, and does matching men to different treatments produce better outcomes—namely, a reduction in violence? Conventional batterer programs assume either that the commonalities of the men are more influential than their differences, or that the cognitive-behavioral approach is suitable for a wide range of men. As mentioned throughout the previous chapter, I continue to be impressed by both of these possibilities.

In our multisite study of batterer programs, a wide variety of men did appear to eventually stop their violence and reduce their nonphysical abuse, according to their female partners (Gondolf, 2000b; Gondolf, Heckert, & Kimmel, 2002). The subgroup of men who repeatedly and severely abused their partners did not fall into a discernible category in terms of psychological profile, pattern of violence, relationship status, and so on (Gondolf & White, 2001). The variation in program approach and format across the study did not seem to make much difference. Yet as others in the field argue, several innovations might at least give batterer programs a boost: treatment tailored to certain batterer types, motivational interviewing in response to stages of change, couples counseling for mutually violent partners, and culturally focused counseling, especially for African American and Latino men. For the most part, these innovations can be implemented as additions to conventional batterer programs, rather than as replacements to them. The challenge is how best to determine what men most need, and who would be most responsive to these alternatives or add-ons. Does the extra effort of assessing for the differences, and tailoring treatments to them, make a substantial difference in program outcome?

Extending the New Psychology

For the most part, the efforts to categorize batterers are an extension of the new psychology discussed in the previous chapter. Basically, proponents of more psychodynamic approaches contend that individual assessment of a man's history and personality will help to expose underlying issues in need of special attention and therapy. They claim that the gender-based, cognitive-behavioral approaches are naïve and resistant to these sorts of issues with their "here and now" focus on the men's behavior. But our review of the clinical observations and research suggests that gender-based, cognitive-behavioral programming is appropriate and at least as effective as the alternatives. The door remains open, however, to proposals for what can be done with the subgroups of men who tend to fall through the cracks—the men who are less responsive to the conventional approach, or to any approach. In particular, how do we reduce the high dropout rate?

One less sweeping view is that some program participants stand out in discernible and important ways. Those men need to be identified and given supplemental treatment. That is, programmatic innovations that don't necessarily replace batterer programs might be implemented for these categories of men. Interestingly, the different categories that are being put forth don't necessarily coincide with one another. As yet there is not a clear hierarchy of differentiation—that is, which categories might have priority over others, or what combination of differences might be most relevant. In general, the innovations are derived from psychological or personality characteristics that point to compounding or complicating problems. The proponents of the psychodynamic approach, as discussed in the previous chapter, argue that the range of individual needs is best assessed and treated in an alternative approach. However, it may be that some men merely need extra help.

The popularity of differentiating among patients is by no means unique to the domestic violence field. Differentiation has strong clinical support in addiction and sexual assault treatment as well. Stories in the news and movies portray a variety of peculiar and idiosyncratic cases of violence, as do the cases that come before the courts or into treatment programs. Similarly, domestic violence does not appear to be a unitary phenomenon. But are there common themes and issues across these cases? Are we accentuating the variations to help us bring order to a complex world?

For years, researchers on cognitive decision making have studied the human tendency to divide the world around us into categories and draw inferences from them (see Macrae & Bodenhausen, 2001; Turk & Salovey, 1988). Our categorical thinking has us see good guys and bad guys, good patients and unco-operative ones, hard workers and goof-offs, and winners and losers. Then we expect certain behaviors from one category or another—and we often get what we expect. One theory suggests that the human brain may be "hard-wired" to think in this categorical way. The fact is that the world is a set of probabilities, tendencies, and dimensions that more often belie neat categories and types (Monahan & Steadman, 1996).

The attempt to categorize patients has a deeper motivation as well. The humanistic values of the helping professions would have us acknowledge the individuality, specialness, and needs of each person (Elkins, 2009). Recognizing the uniqueness and differentness is a matter of respect for the whole person. It helps us to see beyond the behavior that led him or her to treatment and to assess his or her strengths as well as needs. It offers a more complete diagnosis and a more appropriate prescription. Appreciating differentness also helps us to engage and motivate people. Individuals are more likely to feel worth and hope if we give them respect and understanding—to be less resistant and more open to change. This is the logic of humanistic values and treatment (see C. Rogers, 1992). The previous chapter noted similar themes in the promotion of compassion and caring for batterer program participants, and also saw some practical concerns and weak substantiation of these approaches. Such values can be, and generally are, expressed in a conventional batterer program, but is that sufficient? Or are innovations and specialization needed to make a greater impact?

Almost all of the innovations recommended for batterer programs have been used in addiction treatment and also other mental health, physical health, and offender programs. They have their ardent proponents, as well as their detractors. They are bolstered by assessment instruments and special curricula. There is also a spate of research used to substantiate each innovation. However, a hard look at this research reveals a paucity of favorable outcome studies. There are correlate studies showing the association of one differentiation with varying treatment outcomes, but generally there are few clinical trials with supportive results. Some research reviews conclude with an outright dismissal of one innovation or another. Others acknowledge the innovation's weaknesses and inconsistent evidence for its success, and point to the need to advance the concepts and do further the research. Even if there is an effect from differentiated treatments, the boost provided by one innovation or another is unlikely to make a dramatic difference in program effectiveness overall.

Nonetheless, innovations in the domestic violence field have their followers and selective bodies of research. Some practitioners can read hopeful signs into the available research, but others can just as easily argue against each innovation. Interestingly, the experimental findings from evaluations of batterer programs are frequently used to further justify the innovations. The familiar claim that batterer programs don't work or show little effect is used as the reason for considering one innovation or another. However, the research used to advocate for an innovation falls short of the experimental standard applied to research on the batterer programs. Various innovations obviously need to be further developed and substantiated. In the meantime, a case can be made that batterer programs should be respectful of and alert to the variations of the men before them.

Batterer Typologies

The Prevailing Batterer Types

Throughout the study of batterer characteristics, there have been references to different types of batterers who may warrant different kinds of treatment or programmatic approaches. On the surface, this appealing notion represents a resolution of the divergent explanations of men's violence. Some researchers argue that a subgroup of men might be more appropriately served by psychodynamic approaches tailored to attachment issues, while other men are better suited for cognitive-behavioral approaches focused on antisocial violence. In fact, Amy Holtzworth-Munroe established a batterer typology in her review of the research on batterers' personality traits and behavioral patterns over a decade ago (Holtzworth-Munroe & Stuart, 1994). Her subsequently tested typology includes family-only, dysphoric/borderline, and generally violent/antisocial batterers (Holtzworth-Munroe, Meehan, Herron, Rehman, & Stuart, 2000, 2003). (A less severe antisocial subgroup was identified in further analyses and added to the typology [Holtzworth-Munroe & Meehan, 2004].)

These categories suggest different types of batterers, categorized according to the degree of violence, and whose behavior has different causes. The antisocial type was predicted to be the most severely abusive and generally violent—that is, violent toward others as well as the man's partner. The dysphoric/borderline type was characterized by dependent tendencies that include fears of abandonment, avoidant reactions, and explosive violence. The family-only type shows little or no evidence of psychopathology and lower levels of violence.

The batterer types reflect the clinical observations that some incidents appear more emotionally driven than others, especially those that seem calculated and deliberate (Holtzworth-Munroe & Meehan, 2004). In fact, some men appear just plain angry as opposed to downright mean.[1] At least on the surface, the types reflect the familiar expressive versus instrumental categories of violence and suggest that specialized treatment may be warranted (Berkowitz, 1969, 1993). Amy Holtzworth-Munroe and Jeffrey Meehan conclude: "The clinical implication of these findings is that treatment outcome might be improved by matching intervention to batterer subtypes" (Holtzworth-Munroe & Meehan, 2004, p. 1385).

Several assumptions, however, underlie the implications of the batterer typology: (1) the types represent distinct categories of men in batterer programs, rather than tendencies that may vary over time; (2) the types are predictive of future violence; and (3) the types are responsive to specialized or differentiated treatment. In other words, do certain types of men do better in certain programs? Despite the wide appeal of batterer types and apparent clinical support for categorization, research has yet to establish the typology as a diagnostic tool to sort batterers and prescribe their treatment. The batterer types do remind us that, at the extremes, some men appear at times explosively violent and others appear outright sadistic.

As Holtzworth-Munroe and colleagues concede, debate persists over these points (Holtzworth-Munroe & Meehan, 2004). Rather than distinct types, the observed variations may be represented as dimensions among men who batterer. The differentiation is more of a continuum, with men being more or less severely violent and showing greater or lesser extents of psychopathology. Furthermore, these tendencies may vary over time rather than be stable or fixed. Most important to the question of which batterer program approach is best, the types may not be substantially predictive. For instance, the antisocial type may not necessarily be more likely than other types to drop out and assault their partners again. It is also unclear whether treatment tailored to the different types would substantially improve outcomes.

The Research Evidence

A study based on a sample of 102 men from the general population of one community offers some support for distinct and somewhat stable types (Holtzworth-Munroe & Meehan, 2004).[2] Follow-up studies with a 199 batterer program participants in Texas (Eckhardt, Holtzworth-Munroe, Norlander, Sibley, & Cahill, 2008) and in an experimental evaluation of 136 men in a Midwestern program (Saunders, 1996) also offer tentative evidence for tailored treatment. However, analysis of the data on 662 men in our multisite evaluation of batterer programs showed that personality types derived from the MCMI-III were not predictive of subsequent assaults, including their levels of violence and abuse (Heckert & Gondolf, 2005). And a study conforming more to the Holtzworth-Munroe typology found inconsistent results among 175 men across batterer types in terms of batterer program completion, treatment response, and recidivism (Huss & Ralston, 2008). For instance, generally violent antisocial batterers showed the greatest reduction on anger and partner violence scales, and evidenced levels of empathy after treatment similar to the other types—contrary to expectations. However, they were the most likely to be re-arrested, as might be expected given the arrest history associated with this category.[3]

The stability of the types is increasingly in question, as well. The Holtzworth-Munroe team did find some inconsistencies when they tried to replicate the types in their original community sample of 102 men over a three-year period (Holtzworth-Munroe, Meehan, Herron, Rehman, & Stuart, 2003). Additionally, our research team found evidence in our multisite evaluation that violence and abuse patterns were much more complex than categories of severity and frequency (Ip, Jones, Heckert, Zhang, & Gondolf, 2010; A. Jones, Heckert, Gondolf, & Zhang, 2010). A trajectory analysis of abuse over periodic follow-ups—which incorporated a constellation of controlling, verbal, threatening, and physical abuse—revealed at least four discernible patterns of violence over time. Not surprisingly, men at the lowest levels of abuse maintained a relatively constant level throughout the follow-up period, and those with the highest levels of abuse and violence maintained the most extensive abuse. A substantial portion of men, however, varied their level of abuse over time. These findings echo the mixed escalation and de-escalation of violence among the arrested domestic violence perpetrators in the multisite replications of the noted Minneapolis police study (Piquero, Brame, Fagan, & Moffitt, 2006).

Moreover, our analysis of the individual profiles suggests a wider variety of psychological problems than the batterer typology considers (White & Gondolf, 2000), as have other analyses using the MCMI-III (Hamberger, Lohr, Bonge, & Tolin, 1996). These profiles included men with symptoms associated with borderline personality disorder and antisocial tendencies. Psychopathology in general was associated with dropout and re-assault during the follow-up period, as was the severity of past violence (A. Jones, D'Agostino, Gondolf, & Heckert, 2004). However, this association appears to be more like two separate dimensions of greater or lesser degree, than categorical types. The strongest predictor of the outcomes, controlling for other characteristics, was the extent and severity of previous violence. That past violence is the best predictor of future violence is a time-honored axiom in criminology (Gendreau, Little, & Goggin, 1996).

The batterer types could also be translated into the familiar idea that more disturbed men tend to be more violent. Holtzworth-Munroe and colleagues did attempt to replicate the batterer typology using our multisite data and their specifications (Clements, Holtzworth-Munroe, Gondolf, & Meehan, 2002). They found that men both in the borderline personality disorder and antisocial types were more likely to re-assault their partners during follow-up than the family-violence-only type (the group with little evidence of psychopathology). It would appear from this finding that psychopathology in general was an issue. Furthermore, a substantial portion of both troublesome types were not violent and were apparently responsive to the conventional batterer program; nearly 60 percent of both the borderline and antisocial men were not physically abusive in the fifteen-month follow-up, according to their partners' reports.[4]

Similarly, in a study of approximately 200 men arrested for domestic violence in Dallas, Chris Eckhardt and his colleagues (Eckhardt, Holtzworth-Munroe, Norlander, Sibley, & Cahill, 2008) found that both the borderline and antisocial types were more likely to drop out of a six-month cognitive-behavioral program and be re-arrested during the six-month post-treatment follow-up period. The low-level violent type (family-only) had the lowest rates of dropout and re-arrest. However, the arrest outcome included all assaults, not just against female partners. Additional outcomes were unreliable, given the fact that only sixty-five female partners were contacted through the follow-up period. Interestingly, 30 percent of the men fell into the family-only type with lower-level violence and little psychopathology, and over half of the sample was classified as the lower-level antisocial or generally violent antisocial types. Only 20 percent of the men were classified as the borderline type, and thus would have theoretically benefited from a more psychodynamic approach.

Specialized Treatment

The more difficult question to answer—and the most relevant one to issues of program approach—is whether matching treatment to batterer type improves outcomes. So far the research has confirmed the obvious fact that more problematic men are more likely to drop out and commit subsequent offenses. Only one controlled study from the early 1990s has compared the outcomes of a psychodynamic versus a gender-based, cognitive-behavioral approach (Saunders, 1996). The study followed 136 men who had completed four to five months of weekly sessions of either treatment approach. The outcome of violence was based primarily on the reports from 107 women over an average of two years post-treatment. The most impressive finding was that the outcomes for both treatment approaches on a variety of indicators were equivalent: the gender-based, cognitive-behavioral approach was at least as effective as the psychodynamic approach.

Proponents of diversifying treatment, however, highlight the apparent interaction of treatment and personality traits. The men showing evidence of dependent personalities (that is, borderline personality disorder or tendencies) based on the MCMI-I had better outcomes in the psychodynamic approach (33 percent were violent during the follow-up period) than in the cognitive-behavioral approach (52 percent violent). However, the men with antisocial personalities did better in the cognitive-behavioral approach (36 percent versus 53 percent). It is hard to know, from this one study of such a small sample in a Midwestern city, how far to generalize the findings, considering the much larger portion of men with antisocial tendencies in the programs in our multisite evaluation (Gondolf, 1999c) and the Dallas study of batterer types (Eckhardt, Holtzworth-Munroe, Norlander, Sibley, & Cahill, 2008). The cognitive-behavioral approach would appear best suited for them.

We did not find an interaction between personality type and program approach in our multisite study. The major batterer types showed similar re-assault rates for the fifteen-month follow-up period across the two didactic programs versus the two process-oriented programs (Gondolf & White, 2000). (However, the didactic and process-oriented approaches in our study, varied more in format than in explicit modality, and they were not monitored for conformity to a specific treatment approach.) Dan Saunders, moreover, cautions that the personality findings in his study were based on personality traits rather than discrete batterer types. He explains: "Dimensions have more variability than types and thus are likely to produce significant findings" (Saunders, 2004, p. 1391). This caveat takes us back to the question of whether we really have predictive categories or compounding personality problems.

The most impressive research regarding matching treatments comes from two extensive multisite experimental evaluations—one studying depression (Elkin, Shea, & Watkins, 1989), and the other addiction treatments (Project MATCH Research Group, 1997).[5] These studies randomly assigned patients to a variety of treatment approaches and compared the outcomes of the behaviors of concern. The depression treatment study, for instance, compared cognitive-behavioral therapy, interpersonal psychotherapy, medication with clinical management, and a placebo with management ($n = 250$ in each option from several settings), and the alcohol treatment study included sixteen different approaches from multiple sites. The expectation was that different types of patients, in terms of psychological diagnoses and behavioral patterns, would do better in treatments tailored to their type.

In both of these extensive projects, similar outcomes appeared across treatment approaches, much as they did in Saunders's batterer treatment comparison, and interactions with types were not substantiated. According to the director of the National Institute on Alcohol Abuse and Alcoholism, "patient-treatment matching, as exemplified by the 16 combinations of patient characteristics and treatments studied in Project MATCH, adds little to enhance the outcome treatment" (Gordis, 1997, p. 3). The only exception was for individuals with severe psychiatric disorders, who did not perform well in any of the treatments (Project MATCH Research Group, 1997). Interestingly, several previous single-site studies had suggested that there might be some benefit to matching psychological behavioral types with treatments.

In sum, the research on batterer types does highlight some distinctive needs and problems among batterer program participants. However, the predictiveness of types remains in question, as does the effect of tailored treatment approaches. The typology proponents, in fact, concede in their research update: "These study findings do not conclusively resolve the debate regarding how different the borderline and antisocial subtypes are from one another" (Holtzworth-Munroe & Meehan, 2004, p. 1378).

Even if the types are valid, the majority of cases appear appropriate for the cognitive-behavioral approach—that is, the family-only and antisocial batterers, who comprise almost 80 percent of batterers, according to two studies (Eckhardt, Holtzworth-Munroe, Norlander, Sibley, & Cahill, 2008; White & Gondolf, 2000). The remaining borderline personality type had outcomes that were at least similar to the antisocial type in the gender-based, cognitive-behavioral approach employed in the batterer treatment experiment (Saunders, 1996) and our multisite study (White & Gondolf, 2000). Therefore, the increased effect of sending such men to a psychodynamic option is likely to be relatively small overall.

The Future of Batterer Types

Rather than dismiss the batterer typology based on its limitations, one might view it as a promising direction for research and eventually practice. Meaningful types may simply require more complexity than offered in the current two-dimensional typology of personality traits and extent of violence. For instance, Holtzworth-Munroe and other researchers have proposed developing further types that incorporate women's aggression (Capaldi & Kim, 2007; Holtzworth-Munroe & Meehan, 2004). And Michael Johnson (2006) has attempted to align his typology of domestic violence, based on the interaction of couples, with the batterer types of men's personality and violence severity. Saunders (2004) has outlined an ecological framework that incorporates situational factors, such as drinking or relationship status, into batterer types and also includes the cultural reinforcement—including patriarchal attitudes—that a man experiences or seeks.

The ultimate question for batterer programs, however, is whether the increased complexity of types will improve prediction and prescription—that is, serve a diagnostic function. As discussed in the next chapter, the prediction of violence itself is a difficult task that raises a separate enterprise of assessment and management beyond the current debate over program approach.

Practical considerations also persist with the development of a typology. The most central challenge, which spills over into the risk assessment reviewed in the next chapter, is how to get reliable information about men's history of violence. The frequency and severity of violence is a key component of the types, but criminal records are frequently incomplete or insufficiently detailed; women's reports are difficult to obtain, especially amid the crisis of a man's arrest and court appearance; and the men too often deny or minimize their violence.

The psychological tests used to assess the men's personality traits are also tedious, costly, and difficult to administer. Many of the men have lower cognitive and reading skills that hamper their ability to respond to such tests, and many are either resistant to treatment or "playing good" at program intake. Additionally, the practicality of multiple treatment approaches is in question. Tailored treatments would require differently trained counselors and specialized treatment groups in what are already understaffed and underfunded programs. The extra benefit of the tailored treatments would have to be quite substantial to justify such an overhaul of current programs.

In the meantime, the borderline personality disorder and antisocial types may be more appropriately used as a heuristic than as a diagnostic tool—that is, they may be best considered as an exploratory aid. Holtzworth-Munroe and Meehan (2004), in fact, caution against a rigid use of batterer types that is likely to mislead battered women as well as confuse intervention. For instance, the typology could be misused or misunderstood to suggest that a batterer program participant is not a threat because he appears to be a "family-only" type. Despite the human tendency of categorical thinking, sorting out the good guys from the bad guys, the world might be more appropriately seen in terms of tendencies and probabilities. It is not surprising, then, that what is often referred to as the taxonomy-dimensional debate—types versus tendencies—continues in other fields as well as with domestic violence.

In sum, the state of the typology research returns us to a recurrent theme in this book: there are clearly problematic men who are more likely to drop out of treatment and assault their partners again. Those men cut across batterer types, however. One type after another failed to characterize the repeatedly violent and most dangerous men in our multisite study (Gondolf & White 2001), as was also the case with studies of chronically violent adolescent offenders (Piquero, Fagan, Mulvey, Steinberg, & Ogden, 2005). Moreover, the extensive clinical trial of addiction treatment approaches identified a subgroup of men who were unresponsive regardless of the treatment (Elkin, Shea, & Watkins, 1989). That subgroup also did not fit a distinctive profile, but it did show evidence of compounding psychological disorders in general. The most pressing question becomes what to do about these sorts of men. It is unlikely that merely changing the approach would substantially improve their outcomes.

Change Stages and Motivational Interviewing

Stages of Change

Popular but Questioned

Another typology of batterers has been devised through the so-called transtheoretical model of stages of change (Prochaska, 1984). Clients in any sort of treatment are assumed to move sequentially through four major stages, from less to more readiness to change: the precontemplation, contemplation, action, and maintenance stages (Prochaska & DiClemente, 1985). The stages are based largely on attitudes of resistance versus motivation, blame versus acceptance of responsibility, and unresponsiveness to treatment versus being proactive. The conception has particular relevance to batterer program participants for two reasons. First, the high program dropout rates signal a lack of readiness that warrants identification and remediation. And second, matching treatment to a clients' readiness to change improves their compliance with the treatment and ultimately the therapeutic outcomes (Wierzbicki & Pekarik, 1993). Identifying a client's change stage and tailoring treatment to his or her readiness has been applied to alcohol addiction, smoking cessation, and weight loss programs with some apparent success.

Like the other innovations being transferred to domestic violence intervention, the change stages show some promise, but they also face conceptual cracks and a shortage of evidence. Conceptually, the transtheoretical model is based on developmental theory, which posits how one interacts with the world to form perceptions or cognitions of self and others. Over two decades ago, I wrote a paper applying the stages of change theory to batterers and batterer treatment (Gondolf, 1988). The critical reviews of the paper raised some now familiar alternative explanations for resistance and change. Some personality traits, particularly antisocial tendencies, appear to defy the transtheoretical change process, and sanctions or circumstances may prove to motivate or activate a person regardless of his or her stage.

A more technical concern is that the readiness tests do not appear to register distinct stages (Sutton, 2001). Rather, the scores are clustered to represent groups of characteristics that tend to overlap across subgroups. These clustered subgroups are then interpreted as sequential stages and substages. In the several analyses that have been done with batterer program participants, different configuration of substages have also been produced (see C. Murphy & Maiuro, 2008). Researchers continue to debate whether these inconsistencies are the result of a measurement problem (that is, more fine-tuned instruments to identify stages are needed), or merely a reflection of the more complex reality of change.

The more pertinent issue has to do with the research findings overall on the stages of change. Do they in fact help to predict program outcomes? Change stages have been especially popular in alcohol and smoking treatments, where there have numerous studies on the sequencing of stages and longitudinal prediction of stage change, and experimental studies of treatment matching. However, a critical review of this research concludes: "Current evidence for the model as applied to substance use is meager and inconsistent" (Sutton, 2001, p. 187). It should be said that the proponents of change stages have a more positive interpretation: they see at least some tentative indications of differences in stage outcomes (for example, Prochaska & DiClemente, 2005).

Weak Research Support

Despite the prominence of the stages of change model across clinical practice, the scientific critiques of it have been somewhat harsh. A review of the research on the application of change stages to criminal offenders concludes: "We demonstrate the problems that the Stages of Change Model has with its predictive accuracy, internal coherence, and explanatory depth. Consequently the Stages of Change Model may not be an adequate model for measuring readiness to change offending behavior and may not provide a useful basis for developing interventions to improve readiness to change" (Burrowes & Needs, 2009, p. 42). Researchers in the public health field arrive at a similar assessment: "The model occupies a status unwarranted by the conventions of scientific outcome evaluation. Internal and external validity problems with the model have not been adequately addressed by researchers and practitioners, as well" (Burton, Baldwin, Flynn, & Whitelaw, 2000, p. 66). In both cases, the authors argue for alternative frameworks for readiness to change that incorporate race, gender, and class differences, and also contextual circumstances and ethical considerations.

The research on the contribution of change stages to batterer program outcomes is also weak at this point. There are few substantial outcomes studies available on the predictive utility of stages, and those that do exist show little or no relationship between change stages and program outcomes. The studies that use men's report of their abuse tend to show that men in the lower precontemplative stage report less abuse than men in the higher stages (for example, K. Scott & Wolfe, 2003). This tendency, however, may be an artifact of reporting bias—that is, the men in the higher stages are more likely to disclose, and be more honest about, their abusive behavior. Katreena Scott and David Wolfe (2003) tracked the change stage and communication, empathy, and abusive behavior at the beginning, middle and end of a six-month batterer program (119 men completed the program). The men in the higher stages showed more positive change in the designated outcomes during the initial ten weeks of the program. After that, change was similar across the stages. The abuse reported by the woman showed no significant difference and was difficult to interpret given the low response rate (at the end of the program, only seventeen women responded). The researchers conclude: "Interpretation is complicated by pretreatment differences that draw into question stage-related patterns in the final outcome" (p. 879).

In three recently reported studies of program outcome, the change stage did not predict program completion, although the researchers had expected that it would. The studies were conducted in very different settings: intake at an urban batterer program in Canada (Brodeur, Rondeau, Brochu, Lindsay, & Phelps, 2008, $N = 302$), initial contact at a suburban program in Maryland (Alexander & Morris, 2008, $N = 210$), and a domestic violence court in a Texas city (Eckhardt, Holtzworth-Munroe, Norlander, Sibley, & Cahill, 2008, $N = 199$). In the Maryland program, men in the higher-stage cluster again showed some predictable improvements in symptoms—specifically, depression, anxiety, and anger—but no significant differences in partner-reported violence at the end of the program. However, only fifteen women responded.

The outcomes of the Texas court study are more difficult to interpret. Chris Eckhardt and colleagues (Eckhardt, Holtzworth-Munroe, Norlander, Sibley, & Cahill, 2008) found that the stages did not predict re-arrests, but that one of the lower stages was associated with higher rates of violence based on the reports of the men or their female partners during a thirteen-month follow-up after a court hearing (the researchers had reports on seventy-two cases from either the men or the women). Also the scores on the precontemplation scale (as a continuous measure) were related to continued violence. However, the low response rate, especially from women, make this finding preliminary at best (C. Murphy & Maiuro, 2008). Moreover, Eckhardt and colleagues (Eckhardt, Holtzworth-Munroe, Norlander, Sibley, & Cahill, 2008) found an inconsistent relationship between the stages of change and the predominant batterer typology. Contrary to expectations, the precontemplative resistant men were overrepresented in the "family-only" violence type.

In sum, there is no doubt that offenders' denial and resistance to treatment are major problems in batterer programs, and criminal justice interventions in general. It is questionable, however, that change stages—at least, in the theory's current state of development—have a practical application. Although the stages have been partially replicated in various studies, they are currently based on clusters or a mixture of attitudes, rather than distinct or pure categories. The statistical steps in determining and analyzing the subscales from a stage test, and their minimal prediction of program outcomes, make stage assessment less than useful. It may be that further research incorporating more complexity will produce an assessment showing better rates of prediction. But based on the research reviews in other fields, and the challenges in assessing stages, that does not seem very likely to happen any time soon.

Motivational Interviewing

Broad Use and Encouraging Research

An equally popular and widely applied innovation, especially in healthcare fields, is motivational interviewing (see Rollnick, Miller, & Butler, 2008). One pair of researchers characterized it as "empathic dialogue" to facilitate conversations about behavioral change (C. Murphy & Maiuro, 2008, p. 532). Basically, motivational interviewing is client-centered, nondirective, Rogerian counseling used to disarm resistant clients or patients (W. Miller & Rollnick, 2002). In the process of airing their side of the story and identifying their wants for change, clients feel validated, respected, and more likely to take action (Anderson & Stewart, 1983). Motivational interviewing thus leads clients to buy into the process, so to speak, and builds on their initiative. This interviewing also can be empowering, in that it encourages clients to take responsibility for their recovery or change. Proponents of this approach highlight its contrast to the directive and confrontational approaches associated with batterer programs, particularly a stereotyped version of the Duluth model (Dia, Simmons, Oliver, & Cooper,

2009). They especially point out its usefulness in reducing the high dropout rates in batterer programs, and in ultimately improving program outcomes.

Motivational interviewing is most commonly implemented as a supplement to treatments: a program staff member interviews new participants in an individual session prior to their entering the group sessions of a program. Motivational interviewing may also be introduced to reengage clients who are not responding to the group work, or who have stopped attending the group sessions. It has also been developed into an integrated treatment approach often referred to as "motivational enhancement therapy." Both the interviewing and the therapy have adopted stages of change theory to guide the interactions between therapist and client. The techniques and focus of the interviewing may vary to address the client's readiness and theoretically advance that person faster toward the action stage. Additionally, this approach theoretically furthers a therapeutic alliance, or client rapport with the staff member, which has been associated with improved program outcomes (Taft, Murphy, Musser, & Remington, 2004).[6]

The research reviews of motivational interviewing in other fields have generally been favorable, compared to reviews of its theoretical partner, stages of change. There are now four meta-analyses of the growing number of studies of motivational interviewing (for example, B. Burke, Arkowitz, & Menchola, 2003; for a review of all the meta-analyses, see Lundahl & Burke, 2009). Depending on their topical focus, the number of studies reviewed ranges from 15 that assessed individual interviewing for addiction treatment to an all-inclusive 119 studies of motivational interviewing or therapy for health-promoting services in general. Overall, the meta-analyses found low to moderate effect sizes, but there were some exceptions. The authors of the most recent and extensive meta-analysis conclude: "Our analyses strongly suggest that motivational interviewing does exert small though significant positive effects across a wide range of problem domains, although it is more potent in some situations compared to others, and it does not work in all cases" (Lundahl, Kunz, Brownell, Tollefson, & Burke, 2010, p. 151). There were some differences with regard to the effects fading over time, program participants' not doing as well as those in other treatments relying on manuals, and effects being low with members of racial minority groups.

For instance, the multisite clinical trial of additional treatments demonstrated the "dodo bird" effect—that is, all the counseling approaches are equally effective because they include similar components, structures, or interactions— that also appeared for motivational enhancement therapy. The outcomes for patients randomly assigned to that option were comparable to those assigned to the other options, including cognitive-behavioral therapy (Luborsky, Rosenthal, & Diguer, 2002). The reasons for any link between the motivational approach and improved outcomes are also not clear; the explanation could be as simple as giving clients more chance to talk (B. Burke, Arkowitz, & Dunn, 2002). One relevant caution with all these results is that few studies have been done using motivational interviewing or therapy with violent criminals who may bring a different level and kind of resistance to programs.

Batterer Program Studies

The psychologists Chris Murphy and Laura Ting (2010) make a strong case for motivational interviewing with batterers in their review article of research on batterer programs. Unfortunately, the research is limited to a few studies with small samples and limited effects. Barbara Kistenmacher and Robert Weiss (2008), for instance, randomly assigned thirty-three men to two sessions of motivational interviewing before they joined groups. The participants who received motivational interviewing reported greater increases in their efforts to change and in taking responsibility for their abusive behavior. The measures, based on questionnaires administered before and after the motivational interviewing, were compared to the responses of a small control group of men who did not receive the interview sessions. It is hard to know whether the men's professions about change were parroting the session lessons, or actual intentions to complete the program and stop abuse. This is especially the case since the study does not address the batterer program's outcome.

A more substantial study of 108 men compared motivational interviewing (one forty-five minute session) to a structured intake prior to participating in batterer groups (Musser, Semiatin, Taft, & Murphy, 2008). The researchers considered a broader set of short-term and long-term outcome measures. The participants with motivational interviewing had significantly higher compliance with homework and significantly higher therapist ratings on working "alliance." They were also engaged in more help seeking outside of the program than the control group. However, no treatment differences were found in program attendance or on a self-administered measure of readiness to change. Women's reports of abuse were lower for the men with the interviewing during a six-month follow-up, but the difference was not statistically significant. The low response rate (sixty-five women, or 66 percent, responded) during the follow-up made it difficult to conclude much regarding this main outcome of concern. The authors assert that the "findings indicate that treatment of partner-violent men can be enhanced by intervention strategies that are sensitive to the client's readiness for change" (p. 554). One can just as easily argue that the evidence is fairly weak, at face value.

Two other outcome studies of applications of motivational interviewing have their limitations as well. One study is an evaluation of a computerized stages-of-change assessment and tailored workbook assignments, which has shown "acceptability" among batterer program participants that used it (Levesque, Driskell, & Prochaska, 2008, p. 432). In other words, the vast majority of the men found the assessment to be "easy to use" and "helpful" (p. 432). To test the outcome of the assessment, five hundred men were randomly assigned either to the computerized preprogram sessions or to a group with study assignments but no computer session. A six-month follow-up with seventy-four of the men's partners—a 15 percent response rate—suggested that the men in the computerized session were less likely to threaten or physically abuse their partners. However, the results are not statistically or clinically significant without more information, and any claims from them are questionable at this point.[7]

Another study examined the effects of a stages-of-change program that incorporated motivational principles, compared to a gender-based, cognitive-behavioral approach ($N = 528$) (Alexander, 2007; Alexander & Morris, 2008). Once again, the men's reported levels of readiness to change and abusive behavior at the end of the group program were not significantly different across the compared treatment approaches. The women's report of abuse, moreover, suffered from another very low rate of response (20 percent; $n = 125$), leaving the outcome uncertain.

An Experimental Outcome Study

The most recent and most ambitious study examined a motivational curriculum in an experimental comparison of a conventional Duluth-type curriculum and a conventional cognitive-behavioral approach enhanced with motivational techniques. The experimental motivational groups included open-ended questioning, listening reflectively, and affirming the client's efforts to change. In the authors' words, there was more emphasis on "nurturing the group" (Alexander, Morris, Tracy, & Frye, 2010, p. 575). Both approaches required attendance for twenty-six weeks. Over 500 male program participants were randomly assigned to forty-nine different groups that used either the Duluth or the motivational approach. (Only a small portion of the group sessions were monitored for treatment integrity, using audiotapes.) A follow-up with the men's female partners at six and twelve months, however, managed only a 22 percent response rate (118 out of 528 women). Only ninety-one women's follow-up reports could be used in the logistic regressions.

The female partners of the men in the motivational group reported a significantly lower level of physical abuse than the partners of men in the Duluth-type group. However, the men's reports of both nonphysical and physical abuse did not differ, nor did the women's reports of nonphysical abuse. The men showing low readiness to change on the initial testing were less likely to have been physically aggressive toward their partners in the motivational group, according to the partners' report. Therefore, the authors conclude: "Results suggest the importance of tailoring abuser intervention programs to individuals' initial readiness to change" (p. 571). The analysis supporting this recommendation, however, is not entirely clear in light of the principal outcomes and study limitations.

To their credit, the researchers note several major limitations of the study. For one thing, the overall results are clearly mixed, as in previous studies on motivational interviewing. The results may be affected by the low response rate of the women versus follow-up reports from most of the male subjects. The diversity of the large number of groups and staff may also confound the results. The other curious finding, reflected in previous change stage studies, is the lack of any difference in change stage across the comparison groups. That is, the men in the motivational interviewing group did not appear to change more than the men in the Duluth group.

This leaves open the question of what accounts for the outcome. As the researchers acknowledge, it may be the group leaders' enthusiasm for the flexibility of the motivational interviewing approach. It gives them more freedom to interact with the subjects. The more rigid procedures imposed on the Duluth comparison group may make for an artificial difference in approaches. (In the discussion of the Duluth model in chapter 3, the Duluth program trainer endorsed supportive discussion as part of the Duluth approach and criticized the rigid application and overly confrontational misuse of the Duluth curriculum.)

In sum, the study is an important one, given its ambitious efforts to establish an experimental design. But the mixed results, low response rate, constricted Duluth approach, and variety of groups in the study raise some cautions, especially considering the mixed findings of the previous motivational interviewing studies. Although the study used an experimental design, its results leave us with more questions than answers. But the features of motivational interviewing—represented in the efforts to engage and support men—do deserve more consideration, as suggested above.

Practical Concerns and Limitations

The practical concerns about readiness to change echo those associated with using psychodynamic instead of cognitive-behavioral approaches to treat domestic violence. Is a more compassionate, client-centered approach more appropriate than a directive victim-centered approach? As part of an evaluation of motivational interviewing, I recently participated in a two-day training session on motivational interviewing for mental-health caseworkers. Coincidentally, one of the filmed case studies used to illustrate the approach was of a man who had verbally and physically abused his wife. There was a mixed reaction from the largely female audience of caseworkers. Several of the women felt that the interviewing approach allowed the man to make excuses for his abuse and inadvertently reinforced them. Others added that the man appeared to be manipulating the counselor into feeling some sympathy for his case. A few of the women and the instructors highlighted, instead, the man's reduction in apparent hostility and his increased disclosures during the course of the interview. One might infer from this admittedly tenuous anecdote that motivational interviewing should be weighed against the experience of the men's partners.

Although there is research support for motivational interviewing in addiction and health-promoting treatments, the evidence for effects of motivational interviewing in the domestic violence field remains limited. The most optimistic impression suggests that motivational interviewing might offer a slight boost to batterer program outcomes. At least the few studies of interviewing have not revealed any adverse effects. What remains unclear throughout the research is what specific elements might contribute to improved outcomes. Rather than change stages or motivational techniques, individuals may simply be responding to the empathy and respect conveyed in the special sessions (Anderson & Stewart, 1983). Interestingly, preprogram orientation sessions in general have improved attendance in batterer programs, as well as in addiction treatment (Tolman & Bhosley, 1990). Incentives and penalties have also been shown to improve compliance with treatment patients and program participants (for example, K. Burke, 2010).

As mentioned with regard to change stages, our study of court monitoring of program compliance illustrates the motivational impact of external sanctions on batterer program attendance. The percentage of court referrals that completed the program rose from 48 percent in the year prior to implementing the court review to 65 percent in the year following the implementation ($N = 321$) (Gondolf, 2000c). The court review, moreover, goes further in catching the high percentage of men who never appear for even the initial program intake or motivational session. The impact of coercion on compliance has been further documented in the more extensive research on drug courts (D. Wilson, Mitchell, & MacKenzie, 2006). The court in the alcohol and drug cases monitors the men's attendance at addiction treatment sessions and offers swift penalties for not attending them.

There is also the question of whether motivational interviewing reaches the more problematic cases, especially the more violent men with antisocial tendencies. According to some clinicians, those men are more responsive to firm, directive assertions and clear, decisive boundaries. To respond otherwise may actually feed their self-centeredness and narcissism rather than genuinely move them toward change (for example, Loza & Loza-Fanous, 1999a). At the same time, it is clear that antagonizing potential clients with insinuations, veiled threats, or suspicion will usually result in further resistance and even defiance (Anderson & Stewart, 1983).

In sum, research on motivational interviewing with batterer program participants thus far shows little—or, at best, inconsistent—impact on program attendance. The current follow-up studies have ended up with too few respondents for us to derive significant or meaningful results from them. However, further studies may reveal some lessons about approaching and engaging program participants. Research in other fields suggests that motivational interviewing may at least provide a small boost to batterer programs' outcomes, but it certainly will not solve the deeper problems of particularly dangerous and defiant men. Oversight, sanctions, and incentives may be needed to motivate and contain these men.

Couples Counseling

A Specialized Approach

As discussed throughout the previous chapters, couples counseling has been increasingly promoted as a treatment for domestic violence, in spite of long-standing opposition.[8] Supporters of couples counseling view domestic violence as an outgrowth of the dynamics between a man and a woman and assume that gender-based batterer counseling is ineffective with at least certain types of cases (McCollum & Stith, 2008). The opposition, mainly from battered women's advocates, has been based primarily on the concern that couples counseling too easily puts the woman in jeopardy and reduces the man's sense of responsibility, allowing him to say it's really her fault (D. Adams, 1988; Bograd, 1984). The woman may fear retaliation for disclosing information about her partner or challenging him in front of the counselor. The woman may also be pressured, coerced, manipulated, or even threatened by the man to get her to attend couples counseling. However, proponents of couples counseling argue that training over the years has made couples counselors more aware of such issues, and therapeutic approaches have addressed many of the concerns associated with domestic violence cases (McCollum & Stith, 2008). Screening, assessment, and monitoring of couples also help to ensure the women's safety and the choice of an appropriate approach (Bograd & Mederos, 1999).

In the context of evidence-based practice, of course, the issue is what research is there to support these assumptions and document the effectiveness of couples counseling compared to conventional batterer programs. Interestingly, the evaluations of couples counseling rest on programs that have extensive screening to include couples with only low levels of violence, individual sessions for further support and debriefing, and cognitive-behavioral skill building for the couples (Stith, Rosen, McCollum, & Thomsen, 2004). In other words, the tested couples counseling accommodates many of the features developed and promoted in conventional gender-based batterer programs. One couples approach in fact follows several weeks of having the man and woman attend separate group sessions. Much of the debate over couples counseling appears to be more about mainstream couples therapy that may not include the precautions and safeguards of these specialized approaches.

Moreover, a closer look at the couples counseling research shows a weak case for substituting couples work for gender-based batterer programs, and raises some practical concerns about implementing this approach for domestic violence cases. The samples in the evaluations of couples counseling are all highly selective as a result of the extensive screening, and not representative of court-mandated cases in general (Gondolf, 1998a). Not only are they composed of couples with low levels of violence, but also of couples in intact, committed, or stable relationships. In fact, men in these sorts of relationships have very positive outcomes in the batterer programs evaluated in our research (A. Jones, Heckert, Gondolf, & Zhang, 2010). Batterer programs appear suitable for this very select subgroup without the extra training, heavy screening, and safety monitoring that couples counseling would entail—and the risks that remain (see Almeida & Hudak, 2002; Rivett & Reas, 2004).

A recent review of the research on couples counseling for domestic violence identifies three different couples programs that have been evaluated in a series of studies (McCollum & Stith, 2008).[9] The Navy experiment that included a couples group was also cited, but as discussed in the chapter 2, its military setting makes it difficult to interpret and generalize the findings (Dunford, 2000b). Only one other program has been experimentally tested against a gender-based batterer program, and all the other studies rely on very small samples as a result of the intake screening and follow-up attrition (approximately fifty couples for as many as three comparison groups).

Selective Samples

An evaluation of the Domestic Conflict Containment Program compared a primarily cognitive-behavioral treatment for multiple couples in a group session with a gender-based batterers program with a similar cognitive-behavioral approach (Brannen & Rubin, 1996). In this study, forty-nine men ordered into treatment by the court and their partners, after heavy screening, were randomly assigned to the couples program or a conventional batterers program. The female partners of the batterer program participants attended separate group sessions designed to increase their safety and sense of empowerment. The women in the couples group had a special orientation session prior to the program, additional debriefing after sessions, and telephone follow-up if they appeared stressed. The researchers reported no significant difference in dropout or recidivism rates for the small remaining sample. In a subsequent comparison of the same couples program, once again "neither form of treatment was superior to the other in terms of safety and effectiveness for volunteer, intact, and physically aggressive couples" (O'Leary, Heyman, & Neidig, 2002, p. 475). Although proponents of couples counseling cite these results as justification for such treatment, the results also suggest that conventional batterer programs do equally well with this small subgroup of exceptional cases.

The most recent study being used to promote couples counseling is an experimental evaluation of a multicouple group, individual couple therapy, and a small control group without treatment (Stith, Rosen, McCollum, & Thomsen, 2004). This is the only couples evaluation with a no-treatment control group. The counseling in both the group and individual couples treatment is characterized as focused on family violence, much as previously outlined (Neidig, 1985; Geffner & Mantooth, 2000; Mills, 2009). According to the researchers, the couples treatment specifically addressed the interactions of the couple and the woman's abuse or violence as well as the man's. Additionally, the men and women met separately in gender-based groups for six weeks prior to the twelve weekly couples sessions, and they were interviewed after couples groups for any distress or discomfort from the couples counseling.

The study compared the outcomes in terms of re-assault and aggression, marital satisfaction, and battering acceptance for completers of the couples group treatment (n = 16), individual couples counseling (n = 14), and the smaller comparison group without treatment (n = 9). The men's physical aggression reported by their female partners was less for the couples groups at six-month and two-year follow-ups, but that result was based on a 60 percent response rate, leaving only twenty-five couples in the three-way comparison.[10] Other pre- and post-treatment indicators, such as marital satisfaction, improved for the multicouple group but not for the other groups. However, there are several limitations to the study that persist from the previous research on couples counseling.

Those eligible for the couples counseling amounted to less than 6 percent of the initial self-selected pool. More specifically, out of 700 calls responding to recruitment efforts, 364 completed an intake interview, 89 completed a pre-treatment screening, and only 39 were included in the final analysis. In a study my research team and I did many years ago, we found that 20 percent of the battered women surveyed in a domestic violence court indicated some interest in a couples education program. Yet out of over 1,000 women contacted about the option after leaving the court, only a handful pursued it, and none attended the couples group for more than a few sessions (Gondolf, 1998a). In the experimental San Diego naval study, only two out of ten partners attended any one session of a randomly assigned couples group, and this was a more highly motivated and stable sample than those from civilian batterer programs (Dunford, 2000b). The sample of the couples counseling evaluation appears, therefore, to be much more highly motivated and less violent, as well as having fewer criminogenic characteristics (factors associated with high-levels of criminal behavior), than any set of batterer program participants (see Gondolf, 1999a).

Continuing Concerns

Some researchers also support couples counseling because conventional batterer programs apparently fail to have any impact on some men and because some of their partners are also allegedly violent.[11] The "unresponsive" men in the batterer programs, however, are clearly not the men eligible for the couples counseling study (Gondolf & White, 2001). They are the most violent and dangerous men, who tend to be in relationships that are hardly "intact." Moreover, the violence among female partners of batterer program participants tends to be in response to the most violent and volatile men—again, totally outside of the couples study's parameters (Gondolf, in press). These women are generally referred to specialized women's programs for additional help. The court typically has little leverage to require women with low levels of violence to treatment programs for couples or otherwise.

The main concern is how to implement couples counseling safely. Sandra Stith and colleagues acknowledge this issue in their couples counseling study: "We do not mean to minimize the risks that are inherent in working with violent couples, nor the need for victims to be protected from their abusive partners" (Stith, Rosen, McCollum, & Thomsen, 2004, p. 316). In fact, they devoted a two-hour individual interview with each partner along with other screening devices to ensure that the couple was suited for the counseling. It seems highly impractical to devote so much energy and resources to recruiting and identifying such an exceptional group. Moreover, getting reliable information about the men's violence at program intake, as well as from women in crisis or under threat, is problematic (see Heckert & Gondolf, 2000a, 2000c). Risk assessment itself remains risky business, as we shall see in the next chapter.

Clinical assessment of the nature and extent of domestic violence "requires specific skills and knowledge," as the therapists Michel Bograd and Fernando Mederos carefully lay out in their recommendations to couples counselors, especially those who encounter domestic violence in addiction treatment and family services (1999, p. 292). They recommend not only extensive preconditions to assessment, but also a sequence of assessment meetings and assessment criteria. The feasibility of couples counseling for a particular couple, the response to reported violence during counseling, and cautions about a false sense of security need to be considered. The Bograd-Mederos protocol is mainly for couples seeking help for different problems and is not an endorsement for court referrals of domestic violence cases to couples counseling. It may in fact be a conflict of interest for family therapists to be doing the screening in those cases. Their unintended interest might be to let more couples into their programs than to screen out the bulk of them as not eligible.

There are some programs that use couples work with motivated voluntary couples as a supplement to gender-specific groups. The cultural context model in northern New Jersey, for instance, employs separate "cultural circles" for men and women before and during couples therapy (Almeida & Hudak, 2002, p. 3). The New Jersey program has an explicitly feminist perspective in the circles, which operate much like the consciousness-raising approach of the Duluth program. The New Jersey program develops a broader sense of accountability beyond court sanctions (for example, reports of relatives, friends, and neighbors) and links the couples' problems to the larger community. In a sense, the couples counseling is encased in a Duluth-type batterer program, or at least the main components of it.

In sum, these innovations and the evaluated couples programs are conducted with layers of preconditions, assessments, and monitoring. They are used with an exceptional subgroup of couples and are therefore not an endorsement for couples counseling with domestic violence in general.

Culturally Focused Groups

Culturally Oriented Approaches

One more clear-cut differentiation among batterers is according to race and ethnicity. Research reviews and clinicians' recommendations uniformly acknowledge the different perspectives and social needs that African American and Latino men in particular bring to batterer counseling programs (for example, Saunders, 2008). This is no small matter, since in many urban areas, African American men comprise at least half of the men arrested for domestic violence and referred to batterer programs (Gondolf, 1999a). The dropout and re-arrest rates of these men tend to be higher than those of Caucasian men in the same programs. In response, African American researchers and practitioners working on domestic violence have argued that the conventional cognitive-behavioral approach, developed primarily with Caucasian men, needs to be revised in order to improve outcomes (for example, Blake & Darling, 1994; Hampton, Carrillo, & Kim, 1998; Oliver, 1994; O. Williams, 1998). The Institute on Domestic Violence in the African American Community (Nelson, 1999) and the African American Task Force on Violence Against Women of New York City (Garfield, 1998) have specifically endorsed culturally focused counseling for African American men arrested for domestic violence. Batterer program conferences and workshops have also included examples of culturally focused groups and promoted cultural approaches.

There appear to be several variations of cultural approaches for African American and Latino men, and also some for Asians and Native Americans. To illustrate the issues involved, I focus here on cultural approaches with African American men, since the most developed research and practice has been with these men. The approaches include loosely categorized culturally sensitive, culturally competent, and culturally focused approaches to group work (see O. Williams, 1994). The "sensitive" approach suggests that group leaders be aware of cultural differences and respond to them in the course of group sessions. "Competency" refers more broadly to the inclusion of program organization and counseling skills that support racial minorities. For instance, a diverse counseling staff, regular staff training on cultural issues and racism, and linkages to neighborhood centers working with African American families increase cultural competence in batterer programs.

The culturally focused approach generally indicates structured and systematic counseling that specifically addresses racial and ethnic differences. It is most often conducted in racially homogeneous groups with a counselor of the same race as the participants, and it follows a curriculum that identifies issues facing that particular group of participants. For African American men, this approach might include a session on prejudice in the criminal justice system, violence and crime in inner-city neighborhoods, and conflicting images of black manhood (O. Williams & Donnelly, 1997). The culturally focused approach is arguably the most likely to show effects on batterer program outcomes, since it most explicitly addresses cultural issues among the group participants.

By contrast, conventional batterer counseling, promoted in most state guidelines for batterer programs (Austin & Dankwort, 1999), follows the principles of gender-based, cognitive-behavioral treatment that might be considered colorblind (O. Williams, 1999). The counselors generally attempt to stay focused on the behavior of concern and not let tangents or rationalizations divert the group from this objective. Commonalities of woman battering are assumed to underlie the violent behavior, regardless of race and ethnicity, and discussions of cultural issues could digress into rationalizations like "prejudice [of the police or my neighborhood] made me do it." Some manuals for conventional counseling do recommend responding to cultural issues as they emerge in group discussion (Pence & Paymar, 1993). However, a survey of batterer programs approximately two decades ago indicated that few programs—142 out of 212 selected for the study—had adopted features of cultural competence (O. Williams & Becker, 1994), and our more recent observations of numerous batterer groups in several outcome studies confirm the prevalence of colorblind batterer counseling (for example, see Gondolf, 2002a).

Mixed Research Results

A lengthy academic discussion both outside and inside the domestic violence field has explored the impact of cultural differences on treatment participation and outcomes. Social workers and psychotherapists, for instance, suggest that cultural differences contribute to the poor outcomes of African American men in conventional counseling (for example, Blake & Darling, 1994; Franklin, 1999; Logan, 1990; Rasheed & Rasheed, 1999; Thorn & Sarata, 1998). Many African American men draw on a more personalistic culture, leading them to rely more on kinship and friendship networks for support rather than strangers in group counseling. Some African American men are simply confused by the demands to change the violent attitudes and behaviors that seem essential to surviving in a crime-infested neighborhood. Moreover, some African American men are suspicious of social services in general because they tend to be dominated by whites, who are often unfamiliar with and unsympathetic to African Americans' social reality and experiences (for a full review, see Gondolf & Williams, 2001).

The outcome studies supporting these observations, however, are fewer than one might expect for a topic of such concern, and they have produced mixed and less than supportive results. The latest overview of cultural approaches for psychotherapy cites two meta-analyses of a variety of outcome studies that included some cultural or racial component (Sue, Zane, Hall, & Berger, 2009). The most extensive of these meta-analyses examined seventy-six studies of mostly mental health treatment, regardless of their methodological rigor. It included treatments of men and women, youth and adults, and various minority groups. The authors identify a modest effect overall for the cultural approaches, compared to other approaches or control groups. However, they qualify that finding with several caveats regarding the weak study designs and variety of treatment approaches (Griner & Smith, 2006). The meta-analysis does appear to corroborate a previous narrative review of the racial and ethnic outcome research. That review found that culturally oriented counseling produces more positive changes than counseling that does not explicitly consider cultural factors (Sue, Chun, & Gee, 1995; Sue, Zane, & Young, 1994).

On the other hand, a more selective review of culturally competent counseling for adolescents reached a blatantly negative conclusion: "There is no compelling evidence as yet that these adaptations actually promote better clinical outcomes for ethnic minority youth. Overemphasizing the use of conceptually appealing but untested cultural modifications could inadvertently lead to inefficiencies in the conduct of treatment with ethnic minorities" (Huey & Polo, 2008, p. 292). Several other early narrative reviews of the studies appear to support the opposition to culturally focused counseling. For instance, reviews of the few outcome studies of conventional treatment groups for mental health or alcohol addiction found that African American men do not necessarily have poorer outcomes in such groups compared to Caucasian men (Brown, Joe, & Thompson, 1985; Sue, Fujino, Hu, Takeuchi, & Zane, 1991). The limited research on African American–only groups and groups with counselors of the same race as the participants has, furthermore, produced inconclusive results in mental health and addiction treatment (for example, E. Jones, 1982; Rosenheck, Fontana, & Cottrol, 1995).[12]

The lack of outcome studies supporting cultural approaches has brought accusations that cultural differentiation in psychotherapy is based on identity politics or political correctness (Weinrach & Thomas, 1997; Satel & Forster, 1999). Cultural approaches threaten to confuse and discredit conventional treatments that are effective across the board, say the critics. The leading defenders of cultural approaches, however, attribute the lack of research support to the complex and diverse conceptions of culturally based treatments, the shortage of funding for such research, and the difficulties confronting real-world implementation (Sue, 2003). They refer to funding allocations that show "little or no special effort to understand or accept the needs of minority populations" (p. 966). The lack of support has contributed not only to insufficient research, but also to underdeveloped and poorly implemented cultural approaches to treatment.

An additional line of research suggests that the lack of evidence supporting specialized counseling for African American men may be due to the cultural diversity within the African American community. Acculturation, cultural commitment, and racial identity development all appear related to preference for a racial match in counseling (Atkinson, Fulrong, & Poston, 1986; Coleman, Wampold, & Casalie, 1995). Mismatching is cited as a cause of misunderstanding, miscommunication, and cultural biases that lead to poorer outcomes (Erdur, Rude, & Baron, 2003; Sue, 1998). However, a meta-analysis of ten studies—mostly quasi-experimental—of matching African American and Caucasian clients in mental health services with clinicians found no effects for the racial matching (Shin, Chow, Camacho-Gonsalves, Levy, Allen, & Leff, 2005). How well a client's cultural attitudes are associated with his or her racial and ethnic background may need to be considered in assessing counseling outcomes beyond the broad classification of race.

Some Distinguishing Characteristics

Research in the domestic violence field on cultural approaches is especially limited, despite the broad support for specialized counseling—particularly for

African American men. At least a few studies compare the characteristics of African American men to Caucasian men in batterer programs. Not surprisingly, the African American men in our studies are more likely to have lower socioeconomic status and less likely to be married than the Caucasian men (Gondolf, 1999a). African American men are also likely to have experienced more violence themselves and disproportionately suffer from the effects of trauma, given the crime and gang activity in some of their neighborhoods. As a result, it may be appropriate in their treatment to address the hurt and anger from this community violence in order to lessen their violence toward their female partners (O. Williams, 1998, 1999).

According to a self-report checklist of exposure to violence, the vast majority (between 85 percent and 90 percent) of the 501 African American men in a batterer program had been exposed to interpersonal violence throughout three designated periods of their lives—as preteens, teenagers, and adults (Gondolf, 2005). There was no significant difference in overall exposure between the African American men and Caucasian men in the program, but the African Americans were more likely to have been threatened with guns or knives or to have witnessed shootings or stabbings (for example, 54 percent of the African Americans as teenagers versus 30 percent of the Caucasians). Both the African American and Caucasian men were also much more likely to have been exposed to nonfamily violence than to family violence in the past. Only a quarter of the men had been victims of family violence, and a third had witnessed violence among family members during their childhood or adolescence.

Furthermore, the African Americans in the batterer program were more likely to have been arrested previously. According to arrest records, over 80 percent had been arrested at least once prior to the arrest that brought the men to the batterer program. Fifty-nine percent had three or more prior arrests, and 37 percent had six or more. Forty-five percent had been previously arrested for domestic violence or other violent crimes, and 21 percent had been arrested four or more times for previous violence. (Sixty percent also had alcohol- or drug-related arrests.) Not surprisingly, these high rates of prior arrests for violent crimes correspond to the fact that 54 percent of the men reported having been threatened with a knife or gun, or having witnessed someone else being threatened, while a teenager. The violence experienced by these men and the high portion of them with previous arrests naturally raise questions about the social circumstances that contribute to these problems, and our reliance on the criminal justice system to deal with them. At face value, however, they also reinforce the call for specialized counseling that is at least sensitive to the experiences of violence and the impact of frequent periods in jail.

Batterer Program Evaluations

Only a few outcome studies of conventional batterer counseling and one preliminary study of culturally focused counseling were conducted prior to 2000. They offer only some preliminary support to the call for specialized counseling. In our multisite evaluation of batterer intervention systems (Gondolf, 2002a), the African American men were more than twice as likely as the Caucasian men to be re-arrested for domestic violence during a fifteen-month follow-up period (13 percent versus 5 percent of the 210 men at the Pittsburgh site). Their rate of re-assault reported by their female partners was, however, similar to that of the Caucasians throughout the full four-year follow-up (the reports are based on phone interviews every three months, with a response rate of approximately 70 percent for thirty months after program intake, and 60 percent for the full four years). The higher re-arrest rate of the African American men, while showing a similar victim-reported re-assault rate, may be the result of more aggressive policing in the African American neighborhoods of the inner city.

An additional study compared the pre- and post-test results on the Domestic Violence Inventory (DVI) of African American men and Caucasian men in a conventional twelve-week batterer program in the deep South (Buttell & Pike, 2003). The DVI is a 142-item test with six scales (truthfulness, violence, control, alcohol use, drug use, and stress coping) that are associated with recurring and severe re-assault. The fifty-two African Americans and thirty-eight Caucasians showed no difference in score changes across the DVI scales, leading the researchers to conclude that "the standardized cognitive-behavioral treatment program works equally well for African-American and Caucasian batterers" (p. 690).

However, a preliminary study of culturally focused batterer counseling revealed some positive results (O. Williams, 1995). African American men in culturally focused counseling reported feeling more comfortable talking to other men in the group and were more likely to develop friendships that carried over to life outside of the group, according to in-depth interviews with the forty-one program completers. They were more positive about the counselor as well. An experimental clinical trial of culturally focused batterer counseling for African American men was needed to test the outcomes of this approach against conventional batterer counseling. Such a trial took place in 2005, with our study of specialized counseling for African American men in Pittsburgh (Gondolf, 2007b, 2008a).

A Randomized Clinical Trial

We compared a culturally focused approach with an African American counselor and a group of African American men to conventional cognitive-behavioral counseling in groups of African Americans and in racially mixed groups (the number of the men was 501). The batterer program participants referred by the court were randomly assigned to these options at program intake, with very few refusals and overrides. There was no significant difference in the re-assault rate (23 percent overall) reported by the men's female partners over a periodic twelve-month follow-up (333 women, or 66 percent, responded). During that period, men in the racially mixed groups were unexpectedly half as likely to be re-arrested for domestic violence as the men in the culturally focused groups.[13] The men's level of racial identification, according to the Racial Identity Attitude Scale, did not significantly affect the outcomes of the counseling options. Interestingly, the men with high racial identification were much more likely to complete the sixteen-week program in the culturally focused and conventional groups of African Americans (63 percent and 65 percent completion, respectively) compared to the men with high identification in the racially mixed groups (40 percent completion) (Gondolf, 2008b).

We considered several other explanations for the lack of any additive effect from culturally focused counseling. The results may reflect the "dodo bird" effect mentioned above—all the approaches are equally effective because they include similar features (Luborsky, Rosenthal, & Diguer, 2002). Each counseling option in our study had, for instance, a clear message of change, directions on how to change, and group support for change. Furthermore, the counseling options may merely reflect the comparisons between process (discussion-oriented) and didactic (instructional) formats, or between psychodynamic and cognitive-behavioral modalities, that have shown similar outcomes in depression and alcohol treatment (Elkin, Shea, & Watkins, 1989; Project MATCH Research Group, 1997), as well as in batterer counseling (Saunders, 1996).

As I discussed in chapter 2, several implementation issues may have influenced the results as well. First, our monitoring of treatment integrity found some evidence of treatment convergence. The debriefing interviews with the counseling participants reported similar amounts of discussion across the counseling options but also confirmed that the culturally focused groups were much more likely to address African American issues than the other groups. And second, the counselor leading the culturally focused groups may have been deficient in group skills and counseling experience, but the training consultant consistently rated the counselor as adequate, and substantially more men in the culturally focused groups rated their counselor as "very effective."

The threats to external validity caused by the agency context of the culturally focused groups are of greater concern. The culturally focused counseling was an appendage to a social service agency that otherwise relied exclusively on more conventional counseling. As debriefing interviews with program staff suggested, the agency did not appear to be as supportive of culturally focused counseling as another agency with a different approach might have been. The program's close relationship with the court and enforcement of compliance may also have heightened the perception that the counseling, regardless of the approach, was an extension of the criminal justice system and to be viewed with suspicion.

Moreover, the broader social backdrop of racism, discrimination, and prejudice in society at large has been particularly visible in Pittsburgh, the research site for the study. In the mid-1990s, a federal human rights commission investigated the police department in response to a highly publicized case of police brutality and put the police department under federal supervision. This context may increase the resistance, resentments, and rationalizations that affect program outcomes. The culturally focused counseling at this particular site may, therefore, need to address such issues more explicitly. Programs that take more of a peace-building or healing approach, rather than using punitive or containment tactics, might be more effective in connecting with these men, as well.

Treatment Implications

At face value, culturally oriented counseling in general does not seem worth the extra resources required to recruit and train qualified staff, maintain specialized groups along with conventional counseling groups, and negotiate the intra-agency tensions that may arise from its introduction. However, culturally focused counseling appears to be as effective as conventional batterer counseling in terms of the partner reports. It might be offered at least as an option that men could choose, rather than be assigned to a counseling group. But as the previous research in other fields suggests, more funding to support the development and implementation of cultural approaches is ultimately needed before we can reach a verdict on the usefulness of culturally focused counseling (Sue, Zane, Hall, & Berger, 2009).[14]

The identification, training, and support of appropriate African American counselors certainly warrant more attention. Culturally focused counseling might also be improved by linkages with resources and services in the African American community, and in that way might more concretely address the issues that emerge from the curriculum. Furthermore, embedding culturally focused counseling in a community-based agency operated primarily by African Americans might enhance program support and service referral. It might also help to reduce the impression that the counseling is simply an extension of the criminal justice system. Finally, benefits from culturally focused counseling in racially mixed groups might be achieved through a culturally diverse staff, trained in cultural sensitivity (Sue, 1998; O. Williams, 1999). What might ultimately be needed is what some in the field refer to as a culturally competent organization that is equipped to address a diversity of men (O. Williams and Becker, 1994). This approach alleviates the resource demands of establishing and supporting separate groups for men of different racial and ethnic backgrounds, and it may better integrate the advantages of culturally focused and conventional cognitive-behavioral counseling.

In sum, the limited research on cultural approaches to treatment and counseling present a mixed picture in terms of outcomes. Our clinical trial of specialized batterer counseling suggests further that simply adding a culturally focused counseling group to domestic violence programs does not in itself improve outcomes. However, self-selection into specialized groups, increased organizational cultural competence, and more sensitivity in general to the distinctive circumstances of program participants may lead to some discernible improvements in outcomes. Culturally focused counseling for African American men may prove to be more effective especially within community-based organizations tied to local services and supports. Strong program links to the criminal justice system, which is often seen as racist or discriminatory by African Americans, may be offsetting some potential effects.

Conclusion: Toward More Engagement and Help

A Potential Bridge

In one sense, the innovations that address different categories of batterers represent a bridge over the psychodynamic and cognitive-behavioral divide. They recognize that some batterers may not do as well as others because of special needs, acute problems, or social circumstances. In response, the innovations offer techniques or approaches to address those needs. They account in part for the emotional aspects that psychodynamic approaches attempt to address, but in the context of a cognitive-behavioral approach. The differentiations additionally require assessment to identify categories of concern, even though not to the extent recommended in the psychodynamic approaches. They implicitly acknowledge that the gender-based, cognitive-behavioral approaches are suitable for most men; such programs just need a booster for some subgroups. The research supporting the innovations, however, is generally insufficient, inconclusive, or simply weak. In most cases the innovations, although of interest, are not sufficiently substantiated for widespread adoption. That is, they warrant further development and require extensive assessment; also, their implementation means additional costs but no sizable payoff.

The batterer typology, as the most discussed and researched of the innovations, illustrates their potential and limits. The batterer typology includes a borderline/dysphoric type that more directly reflects the abusive personality described in the previous chapter. As discussed in this chapter, the distinctness of the types is still debated, and the typology's prediction of program outcomes is suspect. In other words, the types are not necessarily diagnostic. According to one clinical trial of competing batterer treatments (Saunders, 1996), a subgroup with tendencies toward borderline personality disorder may respond better to a psychodynamic approach. That subgroup is relatively small, considering the men with those tendencies who did well in the conventional batterer program. This study is also not a true test of types, but rather of tendencies on two personality dimensions. A more detailed profile combining a variety of personality traits with violent histories, as the batterer typology attempts to do, might present a different picture. Our interpretation in light of the profiles from our multisite study is that program participants with psychological problems, or personality dysfunction in general, are more likely to assault their partners again. The strongest predictor of subsequent assaults overall is the severity of violence in a man's past. What we may have, then, is more a set of problematic dimensions than types.

The typology does echo what many practitioners observe—that batterers have various behavioral patterns. How distinct those types are, as well as how much they affect program outcomes, has not been convincingly demonstrated by the research. In the meantime, it would make sense to offer some men emotional-regulation techniques within a group setting or individual sessions in addition to a batterer program.[15] Many programs already teach positive self-talk and strategies to monitor one's emotions. These would particularly aid men who are noticeably volatile, angry, or irritable at program intake or in initial group sessions. Many conventional programs already include group sessions devoted to regulating emotions. Other, more clinically oriented programs like Emerge have the staff keep notes of their observations and respond strategically to men who exhibit special problems, apparent resistance, or noncompliance—all within a gender-based, cognitive-behavioral approach. In extreme cases, men may be referred to additional psychological services.

More Potential Contributions

The research on stages of change is particularly discouraging both inside and outside the domestic violence field. Its popularity does speak to one universal challenge in treatment—namely, resistance and dropping out. The discussions about resistant, difficult, or defiant clients are extensive throughout addiction and offender treatments. A variety of interpretations and accompanying techniques have been put forth (for example, Anderson & Stewart, 1983; Newman, 1994; Rooney, 2009). The change stages add a more delineated, theoretical, and progressive model to this mix. The concept helps the therapist discern signs of progress in a client and accordingly appeal to the client's shifting attitudes to further the change. But the extent and nature of resistance may be much more complex than that, and more engrained in the problematic men who do not benefit from batterer programs. The stage studies of batterer program participants show them generally at lower stages of change, which could be a reflection of the minimization, denial, and projection that appear to accompany their violence. The apparent stage may be more a reflection of a larger mind-set and belief system of violence, or narcissistic and antisocial tendencies.

In any case, motivational interviewing has some support for getting resistant clients to invest in treatment. The willingness to hear clients out with nondirective, nonjudgmental, reflective listening is recognized as one means of further engaging a person in the treatment process. It also leads a client to take more initiative and responsibility for his recovery or change. Although the research evidence in the alcohol field and the fledging studies with batterers is less than compelling, motivational interviewing reminds us that more can be done individually to involve men in program activities.

There is some concern in the domestic violence field that motivational interviewing might give credence and reinforcement to some men's excuses and justifications for their violence. That might be checked, however, within the batterer program that a man subsequently enters. The larger message may be that orientation or introductory sessions are worthwhile. They too can demonstrate respect, concern, and encouragement for potential participants. As I have pointed out in this and previous chapters, outright putdowns, belittling, confrontations, and antagonism are likely to be counterproductive, but they have more to do with staff inadequacies or incompetence than with program approaches.

A striking contrast in endorsement surfaces for the last two innovations discussed in this chapter. There has been outright resistance and even dismissal of couples counseling. However, a vocal faction promotes couples counseling to address the mutual violence in some couples and the couple dynamics that may contribute to the violence. The couples counseling that has been studied so far largely follows a cognitive-behavioral approach and has been conducted with a highly selective group of couples following extensive assessment and screening. Moreover, the portion of men eligible for the couples counseling—those with especially low levels of violence, and willing and accepting partners—is a very small subgroup of batterer program participants. It is a group that tends to be very responsive to the all-male batterer programming. The expansion of accompanying groups for violent women also lessens the layers of safety assessment and monitoring involved in couples counseling. Why make all this extra effort for such a small subgroup, and also open the door to potential misuses? Already some family clinics are claiming to do couples counseling for domestic violence cases (B. Adams, 2010), but without the extensive screening, monitoring, and sensitivity implemented in the couples studies and recommended by experts (Bograd & Mederos, 1999).

Finally, the most uniformly recommended innovation for batterer programs is culturally oriented approaches with ethnic and racial minorities. The aim here is also to enhance the gender-based, cognitive-behavioral programming with more discussion of issues facing African American men in their communities. It also is important to acknowledge the trauma and distress caused by men's witnessing violence and being victims of it themselves. The disproportionate frequency of their encounters with police, courts, and jail is also likely to have heightened their suspicion of the criminal justice system and resistance to programs. Interestingly, studies of culturally oriented counseling are relatively few, and the counseling of this type warrants further synthesis and development. Our own randomized clinical trial showed one version of culturally focused counseling with rates of re-assault similar to conventional batterer programming. It also raised several questions about the implementation of specialized counseling that needs more attention and study. The balance of counselor and community experience, and the program linkage to community supports rather than to the criminal justice system, stand out in this regard.

Popularity versus Research Results

Two somewhat contradictory themes emerge from a review of the research. The promoted innovations thus far fall substantially short of evidence-based practice, while using evidence-based practice standards to question stand-alone batterer programs. This apparent double standard may be due in part to the lack of available research on the innovations. We are left to wonder about the enthusiasm for the various innovations, given their weak research support in the domestic violence field and other treatment areas. Of course, one possibility is that the outcome research is simply underdeveloped and difficult to conduct. The so-called evidence-*supported* treatments, based on practitioner-oriented, real-world studies, may therefore be given more attention and credence than evidence-based practice (Sue, Zane, Hall, & Berger, 2009).

The research support is no doubt increased because the researchers of the innovations, for the most part, tend to be devotees of the approaches they are studying. Some have overstated their findings and the promise they hold. But the yearning among practitioners for any help with a difficult clientele has an influence as well. Our seeking a breakthrough, something fresh and new, a quick fix, or even a simple sorting mechanism for our clinical observations may have us jump at a plausible typology of batterers. None of the innovations present a problem in themselves, and some may help us realize the possibilities we seek. However, they could diffuse the focus of existing batterer groups and lead us on tangents.

In any case, the exploration of different categories of batterers reinforces the evolution in batterer programs. It reminds us that within the group of men who batter, some have different motivations, needs, and circumstances that may warrant special attention. It moves us further from the stereotypic thinking that all batterers are monsters and won't change. Men may differ in their readiness to change, need for validation and rapport, mode and severity of violence, and social experiences and outlook. One can make an argument that these variations warrant some attention merely on humanistic grounds. Discerning where men are "coming from" and where "they are at" is an essential part of any counseling or educational effort. Although the evidence to support a major conceptual shift or program overhaul is lacking, respect and care for individuals in a program is part of building rapport and engaging them in the program's goals. The challenge of doing that without being manipulated by the participants, or inadvertently colluding with them, is part of the work (Milne, Leck, & Choudhri, 2009).

Batterer programs continue to try new ways to increase participation. For example, Alternatives to Domestic Abuse, in East Lansing, Michigan, uses a program with three main phases or stages. It begins with several didactic sessions and progresses toward more discussion-oriented sessions and peer support. Many other programs have orientation sessions that help men transition into the group sessions. In some jurisdictions, probation officers act as case managers, often following up with program absentees in a motivational conversation.

The Domestic Abuse Counseling Center, in Pittsburgh, has a program liaison in the court who talks with the men individually when they are referred to the program and helps identify each man's motivations and goals for the program. It had a staff person who called no-shows as well, and it convenes its group meetings in neighborhood churches and community centers around the city. The multiple locations make the program more accessible to low-income and minority men and results in more homogeneous groups. Furthermore, the program uses homework assignments to increase involvement and extend each session's impact.

As I explore further in the next chapter, court oversight, case management, swift sanctions, and coordinated services may contribute even more to program compliance and, for that matter, engagement. But programs also need to convey their desire to engage and help men in order to extend this effort. Our research team's observation is that most programs, regardless of approach, are trying to do that in various ways, but they are often caught in the tension between accountability and treatment, and between ensuring women's safety and caring for men. As discussed in the opening chapter, the intersection of criminal justice expectations and therapeutic intentions poses some underlying conflicts. Many men in batterer programs are in great need of more structure and less wiggle room, given their dysfunctional lifestyles and inconsistent behavior. It may be a matter of finding the right dose of tough love—of being firm, decisive, and direct, as well as being caring and supportive. Exploring ways to do this continues to move the field forward.

In sum, the case for "one size fits *most*" can still be made amid the array of efforts to categorize batterers. The gender-based, cognitive-behavioral programs appear to accommodate many of the designated differences, except for a subgroup of problematic men who fall outside of the current categorizations—

or, rather, cut across many of them. The overlap and intersection of the current types, stages, dynamics, and racial differences has also not been integrated either practically or theoretically. It is hard to say what is primary or most influential in a particular case of battering, and assessing all these possibilities remains complicated and time-consuming. The features or dimensions that deserve the most attention—the ones most likely to predict outcomes and contribute to prevention—are the focus of risk assessment efforts. Responding to that risk goes well beyond the program itself and different types of batterers. This consideration is the topic of the next chapter.

III | THE SYSTEM MATTERS

5 | Risk Management in the Intervention System

The Uses and Misuses of Risk Assessment

System Failures

I have implied throughout this book that the key question with regard to batterer programs is how to improve them. The previous chapters present at least some evidence supporting the conventional gender-based, cognitive-behavioral approach. There is, however, a subgroup of men who remain unresponsive and resistant to batterer programming, regardless of approach. The proposed alternatives, like couples counseling or stage-based approaches, do not appear sufficient or well-suited for these men, who also tend to be the most dangerous participants in batterer programs. In fact, these men are likely to be screened out of such alternatives or to be resistant to them. The challenge facing batterer intervention in general is how to better contain these men and protect their partners.

Our multisite study made this point crystal clear (see especially Gondolf & White, 2001). It identified a subgroup of men (about 20 percent of our sample) who physically abused their partners early in the follow-up period and repeated their violence later. These repeaters were responsible for almost all of the physical injuries reported during the follow-up. Moreover, a portion of these men produced utter horror stories, according to a qualitative review and coding of the narrative portion of the follow-up interviews describing violent incidents (Gondolf & Beeman, 2003). About 5 percent of the overall sample of men was unrelenting in their violence and used tactics that were over the top. Their partners were less likely to seek further help because of fear of possible retaliation, or frustration with an intervention system that had failed them. One of these men chased his partner to a neighbor's house with a baseball; another man held a knife to his partner's throat and threatened to cut her into little pieces and throw her to the fish. If these kinds of men were identified and contained, the overall outcomes of batterer programs would appear amazingly effective.

As mentioned in the previous chapter, the subgroup of repeatedly violent men doesn't fit into a neat category. They don't match a distinct personality type; they aren't predominantly psychopathic or crazed addicts (White & Gondolf, 2000). Not surprisingly, these men are likely to have more violent and criminal pasts and show evidence of psychological problems—but they do not have a distinguishing profile or profiles. As mentioned above, research with chronically violent juveniles and other violent criminals produces almost identical findings (Piquero, Fagan, Mulvey, Steinberg, & Ogden, 2005; Mulvey et al., 2010).

When our research team found how difficult it was to identify the particularly dangerous men using their reported characteristics and behaviors, we reviewed more fully the information collected in interviews with the men and women in our multisite evaluation (Gondolf, 2002a; Gondolf & Beeman, 2003). It was clear that what failed was not so much the batterer programs as intervention systems overall. The severely violent men were predominantly program dropouts who were not sanctioned further by the court. In other words, little was done in response to the most glaring of risk markers—dropping out of a program. Moreover, the high-risk men did not receive supplemental treatment for psychological problems and addictions that may have compounded their violent behavior and resistance to change. Nor, for the most part, did their partners receive further assistance or support. In fact, only 8 percent of the women had any contact with battered women's centers or other social services after the first three months of the follow-up period (Gondolf, 2002b). Yet the rate of repeat violence was lower in cases where the court reviewed program compliance, programs included addiction treatment for some men, and women had follow-up contact with shelters (Gondolf, 1999b, 2000c; Jones & Gondolf, 2001).

One way to improve batterer program outcome appears, therefore, to lie in enhancing our response to high-risk men—the men who are unresponsive to batterer programs regardless of approach. This chapter reviews the efforts afoot to better identify the dangerous men and contain them. It discusses the approaches and instruments that have been developed to better assess risk. As victims' advocates have claimed for years, the emerging risk assessment necessitates a coordinated community response. The coordination is essential not only to obtain assessment information, but also to tailor strategies to interrupt the men's violence and to create safety plans for their partners. In other words, a working intervention system is ultimately needed.

The Emergence of Risk Assessment

The holy grail of much of the criminal justice system these days is risk assessment (Hanson, 2005). The use of instruments to identify the most dangerous offenders and those most likely to commit subsequent offenses has become a major innovation for a variety of reasons. One reason is certainly the need to identify those offenders who are most likely to continue harming others, and to do more to contain those men and better protect their potential victims. Another propelling reason is to more efficiently apply interventions and the resources they represent to the cases most in need of them. As state budgets face major deficits and criminal justice costs continue to rise, risk assessment represents a means of reducing costs while increasing effectiveness. Risk assessment basically serves as a form of triage, sorting out the most urgent and neediest cases for special attention.

A variety of uses for risk assessment has emerged in the field of domestic violence. Some courts want to use it to identify the men who warrant more intensive supervision and possible jailing, as well as those for whom a shorter stint in a batterer program might suffice. Batterer programs, in turn, find risk assessment a helpful tool in identifying men who warrant more intensive programming (for example, several sessions a week rather than the typical once a week approach), or additional services and treatments. In fact, 82 percent (thirty-one out of thirty-eight) of the current state standards for batterer programs indicate that program staff should assess batterers for risk of further violence and lethality.[1] There are, however, no consistent or detailed specifications for how that should be accomplished or what should be done with the results.

Victims' advocates, in contrast, use risk assessment as a way to help a woman decide whether she should return to her abusive partner, allow him to visit her, or get a protection order to keep him away from her. Risk assessment is the basis of the safety planning that has become routine for most battered women's services (see Davies, Lyon, & Monti-Catania, 1998). There are also now shortened risk assessments for police to use in gathering firsthand information on offenders and to assist in making initial decisions about a case (Hilton, Harris, Rice, Lang, & Cormier, 2004; Kropp, Hart, & Belfrage, 2005). The added information that risk assessment brings to decision making at all levels has to be helpful, but with it comes the potential for misuses that can be counterproductive and even increase women's danger.

There is a tendency to use risk assessment in a mechanical and expedient way rather than with caution about its limitations, variations, and shortcomings (R. Rogers, 2000).[2] Most important is that risk assessment instruments are generally weak predictors of future behavior. In a comprehensive article, Randall Kropp reviews the psychometric properties of the most extensively developed instruments for assessing domestic violence—the Danger Assessment Scale (DA), the Domestic Violence Screening Inventory (DVSI), the Ontario Domestic Assault Risk Assessment (ODARA), and the Spouse Abuse Risk Assessment (SARA), which are discussed below. Summarizing their reliability and validity, he concludes: "These instruments still only yield modest associations with recidivism (i.e., correlations roughly between .30 and .40), and this is unlikely to improve as we simply do not possess the technology to accurately predict violent behavior" (2008, p. 211).[3]

Several other reviews of risk assessment in the domestic violence field admit this key limitation and point to the research challenges that underlie it (Cattaneo & Goodman, 2009; D. Dutton & Kropp, 2000; Hilton & Harris, 2005; Roehl & Guertin, 2000). The reviewers note several methodological problems involved in establishing and testing risk assessment instruments. First, there are a number of ways to identify the items and factors that should go into a risk assessment instrument. Some items have been identified based on theoretical assumptions, such as the impact of certain psychopathologies on perception and behavior. Others are based on empirical findings regarding the characteristics that correlate to crime.

Second, it is difficult and costly to follow up with criminal offenders, particularly domestic violence offenders, in order to test the prediction of the instruments. The offenders are hard to reach, their victims are often reluctant to report their partners' abuse, and self-reports of violence in general tend to be unreliable. Third, what is being predicted varies across the available studies (Kraemer, Kazdin, Offord, Kessler, Jensen, & Kupfer, 1997): Is it any re-assault, severe re-assaults, or attempted and actual murder that we most want to predict— or a more nuanced impact of psychological or verbal abuse? Is the potential new offense in the short term, the long term, or something in between? Different factors and instruments are better predictors of some outcomes than others.

The main challenge to the conception of most risk assessment instruments, which I return to further below, is the dynamic nature of risk: violence is more a process than a discrete event. Risk researchers generally accept that dynamic factors—those that vary over time—contingencies, and changes in status are key to improving prediction (K. Douglas & Kropp, 2002; K. Douglas & Skeem, 2005; Hanson, 2005; Hanson, Bourgon, Helmus, & Hodgson, 2009; Mulvey & Lidz, 1995). However, such factors are generally not available at an offender's arrest, court appearance, or program intake. Partner contact, drinking patterns, and employment status, for instance, are all subject to change over time. As has been reported throughout the research on outcomes of batterer programs, compliance with the batterer program and additional referrals also has an impact on future violence and danger to victims.

The most obvious concern in testing risk assessment is, therefore, the impact of intervention on outcomes—what is being predicted. It is hard to separate out the mediating factors that might interrupt the potential risk. A man might appear to be very dangerous but not act violently, because his partner is protected in a shelter, or because he ends up in jail. As a result, risk assessment may be more about the potential for re-assault, rather than about its actual occurrence (S. Hart, 2008). Potential is something much more subjective and more difficult to calibrate.

Practical Concerns

Risk assessment raises a number of practical concerns, especially in the domestic violence field. Jackie Campbell (2005), who created the DA, lays out the key questions to be considered in using risk assessment: when is the risk assessment to be conducted, who is to administer it, how is the assessment information to be obtained, how is the assessment to be used, who is to receive the results of the assessment, and what is to be done about the results? The answers to these questions will probably influence the accuracy of the assessment and its impact. For instance, an assessment of a man's violence conducted with a female victim is likely to differ from that done with the perpetrator. The perspective of probation officers may lead to a different emphasis in information gathering and recommendations, compared to the perspective of victims' advocates or batterer program staff. Are the assessment results primarily to be used by the courts in sentencing decisions, by batterer programs for supplemental service referrals, or by victims' advocates to help formulate safety plans? All of these uses need a different scope and kind of information.

The overarching concern raised by researchers and practitioners alike is how to conduct such assessments without inadvertently endangering or upsetting victims, instead of helping them (J. Campbell, 2004; Cattaneo & Goodman, 2009; Davis, Taylor, & Maxwell, 2000). The victim is usually the best source of the information about battering, for a variety of reasons, but also has the most to lose by disclosing it. A batterer is likely to assume that his high-risk rating and the consequences that go with it are the result of his partner's "telling on him." He may respond with retaliation and intimidation. Additionally, reviewing all the details and history of abuse for a risk assessment can have a disturbing emotional impact on some women. The questioning associated with risk assessment can feel similar to a partner's interrogation and control.

A study by the Vera Institute in New York City (Trone, 1999), based on interviews with thirty practitioners who administered risk assessment instruments, recommends several precautions to improve the results and protect victims. The steps associated with acquiring more accurate information include drawing from a variety of sources (for example, offender and victim interviews, police reports and court records, agency staff observations, and other witnesses and family members). The resulting risk assessment scores might then be weighed against the victim's overall perceptions, consultation with victims' advocates, any other documentation, and the offender's response to and compliance with treatment.

Rather than use risk assessment as a college might rely on an SAT score alone to eliminate applicants, risk assessment needs to be considered as one piece of information among many others. To extend the analogy, college admissions offices generally consider SAT results along with letters of recommendation, high-school grades, essays, student activities, and the status of the student's high school. For battered women, using a range of information sources not only improves accuracy in decision making but also diffuses the potential of retaliation against the woman for disclosing past abuse.

Despite the limitations of risk assessment, it can still make an important contribution to domestic violence intervention and improve the outcomes of batterer programs. A long history of research comparing unstructured professional judgment (basically, relying on one's intuition or general impression) with structured ratings and actuarial instruments bears this out (Grove & Meehl, 1996; Litwack, 2001; Quinsey, Harris, Rice, & Cormie, 1998). Overall, this research shows that risk assessment with structured ratings or actuarial instruments is superior to unstructured approaches (Hanson, 2005; Kropp, 2008). In fact, clinicians, parole officers, and judges tend to have only a 50 percent chance of predicting violence outcomes correctly—no better than tossing a coin. Prediction improves for short-term outcomes and when contingencies are considered (for example, whether a batterer with psychiatric problems enters treatment or not) (Mulvey & Lidz, 1995), but this sort of prediction may be more of an extrapolation or extension of the moment. One clinician many years ago called this kind of short-term assessment "a matter of common sense rather than prediction (Sonkin, 1986, p. 7).

The second main advantage of risk assessment is, as its reviewers conclude, that it promotes communication across and among agencies and services (D. Dutton & Kropp, 2000; Roehl & Guertin, 2000). In order to obtain the information to complete a risk assessment, the assessor needs to draw from external sources such as police records or a victim interview, rather than just relying on instinct. The process also raises awareness of factors associated with risk and helps practitioners be more alert to potential danger in general.

The remainder of this chapter elaborates on the different instruments and approaches used in risk assessment; the research indicating the limitations of static, or one-time, assessment; and the need for a collaborative process focused on prevention of further violence and safety for the victims. Risk assessment to identify the most dangerous and problematic men is becoming a tool more for prevention than for prediction. It can help to increase collaboration in the sharing of information, and supervision of some batterers and support of their partners. However, it requires a broader view of intervention beyond just the batterer program, and ultimately a different mind-set among community services as a whole. Simply rolling out instruments with cutoff scores and risk categories is not only not enough, but may be downright misleading.

Choices in Assessment and Instruments

Actuarial Instruments versus Structured Judgment

The assessment business has exploded in the criminal justice field, with as many as forty assessment instruments developed for sexual assault and several others specifically for child abuse, prisoner assignments, and inmate parole and re-entry (Hanson, 2005). About fifteen risk assessment instruments are circulating in the domestic violence field, but not all have been substantially validated— that is, tested against outcomes during a follow-up period. Some have been substantiated mainly by concurrent validity that correlates the risk assessment results to scores on comparable or associated measures, such as expressed anger (for a full review, see Kropp, 2008; Bowen, 2011).

The most widely used and most extensively tested—although with research limitations—domestic violence instruments are divided into two different approaches: those using structured professional judgment, and those using actuarial measures. The former relies on clinician or practitioner ratings on the items or factors of concern. A practitioner interviews a client and reviews his or her records to derive a high to low rating on each item, finally submitting an overall rating based on his or her global impression. The SARA (Kropp, Hart, Webster, & Eaves, 1999) and MOSAIC (DeBecker, 1996) are the most prominent examples of this approach. Actuarial instruments, such as the DA (J. Campbell, 1995) and Domestic Violence Inventory (DVI) (Risk and Needs Assessment, 1997), are based on a checklist of items that is usually self-administered. These risk factors are primarily behavioral characteristics and symptoms that have been correlated with violence. The responses are tallied and weighted produce an overall total score.

By and large, the predictive strength of the two approaches is similar—with some variation across instruments in different settings with different outcomes, such as a physical assault versus an attempted murder (Kropp, 2008; Roehl, O'Sullivan, Webster, & Campbell, 2005). The proponents of structured ratings argue, however, that this approach does much more to engage the assessed individual, helps the practitioner know the client better, and most important, identifies specific areas in need of attention (for example., alcohol addiction and symptoms of depression).

Although the actuarial instruments do not specifically expose areas of need, they are much more efficient and economical to administer. Program staff can give the assessments to a group in shorter time periods, and the assessments don't require the extensive training needed for structured ratings. The most efficient instrument to date is the thirteen-item ODARA (Hilton, Harris, Rice, Lang, & Cormier, 2004). It is designed to be easily administered by police as well as social service practitioners. The developers claim that the thirteen items are as predictive as other larger sets of items that have previously been used. A shortened version of the SARA, the Brief Spousal Assault Form for the Evaluation of Risk (B-SAFER), has also been developed especially for police, but it requires additional training to formulate the structured ratings used in the assessment (Kropp, Hart, & Belfrage, 2005).[4]

Two other approaches to risk assessment include screening tools with a checklist of items that practitioners associate with high risk. These screens are a big net that tends to produce a large percentage of false positives, but fewer false negatives. They are useful as a first cut, to be followed up with more extensive individual evaluations. The Lethality Checklist (B. Hart, 1989) and the Kingston Screening Instrument for Domestic Violence (K-SID; Gelles & Tolman, 1998) are two such examples. Other risk assessments have been developed and used for identifying high risk for recurrent violence in general, not just domestic violence—for example, the Level of Service Inventory—Revised (LSI-R), Violence Risk Appraisal Guide (VRAG), Historical-Clinical-Risk Management-20

(HCR-20), Psychopathy Check List (PCL), MOSAIC, and Static-99). The most popular of these instruments is the fifty-four-item LSI-R (Andrews & Bonta, 1995) which is widely used by probation officers to determine the extent and nature of services warranted in a criminal case, and to help with intervention placement in general. More basically, LSI-R results suggest the level of supervision and containment that an offender warrants, such as jail, a half-way house, or electronic monitoring.

A possible limitation here is that domestic violence situations and dynamics frequently differ from those of general violence. In fact, as I pointed out in the previous chapter, a major portion of batterer program participants have not been violent to people outside their families. Also, batterers usually have direct access to their victims and use a variety of abusive tactics that are not necessarily captured by the LSI-R. As a result, generic assessment instruments are less predictive of domestic violence than specific ones— namely, domestic violence risk assessments (Kropp, 2009). This shortfall has led some probation departments to administer a domestic violence risk assessment along with the LSI-R. Then there is the challenge of interpreting any conflicting results and deciding on appropriate cutoff score for batterer programs or women's services. The biggest issue with the LSI-R has probably been the formulaic way it is frequently applied. Certain scores alone are used to prescribe a narrow set of responses, such as requiring an offender to attend a program for a month.[5]

Administrative Challenges

The available risk assessment instruments rely heavily on some measure of past violence, criminality, or abuse as a central item of the scale or inventory. As most practitioners have observed and numerous studies have documented, previous violence is one of the strongest predictors of future violence (Cattaneo & Goodman, 2005; Riggs, Caulfield, & Street, 2000). However, obtaining this crucial information can be one of the main barriers to more accurate prediction. Arrest and court records are often incomplete, have been expunged, register only partial counts, and seldom capture the extent of offenses. As mentioned above, victims' reports are also often incomplete out of fear of retaliation or complications, or a desire to forgive or protect one's partner from criminal consequences. Victims also may not know the full story of the offender's abuse of other women and violence toward people outside the family. An assessment study in Denver illustrated this problem. Up to 30 percent of the female partners were either unavailable or refused to report on their partner's violence during a court-based risk assessment (K. Williams & Houghton, 2004). We found in our multisite study that this sort of response rate improved over time, as interviewers developed rapport with the women and the interviews were further from the crisis period at the time of the court appearance (Gondolf, 2000b).

Another challenge in risk assessment is interpreting the scores. Most of the instruments indicate a set of cutoff scores that identify those cases considered high risk, as compared to medium or low risk. The scores provide a categorization system that can then be acted on. But amid the volume of cases and issues facing services, the categories can easily become ossified. The reality is that any such categorization has a substantial set of false negatives and false positives, due to all the prediction and practical problems mentioned above. That is, the low-risk category is likely to contain a substantial portion—approximately 30 percent to 40 percent in one of our studies (Heckert & Gondolf, 2004)—of false negatives, or high-risk men. Overreliance on the scores themselves, then, can inadvertently result in misleading responses, such as a victim's letting down her guard or receiving fewer protections because of a false low-risk classification. Also, an offender may use his low-risk classification as a reason to avoid further treatment or to manipulate his partner: "See, I told you I didn't have a problem," or "I'm not as bad as you claim." The developers of one assessment instrument have, as a result, revised their categories to be "high priority" to "low priority" (replacing "high risk" and "low risk") as a way to lessen the potential misuse of the categories (Kropp & Hart, 2000).

Research on Batterer Risk Assessment

A few major studies have compared the prediction of domestic violence assessment instruments and, more important, explored ways to improve prediction overall. Although the studies do not identify one instrument or approach as necessarily superior to another, they do verify the complexity of risk assessment, the need to consider dynamic factors, and the contribution of women's perceptions to prediction. The first of the studies is with battered women from several settings (Roehl, O'Sullivan, Webster, & Campbell, 2005), and the second was conducted with partners of batterer program participants (Heckert & Gondolf, 2004). In the first study, researchers administered the actual risk assessment instruments as would commonly be done with battered women seeking services. The second study, however, used only simulated scores derived from a data based on women's reports.

The most extensive comparative study examined the prediction of four risk assessment instruments from battered women recruited from six different sites (Roehl, O'Sullivan, Webster, & Campbell, 2005). The Risk Assessment Validation Experiment—or RAVE study, as it is commonly called—randomly assigned 1,307 women to various combinations of four risk assessment instruments: the K-SID, DVSI, DA, and DV-MOSAIC (a special version of MOSAIC for domestic violence cases). The women were interviewed again nine months later about a variety of abuse outcomes ($n = 782$, for a 60 percent response rate). Although all the instruments were more accurate than chance in predicting the reported outcomes, there was no clear-cut winner among the approaches. Some instruments predicted a certain outcome better than another outcome, leading the researchers to warn that "no one instrument should be relied on exclusively" (p. 17).

But the accuracy of prediction was still relatively weak overall, in what the researchers conclude is still a "young science" that needs to be applied with great caution. Like so many others in the field, they call for risk management rather than solely prediction: "Risk assessment should be used as a guide to develop effective interventions to be implemented by the system and/or by the victim" (p. 18). However, this study, as broad as it was, did not focus on the risk from men in batterer programs, but rather the partners of women in hospitals or shelters, women who made domestic violence calls, and women who appeared in family court—men who were most likely not in batterer programs.

Using data from our multisite study of batterer programs, the sociologist Alex Heckert led an analysis of three simulated assessment instruments and women's predictions of abuse ($N = 499$) (Heckert & Gondolf, 2004). The study compared the prediction of multiple outcomes, including repeated re-assault, over fifteen months after batterer program intake.[6] Comparable items from our data were used to reconstruct the scoring of the K-SID, SARA, and DA. These scorings, along with women's ratings of the likelihood of repeated re-assault, were used as the predictors for the multiple outcomes. The sensitivity of the simulated instruments—that is, the percentage of correct predictions of repeat re-assault—ranged from 11 percent to 64 percent. This sensitivity was increased when the women's perceptions of risk were included; moreover, the predictive ability of the women's perceptions *by themselves* was nearly as strong as or stronger than the simulated instruments.[7] As in the RAVE study, the DA was the strongest predictor of more severe violence, but all the instruments, actuarial data combinations, and women's perceptions were relatively weak predictors overall. The findings also corroborate the results of a previous study that found women's perceptions to be a better predictor than the DA items (Weisz, Tolman, & Saunders, 2000). This latter study, however, used a much smaller sample ($N = 177$) and only a four-month follow-up period.[8]

There is also concern that a one-time or static risk assessment fails to capture the dynamic factors associated with violence. The risk-related circumstances of a batterer, for instance, are likely to change over time, including employment status, drinking patterns, access to his partner, and additional treatment or interventions. As mentioned above, numerous researchers have brought out the importance of considering these dynamics or time-varying factors to improve prediction (K. Douglas & Kropp, 2002; K. Douglas & Skeem, 2005; Hanson, 2005; Hanson, Bourgon, Helmus, & Hodgson, 2009; Mulvey & Lidz, 1995). In one analysis accounting for several three-month follow-up intervals, our statistician, Alison Snow Jones, found that the risk factors assessed at program intake (such as demographic factors, psychological problems, and alcohol use) were relatively weak or insignificant predictors of re-assault, compared to factors assessed during the follow-up periods (Jones & Gondolf, 2001).[9] Specifically, information about the man's dropping out of a batterer program, the woman's contact with shelter services, and the man's contact with alcohol treatment improved the prediction somewhat. Another analysis used multiple outcomes cumulated over a fifteen-month follow-up period and showed that the dynamic factors did not substantially improve prediction (Heckert & Gondolf, 2005). (The multisite outcome categories were no abuse; verbal abuse or controlling behavior, but no threats or physical violence; threats, but no physical violence; one physical assault; and repeated physical assaults.) However, using the multiple outcomes did improve prediction over the usual dichotomous outcome of re-assault versus no re-assault.

The lesson appears to be that prediction remains difficult even with the most severely violent men, but using a more complex set of factors and outcome measures tends to improve risk assessment. The limits of prediction continue to point researchers and practitioners to cautions about the bottom-line use of one-time risk assessment instruments and to recommend a shift toward risk management. This is in part why risk assessment is being viewed as a process that must include a broader range of regularly updated information. An essential consideration in all of this is the woman's perceptions of her situation and the development of responses that support her decision making and safety. Battered women also tend to anticipate what they may or may not do in response to the violence and how that might affect the outcomes—thus improving prediction. Admittedly, they may need some help articulating and recognizing their assessment and, in some cases, broadening or revising them with new information (J. Campbell, 2004).

The ultimate objective is to translate the assessments into a safety plan—a set of strategies—that is practical, realistic, and effective (Davis, Taylor, & Maxwell, 2000). As both advocates and risk researchers have noted, this ideally requires scenario thinking about risk rather than mechanical referrals or sentencing. It starts with identifying abuse sequences and escalations, the victim's possible responses and resources, and the possible reactions of the batterer. Then advocates help the woman to outline steps to take and services to contact in response to certain situations. In fact, scenarios are more generally considered to be a good way to assess risk in the arena of public safety, international diplomacy, and product development (S. Hart, 2008). What is the most likely scenario, for instance, if such and such happens?

Domestic Homicide Assessment

Risk assessment tends to be most difficult when it comes to the outcome of greatest concern: homicide. That is in part because the overall rate of murder by men who are actually enrolled in batterer programs is very low. In our multisite study, we identified only two murders over four years from 854 batterers (an annual murder rate of 0.2 percent). This number was derived not only from tracking the men and their initial and new partners, but also by monitoring local newspapers and program feedback. The low number may also be influenced by the intervention and preventive steps taken along the way. Consequently, assessments for homicide tend to substantially overestimate the danger. Another problem is that so many of the already violent men in batterer programs have many of the same characteristics associated with men who have murdered their partners. It is less difficult to distinguish extremely violent men from the population as a whole than it is to distinguish them from other men who tend to be violent.[10]

These difficulties do not mean, however, that we should not assess men for lethality, or risk of committing murder. Obviously, some batterers are extremely dangerous and warrant decisive intervention. The research on domestic homicide has produced several risk factors that provide an important step in understanding the mind-set and behaviors associated with domestic homicide. They offer at least some warning signs that might increase alertness and extend intervention. Interestingly, there are some apparent contradictions in the findings from two of the studies with imprisoned murderers that call for further interpretation.

One line of research has investigated the records of homicide cases and interviewed family members of the victims. Jackie Campbell and her team of researchers, for instance, identified several risk factors that suggest domestic homicide is often an extension previous threats and violence (J. Campbell, Webster, Koziol-McLain, Block, & Campbell, 2003a, 2003b). (The eleven-city study was based on 220 interviews with family and friends of murder victims and with 343 women who had been abused.) They found that, compared to abused women, murdered women were much more likely to have been threatened with a gun, to have faced general threats of murder, and to have had sexual acts forced on them. Stalking and estrangement from one's partner were also highly associated with partner murders. As a result, the DA, which includes such items, tends to produce higher scores for potential murder cases (J. Campbell, Webster, Koziol-McLain, Block, & Campbell, 2003b).

An in-depth look at the men who murder adds further nuance to the motivations, while confirming the tendency for escalating control and violence. In *Why Do They Kill? Men Who Murder Their Intimate Partners*, David Adams (2007) reports on extensive interviews with thirty-one men who killed their female partners and twenty men who attempted to do so. The men were recruited in six different prisons in Massachusetts. Adams identified several different categories of motivation for the men: jealousy, depression, material gain, addiction, and general criminality. There was also a common exposure to violence, distrust of women, availability of and familiarity with guns, and an escalating pattern of threats and violence. The men also report emboldening themselves—getting psyched up for the act. The central recommendations that come from the study are for a more systematic use of risk assessment to identify potential escalation of violence, and services that are more responsive to battered women.

However, a study in Britain led by Russell and Rebecca Dobash raises some unexpected contradictions to other research on risk factors associated with men who kill their partners (Dobash, Dobash, Cavanagh, & Medina-Ariza, 2007). The researchers compared information collected in interviews with 122 men convicted of domestic violence to information from case records of 106 men who killed their partners. The latter "killer" sample was drawn from a national study of murders over a ten-year period. Although most of the familiar risk factors were confirmed, the men who killed their partners were *less* likely to have problematic backgrounds, a pattern of escalating violence and abuse before the murder, and a pattern of drunkenness at the time of the murder. These findings "raise some dilemmas for the growing area of risk assessment" (p. 329). The contradictions to the previous profile may reflect an overrepresentation of so-called overcontrolled murderers who contrast with more problematic undercontrolled murderers in the previous sample.

Neil Websdale's *Familicidal Hearts* (2010) reveals yet another difference. His research was based on 211 case studies of domestic homicides, drawn from his involvement in death review panels around the country. Websdale reviewed newspaper reports and police and court records, and he interviewed people familiar with the cases. He noted across his case studies a familiar continuum of undercontrolled ("livid-coercive") to overcontrolled ("civil-reputable") murders—that is, murderers who are explosively angry and those who appear cool and deliberate on the surface. But at the center of the vast majority of cases was a sense of shame that impelled especially the men (in twenty-one of the cases, women killed their partners), rather than a need for power and control.

The shame was related to the failure to live up to gender role expectations or ideals, as distorted as those may be. The implication is that more needs to be done in social services, particularly in batterer programs, to identify men's emotional struggles and to help relieve them before they lead to severe and possibly murderous violence. This contrary view to previous profiles of possessive men takes us back to the discussion in chapter 3. It brings up the debate over the psychological characteristics of violent men, how to interpret those characteristics, and what they imply for intervention.

There is a general consensus that severely violent batterers share a sense of "proprietariness" or possessiveness, which was identified in early homicide studies from criminal justice data (M. Wilson & Daley, 1996; Serran & Firestone, 2004). There is also the recurring portrayal of righteous murder, in which the murderer feels absolutely justified in his actions. In fact, he convinces himself that what he is doing is morally necessary to set things right in the world (Katz, 1988). This is much like what happened in the emboldening process identified in Adams's prison study. But as some of the contrary findings suggest, men who kill do not necessary fit in a neat box. Risk assessment, as both Adams and Campbell point out, helps to increase awareness of potential danger, but it is not sufficient in itself. It may even be misleading in the case of overcontrolled murderers.[11]

Risk Assessment as a Process

The Need for Some Professional Discretion

The fundamental challenge facing risk assessment today is how to interpret and apply the results. What is to be done once risk has been identified remains very much up in the air. Given the limits of prediction and the need for prevention, researchers and practitioners alike have been promoting a movement toward risk management rather than merely risk assessment (Cattaneo & Goodman, 2009; Heilbrun, 1997; K. Douglas & Kropp, 2002; Kropp, 2009; Roehl, O'Sullivan, Webster, & Campbell, 2005). This shift involves a form of ongoing risk management that not only updates and revises risk according to circumstances, but also identifies a variety of coordinated interventions and supplemental treatments for high-risk cases. A risk assessment may be introduced at the initial contact with the criminal justice system or domestic violence service, but this assessment serves as just the start of a broader and continuing process. Regardless of whether an actuarial instrument or professional ratings are used for the assessment, risk management inevitably requires the use of professional discretion (Kropp, 2008). Decisions have to be made about the instrument's results, considering additional information from other sources and the available resources. Decisions also have to be made regarding the accuracy or thoroughness of the information used for the assessment, and the communication and distribution of the results.

As Randall Kropp (2008) outlines in his overview of risk assessment, there is an urgent need to develop a minimal qualification for risk assessors, identify the best practices for applying the assessments, and train staff to monitor assessments. Assessors clearly need "a considerable knowledge of the dynamics of domestic violence" (p. 213), as well as guidance on the practical steps involved in implementing a response. There is also the important challenge of communicating risk (Grisso & Tomkins, 1996; Hilton, Harris, Rawson, & Beach, 2005). The language of risk needs to be more specific, going beyond a vague "likelihood" of violence toward a sense of imminence, severity, and circumstance. A concise set of main factors or reasons for the risk should be communicated, followed by practical implications for safety planning.[12] Furthermore, the assessment itself needs to be qualified in terms of the accuracy and reliability of the information and its results. In other words, global or general statements about the risk being high or low don't tell us much and may end up being a disservice to potential victims (see especially Cattaneo & Goodman, 2009). As a result, there are increasing calls for practice standards for conducting risk assessments and guidelines for how to use their results.

The Assessment Process for Battered Women

Research from the women's point of view raises another set of fundamental concerns that the research on women's perceptions supports (Cattaneo & Goodman, 2009; J. Campbell, 2004). The ultimate goal of risk assessment is ideally the empowerment of the victims rather than just prediction that puts them on edge. Lauren Cattaneo and Lisa Goodman define this empowerment as the capacity to know oneself and one's worth, to have the confidence to give voice to one's needs, and ultimately to gain control of and influence one's environment (2009, p. 60). In this women-defined advocacy, assessment is used to support women rather than only to protect them, or to impose on them. As studies of prosecutions of domestic violence cases suggest, women's involvement in the assessment of batterers and decision making about their cases is associated with less recidivism (Ford, 2003). Our research adds that their perceptions also substantially improve predictions (Heckert & Gondolf, 2004). Studies of women's prediction-making processes show, furthermore, that battered women are constantly involved in formulating assessments of their own, making observations, and testing out their appraisals (Cattaneo & Goodman, 2009; Langford, 1996; E. Stuart & Campbell, 1989). They obviously have access to information about a broader range of factors, unique circumstances, and changes in these over time.

A couple of qualitative studies bear out this process of assessment. Ellen Stuart and Jacquelyn Campbell (1989) explored factors that women say they used in assessing danger. The researchers conducted a thematic analysis of women's responses to an open-ended question that asked how the women determined that their relationship was extremely or very dangerous ($N = 24$). The researchers concluded that the women drew on a variety of cues, such as rapid changes in the partner's mood, increases in death threats, their own dreams about violence, the partner's nonverbal gestures and expressions, and his show or use of weapons. Another small qualitative study ($N = 30$) also found that women use cues that are often quite subtle to predict the onset of violent episodes (Langford, 1996). Such cues include physical changes in the eyes, facial expressions, posture, and tone of voice. Furthermore, women, respond to triggering events, such as their partner's drug or alcohol use.

We went further to explore the determinants of the women's perceptions— what were they basing the perceptions on, and how were they substantiated (Gondolf & Heckert, 2003). Regression analyses using batterers' characteristics, relationship status, and behaviors indicated that the perceived likelihood of reassault increased with familiar risk factors: men who were divorced or heavy drinkers, and who had been severely abusive in the past. When the women were asked directly about the reasons for their assessments of risk, they professed reasons that corresponded to these risk factors associated with re-assault. The women's perceptions appeared, therefore, to be grounded in practical circumstances and to correspond to actual re-assault.

As the qualitative research suggests, battered women assess risk through an ongoing process of observations, cues, intuitions, and updates that go well be-yond a set of correlated risk factors (Langford, 1996; E. Stuart & Campbell, 1989). Ideally, practitioners conducting risk assessments might learn more about women's assessment processes and attempt to approximate, or at least better support, them. A few studies in the domestic violence field show that even advocates drawing on women's reports (Cattaneo & Goodman, 2009) and batterer counselors observing men in treatment (Gondolf & Wernik, 2009) tend to base their assessments on different factors than the ones that battered women emphasize—and fall short on predictive accuracy.[13]

These sorts of findings further reinforce the need to work more closely with battered women in order to formulate risk assessment and risk management. They also remind us of the complexity involved in more accurately assessing risk.

Toward a Coordinated Community Response

Two Prevailing Approaches

Responding to High Risk

There are already at least two approaches to responding to risk assessment re-sults. One approach, promoted in community corrections, represents a kind of graduated sentencing, in which more intensive and extensive batterer treat-ment is given to high-risk men. The state of Connecticut, for instance, devel-oped such an approach that was based largely on prior offenses and severity of violence. The more violent repeat offenders were mandated to attend a batterer program for a full year, while first-time misdemeanor offenders were sentenced to as short a time as three months. This approach rests largely on the results of a one-time risk assessment or set of assessments, and on the assumption that the longer treatment and surveillance would improve outcomes. The approach is particularly straightforward and efficient and has at least some evidence of outcome benefits, as illustrated in the example later in this chapter.

The other approach relies more heavily on case management by specialized probation officers. The officers respond not only to the initial risk level sug-gested in an assessment, but also to other treatment needs that the assessment may suggest. By implication, the approach includes more structured profes-sional judgment, whether or not the officers use an instrument like the SARA. The officers monitor the men's behavior and compliance and modify the proba-tion referrals and requirements accordingly. If noncompliance or a new offense is detected, the man's probation is likely to be revoked and he will probably re-

turn to jail. Of course, these two approaches can overlap, with probation officers making additional referrals in response to recommendations from the
batterer program staff, or to the officer's own observations or review of the case.
However expanded the risk management in this latter approach may be, it is
still primarily confined to the operation of the criminal justice system and related services for the offender.

Multilevel Treatment

One version of the first approach is documented in an evaluation of what was
termed multilevel treatment in response to batterer risk assessment in Florida
(Coulter & VandeWeerd, 2009). Batterers were assigned to one of three levels of
treatment, primarily according to their prior violence and to mental health issues and substance abuse problems as assessed at program intake. First-time
offenders with no apparent emotional dysfunction, psychiatric problems, or prior
convictions for violence were referred to level 1. Individuals with some recurrent
history of violence, evidence of intimidating and dominating their partner, and
committing physical or sexual violence were sent to level 2. They may have had
some psychological or alcohol problems but did not have a history of treatment
failures. Level 3 programming was for men who most chronically behaved violently, as shown in their use of weapons, their infliction of severe injuries, their
stalking their partners, and their violent criminal histories in general.

The multiple levels basically represent a progression to longer batterer program attendance and supplemental services. Level 1 was a shortened version of
a psycho-educational batterer program, lasting eight to twelve weeks. Level 2
provided twenty-six weeks of the batterer program, incorporating the Duluth
Power and Control Wheel and referral to additional services as appropriate. At
level 3, batterer program attendance was extended up to one year, with accompanying psychological or psychiatric treatment. Licensed mental health profes-
sionals conducted the level-3 batterer groups and administered a reassessment
of the men at twenty-six weeks.

The evaluation found some encouraging outcomes in terms of re-arrest
rates. It was based on the intake and arrest records of approximately 18,000
men across a Florida county from 1995 to 2004, but included no comparison to
rates prior to the innovation or to other sites without the multilevel treatment.
Probably the most relevant finding is that approximately 17 percent of the men
qualified for level 3. The level 3 assignments increased from 8 percent in 1995 to
26 percent in 2004. The decline in the total annual referrals for batterer inter-

vention (from 2,592 in 1995 to a low of 1,242 in 2002) may have meant that more severe batterers were being arrested and referred to batterer intervention. At each of the three levels, re-arrests for domestic violence during the following year were approximately 8 percent for men who completed the program, compared to 21 percent for the dropouts. It is difficult to interpret the impact of the level assignment on these results. It is, nonetheless, encouraging to see comparable low arrest rates for the level-3 batterers who were at high risk and therefore were expected to be re-arrested at higher rates.

Probation Case Management

Compared to the first approach, the second puts the responsibility for supervision and service referrals more squarely on the probation department and allows for more discretion. It generally follows the trend in so-called community supervision and specialized case management in probation (for example, Harris, Raymond, & Whittaker, 2004). The idea of using risk to help determine the intensity and scope of program supervision makes a lot of sense financially as well as practically. Overloaded probation officers can devote more time to the cases that most need the extra time, if some cases are deemed less needy. This approach can become overly routinized amid the paperwork of probation. There are assessment forms to complete, scores to calculate, classifications to be determined, and decisions to be made about referrals (often based on a chart that matches the risk classifications to services). But overall, the trend helps to shift the attention more toward managing risk than looking for probation violations.

One recently publicized example of this probation approach is the overhauled system of case management for criminal offenders in Travis County, Texas (Sprow, 2009; Yeung, 2010).[14] Following a risk assessment that includes ratings from a probation officer, the offender is not only classified by risk, but is also sent for further evaluation of individual problems that may have surfaced in his records or his assessment. Those offenders assessed as having a lower risk of committing new offenses receive training in problem-solving techniques, with the officer intervening selectively as needed. Those deemed to have a higher risk receive intensive attention from a caseworker, with zero tolerance for noncompliance or further crimes. The sanctions can vary from costly fines to jailing.

In other words, the probation officers assume the role of a social worker using motivational interviewing and problem-solving approaches to move the offender toward the learning and treatment intended to change the behavior of concern. There are also more extensive staff meetings to review cases and consider additional responses, but overall the approach is one of intensified supervision that includes tailored treatments and revised referrals. An evaluation of the probation reform showed a drop in the annual recidivism rate from 29 percent in 2005, before the reform, to 24 percent in 2008, after the reform (a 17 percent decrease). There also was a reduction in the number of men whose probations were revoked after they committed a felony, from 1,052 in 2005 to 846 in 2009 (a 20 percent decrease), according to official records. The drop in "technical revocations" was nearly 50 percent. (This kind of revocation is for minor violations, such as failure to pay fines, tardiness at probation officer meetings, and failure to participate in a court-ordered treatment program.) The state budget board estimated that these results amounted to a saving of $4.8 million over three years. However, the recidivism decrease for the high-risk cases was much lower (9 percent) than that for medium- and low-risk cases (77 percent for low-risk offenders). The high-risk offenders remain the most difficult to reform. As a result, officials wonder what else might be done protect the potential victims of these men.

The encouraging findings aren't too surprising, given the research on case management in criminal cases overall. Case management has also been shown to reduce dropout rates and improve outcomes in substance abuse treatment (Siegal, Li, & Rapp, 2002; Shwartz, Baker, Mulvey, & Plough, 1997). People with a substance abuse problem additionally tend to stay in treatment longer when motivational case management is used, compared to similar people assigned to treatment without it (Rapp, Otto, Lane, Redko, McGatha, & Carlson, 2008).

However, case management of this sort requires highly trained, competent, and proactive staff (Harris, Raymond, & Whittaker, 2004)—what are sometimes referred to as "social work types." It also necessitates having referral sources and compliance feedback to support the casework. In the Texas project, some probation officers resisted the change to the intensive case management model, and a few judges were concerned about allowing the level of risk, rather than the crime, to determine probation conditions. Of course, with domestic violence cases, supervision of men with direct access to their potential victims, and with some distinctive dynamics and risk factors, warrants further expertise and training than work with criminal offenders in general.

Ongoing Risk Management

The increasing evidence from risk research points to the advantage of even more complex ongoing risk management. As discussed above, the familiar one-time or static risk assessment offers an improved but still very limited ability to predict subsequent assaults. Dynamic factors observed over time improve predictions further, and some level of professional interpretation and discretion is warranted to communicate and apply assessments. Risk management is ideally a process of formulating risk assessments and scenarios of contingencies and circumstances, and then communicating the level of risk to the appropriate individuals for varying purposes. It continues with the implementation of plans to contain and reduce risk, and monitoring to gain feedback to revise plans and improve procedures (for example, Kropp, 2008; S. Hart, 2008). Making all this happen and figuring out what to do with the information requires a special mind-set, say the experts.

A training workshop that I attended on risk management guidelines used in hospitals, mental health clinics, and prisons in the United Kingdom emphasized this different mind-set (Haque, 2008). The staff member needs to accept interacting and communicating with clients' family members. He or she must not only use procedures and networks for information sharing, but also must establish relations of trust and rapport for informal and open exchanges. This sort of process leads to increased alertness to warning signs and risky situations, and an awareness of what might be done about them. It also includes critical reflection on what has worked well and what has not, thus improving as well as guiding professional discretion. All of this needs to be done while observing the ethics of confidentiality and the inclinations of potential victims.

The components in orchestrating risk management might be summarized as monitoring, treating, supervising, and planning for potential victims' safety (Kropp, 2008). Monitoring includes review and surveillance of a case through, for example, a victim advocate's contact with the woman, a probation officer's ensuring that the man complies with treatment, and a batterer program's reporting to the court about the man's attendance and behavior in group sessions. Treatment of course includes referral to a batterer program and additional services, and also the extension or intensification of any treatments in response to the monitoring or initial assessments. Supervision tends to be more intrusive than monitoring, in that it regulates a person's activity in some way. It might entail restricting contact with a partner, limiting the ownership of weapons, or adding an electronic monitoring device or more probation visits.

Of course safety planning, as mentioned above, means working with the victim to develop contingency plans of escape, support, and protection. Ideally, safety planning is a means of what has been referred to in other protective work as target hardening—making a victim less vulnerable to attacks or escalations of them. Obviously, these options require a cooperation, collaboration, and co-ordination of police, courts, probation officers, batterer programs, referral agencies, women's services, and additional support and treatment agencies. A coordinated community response is an essential and inevitable part of risk management.

Conclusion: Using Assessment Wisely

The Obvious Need for Risk Assessment

Cutting across the debates over program approach and differentiation among batterers is a more fundamental issue of who are the men who drop out of pro-grams and continue their abuse and violence. The outcomes of batterer pro-grams would obviously be substantially improved if these men were identified and contained, and their partners could be further supported and protected. The repeatedly violent men appear to fall through the cracks of the intervention system in general, and there is some evidence that their partners do, too. The challenge, as this chapter highlights, is how to stop or at least lessen this part of the system's failure. As noted in chapter 4, the innovations of differentiated treatments for batterer types, stage-based or motivational counseling, special-ized counseling for ethnic groups, and couples counseling may offer some additional help for certain groups of men. However, the problematic cases of repeated and severe violence appear to cut across these sorts of differentiations, and they are simply untouched by the popular innovations.

The real challenge seems to be how to identify and treat the unresponsive and dangerous men who are being arrested, appear in court, and are sent to batterer programs. One might even argue that the preoccupation with batterer program approaches is a diversion from this more crucial challenge, especially since the vast majority of men appear to de-escalate or stop their violence fol-lowing the intervention of batterer programs (Gondolf, 2000d). This sugges-tion is by no means intended to promote some sort of satisfaction with batterer programming as it is, but rather to say that the men giving batterer programs a bad name need more than a new therapy. The research reviewed in the previous two chapters suggests that the alternative approaches have not been convinc-ingly substantiated, and they are no more likely than traditional batterer pro-grams to "fix" the dropouts and repeat offenders on their own. In fact there is some counterevidence that this type of batterer is in fact more responsive to cognitive–behavioral approaches rather than to insight or introspective therapies (D. Wilson, Bouffard, & MacKenzie, 2005).

The use of risk assessment appears to be the logical answer. It is an approach that is a constant in our personal lives as well as our professional work. We regularly sort out the good guys from the bad guys. In fact, we tend to think in categorical terms—put people in boxes, so to speak—rather than consider the probabilities that prediction actually produces for us (for example, that a person has a 70 percent chance of re-assaulting his partner within six months). Drawing on individual risk factors, such as addiction or psychopathology, also are insufficient by themselves.

Research over the years has shown that outright impressions are usually insufficient and too often wrong. There are, of course, the constraints of common sense and the consequences of recklessness, but making general predictions about who is good and who is bad is tricky business. Combinations of factors must be weighed, together with circumstances and contingencies. As the research on risk assessment further shows, even our professional judgments can be substantially improved with a set of consistent indicators associated with violence—what has come to be called actuarial assessment and structured ratings, or structured professional judgment (Kropp, 2008).

The risk assessment instruments for domestic violence that have been developed do increase the accuracy of predictions of re-assault and severe re-assault, but those predictions still include a high percentage of false negatives—men who are not deemed to be high risks but who do commit new offenses. This is in part because prediction remains a complicated process—similar to predicting the weather, as one set of researchers has pointed out (Monahan & Steadman, 1996). We certainly do better at tracking hurricanes, for instance, when we use additional information from sources like satellites. However, weather prediction is still far from an exact science, as both those hit unexpectedly by hurricanes and those who were evacuated and found their homes passed over by a storm can attest.

In any case, risk assessment increases the communication, alertness, awareness, and attention of those working with batterers and their partners. And all of these changes can help improve the response to high-risk men and reduce recidivism. Although not an end in itself, risk assessment today appears to be an essential next step for batterer intervention. Or rather, one could say, it is an extension of something that women's advocates have long recommended. The lethality checklist that they developed and promoted as early as the 1980s succeeded in getting services and the court to pay more attention to women's safety (B. Hart, 1989).

Improving Risk Assessment

The efforts to further improve risk assessment point to a number of key points, some of which may seem obvious. The main one is to see risk assessment as a process that goes beyond a score or rating on an instrument. To gain sufficient and reliable information, the assessor needs to enage the victim of violence in a supportive way (J. Campbell, 2005). Assessment is further enhanced with the use of dynamic factors of behavior and circumstances that vary over time. Multiple sources of information at different times are therefore essential, and women's response to and revision of assessment outcomes needs to be considered. The research on prediction demonstrates the impressive accuracy of women's perceptions of their own safety, and women's ongoing observations to verify and revise their perceptions (Cattaneo & Goodman, 2009). These points caution against using risk assessment as a mechanical routine—a kind of "paint by the numbers" exercise.

Some practitioners argue for a shift in focus from triage—that is, from sorting offenders into groups that will receive less or more supervision and treatment— to victim empowerment (Cattaneo & Goodman, 2009). The idea is that risk assessment needs to be tailored more to the experiences of women and used as an aid to further their decision making and access to services. It can help to reinforce and broaden the women's own perceptions, rather than imposing decisions on their situation from outside. At a minimum, most victims' advocates turn to safety planning as an extension of assessment (Davis, Taylor, & Maxwell, 2000). They develop strategies with battered women in response to the possibility of renewed abuse and violence—what to do when their safety appears in jeopardy. The women's experiences, observations, resources, and circumstances all are weighed in what is a planning process rather than a set directive. Of course, the other side of this approach is having the appropriate services and skilled staff in place to respond adequately when the need for them arises.

The main challenge for the risk assessment effort is what to do about the results of assessment. The best responses to different levels of risk are not yet definitively mapped out. In some jurisdictions, high-risk men are required to attend batterer programs longer than other men; in other jurisdictions, high-risk men are expected to attend program sessions more frequently. In still other places, an initial assessment of high risk may lead to further diagnostic work for psychological or addiction problems, and supplemental referrals following those results. Being rated as a high risk could mean more support and protective services for the man's partner, as well. And sometimes a combination of options is invoked.

In this chapter, I presented two examples of response strategies that have been tested. One is the multilevel approach that puts the responsibility for prevention primarily on different intensities and extents of batterer programming (Coulter & VandeWeerd, 2009). The other gives the responsibility to a probation department that conducts differentiated case management (Sprow, 2009). In both cases, the high-risk men basically receive tighter supervision, swifter and more certain consequences for noncompliance, and supplemental treatments for psychological and addiction problems as needed.

The limits of risk prediction and the need for prevention planning have long reinforced the ideal of a coordinated community response (see Pence & Shepard, 1999). As noted in reviews of risk assessment instruments, one of the sure benefits of risk assessment is the communication and awareness it promotes among the criminal justice system, service providers, perpetrators, and victims. Multiple sources are needed to maximize the predictive powers of the assessment and also the response to it. The channels for obtaining, sharing, and acting on assessments need to be established and sustained. In order to incorporate the key points of assessment—especially the dynamic factors and risk revision they imply—ongoing risk management is needed.

The shift in the risk research and application at this point is from prediction to prevention. This means that observations as well as responses from a variety of services need to be considered. As these change, the risk changes and new strategies are introduced in what some researchers have referred to as responsivity (Hanson, 2005; Hanson, Bourgon, Helmus, & Hodgson, 2009): The goal is to assess risk, identify needs, respond with services, reassess, and revise—all with supervision and accountability. In fact, some experts in the field recommend that risk assessment occur at many contact points of intervention: at arrest, court sentencing, batterer intake, advocate contact, custody hearings, child services, other services, and so forth (J. Campbell, 2009). A functional system, with established procedures, policies, and linkages, is obviously essential for this to happen. More than the batterer program is needed to take into account the women's safety, needs, and empowerment, along with the men's potential for committing repeat offenses and compliance with referrals.

Implications for Batterer Programs

Unfortunately, there are no clear, definitive guidelines for risk assessment in what is still a developing field. What, then, does all of this mean, especially for batterer programs? It implies that batterer programs should be a part of the risk assessment process, and even a facilitator of it. Most of the programs collect information at intake that is relevant to risk assessment and that needs to be shared or pooled with other sources. The caution here is to selectively collect information that is directly related to risk and compile it so other parties can use it. Some programs have gone to such an extreme in their data collection that it is hard to see the forest for the trees; most of the information just sits in a file cabinet or on a computer. There is also a tendency to record more subjective clinical information—which is often difficult to analyze and convey—than calibrated information and ratings. Obviously, structured risk assessment instruments assist in determining what information is useful.

Batterer programs also must select instruments and decide who will administer them. Most of the reviews of available instruments conclude that there is no one overwhelming winner among the validated instruments. They assess different risks (for example, of committing a new assault, severe assault, or homicide), and they have different approaches (actuarial checklist versus structured ratings) and primary sources (police and court records, batterer interviews, and victim responses). The choice may depend in part on the program's staffing and other resources, as well as on how the results are going to be used. The SARA, for instance, requires trained staff to do individual assessments and therefore takes more time and funds to use. However, it provides more explicit implications for intervention (such as the need for addiction treatment) and direct involvement in formulating a treatment plan. All of the instruments have such tradeoffs.

Who administers the risk assessment appears to vary across jurisdictions. Many batterer programs are doing some form of risk assessment at program intake, as most state standards recommend. But in other places, the probation officer does the assessment and manages the case. A court-based forensics department is another option, as is court referral to a mental health clinic for an evaluation. There would seem to be an advantage in having people with domestic violence training and experience with batterer programs directly involved in the assessment and the decision making in response to it. As we see from the research, a woman's perspective and experience contributes to more effective assessment; therefore, those closest to that perspective have an important role to play in the assessment process (Gondolf & Heckert, 2003; Heckert & Gondolf, 2004). A special set of skills and experience is also required to meaningfully interpret and communicate risk assessment findings in a way that benefits the victim and not just the system (Grisso & Tomkins, 1996; Hilton, Harris, Rawson, & Beach, 2005).

Another point that stands out is the importance of being part of a larger process of assessment and management, with the collaboration and coordination that such a larger process entails. Batterer programs can be an essential facilitator, sharing information and observations with the court for its monitoring role and with women's services for their safety planning. Of course, the sharing needs to be done ethically and in a safe and secure way. The most obvious contribution of the programs comes in developing clear attendance policies and communicating violations of those to the court and probation officers. After all, not complying with a program and dropping out continue to be among the strongest predictors of repeated violence (for example, Heckert & Gondolf, 2005; A. Jones & Gondolf, 2001). The batterer program is also in a position to assist with additional referrals for a batterer and to ensure that those referrals are supportive of the domestic violence programming and message. Even when a system, network, or linkages are weak or not in place, a program's risk assessment can help to prompt more involvement and response from other agencies, including the criminal justice system.

An understandable argument against risk assessment is that all men sent to batterer programs have the potential to be violent again—and in fact many are. The fact that a man has been arrested and sent to a batterer program is evidence in itself that he can be violent. This argument is supported by the fact that it is difficult to predict which men among a relatively homogeneous group will be violent, and incorrect predictions could endanger others rather than be helpful. Some advocates even suggest that battered women may be better off if they are left to make their own plans for safety in response to the likelihood of violence, rather than led to expect a risk assessment of their partner to take care of them. Continuing the logic, the batterer program, like the courts, should stay focused on the task of impressing on all the men the need to change for their partners' and their own sakes.

Despite this reasoning, batterer programs are currently caught in the middle of debates over their effectiveness and are being pressed for ways to improve their outcomes. By default they are charged with the responsibility of "fixing" the men who are sent to them. Risk assessment is at least one means of broadening and sharing that responsibility, and of dealing more efficiently with the men referred to the programs. Moreover, risk assessment is likely to reduce recidivism overall in a way that improves the safety and well-being of women. This means more coordination of court and other services than is the case without risk assessment.

What this coordinated response should look like, how to achieve it, and how effective it will be in preventing severe violence and escalated abuse remains to be examined. Several studies show improved outcomes from coordination, but a few raise questions about the effectiveness of coordinated community response, especially when it is only modestly implemented (for example, Visher, Harrell, & Yahner, 2008). But new efforts to achieve coordination beyond collaboration have appeared, and there is the possibility of making batterer programs less of a Lone Ranger in dealing with high-risk men.

The next chapter considers the importance and challenge of this approach in furthering risk management and dealing with domestic violence cases in general. Risk management within a fully implemented coordinated community response becomes the function of the intervention system as a whole. It goes well beyond scoring an instrument, making referrals, and monitoring compliance. In sum, a coordinated response is needed to do risk assessment thoroughly, wisely, and effectively.

6 | Implementation, Implementation

The Call for Systems Thinking

The Need for a System Perspective

System Failures with Battered Women

As my research team asserts in the book that summarizes our multisite study, *Batterer Intervention Systems*: "The system matters!" (Gondolf, 2002a, p. 199). This is not a novel idea in criminology, nor is it unique to the domestic violence field. But it has been somewhat overshadowed by the biomedical model imposed on batterer programs amid the evidence-based practice movement and the experimental evaluations it promotes. It is essential for batterer programs to be held accountable for their work, derive feedback to develop and improve, and test out innovations and new developments.

As chapter 4 pointed out, much of the subsequent research on program innovations is methodologically weak and limited in extent. The even more pressing need is to develop systems thinking that puts program-based findings in context and interprets them more meaningfully. Systems thinking is also essential to better understand what is really going on and what needs to happen in intervention. It also gives practitioners a broader perspective and helps them coordinate their efforts with other components of the intervention—the courts, probation officers, victim services, addiction treatment, and so on. Ideally, a coordinated community response helps batterer programs, and intervention more broadly, to be more effective. And a batterer program in turn can enhance the community response.

Our 1980s study of intake data from over 6,000 women in the fifty Texas shelters made me realize the importance of a systems perspective on domestic violence intervention (Gondolf & Fisher, 1988). At the time of the research, the popular view of battered women in shelters was that they acted out of learned helplessness, much in line with behavioral findings in animal experiments

(L. Walker, 1979, pp. 49–50). A psychological profile emerged of cognitive dysfunction, resignation, depression, anxiety, and even masochism. The implication was that battered women were responsible, in a large part, for their partner's abusing them. Although such symptoms are experienced by many battered women and victims of violence in general, they don't tell the full story.

We found that a more accurate view of the women was that they were in survivor mode: the women in the shelters tended to seek out a greater variety and number of sources of help in response to more severe violence, rather than succumbing to it. In fact, on average each woman had contacted eight different sources of help, often making multiple contacts per source, prior to leaving her partner and entering a shelter. Our research team also found, that when the battered women received resources and social support, they were more likely not to return to their abusive partner after leaving the shelter (Gondolf, 1988). The evidence in our analyses suggested that the availability, sufficiency, and effectiveness of help sources were inadequate. Ending up in a shelter was more the result of system failures than a woman's learned helplessness, as a few other studies at the time also suggested (for example, Bowker, 1983). Although the response to battered women has improved over the years, recent studies bear out the help-seeking attempts of battered women and the challenges that remain (Cattaneo, Stuewig, Goodman, Kaltman, & Dutton, 2007; Postmus, Severson, Berry, & Yoo, 2009).

A System Perspective on Complex Problems

Our society is replete with examples that reinforce the need for a systems perspective to understand and intervene in complex problems. For instance, the near collapse of the U.S. economy has been attributed to different components along the way: the lending patterns of banks, the derivative securities sold by Wall Street firms, the interplay of computerized trading, the failure of federal oversight, the deregulation of the financial sector, the greed of investors, the irresponsibility of mortgage holders, and so on. The ultimate cause was all of these and their interactions with each other. One recent commentator explained: "No one cog in the federal government's regulation or in the financial sector let down the country by failing to prevent the latest shakeout on Wall Street. The entire system did" (Lightman, 2008, p. 1).

One of the most vivid illustrations of a system failure, in what initially appeared to be a freak breakdown, was the explosion of the space shuttle *Challenger* in 1986. That disaster is now widely used in teaching engineering safety, ethics, and system analysis (for example, Hoover & Wallace, 2008). The explosion could have easily been left as a failure of the O-rings in the booster rockets, rings not suited for the cold temperature of the launch day. However, the presidential commission studying the disaster found that the National Aeronautics and Space Administration's (NASA) "organizational culture and decision-making processes" were the key reasons for the accident (Rogers Commission, 1986). NASA managers had known since 1977 that the O-rings contained a potentially catastrophic flaw, but they failed to address it properly. They also disregarded warnings from engineers about the dangers of launching in such low temperatures, and they failed to adequately report these technical concerns to their superiors. In addition, political and budget pressures helped push the flight to a premature launch. In sum, NASA's organizational structure and operation needed to be overhauled, rather than just the space shuttle.

Of course, there are other examples of systems thinking that directly affect our personal lives. Much public attention has been focused on our homeland security system since 9/11. Its breaches or failures have very much been in the news and scrutinized for potential repairs. But the system is more than baggage checks and metal detectors. It includes another dimension: awareness. Any traveler hears numerous broadcast messages to report unattended bags, and not to put certain things in a suitcase. Messages encouraging vigilance and self-monitoring have been promulgated, and there have been clear changes in passengers' routine behavior. Not only have violators and real terrorists been apprehended, but there has also been a new outlook about assessing risk and risk management. We are all participants in the process, and although there are still breakdowns, overall safety has arguably been increased.

So systems can do more than carry out a certain function, like capturing a terrorist or making it harder for a terrorist to achieve his goal. A system can help to change norms through the engagement of bystanders and, in the process, broaden its extent and impact. This is not to suggest that we should put metal detectors at people's front doors to reduce domestic violence, particularly homicide. It does say something about the potential of a systems approach to true "homeland" security—security and safety in our individual homes. The use of more systematic screening and attention to risk markers in general has a precedent, and a contribution to make. The consistent and coordinated response to offenders, the ensured revising of behavior in response to noncompliance, and the extended awareness of the public (in the case of domestic violence, neighbors and relatives) are necessary and accepted. As a result, security has become a commonplace concern and activity.

Examples of Coordinating Responses

There are documented examples that illustrate the importance of a systems approach in child welfare, homelessness, and poverty programs, as well (for example, Sampson, 2008; Schorr, 1997; Smyth, Goodman, & Glenn, 2006). One such example is the Full Frame Initiative, developed and applied to two model programs for marginalized women—those who are homeless, poor, or otherwise "unstable or crisis-prone" (Smyth, Goodman, & Glenn, 2006, p. 489). One program is the ROAD (Reaching Out about Depression) project, a grass-roots mental health and organizing project for low-income women with symptoms of depression. The other is the On the Rise program for women who are homeless or at risk for homelessness, and who have not been able to meet their needs through mainstream services. Both are located in the Boston area to address women who have fallen through the cracks, according to their founders.

The programs are a response to an increasing overspecialization of services that tends to separate a series of problems from their community context and social roots. It is fashionable to observe that services work in silos, with differing perspectives, agendas, and approaches. Consequently, treatment is of discrete problems across several differentiated services. A low-income person may end up going to an employment agency, welfare office, addiction counselor, mental health clinic, and housing authority—all to avoid becoming homeless. The proponents of the Full Frame Initiative argue that this sort of treatment fragments women's lives and thus undermines the development of a consistent and strengthening sense of self. It is that sense of self that the women so need in dealing with adversity.

The proponents believe that the best way to counterbalance the specialization and to coordinate services in a supportive way is to start at the receiving end—with the women consumers or clients. Building up from the women's experiences toward an integrated approach, the initiative is more than just a collection of agencies and programs connected through referrals and bent on service delivery. Each specialized program forms a kind of double helix with other programs and components of the community, reinforcing and strengthening one another (Smyth, Goodman, & Glenn, 2006, p. 490). The shift toward this ideal reflects the client-centered, recovery model on the rise in case management with adults who are addicted to drugs or mentally disabled.[1]

Rather than lead consumers to one agency and then another, the aim is to work with the person to identify his or her needs, wants, strengths, and motivations. The case manager then supports the consumers as they formulate and implement a plan. Of course, this is not as simple as it sounds, but these sorts of projects are making some progress with even the difficult cases that have otherwise not been resolved. The approach also helps to build relationships across and within services that the consumers use. According to this perspective, those sort of relationships form and transform any system.

This kind of coordinated community response requires a different sort of evaluation to substantiate it than the more narrowly focused biomedical treatment experiments at the center of the evidence-based practice movement. The widely circulated editorial by Lisabeth Schorr (2009), a Harvard researcher, and an accompanying paper written with her colleague Katya Fels Smyth, from the Full Frame Initiative (Smyth & Schorr, 2009), argue that experimental evaluations simply don't fit the reality of programs within intervention systems and a community setting. As Smyth and Schorr (2009) write in their report on evaluating two child welfare programs: "The evaluation tools have to be able to incorporate not only a program's work, but how that program fits with other interventions. In other words, some of the very factors and situations that the experimental method controls for may need, instead, to be explicitly folded into an evaluation" (p. 18). The researchers conclude that "the dogma of experimental designs is ultimately detrimental to program development and social intervention" (p. 21).

As I discussed in chapter 2, there are several methodological alternatives that help accommodate this systems perspective on program intervention. "It is a false choice between relying on random assignment experiments versus relying on professions of good intentions, ideology, and a handful of anecdotes," say Smyth and Schorr (2009, p. 19). A variety of methods can be combined for a more complex approach, as a report from the Government Accountability Office (2009) recommends.

For one thing, a team of stakeholders—including representatives from related community agencies and service clients—needs to be involved in formulating and pretesting the multimethod design, rather than relying on one external authority to do so. Case studies, longitudinal follow-ups, network analyses, implementation measures, and statistical modeling have all been developed to assess the complexities that come from such a formulation (see Woolcock, 2009; Cross, Dickmann, Newman-Gonchar, & Fagan, 2009). The integration of qualitative and quantitative methods in evaluation research has also been mapped out in other fields and can be useful in this regard (for example, Vijayendra & Woolcock, 2003). The systems proponents also urge the incorporation of multiple wisdoms (Symth & Schorr, 2009)—that is, input from community representatives not only in developing the research design, but also in interpreting the outcomes. This participation is more likely to create a learning experience all around, one that leads to relevant findings and the actual adoption of a study's recommendations.

The Emerging System and Its Evaluation

As I discussed in the previous chapter, there is a convergence of risk assessment and coordinated community response around batterer programs. Programs by default or intention have a central role to play in this movement toward what victims' advocates have promoted for decades. Most practitioners have been preoccupied with establishing better linkages between batterer programs and the courts to increase accountability through court-mandated attendance at programs and sanctions for noncompliance. There has also been at least a professed effort to collaborate with victim services in some ways, but the increased specialization of batterer programs has led to less of this than increased accountability in many jurisdictions.

Several jurisdictions have compiled definitions of a successful coordinated community response (for example, Sadusky, Martinson, Lizdas, & McGee, 2010; Visher, Newmark, & Harrell, 2008). For instance, a team of criminal justice officials and domestic violence workers formulated a set of components for coordinated community response in British Columbia (Critical Components Project Team, 2008). The components are managing risk and victim safety, offender accountability, specialized victim support, information sharing, collaboration, domestic violence policies, use of specialized expertise, and monitoring and evaluation.[2] These components were derived largely from a review of intervention systems in the province and observations from participants in those systems, rather than more wide-scale research. The team provided practical details and recommendations for the operation of the components, while allowing for adaptations necessary to accommodate community differences. In sum, the project offers one example of many maps of what a coordinated community response needs to entail and how to achieve it.

The remainder of this chapter examines the research on the impacts of such a coordinated community response and its implications for intervention. Evaluations have not as yet fully embraced the complexities of a system in a way that documents the fundamentals for coordinated community response in domestic violence cases. However, the evaluations do reveal the challenges of implementation that lie ahead. Just as in the examples above, there is an increasing effort toward a grounded interaction between service and agency staff, and discussions focused on consumers' experiences and feedback. The aim is more an ongoing process and ultimately a mind-set that promotes a kind of institutional and social change—a lofty sounding ideal, perhaps, especially at a time of financial cutbacks and cynical discouragement. But it is being acted on with apparent results. The next step is to develop evidence that helps to document and share those results. To do so means creatively broadening our application of evaluation methods and our concept of evidence-based practice.

Research on Coordinated Community Response

The Beginnings of Coordinated Community Response

The obvious need and long-standing call for a combination of interventions that represents a coordinated community response warrant some definition and substantiation, especially amid today's evidence-based practice movement. "Coordinated community response" usually refers to a collaborative system-wide intervention—one in which a variety of agencies and services, along with the police and the courts, work together on criminal cases. The courts—more specifically, the judges—are usually considered the optimal center of the system, offering oversight of cases and their referrals. Such a system might be seen as the ideal, as opposed to a dysfunctional or inadequately developed system. In the domestic violence field, coordinated community response was explicitly promoted and supported with the Service, Training, Officers, and Prosecution (STOP) funding from the Violence Against Women Act in the early 1990s. STOP required states to establish a collaborative planning process and disperse funds to support local efforts toward a coordinated community response.

Such a response was an extension of the effort of battered women's movement to develop a more comprehensive intervention into domestic violence cases (see Pence & Shepard, 1999). As I summarized at the beginning of this book, advocates had been working to reform police practices and court action, train other community services to recognize domestic violence, and basically promote a kind of community development that worked against the abuse of women (Schechter, 1982). This approach has received an implicit endorsement in work on many other forms of crime. Coordinated community response is being applied to recidivism, drug-related crimes, child abuse, and other violent offenses. A 1998 meeting of the American Criminological Society, for instance, included at least five academic presentations on the subject. In 2007, a special issue of the *American Journal of Community Psychology* was devoted entirely to coordinated community response with other social and family problems (for example, Foster-Fishman & Behrens, 2007).

Promising Early Research

In the domestic violence field, however, the research on coordinated community response has been much less extensive. The evidence base for such a response remains somewhat sketchy, contradictory, and disappointing on the surface. However, several studies have been conducted of a systems perspective and have shown it leads to improvements in desired outcomes (Bledsoe, Bibhuti, & Barbee, 2006; Bouffard & Muftic, 2007; Gamache, Edleson, and Schock, 1988; C. Murphy, Musser, & Maton, 1998; Salazar, Emshoff, Baker, & Crowley, 2007; Steinman, 1990, 1991; Tolman & Weisz, 1995). Most of this research consists of case studies of a particular coordinated community response or some aspect of it, but without a comparison or control site. Various indicators such as accountability, arrests, and reported re-abuse were compared before and after implementation of increased coordination.

For instance, Denise Gamach, Jeffrey Edleson, and Michael Schock (1988) showed increases in arrests, successful prosecutions, and sentencing men to batterer treatment in three Minnesota communities after the adoption of community coordination projects. Chris Murphy, Peter Musser, and Kenneth Maton (1998) found lower rates of new offenses among batterers who were prosecuted, convicted, sentenced to probation, and then completed a batterer program, compared to those who were not prosecuted. They interpreted this result as at least tentative support for a coordinated community response in Baltimore, Maryland. However, these studies failed to measure the nature and extent of the coordination, relied on very small samples, and used weak measures of re-offense. Most of all, we can't be sure whether other factors in the community contributed to the outcomes over time. Fewer men might have been unemployed at the end of the study, or the police department may have been expanded.

A more recent study of approximately 1,500 cases from three jurisdictions in Georgia used a time-series analysis to statistically control for variations like these. With court records as their data source, Laura Salazar and colleagues demonstrated increased accountability in terms of arrests, prosecutions, convictions, sentencing, and referrals to batterer programs (Salazar, Emshoff, Baker, & Crowley, 2007). They also identified an increase in the arrests of women who had been violent toward their partners. As a result, the researchers conclude with "cautious optimism" about coordinated community response and see their study as a "springboard" for more research along these lines (p. 640).

System Studies of Batterer Programs

The Chicago Multisite Study

A few additional studies specifically examined batterer intervention systems— that is, batterer programs as linked to the courts, probation officers, and other services. They especially demonstrate the influence of the court linkage on batterer program outcomes. The batterer programs appear, as a result, more dependent on the links with the courts than they do in previous studies of the coordinated community response as a whole. However, the previously mentioned studies and these more current ones are nonexperimental in design in that they do not have matching control sites. They also do not consider the impact of an ideal coordinated community response on the rates of re-assault and victims' well-being. But the current studies do open the door further for systems thinking and offer additional evidence in support of coordinated response, or at least increased accountability imposed by the court. These studies are multisite evaluations within Illinois and California, along with ours—which took place in several states. They also present some helpful examples of nonexperimental system evaluation, and suggestions for improving evaluation methods overall.

For instance, Larry Bennett and his colleagues evaluated the program completion and re-arrest rates for approximately 900 arrested men in the Chicago metropolitan area (Bennett, Stoops, Call, & Flett, 2007). The intervention system for the jurisdiction included thirty different batterer programs operating under a set of state standards. A six-month gender-based, cognitive-behavioral program, as well as centralized oversight of compliance by the courts, was the prescribed approach. The researchers analyzed program completion and re-arrests using statistical modeling—in this case, instrumental variable analysis. As discussed at length in chapter 2, the approach uses an extensive set of batterer, program, and community characteristics to control first for program completion, and then uses that program completion equation to help control for program outcome.

In this case, the researchers used partner abuse, substance use, prior arrest, motivation, and demographic variables to control for differences between completers and noncompleters, and ultimately to predict arrests for the two groups. (For the sake of comparison, they also conducted a less sophisticated logistic regression for arrests, using program completion as a predictor, along with the control characteristics.) They found the program completers were 40 percent to

60 percent less likely to be re-arrested—a rate comparable to our multisite findings using instrumental variable analysis (Jones & Gondolf, 2002).[3] The researchers thus concluded: "This study supports previous work finding that batterer program completion reduces domestic violence recidivism" (Bennett, Stoops, Call, & Flett, 2007, p. 50). The study faces the stock criticism, however, of having a quasi-experimental or nonexperimental design, and of using re-arrests rather than victims' reports as the outcome measure.

The California Study

A second current example of system evaluation, at least an indirect one, is the California evaluation of batterer programs. The court administrative office for California examined batterer program completion and arrest records for over 1,000 male domestic violence offenders across five jurisdictions in the state (MacLeod, Pi, Smith, & Rose-Goodwin, 2008). The intervention systems all had scheduled days for domestic violence cases, specialized court procedures, periodic compliance reviews, and largely cognitive-behavioral and Duluth-type programs. The researchers did find small positive changes in attitudes and beliefs for men who had completed the fifty-two-week batterer programs that the state required, as well as lower arrest rates. As in several other studies, re-arrests were most strongly predicted by individual batterer characteristics. Men who had more education, were older, had shorter criminal histories, and did not display clear signs of drug or alcohol dependence were less likely to be re-arrested. Of particular interest is the comparison of the five jurisdictions. There were significant differences in re-arrest rates across the sites—differences that persisted even after controlling for the characteristics of the program participants, which varied across the sites. In other words, even after simulating equivalent participants, the arrest rates still differed across the sites.

The obvious inference is that the difference in the intervention systems may have contributed to the different outcomes. Unfortunately, the researchers did not have sufficient information on the sites, or measures of the system components, to assess the aspects contributing to the difference in outcomes. They point finally to what system evaluations need to consider in the future: "Clearer specification of system intervention measures is needed. System intervention measures such as 'probation contact,' 'court review,' or even 'attendance' at a batterer program are all inherently limited by the variability in how these interventions occur across locations" (MacLeod et al., 2008, p. viii). The researchers also acknowledge the need to know more about the batterer program's organization beyond its counseling approach, including its staffing levels, the staff's training and experience, supplementary services and referrals, and financial and community resources: "Such information is essential to our ability to understand batterer programs in their various organizational forms, as well as to identify promising program approaches and practices" (p. 96).

Our Multisite Evaluation of Intervention Systems

Our multisite evaluation of batterer intervention systems offered a semblance of systems analysis as well (Gondolf, 1999b). The sites were selected based on the batterer program's approach, format and duration; additional services; court action; and linkage between the program and the court. Our research team also considered additional services and interventions into the case—the advocacy contact, victim services, mental health treatment, substance abuse treatment, and subsequent jailing—through initial and periodic follow-up interviews with both the program participants and their female partners. One aspect of the study, then, was a comparison of the different systems' outcomes to gain some insight into the overall effectiveness of the various interventions.

The Pittsburgh site had a three-month didactic batterer program that received referrals from a preliminary hearing. Those referrals were subject to periodic court review of the men's compliance with the program. Program participants were sent to additional services, such as substance abuse or mental health treatment, based on either police records, screening at program intake, or behavior in the program. The portion of men receiving such referrals was 17 percent. All the men's initial partners had contact with an advocate in the court.

At the other extreme was the more extensive and comprehensive intervention of the Denver site. Its nine-month batterer program was a network of therapists conducting more discussion, or process-oriented, sessions following individual assessment. The assessments not only considered the men's background and behavior, but they also tested for alcohol dependence and psychological disorders. Men with psychological problems received individual counseling with program staff in addition to the batterer program; those with alcohol problems were put in a batterer group addressing both alcohol use and partner abuse, and were subject to urine tests and Antabuse medication. (Nearly 30 percent of the batterer program participants reported involvement in alcohol treatment.) At this site, program referral was part of a postadjudication sentence under probation supervision.

Between the Pittsburgh and Denver programs were a three-month process-oriented program in Dallas and a six-month didactic-oriented program in Houston. The referrals at both these sites were postadjudication, but with quicker court action in response to noncompliance than in Denver. Women's service coordinators, affiliated with the batterer program, were available in both Denver and Houston. These staff members contacted the men's partners with explanations about the batterer program and information about support services for the women.

The results were strikingly similar across the four sites on a number of outcome measures, including the women's reports of assaults, threats, controlling behavior, sense of safety, and quality of life, assessed every three months for fifteen months following program intake ($n = 647$ of 840, a 77 percent response rate). However, at the more extensive intervention in Denver, the severity of violence, the repetition of assaults, and the rate of resulting injuries was lower (for example, in Pittsburgh 23 percent of the victims reported new severe violence, compared to 12 percent in Denver). In a logistic regression controlling for an extensive set of demographic, behavioral, and psychological factors that favored Denver, however, the differences were no longer statistically significant (Gondolf, 1999a). The odds of assault and severe re-assault during the follow-up period were still lower at the Denver site, even though not significant. In other words, the tendency remained but could be a chance happening.[4]

In a further analysis of the follow-up data, we found at least tentative evidence of additional factors contributing to the outcome (A. Jones & Gondolf, 2001). After controlling for other background characteristics, by far the strongest predictor of re-assault at any of the four sites was dropping out of the program. Men who received substance abuse treatment and men with partners who had contacted shelter services during the follow-up period were slightly less likely to re-assault their partners. Since these latter two factors were the highest at the more comprehensive Denver site, they may have contributed to the lower severity of the violence there.

But we are left with the question of why the more extensive and comprehensive intervention, especially at the Denver site, did not more substantially reduce re-assault overall and lead to greater improvements in victims' well-being. The most apparent explanation was the lack of the court oversight of noncompliance, which most likely would have increased program completion. The dropout rate for the nine-month program was nearly 50 percent, on top of a high percentage of no-shows (that is, men referred to the program by the court but who never enrolled). Our analyses of the dropouts suggest that they were the men most in need of additional treatment and supervision.

Moreover, the drug court model at the Pittsburgh site appeared to contribute to its comparable outcomes in terms of re-assault rate and victims' well-being, as this approach has done in the reduction of drug-related crimes (K. Burke, 2010; D. Wilson, Mitchell, & MacKenzie, 2006). The domestic violence court referred arrested men to a three-month batterer program under a stipulation of bond and reviewed the case for compliance every thirty days, with information from a program liaison present in the court. Noncompliant men received additional sanctions in the form of jailing for violation of bond (60 percent), being "held over" for a hearing on the original charges (20 percent), and being returned to the batterer program for additional group sessions (20 percent). The men were generally enrolled in the program within two weeks of their arrest, thanks to the practice of convening preliminary hearings two working days after the arrests, and the program liaison instructed men in court on the program's requirements and intake procedures. Cases of aggravated assault or repeated offenses were usually held over for a full hearing and more severe sanctions, which could include jail time, attending the batterer program for nine months, or some combination of the two. (Batterer counseling was also available in the jail.)

This swift response contrasted with the other sites, where batterer program referral followed a full court hearing and was supervised by probation officers. The average time from arrest to program intake at these other sites varied from three to six months, with a lag of a year for some cases. These sites also faced a delayed response to noncompliance. Probation officers had to bring the violators back to the court, which meant a wait of a month or more for a court date. In Denver, only about 30 percent of these cases received additional penalties.

Our research team specifically studied the impact of the swift and certain response, and the role of court monitoring in achieving this impact, at the Pittsburgh site (Gondolf, 2000c). In the mid-1990s, we compared program completion for the year before and two years after the court changed its review procedure, adding a review thirty days after referral to the program on to an established review ninety days after referral. The batterer program liaison could also report noncompliance to the court at any time and have a noncompliant man subpoenaed to appear in court. Most impressive was the reduction in "no shows" to the program following a court mandate to attend it. The no-shows dropped from 35 percent to 5 percent, and the program completion for the enrolled men remained at approximately 70 percent for the twelve-week program.[5] This translates into less than half of all referrals showing up for the program and completing it prior to establishing the court review, and over two-thirds showing up and completing afterward. Under the court review procedure, more men completed the program and fewer men were re-arrested.

The pre-post study left us with an appreciation of the behaviorist axiom that says a swift and certain response improves outcomes. Also, the court oversight of the cases—particularly holding men accountable for noncompliance—is essential in boosting program enrollment and completion, and ultimately increasing the percentage of men who reduce their violence and abuse. In sum, there is some indication here that the system components influenced the program outcome, but we can't be sure what an ideal coordinated community response might do in comparison to what was done at these sites. Each of the studies above highlights the importance of identifying and measuring the relevant system components so we can gauge the strength of their implementation and impact.

Two Quasi-Experimental Studies

The Community Impact Study

Two recent multisite quasi-experimental evaluations compared jurisdictions with enhanced coordinated community response to otherwise similar sites without such enhanced responses. Their more ideal research approach produced mixed or no substantial effects. The first of these studies was conducted through the Centers for Disease Control and Prevention in the early 2000s (Klevens, Baker, Shelley, & Ingram, 2008; Post, Klevens, Maxwell, Shelley, & Ingram, 2010). In this case, the outcome of concern was the impact on the community at large in terms of attitudes about domestic violence, knowledge and use of domestic violence services, and prevalence of domestic violence in the community. The researchers did not specifically track or assess the impact of the coordinated community response on the offenders and victims who went through the system. The communitywide outcome reflects the fact that this was basically a public health study—that is, an investigation of how the intervention affected the well-being of the public at large. In a random-dialing telephone survey (N = 12,039) in ten test and ten comparison sites across the country, the researchers found little evidence that the coordinated community response affected the community attitudes, service use, or violence prevalence. However, the sites with a longer-established coordinated response (six as opposed to three years) did show lower levels of reported aggression in the previous year.

Probably the most instructive part of the study is the extensive qualifications raised by the researchers (Post et al., 2010, pp. 87–91). To their credit, they devote several pages of their published report to enumerating the challenges of implementing such a study, an aspect called for in the previous chapter discussing the experimental evaluations of batterer programs. One limitation of the study was that the subjects were not necessarily matched across test and comparison sites. Demographic differences or other characteristics may have contributed to the blunted effect of the intervention. The quality and extent of the coordinated community response obviously varied across the test sites, and the comparison sites inevitably had some components of a coordinated response that made them more like the test sites. Also, exposure to the intervention was not taken into consideration. It is possible that the coordinated community response affected those who had direct contact with it. Finally, the increased impact associated with the longer-established community response suggests that the development of the intervention system may require more time to produce broad community effects.

The researchers also note specific methodological issues in terms of the sensitivity of the measures used, including asking subjects to recall an entire year, and people's reluctance to disclose personal information in "cold" survey calls. In other words, the expected difference in outcomes may have been undetected due to methodological shortcomings. Furthermore, the researchers caution against generalizing from a sample of sites whose coordinated community response may not be representative of such responses in other cities and communities. They finish with the challenge to "first identify effective strategies for the prevention or control of domestic violence . . . to ensure that we are packaging the best practices in a coordinated effort" (Post et al., 2010, p. 91). As we will see in the next study of the impact on intervention users, there is an even more fundamental challenge—achieving full and effective implementation of coordinated community response.

The Judicial Oversight Demonstration

The most extensive and prominent evaluation of a system intervention in domestic violence cases is the Judicial Oversight Demonstration (JOD) project, funded by the National Institute of Justice and conducted by the Urban Institute of Washington in 2000–2006. The complex study included five sites, multiple agencies, and several outcome measures, and it had a price tag of a few million dollars. It specifically examined the overall impact of an enhanced coordinated community response on service use, attitudes about the intervention, and any arrests of victims and offenders. A percentage of the victims were also interviewed about further incidence of domestic violence and abuse. The ultimate objective was to build a comprehensive collaboration around domestic violence cases and evaluate it through a quasi-experimental design.

At the center of the enhancement was judges' oversight or monitoring of cases, particularly male batterers' compliance with court orders. This was done primarily through follow-up court hearings that reviewed the progress of the case and court action on subsequent reports of further offenses, violations of probation, or noncompliance. Police response, prosecution approach, women's services, probation supervision, and batterer programming were also strengthened through training and additional staffing. Interagency coordinating committees were established to respond to system shortfalls, and data systems were improved to better track cases and coordinate service delivery.

The researchers summarized the JOD project as implementing coordinated victim advocacy and services, strong offender accountability and supervision, and uniform and consistent initial responses to offenses. However, it is important to note that the evaluation did not test the effectiveness of individual components, such as batterer programs. The researchers acknowledge: "The study was designed to measure the overall impact of the JOD intervention and was not designed to assess the impact of individual strategies or component services" (Visher, Harrell, & Yahner, 2008, p. 517).[6]

The quasi-experimental design compared two sets of matched cities and one site with a pre-post design. Specifically, the outcomes of Dorchester, Massachusetts, and Ann Arbor, Michigan, which received the enhancements, were compared respectively to those from Lowell, Massachusetts, and Lansing, Michigan, which did not receive the enhancements. In Milwaukee, Wisconsin, outcomes before the enhancement were compared to those following its implementation. The guiding assumption was that the increased accountability exercised by the courts, coupled with the extended service delivery, would improve outcomes in terms of increased service use, stronger attitudes in favor of the criminal justice system and against violence, and reduced repeat violence during the eleven months following the court's disposition of a case. Over 900 victims were interviewed at the eleven-month follow-up (45 percent of the eligible women) and 366 offenders were interviewed (33 percent of the eligible men) at the four comparison sites.[7] Only police records of re-arrests were used as the re-offense outcome for the Milwaukee pre-post site.

Mixed Results of the JOD Project

Overall, the JOD findings were mixed across the sites and inconsistent across outcomes. The expected reductions in victim reports of further violence were found in the Massachusetts comparison, but not in the one in Michigan. Domestic violence arrests were reduced in Milwaukee following the enhancement there, but not at the enhanced sites of Ann Arbor and Dorchester that measured arrests on all charges. The courts at the enhanced sites did increase accountability in the form of more consistent sentencing for offenses and sanctions for noncompliance, but the men's perceptions of consequences were similar across the sites. The victims at the enhanced sites did receive a wider range of services than the victims at the comparison sites. However, they reported moderately high levels of safety and well-being across the sites, with no difference in safety and well-being between enhanced and comparison sites.

Two other findings drawn from the sample as a whole shed light on the mixed outcomes across the sites. Further violence was less likely when the offender's probation was revoked for noncompliance with the batterer program requirements. Graduated sanctions were applied in the noncompliant cases, which usually meant jail time and an obvious separation from the victim. The enhanced sites also were more effective with subgroups of offenders, particularly those who were younger and had several previous arrests. Interestingly, these findings appear to support theories contrary to coordinated community response: that selective jailing or incapacitation contributes to improved outcomes more than a coordinated response does, and that "stakes in conformity" is not necessarily a factor in the outcomes ("stakes" would suggest that men who are older, employed, in stable relationships, and with fewer prior arrests would have done better, rather than the other way around). The characteristics also are the opposite of those found in a number of previous studies with batterer programs (for example, MacLeod et al., 2008; Gondolf, 2002a). The researchers conclude that "none of the theories of change that underlie the JOD model were supported" (Visher, Harrell, & Yahner, 2008, p. 519). On the surface, this conclusion could be taken as a negative verdict on coordinated community response.

The rather complicated results of the JOD project have opened the door to a range of interpretations—and some confusion as well. The study report that was published in an academic journal (Visher, Harrell, & Yahner, 2008) was accompanied by several responses from other criminology researchers. At one extreme is a rather negative assessment overall. Richard Peterson, the research director at the New York City Criminal Justice agency, writes: "Accumulating evidence shows that only a few criminal justice interventions have even a weak deterrent effect, and many have no effect . . . Little evidence suggests that current criminal justice interventions effectively deter recidivism by domestic violence offenders . . . A stronger conclusion, and one that I think it is time to consider seriously, is that the criminal justice system is ineffective at deterring recidivism by domestic violence offenders" (2008, p. 539).

Two other prominent criminal justice researchers, Joel Garner and Chris Maxwell, counter with a more encouraging view: "We strongly recommend caution in using their findings as a basis to reduce the level of support for efforts to improve coordination in the delivery of services to victims of intimate partner or family violence. First, whether the initial findings are positive or not, they need to be scrutinized closely for logical and empirical limitations . . . Lastly, more and better research is needed" (2008, pp. 530–31). These researchers, along with other respondents, see the research effort as a "beginning" and a prompt for "refining the 'coordinated community response' approach rather than waiting until there is definitive evidence regarding its effectiveness" (Spohn, 2008, p. 492).

Limitation of the JOD Evaluation

Garner and Maxwell (2008) go on to outline some of the more obvious limitations that complicate a simple interpretation of the JOD findings, and the JOD researchers themselves discuss several more (Visher, Newmark, & Harrell, 2008). The most extensively reported are the implementation problems that beset the JOD enhancement. The researchers outline these problems in detail in a separate volume submitted to the funders (Visher, Newmark, & Harrell, 2006) and summarize them in an online booklet published by the National Institute of Justice (Visher, Newmark, & Harrell, 2008). The researchers faced many of the barriers and breakdowns familiar to collaborative efforts. The broader implication of these implementation problems is discussed below.

One of the more pressing questions raised by the research is whether the cases that most needed additional services and supervision received them. Without some procedure for risk assessment and management, many of the more resistant, dangerous, and noncompliant offenders are likely to fall through the cracks or be unresponsive to what is offered to them. Compounding this likelihood, the increased referrals overloaded the system, and service delays and omissions occurred as a result. Funds for additional staffing were sometimes diverted to other operational needs within a program or service. There were also hiring limitations imposed by the court and state rules. Information sharing across agencies and service providers remained limited and in need of automation and updating. Despite the extensive efforts, "integrating community-based service providers into justice system operations proved difficult in all sites because of competing priorities between the two groups" (Visher, Newmark, & Harrell, 2008, p. 11). So what we may have in the end is a snapshot of work in progress that exposes the need for development, rather than a negative verdict on coordinated community response.

Respondents to the published research report note some methodological limitations that further undercut over interpretation of the results (for example, Garner & Maxwell, 2008). The most obvious is that the design was a quasi-experimental one, with comparison cities or jurisdictions as the control groups. These comparison cities already had some level of a system intervention, albeit not as developed as in the enhanced sites. Entrenched interests at the enhanced sites may have limited the implementation there and made them equivalent to the comparison sites. Additionally, the judicial oversight model was grafted onto existing agencies and programs rather than built from the ground up. Although the study does present a realistic picture of the modification of an existing system, it does not test the ideal of coordinated community response. The question of whether this ideal should be pursued and achieved is therefore not really answered.

As the JOD researchers point out, the evaluation was of the system as a whole and not of individual components. Therefore, it is difficult to discern what specific parts or procedures within the system contributed to the mixed outcomes. The researchers do note some internal strengths and weaknesses, such as the positive impact of quick jailing for noncompliant offenders, but overall we don't know which breakdowns or shortcomings contributed to the outcome failures. The implementation problems seem to suggest that it was not that coordinated community response failed, but that aspects of it were inefficient.

Interestingly, the researchers make one claim in this regard that seems to step outside this admitted limitation: "*The results suggest, like those of other studies, that referral to batterer intervention programs does not have a powerful effect in reducing intimate partner violence.* Until progress is made in changing offender beliefs and behavior, the implication is that the justice system must continue to focus on protecting victims and using the authority of its agencies to closely monitor offenders and respond rapidly with penalties when violations of court-ordered conditions are detected" (Visher, Harrell, & Yahner, 2008, p. 520; emphasis added).[8] Although the inference regarding batterer programs appears to go beyond the study's intent, design, and data, the latter part of this statement points to an essential part of a coordinated community response. In fact, the success of batterer programs is arguably dependent on the rapid and decisive response to noncompliant offenders and more comprehensive support and protections for the victims. These aspects are being refined and addressed more efficiently and systematically in the course of risk management discussed in the previous chapter.

Practitioner Response to the JOD Project

The most positive impressions of the JOD project come from the participating practitioners. At a practitioner conference responding to the study, three of the program directors reported that they had not been briefed about the study and did not have an opportunity to reply to it (Funkhouser et al., 2009). One director was particularly surprised by the claim that the batterer programs "didn't work" and had a very different impression of the actual outcomes and reasons for the reported outcomes. An audio conference with judges involved in the study also presented very different interpretations of the results and endorsed the positive impact of the coordinated community response (BWJP, 2008). The conference judges and probation officers were enthusiastic about the lessons learned in the process of enhancing the intervention and about the court's role in monitoring cases.

A specific example of how such insider knowledge leads to a different interpretation comes from the project manager of the coordinated community response training and implementation (Cline, 2009). According to her, one of the more surprising findings was that the victims in the enhanced sites did not perceive themselves as safer than those in the comparison sites, yet the first group actually experienced less physical violence, according to victim reports in Dorchester and re-arrest rates in Milwaukee. The increased accountability and extended services may have prompted victims to be more alert to potential dangers rather than minimizing or denying the seriousness of the abuse. This could also be an outcome of the increased safety planning under the expanded advocacy services. Moreover, the fact that 90 percent to 98 percent of the victims at the enhanced and comparison sites reported a positive view of the court actions may be taken as a further endorsement of the role of the criminal justice system in domestic violence cases, rather than a dismissal of domestic violence courts, as a few judges across the country have suggested.

The contrary practitioner responses seem to reflect the tension discussed in chapter 2 between researchers and practitioners in general. It is understandable that researchers often take a detached position in their striving for objectivity. But in some cases, that leads to neglect of the grounded experiences and perspective of practitioners. In subsequent summaries of the JOD project, the researchers do outline the lessons learned and some of the cautions associated with the findings (Harrell, Visher, Newmark, & Yahner, 2009; Visher, Newmark, & Harrell, 2008). The researchers may be acknowledging the practitioners' observations in these statements, and pointing to some of the positive aspects of the study outcomes. Nonetheless, integrating alternative interpretations and accommodating the complexity of such an evaluation remains an increasing challenge to the field, and to the evidence-based practice movement in general.

The various responses to the JOD project and its evaluation by no means limit the project's importance and contribution. Among researchers, it stands as a pioneering effort of a system evaluation (Spohn, 2008). It raises the design and procedural issues associated with such evaluations and sets a path for researchers to follow in conducting more comprehensive analyses. Although on the surface, the JOD evaluation produced a complicated and confusing picture, it also pushes the field to sort through the complexity of this kind of work. It points to the need for more sophisticated evaluation designs that include network analysis to better understand the system linkages, individual case studies to determine the experiences of individuals across the intervention, and statistical modeling to draw out the contribution of individual components. Perhaps the project's greatest contribution is the verification of the implementation challenges associated with a coordinated community response. These lessons do much to move coordinated community response from a vague ideal toward a set of practical procedures.

Evidence of Implementation Shortfalls

The resounding importance of the JOD project, in my estimation, is the implementation issues it exposed. A booklet published by the National Institute of Justice summarizes these issues and proposes remedies to alleviate them (Visher, Newmark, & Harrell, 2008). However, the study is not alone in suggesting that the intention of coordinated community response often falls short. In fact, a few additional studies show that even the basic linkages between batterer programs and the courts are often not established, not consistent, or not sufficient. These studies include a national survey of batterer programs, a state audit of probation departments, and a citywide evaluation of a collaborative project. The most glaring shortfall is the lack of accountability, especially in terms of noncompliance to batterer programs, and the neglect of a crucial risk marker—namely, dropping out of a program—in the process.

A National Survey of Court Actions

A national survey of batterer programs, criminal courts, and women's centers explored the extent of accountability in batterer intervention (Labriola, Rempel, O'Sullivan, & Frank, 2007). The results of this study by the Center for Court Innovation are not necessarily representative of the country, nor do the opinions of the respondents necessarily reflect what is actually practiced. There was unfortunately a very low response rate to the survey and few details on the questionnaire.[9] The survey nonetheless offers a disappointing picture of the most basic aspect of a system intervention—the court referral and response to batterer program noncompliance. Fewer than two-thirds of the courts reported requiring periodic monitoring of batterer program compliance, and only about half of these did so within the first four weeks.

Moreover, only 40 percent of the courts "always" or "often" imposed a sanction in response to noncompliance, and those sanctions were generally not substantial (for example, "verbal admonishment" rather than being sent to jail or having probation revoked). In fact only one in six batterer programs reported that jail time was imposed "often" or always" in response to noncompliance with the mandate to attend batterer programs, and one in three programs viewed the courts as "inconsistent" overall. The latter concern may reflect the fact that only 12 percent of the courts reported having a written protocol for responding to noncompliance. The researchers are left to conclude that a low percentage of courts promote accountability in practice, despite the fact that the majority of them indicated that it is a main function of the court mandates (Labriola, Rempel, O'Sullivan, & Frank, 2007, p. viii).[10]

A State Audit of Probation Departments

A California audit of probation departments verified many of the survey findings at least in that state (California State Auditor, 2006). The auditors drew on court, program, and probation documents to determine the implementation of statues for the handling of domestic violence cases and especially the response to noncompliance to batterer programs. Documentation was obtained and analyzed for a random sample of 125 batterer program referrals from five county probation departments deemed representative of the state's fifty-eight counties.[11]

Only about half of the men sent by the courts to batterer programs completed the required attendance. Contributing to the high dropout rate was the fact that probation departments had attendance policies that varied from the state statutes and were more leniently imposed than the statues allowed. Rather than notify the courts of noncompliance as required, probation departments were found counseling and referring noncompliant men back to programs. Also, courts often did not sanction the noncompliant men who were reported, even when they had multiple prior violations. Finally, the probation departments failed to consistently conduct on-site reviews of the batterer programs, although the state statutes required the departments to periodically monitor and review the programs in order to approve them for referrals.

This all occurred in a state with clearly legislated guidelines for probation and program operation. In response to the disappointing findings, the auditors recommended establishing a set of consequences or sanctions for violations by noncompliant men, and consistent administration of those policies through the probation departments. This included a limit on the number of violations before a man's probation is revoked and he is jailed. The auditors also promoted periodic court appearances to review a batterer's compliance, and regular, documented reviews of programs along with establishing procedures for the reviews.

In sum, it would appear that the foundation of accountability and the reinforcement of batterer program attendance are weakened by inconsistencies in court and probation oversight of domestic violence cases. As noted in earlier chapters, the outcome of batterer programs is substantially influenced by the court response to noncompliance. Moreover, it is difficult to introduce risk management when program noncompliance (a strong predictor of the commission of new offenses) is inconsistently addressed. According to the California study, even men who repeatedly did not comply with program mandates were returned to batterer programs in many cases. Judging by these sorts of findings, we have a long way to go to reach the ideal coordinated community response.

A Local Collaboration Project

Supplemental Mental Health Treatment

Our research team conducted a local study that exposed the barriers to and breakdowns of implementation (Gondolf, 2009a, 2009b). It also confirmed some of the familiar reasons for the implementation failures and recommended ways to fix them. The study was an evaluation of supplemental mental health treatment for batterer program participants who screened positive on a psychological test, the Brief Symptoms Inventory. Over a two-year period, we directly observed the agencies' procedures, participated in training and supervision meetings, debriefed administrators in formal interviews, and noted informal conversations with staff and clients.[12] The overriding finding was the difficulty in fully implementing mandatory referral to mental health treatment across the collaborating agencies—the courts, mental health clinics, and the batterer program. Despite extensive planning, training, protocols, and support; inconsistencies in the screening and referral processes emerged and undercut the implementation of the mental health evaluation and treatment.

For example, members of the batterer program's staff failed to notify some men that they were being referred to supplemental mental health treatment and how to get it. The schedule of orientation sessions was disrupted by various postponements due to meeting room availability; the clinic missed sending verification of some men's mental health evaluations to the batterer program. The prosecutors in one court excused some men who were noncompliant with their mental health referral because of wanting to move cases along to avoid increasing the backlog, or out of a sense that completing the batterer program alone was sufficient. Several underlying issues were also exposed, as described in chapter 2: administrative absenteeism and turnover, vacancies in administrative staff, client overload, and differing agency priorities.

Gaps in the administrative staff were apparent in complaints about the burden of paperwork and signs of "training decay"—in spite of being trained twice in their role of screening and notification of referral, frontline staff increasingly made procedural slip-ups. A batterer program administrator also diverted some of the funds for project staff to other, more pressing needs, which limited screening and referral oversight within the organization. The most obvious evidence of client overload was at the clinic: each day, its intake unit received up to 100 calls, and each clinician saw as many as fifteen clients in various states of need. Consequently, it was not surprising that the additional court referrals did not always receive the special attention that was planned. Differing priorities led to a less than eager response, as well. The clinicians voiced their preference for voluntary patients who were responsive to treatment. And in contrast to the courts' preoccupation with processing its caseload, the batterer program was concerned with managing 80–100 new participants a month and tracking their group assignments and attendance.

Contributions of a System Coordinator

Several adjustments and modifications to procedures were made during the study to address these sorts of problems, but the most beneficial change was the addition of an experienced case manager and system coordinator to facilitate and sustain the implementation. This person worked directly under the supervision of the principal investigator and was therefore relatively independent of the individual agencies. She was able to monitor the big picture through the ongoing collection of data for our accompanying outcome evaluation, and to remain relatively free of the demands and pressures within the agencies.

Specifically, the case management involved our staff member's tracking the men's compliance with their mental health referrals, and calling men who were not compliant to remind them of the referral and overcome their resistance or other obstacles. System coordination was based, first, on monitoring the number of positive screens for mental problems, notified men, clinic appointments, completed evaluations, and court actions concerning noncompliance. The staff then addressed any decline or gaps in the numbers through interagency meetings, phone calls, and other types of troubleshooting. In a sense, the coordinator was conducting a kind of system audit, identifying inconsistencies and facilitating discussions of how to rectify them (see Pence & McDonnell, 1999). As a result, the percentage of referred men who obtained a clinical evaluation rose from less than 5 percent under voluntary referral based on observed symptoms to approximately 14 percent during the introduction of a mandated referral for positive screening. Under the case manager and system coordinator, the portion obtaining an evaluation rose to 28 percent.

The remaining shortfall was attributable, at least in part, to the inconsistent court response to the men's noncompliance with mental health referrals. This appraisal was drawn from our observations of the court proceedings, debriefing interviews with program staff, and review of the batterer program records. The main reasons for the court's inconsistencies were reportedly the increased number of new judges circulating through the domestic violence court and the tendency to quickly move cases through the system to avoid a backlog.

The enhanced implementation under our case manager and system coordinator, in spite of several unexpected challenges, suggests that coordination and collaboration can be improved with a modest investment. In this case, independent oversight of lapses and gaps in the referral process made a difference, albeit a shortfall remained in the number of men actually receiving treatment (19 percent of the referred men). The outcomes of the current mental health treatment for batterer program participants appear to be related to the shortcomings of referral implementation, rather than to any ineffectiveness of the treatment. More attention clearly needs to be devoted to improving collaboration within coordinated community responses and sustaining them. Legislated procedures like those in the California probation audit, the enhanced court oversight in the JOD project, and the lack of court follow-through evident in the national survey all show that the basic linkages of coordinated community response too often are not realized.

Building a Coordinated Community Response

System Management

The most basic means of maintaining and modifying a coordinated community response comes from a management perspective (for example, Weiner, 1990), much like what was applied in our supplemental mental health referral. Essential to this perspective is ongoing systems analysis using feedback loops of information about the system's functioning. Data on the results of the identified components of the system are regularly tallied and reviewed. Does the flow of cases through the system and the response to them reflect the intended function? What outputs are low or high—and which anomalies are expected or inconsistent with one another? The answers to those questions are used to adjust the system and see if the outputs improve.

For example, the number of domestic violence cases being prosecuted may be particularly low compared to the number of domestic violence calls to the police. Or the percentage of batterers referred to a batterer program may be only a small portion of those actually prosecuted. Very often we find that the number of men actually appearing for a batterer program is a small portion of the men mandated by the court to attend the program. What do these discrepancies say about the system and how it might be improved? One previously cited example is the 30 percent no-show rate of men referred to the Pittsburgh batterer program (Gondolf, 2000c). This led to introducing a court review of compliance thirty days after a referral, and this reduced the no-show rate to 5 percent. Batterer program dropout rates are another convenient—and perhaps the most obvious—indicator of system breakdown. How many of these men are sanctioned in any way by the court for violating the conditions of their probation or other court stipulations?

As a number of reviews have noted, program dropout rates have been reported to vary from 15 percent to 70 percent (Daly & Pelowski, 2000). What could be done in the programs, courts, or probation offices to lower the high dropout rates? Some programs have regularly called absent program participants, assigned a fellow group member to personally check up on absentees, introduced orientation sessions that transition men into the program, or used motivational interviewing at various points. Above, I described the swift and certain response of the Pittsburgh court to noncompliant cases in our multisite evaluation and the impact of that response (Gondolf, 1999b). Other programs have enhanced reporting to the courts or established court liaisons to improve the court response to difficult cases.

This management approach can certainly be used to bring representatives of the different components of the system together to help solve apparent under performance or other problems. For instance, the system coordinator in our supplemental mental health referral project (Gondolf, 2009a, 2009b) monitored the number of men screened as eligible versus the number completing an evaluation. Discrepancies prompted problem-solving meetings with staff members from the batterer program, mental health clinic, and court.

However beneficial, systems analysis of this kind is primarily a mechanical endeavor. It focuses on the outward operation of the system rather than on the assumptions and perspectives that underlie it, and the experiences of individuals involved in it. Staff attitudes and frontline practices may stay the same, or the staff may be overburdened by output-based adjustments. The clients or victims using the system may have negative or frustrating experiences, even when the system is efficient. In fact, simply adjusting procedures rather than changing the objectives can be counterproductive. The most discussed example in domestic violence intervention has been the increase in women arrested for domestic violence in the aftermath of pro-arrest policies. Also, women under "no drop" prosecution policies may be hampered financially by their partner's going to jail, threatened further by their partner's retaliation, or retraumatized by the pressure and questioning of the court (Ford, 2003).

Domestic Violence Councils

Efforts to improve the implementation of a coordinated community response, as well as to promote collaboration in the first place, have frequently involved the creation of councils, coalitions, or other collaborative groups. Domestic violence councils have proliferated for this purpose. The federal STOP grants, initiated in the early 1990s under the Violence Against Women Act, required the formation of a council to develop procedures and policies for domestic violence interventions and services. The councils are generally comprised of leaders from a variety of local agencies—for example, the battered women's shelter, district court, social services, child protection agency, and batterer program—dealing with domestic violence cases who meet periodically to share information, discuss system problems, and consider difficult cases. Some councils reduce the number of such meetings as turnover and absenteeism increase under tight schedules and limited resources, and the groups' productivity may wane as agency representatives turn to posturing or defensiveness against criticisms and failures. A review of the research on the coordinating councils in general concludes that there is little empirical evidence that they achieve the desired outcomes related to system change (Roussos & Fawcett, 2000).

However, researchers in the domestic violence field question this somewhat negative view because of its basis in broad outcomes rather than more intermediate ones, the overuse of quantitative analyses that miss the dynamics of the councils, and the neglect of the specific nature and activity of the councils (Allen, Watt, & Hess, 2008). In a qualitative descriptive study of domestic violence councils, Nicole Allen and her colleagues found a more encouraging picture, especially in terms of more intermediate effects—effects known to facilitate system change. The researchers conducted in-depth interviews of the conveners or leaders of forty-one of the forty-five councils in Michigan about the structure, operation, and impacts of the councils.

Their content analysis of the transcribed interviews identified six primary activities of the councils: discussing issues, sharing information, identifying system gaps, providing training across agencies, engaging in community education, and lobbying. These contributed to several intermediate outcomes: the promotion of knowledge, relationships, and institutionalized changes (that is, revisions in policies and procedures). For example, nearly all the interviewees noted that face-to-face contact was encouraged through the councils, and this contact helped to reduce hostility and misunderstandings between agency leaders. It also led to informal problem solving. These kinds of contacts made for important social ties, or cross-sector relationships, according to other researchers (Lasker & Weiss, 2003). The findings overall led the researchers to conclude "that councils may, indeed, play an important role in improving the community response to domestic violence" (Allen, Watt, & Hess, 2008, p. 71). They acknowledge, however, that the study does not establish or verify the extent of the intermediate outcomes, nor their specific impacts on the system at large.

Allen and her colleagues furthered their investigations through a survey of 511 members of domestic violence councils (51 percent of the "regularly attending" members responded; Allen, 2006). According to the members' ratings, the councils were on average "moderately" effective at accomplishing their goals within the criminal justice system and other community sectors. However, the effectiveness ratings varied considerably across the forty-one councils. In a regression analysis of the responses, organized and skilled leadership, shared power in decision making, and a clear and shared mission were the main predictors of perceived effectiveness.

Leadership has appeared as the strongest predictor of effectiveness in other types of councils, along with conflict resolution, which did not emerge as salient in the case of domestic violence councils. The researchers suspect, as we found in a participant observation study of a rural council, that power imbalances with officials from the criminal justice system account for the need for strong leadership and conflict resolution. Judges and prosecutors often have veto power over the concerns of battered women's advocates, and service providers can be left kowtowing for concessions. Not surprisingly, shared decision making, in one study, was the strongest predictor of effective collaboration with the criminal justice system (Allen, 2005).

The importance of an inclusive climate and diverse active membership is obvious. How to achieve and maintain these characteristics are challenges, especially considering the different personalities, resources, agendas, interests, and politics involved. Notably, one study on this issue found that opportunities to have an influence (a kind of empowerment) both inside and outside meetings were associated with higher member participation, and not with the process of the meetings (Wells, Ward, Feinberg, & Alexander, 2008). At a minimum, the councils provide a forum for building bridges and understanding that open opportunities and permit shared decisions. Ultimately, we also need to find ways to go beyond councils to engage those doing the frontline work, as well as to secure the participation and support of agency leaders.

Accountability and Safety Audits

The broader issue is how to bring a change of perspective and collective action to the entire system. How do we get frontline staff fully involved, along with agency leaders? How do we truly integrate or coordinate the system, rather than merely fine-tune it? There is a long line of research and prescriptions for system change that include school, health, child protection, and criminal justice systems (for example, Kreger, Brindis, Manuel, & Sassoubre, 2007). They consider agency coalitions, collaborations, and partnerships as well as ad hoc networks and large, self-contained organizations. We also hear these days of stakeholder initiatives that bring the consumers of services and agencies into the feedback loop.

Ellen Pence and her colleagues at Praxis International have developed a change model tailored to domestic violence cases that both honors the experiences of battered women and attempts to change the mind-set of staff working in the system (Pence & Lizdas, 1998; for an overview, see Sadusky, Martinson, Lizdas, & McGee, 2010). Their safety and accountability audit collects information far beyond operational feedback through interviews with staff, observations of staff interactions, and text analysis of documents and records. The guiding question is *how* does a specific action enhance or diminish the safety of battered women? The question of *why* one does or doesn't act in a certain way is not as important, and asking such questions can appear accusatory to some staff members.

The system assumptions behind the safety audit are, first, that organizations tend to fall into a kind of institutional maintenance that solidifies around a designated and narrowly focused task, like delivering counseling sessions to batterers.[13] Second, staff in organizations tend to develop their own way of doing things that often is shaped by practicality and efficiency rather than by broader goals. Within human services this tendency has famously been dubbed "street-level bureaucracy" (Lipsky, 1983). Therefore, the staff, as well as the organizational leaders, need to be engaged in a process of sharing and discussing their outlook and tasks. The object is to solve problems together, not just to have another meeting. As staff members rethink their approach from the standpoint of the women they aim to assist, a new mind-set emerges, a collective effort develops, and integrated procedures are identified. The ideal result is what its founders term an "audit attitude"—monitoring themselves and each other to make individual battered women feel and be safer (Sadusky, Martinson, Lizdas, & McGee, 2010, p. 1033).

The safety audit is more than an idealized process that is impractical in the real world. It has been conducted in over seventy-five cities in the United States and informally in many other places (Sadusky et al., 2010). Its most thorough example to date is the Blueprint for Safety established in St. Paul, Minnesota.[14] It is fair to say that the blueprinting was lengthy and tedious work, and some agency representatives were inclined to protect their interests rather than to collaborate. However, the project is the most extensive to have used the principles of the safety audit to totally overhaul the intervention system and achieve a truly coordinated community response.[15]

This kind of process results in a "collective policy, rather than a collection of policies" (Sadusky et al., 2010, p. 1040). Nitty-gritty daily procedures were reexamined at all levels of agencies and services and revised to speed up the response to domestic violence cases throughout the system—and especially to produce a more decisive response to noncompliance and enhance protection against high-risk cases.[16] A newspaper article quoted one of the blueprint participants on the outcome of the project: "The agencies have really come to understand that it's one process. It's a kind of organic process that needs to have everyone understand his or her responsibility in relation to everybody else's responsibility. Definitely it will save lives" (Xiong, 2010).

What's needed next, of course, is research that substantiates the effectiveness of the blueprint process, particularly its contribution to risk management and batterer program outcomes. What conditions contribute to the process: community readiness, organizational capacity, social capital, funding and resources? What does a coordinated community response contribute to a batterer program, and what does a batterer program contribute to it? The implication is that batterer programs, within a fully implemented coordinated community response, are particularly effective in its determining which men need enhanced supervision and supplemental treatments. The programs would provide risk observations to help the court choose its response, especially noting noncompliance that would trigger further intervention and protection. Even at this stage of the research, evidence points in this direction, or rather reinforces a long-held ideal. It also substantiates the claim that batterer programs should continue to evolve within this ideal, rather than be replaced or completely overhauled. The programs in fact can facilitate ongoing risk management, which fuels and requires a coordinated community response.

Conclusion: Facing the Challenge of Coordination

The Need and the Desire

"Coordinated community response" has become such a catchphrase within criminal justice circles, and particularly in the domestic violence field, that you'd think we would have mastered it by now. It clearly has a contribution to make to intervention efforts, including those associated with batterer programs. By and large, the systems thinking that underlies coordinated community response is evident in programmatic and policy development for social problems, like child welfare and homelessness. It is evident in domestic violence projects, particularly those centered on the courts. It is reinforced as well by research on offender rehabilitation, offense desistance, case management, and probation supervision. Moreover, early coordinated community response evaluations in the domestic violence field show reductions in recidivism, albeit with nonexperimental designs.

The critics of batterer programs are mainly preoccupied with evidence of a narrow scope—namely, experimental outcomes of batterer treatment independent of the intervention systems of which the programs are a part. Admittedly, documentation and evaluation of intervention systems, and the coordinated response to which they aspire, are difficult to design, orchestrate, coordinate, and interpret. Multimethod research is being recommended, along with new techniques for measurement, analysis, and interpretation. The preoccupation with treatment experiments is in fact facing outright objections from some researchers, such as Katya Fels Smyth and Lisbeth Schorr (2009), who argue for more complex studies of what in reality are community-based interventions. The next section summarizes the available research evidence for system intervention and the ideal of a coordinated community response, which has been reviewed in detail above. The chapter concludes with the implications of that research, particularly for batterer programs.

Mixed Research Results

The recent research on coordinated community response is mixed, and some would call it discouraging. Two multisite studies, including our own, use statistical modeling to demonstrate a batterer program effect while controlling for system and community variables. Also, a California state study and a part of our multisite evaluation suggest that variation in court linkages to batterer programs and court oversight of participant compliance influence program outcomes. On the other hand, two major comparative studies that use a quasi-experimental design show some similar outcomes across communities with an enhanced community response and others without. Some different outcomes in favor of the enhanced community response did emerge as well.

The first of these quasi-experimental studies examined the impacts on the public at large rather than on the users of the coordinated community response—specifically, the attitudes, knowledge, and overall prevalence of domestic violence in the community (Klevens et al., 2008). The communities with a longer established coordinated response did show lower levels of reported aggression in the previous year, even though there was not much difference on the whole across the ten test and ten comparison sites. The researchers of this study, funded by the Centers for Disease Control and Prevention (CDC), identify an extensive set of qualifications and limitations that make it hard to draw generalizations from its findings.

The most relevant and controversial of the studies, the Judicial Oversight Demonstration project, used two test and two comparison sites, and one site with a pre-post evaluation (Visher, Harrell, & Yahner, 2008). A substantial amount of funding went to staff, training, and information systems intended to establish a coordinated community response, or at least to improve an existing one. Basically, a six-month follow-up showed an increase in the delivery of services to batterers and their victims, but not a consistently lower rate of reported violence and re-arrests at the enhanced sites. There were lower arrest rates where noncompliance was systematically punished, and the enhanced sites appeared more effective with certain subgroups of offenders. The researchers conclude, however, that these particular findings actually counter the theoretical assumptions of coordinated community response. They also assume that the batterer programs were not effective in changing men's attitudes and behaviors, even though they admit not being able to evaluate independent components of the system.

The study triggered a range of interpretations and responses, which probably verifies its complicated findings and implementation problems. Some researchers view the findings as further evidence that not much really works in criminal justice interventions, and that attention and funds should be turned more to prevention (Peterson, 2008). Others continue to see promise in coordinated community response and find support for this in the study (Garner & Maxwell, 2008). Perhaps most telling is the reaction of several of the practitioners working at the research sites. In two conferences, these practitioners have identified the positive impacts of the enhancements and strongly recommended their continuation and expansion (BWJP, 2008; Funkhouser et al., 2009). The varying responses overall illustrate the role of interpretation in applying research findings, and how our vantage point effects what we take from them.

Implementation Problems

The most noteworthy aspect of the JOD study, however, is the implementation issues that it exposed. Despite the funding, planning, and training that went into the study, the intended coordinated response was not fully achieved, and the test sites may have been more similar to the comparison sites than hoped. Several implementation problems were noted, such as knowledge gaps, heavy workload, hiring limitations, data-sharing problems, and criminal justice constraints. Moreover, the improvements that were made contributed to an overload of cases in probation and victim services, and the absence of risk assessment meant that those in most need of extra supervision or treatment didn't necessarily receive them.

A few studies since the CDC and JOD research have further substantiated the shortfalls of implementation, even at the very basic linkage among criminal courts, probation departments, and batterer programs. This linkage seems crucial to batterer outcomes, especially since it is well established that court oversight influences program completion and further containment of noncompliant men. For example, a national survey of batterer programs, along with court and probation representatives, showed court monitoring of compliance was low, and sanctions for noncompliance were inconsistent or insubstantial (Labriola, Rempel, O'Sullivan, & Frank, 2007). The researchers concluded that a low percentage of the courts promote accountability in practice, despite accountability being an acknowledged function of the courts.

The California audit of probation departments reveals a similar lack of follow through, despite state requirements of periodic reviews of batterer program operations and mandated reporting of violations of batterer program requirements to the court (California State Auditor, 2006). The courts also did not consistently sanction the mandated men for the violations that were reported, as the national survey indicated as well. All of this contributed to the high dropout rate from batterer programs, a rate that was over 50 percent, according to the researchers. Last is my research team's local study of the implementation of supplemental mental health treatment for batterer program participants (Gondolf, 2009a, 2009b). Despite the planning, training, and clear procedures, compliance with referral for a mental health evaluation and treatment was terribly low. A system coordinator monitoring the flow of referrals, however, substantially increased compliance. Even with that, the overall percentage of screened men obtaining an evaluation and treatment remained low, in part because of the court's inconsistent response to noncompliant men.

Making It Happen

This sort of evidence leads us to assume that the real challenge facing the field is not so much what new batterer programming should we have, but how we can improve the implementation of existing programs. At a minimum there can be better system management, like that established with a system coordinator in our supplemental mental health study (Gondolf 2009a, 2009b), or with case managers in the Texas probation project discussed in chapter 5 (Sprow,

2009). Monitoring the service delivery, or client flow, in itself would expose breakdowns and barriers that need repair. This would amount to a kind of feedback loop that is essential to sustaining systems. Of course, there still is the challenge of getting people on board with the necessary adjustments.

Domestic violence councils have played a prominent role in starting and maintaining some level of collaboration and ultimately coordination among intervention components. The empirical evidence on coordinating councils in general is not very positive, but the little research available on domestic violence councils suggests that there are notable intermediate effects: discussion of common issues, sharing of information, identifying system gaps, and providing training (Allen, 2005, 2006; Allen, Watt, & Hess, 2008). All of these outcomes contribute to building an informal network that helps in dealing with problematic cases and in formulating procedures that improve intervention in general. Power imbalances, defensive posturing, poor attendance, and personality clashes, of course, can limit the impact of such councils. Moreover, the relationships and problem solving of a council's agency leaders does not necessary trickle down to the frontline staff doing the work.

The most extensive approach—one that facilitates reform of the system and the way it operates—is the accountability and safety audit developed in Duluth, Minnesota (Sadusky, Martinson, Lizdas, & McGee, 2010). It represents a shift in perspective from making agencies operate more efficiently to better serving women in abusive relationships. The audit collects information beyond operational feedback or collaboration issues through interviews with staff, observations of procedures, and analysis of documents and records. The information is then used to engage individuals across the system at all levels in solving problems.

The ideal result is a unifying mind-set, much like that recommended in the process of risk management. The practitioners of the system become aware of their responsibilities and of others' responsibilities as well; they see themselves as part of the whole rather than in separate compartments. As noted above, such safety audits have been conducted in over seventy-five communities, and the St. Paul Blueprint for Safety has maximized a coordinated community response across police, courts, and services citywide (Sadusky et al., 2010). A kind of process-oriented risk management is emerging throughout the system.

System Evaluation

This kind of innovation leads us to the next step in evidence-based practice: substantiating and evaluating these sorts of efforts. We might first conduct more implementation studies that show how coordinated community responses are formed, and how to address the barriers and breakdowns that impede them. There is already a substantial literature on system development and change, as well as on forming collaborations and effective networks. Studies need to consider not only the client flow but also the interactions between the clients and practitioners, and the personal impact of those interactions. As the research on domestic violence councils illustrates, evaluations might focus more on intermediate outcomes and their ties to longer-term ones like recidivism. Overall, there needs to be more systems thinking and systems analysis in order to improve intervention and the impact of batterer programs.

Cost-benefit studies are also essential to the field, especially at this time of financial crisis throughout society. It is assumed that coordinated community response ultimately is not only more effective in reducing violence, but also more efficient in responding to criminal cases. The reduction in the number of cases coming to court and in harm to victims should lead to a cut in criminal justice costs. More efficient operation of the components in the system with less overlap and redundancy should increase savings. The cost study of batterer programs incorporated into our multisite evaluation showed an amazingly low cost per participant compared to alcohol treatment, psychotherapy, and especially jailing (A. Jones, 2000).

The Big Picture of Batterer Programs

This big-picture approach does not mean that batterer programs can afford to neglect their clinical skills, domestic violence knowledge, and familiarity with program research. Of course, they need to ensure the skills and competence of their staff members, and the efficiency and finances of their program operation. But in the process they need to keep an eye on the intervention system as a whole, especially their linkages to the court. As I mentioned in the chapter on risk assessment, batterer programs have a facilitating role in promoting and contributing to risk management, which in turn leads to more collaboration and linkages. The most obvious need at the moment appears to be establishing better linkages with the courts and probation officers. Any shortfall there clearly undermines program completion and containment of men who remain noncompliant.

As batterer programs have become increasingly specialized and infused with clinical psychology, they have admittedly become less attentive to system development. Or they may simply not have the time to do much beyond their own service delivery, and leave that role to the probation department. In some jurisdictions, the batterer program is still left out of the domestic violence council or may be at odds with it. Procedures and policies may already be in place, but the turnover of judges, prosecutors, or victims' advocates may be too much to keep up with. So the program's efforts to engage the system and work toward a community response are weak.

There are, nonetheless, batterer programs that have no trouble seeing their work with men as a springboard for a kind of community organizing—and that are working to build a response that goes well beyond even collaboration with the courts and other social services (for example, U. Douglas, Bathrick, & Perry, 2008). Their staff members use their experience with the men in their groups as leverage with other organizations and the community at large. What they see and learn from the program participants is used in talks, trainings, and forums about intervention. They may also allow police, probation officers, court officials, and victims' advocates to visit their group sessions. A few batterer programs have participants invite a male friend or relative to attend a meeting or two. The treatment is, in this way, *with* and *from* the community. There is some reinforcing energy and sharing of responsibility—synergy—that comes from that process.

Much of what batterer programs do is help to send a consistent message that men who batter can and must change. This can be a motivator in itself, a component of cognitive-behavioral treatment, an aspect of reality therapy, and an essential in deterrence. The challenge, from this perspective, is how to extend that message beyond weekly group sessions. The program participants too often take advantage of the wiggle room that most intervention systems and community norms allow. In fact, many of them are skilled at manipulating others to get their way. A coordinated response helps to reduce that wiggle room and reinforce the batterer program message.

Changing community norms and attitudes about domestic violence is a bigger task, but one that has a broad basis of support. It comes from a process that is at least amplified by a coordinated community response. We've seen that efforts to further or achieve a coordinated community response can activate such a process—which involves ongoing development and an evolving mind-set. Some batterer programs—the Duluth model, Atlanta's Men Stopping Violence, Boston's Emerge, Michigan's Alternatives to Domestic Abuse, and many others—work to promote this sort of process. Books and other writing also outline how psychological therapy can also contribute to social change. This may not only be where programs are headed, but also, to varying degrees, where many are—or would like to be.

Conclusion

A Summary of Batterer Program Evidence

Evidence-Based Issues

This book began with a lament about the apparent disarray among batterer programs. On the surface, they seem faced with a variety of budding alternatives and proposed innovations, and undercut by research that brands them as ineffective. In the midst of the rising demand for evidence-based practice, many programs are being pressured to change or being pushed out by alternatives. They are also facing an increasing funding shortage that leaves many of them struggling to survive, let alone expand or modify their programming. These circumstances make programs appear even less effective, and in turn receive even less support and funding. These days, a downward cycle is likely among many social services unless they can document their efficiency and effectiveness.

A more critical look at the evidence-based practice movement, and the experimental evaluations it favors, offers a different picture, however. Evidence-based practice, as observers in several fields point out, is intended to be an interactive process between practitioners and researchers that helps to develop practice. Evaluation methods need to fit the realities of intervention, and interpretation should draw on a variety of stakeholders and real-world circumstances. A more narrow use of evidence-based practice is in some ways constricting batterer intervention, as its critics claim, with its dogma of experiments and bottom-line message about what works. It also tends to jeopardize low-income neighborhoods that are not ready to be research sites and that need a community-based response to deep-seated social problems.

The bottom lines are subject to misuse in the competition for funding, given the promotion of personal agendas and the increasing simplification of decision making. Determination of what works is certainly an attractive and desirable goal. Many sectors want to use that information to streamline intervention, making it more effective, and to reduce mistreatment of clients. Research can also help to sort through pet theories and assumptions about treatment that proliferate throughout the helping professions in general. The long-standing challenge is how to bring research and practice together in a way that promotes program development rather than antagonism and confusion. Some bridges have been built to this end, but more are obviously needed.

We see this narrow approach to evidence-based practice affecting batterer programs. Five major experiments show little or no effects and are being used to promote a variety of approaches and new directions. As several articles discuss, methodological and conceptual issues make it difficult to interpret and apply their findings. The experimental groups are compromised by a substantial portion of dropouts, for instance, and the impact of the programs' context is not accounted for. The studies' implementation, overall, is too weak to draw inferences from. Also, the narrow approach of evidence-based practice has, for the most part, dismissed statistical modeling with nonexperimental studies. But moderate program effects produced in the modeling are reinforced by a variety of other quantitative and qualitative analyses. The statistical models admittedly have drawbacks of their own. Nonetheless, they attempt to simulate an experimental comparison while accounting for dropouts and context—some of the things the experiments do not do.

Competing Alternatives

At the heart of the contention over batterer programs is the divide between the gender-based, cognitive-behavioral approaches that dominate conventional programs and the more psychodynamic approaches that claim to be more therapeutic and ultimately more effective. A careful review of the evidence, however, shows that many of the claims about the alternative approaches have weaker research and even contradictory findings behind them. And there is substantial generic evidence that cognitive-behavioral approaches are well suited for the men in batterer programs and are just as effective as other approaches, if not more so. The critical characterization of gender-based, cognitive-behavioral programs, such as the Duluth program, has also been shown to be a distorted stereotype. Many of these batterer programs are incorporating therapeutic techniques to better engage unresponsive men. What does emerge from the research is evidence of a subgroup of men who have psychological problems that contribute to program dropout rates and make the men resistant to change. More supervision and additional treatments may be warranted for them.

Although there is certainly agreement that not all batterers are the same, it is less clear how to differentiate among them. How the proposed categorizations—such as psychological typologies, change stages, couples interactions, and racial or ethnic groups—intersect and overlap is still to be sorted out. Also, we don't yet have substantial evidence that matching treatments to different types of batterers would be more effective than the prevailing approach. The recommended alternatives for different batterers include specialized treatments tailored to the batterer types, motivational counseling addressing change stages, culturally focused counseling for African American men, and couples counseling for batterers whose screening shows them to be less violent. The evidence for these alternatives is mixed at best, and there are few experimental evaluations to support them. It is also unclear whether these alternatives in themselves are sufficient or effective with the men who tend to drop out of programs and continue to abuse and assault their partners—the men most responsible for the injuries inflicted following program intake. But proponents of the various innovations affirm that more can be done to engage program participants by recognizing distinctive issues or needs—something most programs are already attempting to do.

Dealing with High-Risk Men

The tough question facing batterer programs, and the criminal justice field in general, is how to identify the especially dangerous men. Several validated risk assessment instruments have been developed to help do this—based on either checklists of actuarial factors or topical ratings for structured professional judgment. All of them have disadvantages, and as yet none is clearly the "best one." The risk instruments do produce more accurate predictions than "gut feelings" and general impressions, even those of experienced clinicians, but they produce an unsettling portion of false negatives. Predicting which are the dangerous or high-risk men based on a one-time assessment is difficult particularly because violence is more a process than a solitary event. It depends on a variety of contingencies and circumstances, as well as psychological and social issues. The shift, therefore, has been from prediction to ongoing risk management that entails repeated assessments, monitoring compliance, and revising interventions along the way.

The most pressing issue for the field at this point is what to do in response to the assessment results. What additional treatments for the men or supports for the women are available and effective? In order to obtain the information needed to make a meaningful assessment, the services to respond to the risk results, and the supervision and accountability to maximize compliance; a coordinated community response is needed. Merely triaging batterers based on a cutoff score, or sending them to longer or shorter programs, could be a misuse of risk assessment, and a misleading one at that. Several researchers argue for making risk assessment more of a process that incorporates the perceptions and experiences of victims. Those considerations have in fact been shown not only to improve prediction but also to increase prevention of new offenses.

What, then, have we learned about coordinated community response? It reflects the systems thinking that underlies much of the way we attempt to address social problems in general. Also, there is evidence across disciplines that coordinated responses improve outcomes, particularly in the criminal justice field. But the research on coordinated community responses to domestic violence has produced mixed results at best. It has also exposed implementation shortfalls with even the most basic links between the courts and batterer programs. There are means to repair and develop coordination that range from systems management and domestic violence councils to accountability and safety audits. The latter add a problem-solving process of engagement across agencies and personnel that not only improves procedures and their enactment, but also develops a mind-set bent on assisting and protecting victims.

Some Final Thoughts

The Future in Past Basics

This book addresses two fundamental issues implied in its title, *The Future of Batterer Programs: Reassessing Evidence-Based Practice*. My response to the first part of the title is that the future is very much here. Within the emerging approaches, alternatives, and criticisms of batterer programs, an ongoing evolution is taking place. It is more a matter of refining and advancing the basics laid down over the years: gender-based, cognitive-behavioral approaches, accountability imposed through court oversight and sanctions, and a coordinated community response to extend batterer programs' impact and victim protections. A backdrop to this evolution has been the sense that institutional reform, community organizing, and, ultimately, social change are needed to reinforce the basics or make them happen. As a result, the context of batterer programs has changed in many cases. Collaborations have been established, and perspectives have converged. In some places, this transition unfortunately has not occurred, or is still not complete.

The second half of the book title speaks to the call for evidence-based practice that affects this program evolution. A narrow view of evidence-based practice, relying on a bottom-line interpretation of experimental evaluations, questions batterer programs' effectiveness. In the process, this view has opened the door on a variety of options that include new treatments, such as couples counseling, or tougher sentences and jailing. As I have attempted to show, a broader consideration of available research, especially from the criminal justice perspective, reveals evidence that supports the evolution of batterer programs and the basics underlying it. The direction is not merely antiscience, ideology, a feminist conspiracy, political correctness, or cultlike thinking at work, as various critics contend. This book has shown that much of the evidence for the alternatives is relatively weak, and certainly no more substantial than the evidence associated with established batterer programs. In fact, there appears to be a double standard in which critics call for rigorous evaluations and selective studies to discredit existing batterer programs, while using less rigorous and less complete research to justify their own recommendations.

The debates surrounding batterer programs are not unique, although they may be exaggerated by some extreme factions. For instance, all of the following issues have cycled through addiction and sexual assault treatment: typologies versus dimensions of offenders, community-based programming versus more medicalized treatments, accountability and supervision versus confidential therapy, and rehabilitation versus punishment and containment. More recently, these other treatment fields have also identified an unresponsive subgroup that needs special attention, and have moved toward risk management with coordinated interventions. There are, as well, debates over the length of treatment and the optimum treatment throughout social services. Victims of drunk drivers or sexual predators are demanding justice, much as battered women are. One might argue that these other treatment fields have been less affected by a critique of society at large and the backdrop of social change than has been the case with batterer programs and the domestic violence field in general. The batterer programs' origins were admittedly intertwined with the feminist movement of the late 1970s and 1980s, and the battered women's movement that resulted from that.

Some Neglected Developments

One of the underlying arguments throughout this book is that batterer programs need to be viewed in their broader context—within the intervention system of which they are a part. The argument goes further, suggesting that the most substantial way to improve batterer programs' outcomes is through a fully implemented coordinated community response. Such a response is likely to maximize accountability by activating a process that better contains unresponsive men, and better supports their partners. However, the book's review of program research neglects many other developments in the field, and in the process somewhat contradicts my appeal for a broader view.

Batterer programs, for instance, have developed sessions, modules, and separate curricula to help men who batter their female partners improve their parenting skills. Additionally, many programs are doing more to explicitly address men's sexual abuse of their partners. Custody planning, supervised visitation, and family courts are all arenas to which batterer programs are contributing as well. Furthermore, work is being done to help military veterans who bear the effects of combat and family separation, and inmates who are reentering society following long imprisonment. Some batterer programs have extended aftercare or support for program participants following their required number of sessions. As indicated earlier, the programming for women who are also violent is expanding as a supplement to the batterer programs for men.

An entirely separate volume could be written on prevention projects, such as the educational efforts of many batterer programs directed toward youth. There is, of course, a host of things going on outside the criminal justice interventions that have been the focus of this book. Those efforts, many practitioners and researchers insist, warrant more attention in order to reduce abuse and violence more broadly and to decrease the number of cases ending up in the courts. All of these are part of the future of batterer programs and are likely to affect the community in ways that make them safer. Many observers believe that prevention on a variety of levels—from the workplace to the streets—is where more programming is ultimately needed (see Tift, 1993).

In addition, this book has not specifically addressed the lingering controversies over state standards for batterer programs. There is little escaping the need for some guidelines and quality control for services that draw referrals in the public arena. However, the nature, extent, detail, and enforcement of the batterer program standards varies considerably across the forty or so states that have such standards. Most standards purportedly draw on research findings to substantiate their mandates, but overall that substantiation has been far from systematic or sufficient. Admittedly, program practices in the past have often been ahead of the research, and influenced by consumer experiences and practitioner perspectives. The evidence-based practice movement is changing that to a degree, thanks to more research and more states' attempting to incorporate that research in program recommendations. However, some states are totally reevaluating their existing standards and opening the door to a variety of alternative approaches as a result.

The research reviewed and interpreted in this book obviously supports the basic parameters that typify most batterer program standards: a gender-based, cognitive-behavioral approach, risk assessment and supplemental treatments for some batterers, court linkages that promote consistent oversight and sanctions for noncompliance, and efforts toward a coordinated community response. Some standards also specify collaboration with victim services, and documentation of service delivery and outcomes. The discussion in this book of evidence-based practice also raises cautions about misusing study bottom lines or single-study findings, and underreporting research limitations and divergent interpretations, in order to promote one position or another. In fact, the book raises an implicit challenge to dogmatic positions—both the scientific and the activist kind. A broader view on all sides is needed, as well as more discussion. This sort of expanded outlook and discussion is already very much afoot in practitioner conferences with research presentations, academic conferences with practitioners participating, and seminars and audio broadcasts with practitioners responding to researchers. I'd like to think that this book reflects—and reports—on the themes emerging in those exchanges.

More Researcher-Practitioner Collaboration

At the same time, much is at stake in the current climate of competing approaches, fiscal constraints, and vying factions. There is a chance that some programs will be identified as clear winners and losers. Some are liable to have their funding or referrals cut further under the pretense of evidence against them. Others may gain more media attention with an appearance of being more professionalized and evidence-based. A few basic recommendations stand out in this regard. These are ones that apply to the evidence-based practice movement in general, and the chance of its misuse.[1]

Batterer programs, as well as other social services, need to be more research savvy in order to respond to evidence-based claims and participate in the broader policy debates that those claims are fueling.[2] Books like this, research-oriented conferences, seminar webcasts, Internet discussion sites, and academic review articles are all sources for this. Keeping abreast of the debates amid the demands of operating and sustaining programs is obviously no easy task. Sorting through the mountains of often contradictory information can seem insurmountable. There are digests, bulletins, and newsletters that attempt to offer convenient summaries. The National Institute of Justice has posted several such bulletins for practitioners that tell at least some of the ongoing story (Klein, 2009; R. Campbell, Damiani, & Menghra, 2004; Visher, Newmark, & Harrell, 2008). Statewide committees and coalitions are also discussing and exploring many of these issues through communications of their own.

Moreover, federal agencies and foundation funders are encouraging collaboration between researchers and practitioners in evaluations. This sort of effort has been a long-standing venture, but often an awkward one due to the different audiences, requirements, and perspectives of the two spheres. It is easy to fall into a kind of detached research that collects signed agreements rather than builds broad participation. The latter is a time-consuming chore that entails establishing relationships and including practitioners in the study design, methodological development, and interpretation of findings. Practitioners need to be versed in research to make this sort of collaboration work, and researchers need to make it clear that they are attempting to develop programming rather than to judge it. Ultimately, some special training for these sorts of roles, and more practitioner-initiated evaluations, would be helpful, along with funds that directly compensate practitioners for their research involvement.

On the other side, researchers are increasingly being expected to convey their research findings in more accessible terms. The risk, of course, is oversimplifying complex results or making recommendations that go beyond the data. Clearly there is a need, as earlier chapters have pointed out, to fully disclose the limits, shortcomings, and qualifications of the research. This step helps to avert overgeneralizations and misuses of the findings. The research and academic ideal is an ongoing discourse rather than the imposition of absolutes, despite the human yearning for the latter. I would like to think that this book contributes to a broadening of that discourse rather than its narrowing. At least, that is the intent.

Notes

Chapter 1

1. The question often arises: "Why not jail batterers first and foremost?" The answer is primarily a practical one. The overcrowding of jails and prisons has led to most misdemeanor offenders being put on probation. Most of the domestic violence cases are classified as misdemeanors. The most severely violent cases are generally classified as aggravated assault, thus becoming felonies. Jail time is more likely in these cases. In the misdemeanor cases, batterer counseling becomes a preferred alternative to putting men on open probation with minimum supervision. The other concern about jailing is the issue of its effectiveness. Jailing a batterer generally ensures some short-term safety for the victim, although jailed men are known to intimidate their partners through letters, phone calls, and accomplices on the outside. There are also publicized instances of jailed men becoming even more hostile in jail, only to stalk and severely attack their partners after being released.

The one available study comparing outcomes of batterer programs to jailing shows that jail time is less effective (Babcock & Steiner, 1999). However, comparative studies of jailing and other options are difficult to implement, since the samples of those in jail versus those in the options are not equivalent. An experimental evaluation would make the samples more similar, but random assignment to jail and other options is not feasible. It is hard to justify putting one man in jail and another on probation for the same offense or circumstances. Under normal practices, the jailed samples tend to be biased toward men with more serious offenses and more severely violent pasts. These are more likely to commit new offenses because of their characteristics, regardless of the options to which they are assigned.

2. One particularly thoughtful overview of batterer programs casts their diversity as a remnant of the progressive development of batterer intervention (Mederos, 2002). Batterer intervention may be an accumulation of lessons, innovations, and circumstances that have varied over time and were launched by the awareness and challenges raised by the battered women's movement. According to this view, a first wave of programs exposed the impositions of male supremacy and compensated for the failure of social service institutions to address it. A second wave of programs developed social service

networks and community infrastructure to support batterer intervention and establish accountability as a criminal justice issue, not just a responsibility of the batterer program. A third wave of batterer programming—albeit not a self-conscious movement in itself—represents a more holistic approach that considers men's own history of victimization, mental health and substance abuse problems, parenting and fatherhood issues, and racial and class influences. Mederos concludes: "These measures will not prevent further assaultive or oppressive behavior, but they will help many of the men who are mandated to batterer intervention programs to establish their lives and thereby enhance their capacity to resist returning to or escalating violent and abusive conduct" (p. 25).

3. "Open probation" refers here to probation with minimum supervision and no additional stipulations other than to not assault one's partner again and to not be arrested for another crime. This is generally the situation for most misdemeanor cases, especially under the heavy caseloads of most probation officers.

4. The diversity of programs and their underlying themes are discussed more fully in chapter 3. The methodology of the batterer program survey, mentioned here, is also reviewed in note 1 in chapter 3.

5. "General deterrence" is the term used to describe the established consequences for an offense that apply to the population in general. The fines for speeding on the highway, for instance, are a form of general deterrence. They may or may not be applied directly to me. I may assume that I won't get caught, or that if I am, I'll beat the rap somehow. "Specific deterrence," which is considered more effective, is when the consequences apply directly to an individual and that person is made aware of that fact. An example would be a judge instructing an offender that he will be sent to jail if he does not attend a batterer program.

6. This ongoing tension between accountability and treatment is discussed further in chapter 6. According to another survey of batterer programs and the courts, interviewees from the courts overwhelmingly saw intervention into domestic violence cases as for both accountability and rehabilitation (Labriola, Rempel, O'Sullivan, & Frank, 2007). The methodology and further interpretation of that survey are found in note 9 in chapter 6.

7. Serious debate continues, however, over the effectiveness of alternative medicine. Larry Dossey (1999, 2008), for instance, has notably critiqued the research on the healing effect of prayer and posed counterevidence to the claims of ineffectiveness (for a review, see Dossey, 1999, pp. 85–118). He outlines the conceptual and methodological problems associated with much of the research in a separate article (Dossey, 2008), and even the researcher of the touted multisite study on prayer effects acknowledges the study's limitations (Krucoff, Crater, Gallup, Blankenship, Cuffe, Guarneri et al., 2005). For one thing, being told that you were to be prayed for might have elevated the fear of patients going into surgery: "I must be really bad off if they have to pray for me." There is also the challenge of obtaining a pure control group free of any prayer, given the high portion of people espousing faith-based responses to disease. A flood of the faithful have

added that the power of prayer—or, in other terms, the mind-body connection—may as yet be beyond the reach of conventional scientific measures (see, for example, R. Lawrence, 2006).

8. Positivism is a philosophy arguing that authentic knowledge is established through the observation and verification of the scientific method. In the social sciences, it is generally associated with empirical and quantitative research and with research designs that minimize research bias and subjectivity.

9. The extent of the overrides, misassignments, or exceptions to the random assignment in the Broward experiment is more complicated than with some of the other experiments. A published article on the study indicates that only 4 percent of the sample was misassigned, and that that low amount had a minimal impact on the results (Feder & Dugan, 2002). A more extensive project report to the National Institute of Justice suggested that a higher percentage of eligible cases may have been omitted from the study (Feder & Forde, 2000). The researchers elaborate on the related difficulties and resistance to the implementation of their study in another article (Feder, Jolin, & Feyerherm, 2000). A later section of this book, chapter 2's "Implementation Back Stories," discusses these broader implementation issues more fully.

10. Another practitioner clash over policy-oriented research has to do with a study of the impact of mandatory arrest on victim safety (Iyengar, 2009). The study, conducted by public health researchers from Harvard University, found an apparent association between mandatory arrest policies for domestic violence and higher homicide rates for women in states with such policies. The study's author publicly called the arrest policies into question in an opinion piece in *The New York Times* (Iyengar, 2007). Battered women advocates, however, had worked for years to establish mandatory arrest policies to help offset the police discretion that too often left batterers free to abuse again. The advocates also believed that arrests send a message to the larger community that domestic violence is considered a serious offense. Several letters to the editor expressed the advocates' concerns about the researchers' claims.

On the broader societal level, the relationship between arrest policies and homicide rates is very likely what researchers call a "spurious correlation." That is, other factors probably also contribute to the differences between states with mandatory arrest and those without the policy. Other factors like access to handguns; levels of other crime, housing density, and poverty; and the extent and nature of drug use also may affect the rates of homicide. At the ground level, focusing on mandatory arrests misses the broader intervention at work. What is done after the arrest has as much to do with the outcome as the arrest does. It is not that arrests cause more homicides, but that many of the more dangerous men fall through the cracks, so to speak, once they are arrested. The issue is how that happens, and what can be done about it.

11. Even among those programs labeled feminist or pro-feminist, there is substantial diversity. For instance, a diversity of emphasis was apparent at a symposium on long-standing batterer programs convened by the Family Violence Prevention Fund and the

National Institute of Justice in late 2009. Representatives from Men Stopping Violence in Atlanta and Volunteer Community Services in New York State argued forcefully for efforts to educate not only men but the community around them. Leaders of the Institute on Domestic Violence in the African-American Community and the National Latino Alliance for the Eliminate Domestic Violence promoted a personal transformative experience for men. Staff members from the Duluth Project emphasized the importance of linkages to the criminal justice system and other community services that reinforce men's participation in batterer groups and that position batterer programs as part of a broader intervention system. Programs like Boston's Emerge and Ann Arbor's Alternatives to Domestic Violence have worked to engage men in a process of change. This includes a more strategic approach that advances through curriculum stages, maintains clinical notes that go to the courts, and responds to individual needs such as alcohol and drug problems. AMEND (Abusive Men Exploring New Directions) in Denver and the Paths of Change men's program in Calgary, Alberta, have developed more extensive psychological and alcohol assessment and enhanced programming for men with those kinds of problems.

What these different programs have in common may be an implicit framework or underlying perspective. They all have a concern for accountability—that is, helping men to take responsibility for their behavior. But as the diversity of programs suggests, this sort of framework does not amount to a straitjacket approach to intervention or to the exclusion of various psychological advances or techniques. Certainly the programs operate at different levels of competence and sophistication. Some no doubt revert to a narrow emphasis or more simplistic approach, leaving other issues to the courts, women's services, and other community agencies. The main point of this overview is that batterer programs can hardly be characterized, praised, or denounced in singular terms. Nor can results from a few single-site evaluations be generalized to them all. Our consideration of effectiveness might, therefore, be broadened to account for this program diversity and the extended efforts that many programs represent.

Chapter 2

1. Although many social science textbooks and research reports refer to a completer versus noncompleter comparison as a quasi-experimental design, others considered it to be nonexperimental. Some researchers consider this frequently used and somewhat convenient comparison to be quasi-experimental because the noncompleters offer some semblance of a control group. The noncompleters have similar characteristics or circumstances to those who complete the program. Additionally, the completers make up an experimental group that receives the treatment in full. This group excludes dropouts, who are incorporated into the treatment groups of many of the experimental evaluations. However, those who view this sort of comparison as nonexperimental argue that the dropouts are not a quasi-control since they actually received some treatment. Quasi-

control groups are more appropriately those who have no treatment contact, such as individuals on a waiting list or offenders or other potential clients who were not referred to the program. The distinction may also reflect whether the goal is to test "intention to treat" or "treatment received"—a matter discussed below in this chapter.

2. A few other experimental evaluations have previously been conducted, but these have more obvious limitations than the later ones. Because of their lesser scientific rigor, they have generally not been included in the meta-analyses of batterer programs. The first of these was a study in Baltimore that randomly assigned arrested batterers to a three-month batterer program and to probation, or to a suspended sentence, without a batterer program ($N = 193$) (Harrell, 1991). The assignment was not truly random since it was based on the discretion and preference of the judges, which was presumed to be random at the time. There also remains some question as to whether the particular program used in the study was somewhat faulty. It was short in duration, a bit disorganized, and had high dropout rates. Moreover, the counseling approach in the program was not representative of the prevailing approach across the country at that time. On several outcome indicators in a six-month follow-up, the batterer program group did no better than those offenders not assigned to a group.

Another study, the Ontario Experiment (Palmer, Brown, & Barerra, 1992), found a significantly lower rate of police reports of physical abuse among those assigned to the batterer program in comparison to the control group (10 percent versus 31 percent). However, the study had a small sample ($N = 59$), and there were questions about the representativeness of that sample.

An Indianapolis experiment randomly assigned subjects to one of three conditions: a sentence to a batterer program; a sentence to probation and a batterer program; or a control condition that went through adjudication but was not sentenced to probation or a batterer program ($N = 347$) (Ford & Regoli, 1993). There was no significant difference in the rate of new assaults reported by their partners (31 percent response rate) in any of the three groups in a six-month follow-up. The authors concluded: "The point, then, is that *any* intervention helps, not necessarily counseling" (p. 157). However, this study was embedded in a broader evaluation of prosecution procedures and sentencing options, specifically "no drop" policies for the cases (that is, the victim cannot have the case dismissed by refusing to press charges or testify). The complicated context of the program assignment makes the results difficult to interpret, and the type and duration of the programs were not specified.

3. A nonexperimental study of subsequent arrests of domestic violence offenders has also been used to question the effectiveness of batterer programs and intervention in general. Klein and Tobin (2008) compiled the arrest rates of 324 offenders over a decade in Quincy, Massachusetts, and found that the majority (60 percent) subsequently abused family members, and almost three-fourths were arrested for subsequent domestic abuse or nondomestic abuse. The authors imply that intervention, including batterer programs, appears to be failing. Short-term follow-ups that suggest lower rates of subse-

quent offenses are likely to be misleading: according to the authors, those rates increase dramatically over time.

The authors acknowledge several limitations of their study—a main one being that the subjects included all of the men brought to court for the first time in 1995–1996. Thus the study includes men whose cases were dismissed; who were incarcerated, put on open probation, or sent to treatment; and who did not comply with sentencing or referrals. It is also not clear what the court response was to any subsequent offense. What we may have, then, is not so much the failure of a particular intervention, but failure to implement consistent and sufficient intervention overall. The Quincy results also reinforce batterer program studies showing that a substantial portion of repeatedly violent men need to be identified and contained early on.

Moreover, the Quincy re-arrest rates clash with those from the multisite study of batterer programs that I led (Gondolf, 2002a). Over our four-year follow-up, only 11 percent of the men mandated to attend a batterer program were re-arrested. That rate includes both men who completed the program and those who dropped out. The four-year rate would have to increase sixfold in the following six years to reach the rate for domestic violence re-arrests in the Quincy study. One explanation, which the Quincy authors concede, is that many of their subjects may not have actually participated in a batterer program. We also don't know the nature of the programs available to their subjects, nor what reinforcement of the programs came from the courts and other services. The Quincy results may, in fact, show that high rates of subsequent offenses are likely when sentencing and services are disjointed and inconsistently applied. In sum, no conclusion about the effectiveness of batterer programs or other specific interventions can be drawn from the Quincy study.

4. The distinction between "intention to treat" and "treatment received" is related to the concepts of "efficacy" and "effectiveness" in psychotherapy research (Nathan, Stuart, & Dolan, 2000). Research on efficacy involves outcome assessments under conditions of high internal validity best achieved in experimental evaluations, which are more likely to represent "intention to treat." Research on effectiveness has high external validity—that is, it considers more fully what actually happens. Studies in the former group not only rely on random assignment but also on monitored treatments that strictly follow a manual. Effectiveness research aims to determine a treatment's feasibility with a wide range of clients in real-world settings. These studies may still use randomization to develop a control group, but they are concerned about the exclusion of clients and the disruption of treatment that may result. Clinicians tend to see the latter type of research as more relevant and realistic. The debate, according to a recent review, is over how best to combine features of the two types (Nathan, Stuart, & Dolan, 2000).

5. A few states, such as Maryland and Texas, require batterer programs to collect standard data and submit a summary to a state coalition of programs or oversight committee. The data are also used to develop reports of program activity and developments statewide. Such standardized data collection offers a foundation for multisite evalua-

tions and comparisons. Maryland has been working on launching some comparative and possibly experimental studies across some of its program sites.

6. We modified our research design into a quasi-experimental approach, as a result. We derived three comparison samples through implementing the mental health referral in phases (Gondolf, 2009b). A quasi-control group was established by first referring the men who screened positive on a voluntary basis; very few sought an evaluation ($n = 182$). Next, there was a transition phase in which referral under a court mandate was partially implemented ($n = 149$), and finally, a subsample of the men who were mandated by the court to seek a mental health evaluation ($n = 148$). This later group was under the fully mandated referral system supervised by a case manager and system coordinator. As it turns out, this approach enabled us also to study the impact of implementation and the barriers associated with it (Gondolf, 2009a).

7. The authors also identify the factors most associated with the variation in implementation: community factors, provider characteristics, treatment stability, organizational capacity, training and technical assistance, and the relationship among the factors. Previous reviews have also identified shared decision making, diffused leadership, insufficient administrator support or attention, and broad coordinated infrastructures as factors that may negatively influence experimental implementation (Durlak & Dupree, 2008).

8. Meta-analyses statistically summarize the magnitude of the effect attributable to the group of programs considered in the analyses. Jacob Cohen (1988) developed statistical calculations for effect size as an alternative to the dependence on and misuse of p values. Cohen's d measures an effect's size as a standard deviation unit difference between treated and control groups, with weighted adjustment for study sample size. In the case of batterer programs, the statistic for effect size considers the difference in subsequent assault rates between the program and the control or quasi-control group, adjusted for the sample size. According to Cohen (1988), effect sizes of 0.20 or less are considered small, 0.50 are considered medium, and 0.80 or above are considered large.

9. In his discussion of statistical inference in meta-analysis, Berk (2007) raises questions about the credibility of confidence intervals in meta-analyses in general.

10. For a detailed summary of the available meta-analyses and their limitations, see C. Murphy & Ting, 2010.

11. The Cochrane Collaboration is a group of over 27,000 volunteers in more than ninety countries who review the effects of health care interventions tested in biomedical randomized controlled trials. The results of these systematic reviews are published as Cochrane Reviews in the Cochrane Library. The Cochrane Collaboration was founded in 1993 in response to Dr. Archie Cochrane's call for up-to-date, systematic reviews of all relevant randomized controlled trials of health care. As a founder of the application of randomized clinical trials, Cochrane established systematic reviews of controlled trials for pregnancy and childbirth care and urged that reviews be conducted and applied more widely. The Research and Development Programme in the United Kingdom promotes and funds this approach for the United Kingdom's National Health Service.

12. To rate the scientific rigor of the evaluation studies, Shannon Morrison and colleagues relied on a guide previously used in the public health field: *Guide to Community Preventive Services: Systematic Reviews and Evidence-Based Recommendations* (Briss et al., 2000; Zaza et al., 2000).

13. Instrumental variable analysis attempts to increase the validity of causal inferences of the effect of the intervention on outcomes by controlling for the bias introduced by potential omitted variables. Instrumental variable estimation seeks to identify a variable or variables that help to isolate the primary predictor's (the program's or intervention's) influence on the outcome (Angrist, 2006; Angrist, Imbens, and Rubin, 1996; Apel, Bushway, Paternoster, Brame, & Sweeten, 2008; Kelejian, 1971; Jones & Gondolf, 2002; Levitt, & Miles, 2006). Instrumental variables have no direct influence on the outcome but have a strong relationship to the predictor variable and therefore are not contaminated by the confounding variables. This approach ensures that the association observed between the intervention and the dependent variable is not due to any other undetected or unmeasured variables. Thus instrumental variable analysis strengthens the causal inference between the intervention and outcome.

14. Regression analysis is sometimes used with experimental data to examine the treatment-received effect. The main problem with simple regressions is that the characteristics used as controls in the equation predict dropout as well as the outcome (subsequent assault, in this case). Yet dropout is entered as the predictor indicating "treatment received." Regression analysis also inevitably overlooks unmeasured characteristics, especially the key factor of motivation. Statisticians therefore often consider simple regression analysis to be naïve and prefer more sophisticated statistical modeling.

15. To examine the influence of referral source (voluntary versus court mandate), we computed regression equations for re-assault that controlled for subject background characteristics, including demographics, prior abusive behavior, criminal history, alcohol abuse, and mental health problems. Men who were voluntary referrals, without court obligations and oversight, were much more likely to commit subsequent assaults during the follow-up. It would appear that the court oversight rather than different characteristics accounted for the difference in the outcomes.

16. Here is a technical description of the statistical approaches involved. There are two possible specifications in an instrumental variable (IV) analysis: full information maximum likelihood (FIML) and two-stage specifications. The FIML specification provides estimates that are more efficient (that is, they have a smaller variance), while the two-stage specification does not require an assumption about the joint distribution of the two outcomes. Both results are presented in order to give the reader a sense of the range of estimates obtained from both specifications. As sample size increases, estimates from both specifications should converge around the true value of the completion effect on re-assault.

In the FIML specification, a bivariate probit model is used to estimate the completion and re-assault outcomes. The bivariate probit model uses a bivariate normal density function since both completion and re-assault are binary ("yes" or "no"). The joint likelihood of the two outcomes is maximized, and standard errors are corrected for correlation between the error terms in the two equations. This specification also provides an estimate of the correlation between the two equations. In the two-stage probit specification, a probit regression of program completion is computed in the first stage. The predicted value of the dependent variable from this regression is then used as a predictor in the second stage re-assault probit regression. Use of a predicted variable as a predictor produces incorrect standard errors; the standard errors are, therefore, corrected using a bootstrap approximation.

The coefficients from the two IV probit regressions are not directly comparable. In order to make them comparable, we calculated the marginal effects for the variable of interest: program completion. (The calculation uses dF/dx, which is the total derivative of the normal cumulative density function with respect to a unit change in program completion.) This transformation makes it easier to compare differences in the magnitude of the effects since all effects are, as a result, expressed in the same units. The marginal effects serve much the same purpose as Cohen's h, which is frequently used in naïve assessments of effect size.

17. Larry Bennett and his colleagues (2007) also used instrumental variable analysis in their study of batterer programs in the state of Illinois. They attempted to reduce the confounding variables between the related behavior of program completion and not committing subsequent offenses versus dropping out and offending again. The "instrument" they used was a composite variable based on demographic factors including the program's percentage of African American participants, the participants' marital and employment status, and whether the participants spoke English, because they found these variables to be correlated with program completion but not with re-arrest ($p > 0.10$). However, this relationship is admittedly unlikely to be stable, because other studies have found a higher likelihood of committing repeat offenses among those who are unemployed and unmarried, and otherwise have a low stake in conformity (Puffett & Gavin, 2004; Labriola, Rempel & Davis, 2005; Feder & Dugan, 2002).

18. A substantial portion of the men received some dose of the program even if they dropped out. Only 27 percent of the dropouts did not attend any counseling sessions, and nearly half (47 percent) attended more than three sessions. One fifth (22 percent) of the dropouts from the nine-month program attended the program for more than three months, the minimum requirement of the shortest program.

19. From his analysis of clinical studies and community surveys, Michael Johnson (2008) identifies four types of intimate partner violence: intimate terrorism, violent resistance, situational couples violence, and mutual violent control. These categories have been particular useful in interpreting the contradictory findings from clinical studies and community surveys. There are limitations to the typology, nonetheless (see Zorza, 2011). Johnson acknowledges one that is particularly relevant here: Situational couples violence is very diverse in terms of causes, such as alcohol abuse or impulsive outbursts,

and severity of the violence. This type of violence may still be injurious and harmful. It also can escalate into intimate terrorism and have undetected aspects of control.

20. Our studies at many different courts appear to substantiate the asymmetry of the violence in terms of gender. Based on the victims' reports, the men's violence has spanned an average of three years and involved severe tactics beyond slaps, pushes, and shoves. About 25 percent of the women partners were also arrested for domestic violence charges, but in the vast majority of these cases, the man was the primary perpetrator, and, depending on the circumstances, the woman was sent to separate services to address her use of force. Only about 5 percent of the total domestic violence incidents studied in one court were perpetrated primarily or exclusively by the woman. Moreover, 60 percent of the women who reported having been physically aggressive or violent had been so out of self-defense. They also were the most likely to have contacted services and interventions in response to the men's violence. The women who were reportedly violent conformed, therefore, to Michael Johnson's (2008) "violent resistance" rather than "mutual combat."

Donald Dutton, however, has claimed that our research indicates that 40 percent of the women hit their partners first. He uses that interpretation as an indication that participants in batterer programs are involved in a kind of mutual combat that warrants a different approach. We are not sure how he derived this percentage. The citation that Dutton uses as his source does not appear to say this. The reference to the women's violence in the citation is a summary of what the men said at program intake about their partner's past response to them. The majority of the men say that their partner was aggressive, using anything from a push or slap to a weapon during their relationship. Women report a much lower level of their violence as indicated in the text here, and they also overwhelmingly gave reasons of self-defense or fear (Gondolf, 1998b).

In addition, very few men reported any kind of injury or impact, whereas 70 percent of the women had been at least bruised, and a third had received medical attention for their partner's violence (Gondolf, 1998b). The vast majority (83 percent) of women who did report aggression toward their partners had been the target of "severe" violence, and a quarter reported being "beat up." Moreover, our comparison of the men's and women's self-reports and the police records of the arrests found the men's reports of women's violence to be inflated and their own minimized, in comparison to the women's and police reports at intake (Heckert & Gondolf, 2000a, 2000c). The discrepancies were minimal on other variables, and the violence discrepancies decreased during the follow-up period. Our interpretation was that the men's reports at intake of the women's violence were inflated largely as a justification at their arrest and entry into the program.

21. In 2010, a series of articles appeared in major newspapers from Boston to Dallas, criticizing batterer programs as ideological and dismissing them as ineffective. The series was largely based on the antifeminist position that women were as violent as men and that intervention, programming, and policy needed to be revamped as a result. One of the proponents of this view, who also heads a men's right organization, was interviewed on National Public Radio.

22. Sherry Hamby (2009) reviews the research on men's and women's violence and acknowledges the wide range in estimates of women's violence in the general population. She poses a "moderate asymmetry," with men's violence against women being the most extensive and extended particularly by sexual assault and abuse. She recommends several measurement modifications that would help to bring the opposing schools of thought on women's violence closer together.

23. The level of knowledge is likely to have increased in the last few years, with more practitioner conferences including updates on the evaluation research and the debates around it.

24. The website, called Aquila, is maintained by the Batterer Intervention Services Coalition of Michigan (see www.biscmi.org/aquila/).

25. The conferences were "Shifting the Paradigm: Strategies for Addressing Batterers as Fathers," sponsored by the Batterer Intervention Services Coalition of Michigan, in Traverse City, Michigan, September 17–19, 2008; and "Bridging Perspectives: Interventions with Men Who Batter," sponsored by the Domestic Abuse Project, in Minneapolis, Minnesota, May 12–15, 2009.

26. Information and updates on the study are available at the Respect website (www.respect.UK.net/pages/evaluation-project.html).

Chapter 3

1. The study results are not likely to be representative of batterer programs in operation, as the researchers readily note. Not only was there a very low response rate from the known programs, but the responding programs were disproportionately concentrated in several states (Price & Rosenbaum, 2009). Over one-third of the programs identified through a number of databases on domestic violence programs were not available at the indicated addresses and may no longer have been in operation. Despite the interest in batterer programs over the last couple of decades, there is no centralized, updated, or complete listing of the programs. Moreover, the survey was administered over the Internet after each program was contacted by phone or e-mail. It is not clear who actually completed the survey for each program, whether that person reflected the program as a whole, and whether there were variations of opinions within a program. As the researchers point out, the results must therefore be considered exploratory, but they represent some indication of batterer programs and are the best information we have so far.

2. I discuss other considerations influencing program approach in the next chapter: neurobiology (Cellini, 2004), gender-neutral interactions (Hamel & Nicholls, 2006), motivational interviewing (C. Murphy & Maiuro, 2009), cultural sensitivity (Perilla & Perez, 2002; O. Williams, 1998). Furthermore, a few recent books promote alternative formats such as individual (C. Murphy & Eckhardt, 2005), couples (McCollum & Stith, 2008), couple groups (Mills, 2009), and client-centered treatments (Stosny, 1995), along

with educational approaches (Sinclair, 1989). These formats contrast to the all-male discussion groups that typify conventional batterer programs, regardless of counseling approach or modality.

3. The study identified 200 of the most-cited authors of research associated with domestic violence (intimate partner violence, sexual assault, psychological abuse, and stalking) during the period 2003–2007. Psychologists accounted for 64 percent of the authors (n = 98 of the 154 authors); an additional 19 authors were psychiatrists. The psychologists published 49 percent of the 584 articles (n = 289) and accounted for 40 percent of the 4,665 citations (n = 1,883). The researcher concluded: "Psychology is by far the most commonly cited discipline in the field of violence against women. Psychiatry, nursing, and medicine were the next most common . . . This analysis reveals that the biomedical and psychological bibliometric databases have experienced the greatest growth in literature volume during the past decades, whereas the sociological, social work, and legal literatures have leveled off or declined" (Jordan, 2009, p. 408).

4. Clatterbaugh (1997) and others (Bowker, 1998; Messner, 1997) have reviewed and critiqued this movement with some concern. Rather than a monolithic movement, they see several strands that include the mytho-poetic, personal development, fathers' rights, and gay rights themes. The strands also vary from self-help or personal growth to an activist social-change orientation. Although the collection of themes has generally been a response to the confining sex roles publicized by the feminist movement, the men's movement has also faced criticism for what some consider a backlash against the women's movement. Some of the men's movement appears to be about reclaiming rights and attention from women and drawing concern to men's emotional needs rather than those of others (Hagan & Steinem, 1992).

5. The distinction has a long history in the study of aggression and is often referred to as hostile versus instrumental aggression, or automatic versus controlled aggression (Berkowitz, 1969, 1993).

6. Some clinicians speak in terms of the more familiar, clear-cut, and established borderline disorder rather than attachment disorder. They are not necessarily the same but do overlap considerably in symptoms and origins (Mauricio, Tein, & Lopez, 2007). Attachment disorders have been diagnosed in children more frequently than in adults. The Mayo Clinic staff summarizes the disorder as "an emotional disorder that causes emotional instability, leading to stress and other problems" and describes its symptoms as follows: "You often have an insecure sense of who you are. That is, your self-image or sense of self often rapidly changes . . . An unstable self-image often leads to frequent changes in jobs, friendships, goals and values. Your relationships are usually in turmoil. You often experience a love-hate relationship with others. You may idealize someone one moment and then abruptly and dramatically shift to fury and hate over perceived slights or even minor misunderstandings. This is because people with the disorder often have difficulty accepting gray areas—things seem to be either black or white" (retrieved May 16, 2011, from www.mayoclinic.com/health/borderline-personality-disorder/DS00442).

7. The televised series of discussions among brain scientists makes it plain that the science is still in its infant stages, and that it is likely to be another ten years or more before its discoveries can be applied in the field (Rose, 2009).

8. See http://en.wikipedia.org/wiki/Cognitive_restructuring.

9. However, the cognitive-behavioral approach may be subject to more misuse because of this assumption. Inexperienced and unqualified staff members can too easily turn it into a rigid directive or a superficial set of exercises. It's not meant to be a mechanical or by-rote type of instruction.

10. This issue of responding to program participants and furthering the group process is discussed in a recent review of the research on group process with criminal offenders in general (Marshall & Burton, 2010). The review highlights the importance of the delivery of treatment beyond skills and technique—although those are important, too. An overdependence on manuals tends to reduce responsiveness to group participants, which—according to the review—has been shown to reduce effectiveness. Therefore the authors recommend that training for group leaders emphasize the importance of delivery in terms of three essential components: characteristics of the therapist (particularly empathy, warmth, and support), the quality of the therapeutic alliance (the effort everyone makes to work together), and the nature of the group climate (the cohesiveness of the group and the level of group expressiveness). According to the research, all of these components are significantly related to the positive benefits that result from treatment. The authors of the review characterize this emphasis on group process as "positive psychology" (p. 145), which is primarily cognitive behavioral in approach but which integrates aspects of motivational interviewing and psychotherapy. (Motivational interviewing is discussed in the next chapter.)

Chapter 4

1. This distinction reflects that of Neil Jacobson and John Gottman (1998), who popularized the batterer categories of "pit bulls" and "cobras." They based their categorization on laboratory studies of couples engaged in an argument. The men who tended to respond angrily showed corresponding physiological responses that made them "pit bulls." "Their emotions quickly boil over," according to the researchers (p. 29). The more restrained men who struck back somewhat unexpectedly also had confirmed physiological cues that led to their label as "cobras." They are "cool and methodological as they inflict pain and humiliation" (p. 30). The study faced some challenges when attempts at replication were not successful (Babcock, Green, Webb, & Graham, 2004; Meehan, Holtzworth-Munroe, & Herron, 2001).

2. Critics have also pointed out the influence of the analytical technique on the persistent formulation of types (Gondolf, 2002a; Saunders, 2004). Specifically, cluster analysis has been used to sort the personality and violence variables into categories. This approach by design produces some groupings, but these are often difficult to interpret,

generally unstable, and subject to interpretation (Aldenderfer & Blashfield, 1984). Clustering is best used as an exploratory tool, which admittedly can hide the dimensionality or complexity of the characteristics. Our analysis of MCMI-III results in our multisite study instead grouped subjects based on their profiles (that is, the pattern of elevated subscales for each case), as recommended by the originators of the MCMI-III (White & Gondolf, 2000).

3. According to the researchers, the findings are limited by the small subsamples that resulted from the attrition of subjects during the study. Only ninety-six men were distributed over the three types for most of the outcome variables.

4. There was an association between batterer type and arrest.

5. Despite the decisive evidence from the "largest randomized clinical trial of psychosocial treatments ever undertaken that took nearly a decade to complete," debate over patient matching continues (Longabaugh, 2003, p. 8). It could be that the theory or methods were inadequate to capture matching effects. But the field has largely endorsed responding primarily to addiction severity and compounding dual diagnoses. There continue to be interesting sidelights in terms of matching, such as the interaction of patient anger and therapist directiveness. Therapists who are less directive with angry patients show better alcohol outcomes, regardless of approach (Karno & Longabaugh, 2004, $N = 140$). Several mismatches on a number of criteria are associated with less favorable outcomes, but "matches, on the other hand, while beneficial, may not be necessary to achieve good outcomes" (Karno & Longabaugh, 2007, p. 587).

6. "Therapeutic alliance" has become a popular concept in psychotherapy. With responses that are tailored to participants' motivation and readiness, therapists are able to increase rapport, cooperation, and responsiveness in a client. A few studies with batterer programs have begun to explore the relationships of readiness to alliance, and of alliance to outcomes (Taft, Murphy, King, Musser, & DeDeyn, 2003; Taft, Murphy, Musser, & Remington, 2004). The first of these did find an association of interest. However, reviews of alliance research in general note the difficulty in relating process variables to outcome, and the especially small effect sizes for alliance variables (Saketopoulou, 1999).

7. The results of the follow-up have yet to be published and are available only at the authors' website (www.prochange.com/domestic-violence). Further findings may be forthcoming and publishable.

8. According to a review of state standards for batterer programs, 68 percent of the forty-four states with standards prohibit couples treatment for domestic violence, at least in cases referred from the courts (Maiuro & Eberle, 2008).

9. The often-cited experimental evaluation of the Families and Addiction Program in Boston and Buffalo is actually of substance-abusing couples who also report physical aggression ($N = 80$) (Fals-Stewart, Kashdan, O'Farrell, & Bircher, 2002). This program also has extensive screening and uses a behavioral approach to treatment. The comparison in this study, however, was with individual treatment that was shown to be less effective. The study may be a sign of the effectiveness of couples treatment with substance-

abusing couples, or a rejection of individual counseling. Some of the effect may be attributable to the accountability taken by the women and the careful monitoring offered by the staff in the couples group. In either case, we are left with an even more exceptional group than the subjects of an alcohol treatment program, and the outcomes for this group have yet to be compared to those for participants in batterer programs using an experimental evaluation.

10. Not only is the sample exceptional from the start, as a result of the strict inclusion criteria, but it ends up extremely small as a result of attrition in the follow-up period. This makes it very difficult to generalize beyond the study and puts the findings themselves in question.

11. In the conclusion of the couples study report, the researchers compare their re-assault outcomes to those in our multisite evaluation of batterer programs. The authors claim that their lower levels of re-assault further endorse the utility of the couples approach. Yet there is no direct comparison. Even if there were, it is a case of apples and oranges: the batterer program participants are much more violent, the women are in more danger, and the men are all coerced by the courts into the batterer programs. Also, the outcome follow-up procedures and measures are different and probably produce different levels of disclosure. Our rates also include both men who completed their program and those who dropped out, while the couples study includes only a highly selective sample of those who completed counseling.

The authors also make the claim that the small sample reinforces the statistically significant differences in favor of the group couples counseling, and of both couples approaches over the comparison group. The opposite argument could be made with such an exceptional sample. The significance applies only to those in the highly selective sample, and the results could be shifted with only one or two couples reporting a different outcome. The actual effect size would be negligible because of the small sample size, as well. Moreover, while the examined characteristics of the subsamples are similar, characteristics of the respective follow-up respondents may differ.

12. A 2008 dissertation compared batterer program participants who were ethnically matched to their group leader to those who were not ($N = 309$) and similarly found no significant differences in the self-reported anger and aggression levels at the end of the program, which lasted ten to twelve months (D. Murphy, 2008).

13. The rate for domestic violence re-arrests in the culturally focused groups was 15 percent; in the racially mixed groups, it was 7 percent. Our research team was not sure what to make of this difference, given the small base rate of re-arrests, the inconsistencies in offense classifications, and the broad category of "domestic violence" arrests. In other words, we had questions about the reliability of the re-arrest data. We speculate that the racially mixed counseling tended to present the consequences of domestic violence more directly and emphatically. As a result, the men in those groups may have been more aware that re-arrest was likely for abusive incidents—and they wanted to avoid arrest even if they were abusive.

14. Reviewers of our initial report on the culturally focused counseling study raised a concern in this regard. They noted that the specific cultural factors that are associated with dropping out and committing new assaults need to be identified. Then treatment components to respond to those specific factors should be developed and tested. As it stands now, the notion of a single African American culture is too broad, and the components of the culturally focused curriculum may not be related to outcomes.

15. Dialectical behavioral therapy has developed techniques for emotional regulation within a cognitive-behavioral approach and has been applied particularly to individuals exhibiting tendencies toward borderline personality disorder (Fruzzetti, 2000). A review of this therapy for abusive behavior shows why its techniques may be useful to some batterers, but acknowledges that there are no controlled outcome studies with batterers to demonstrate the therapy's effectiveness compared to other approaches (Waltz, 2003).

Chapter 5

1. This information comes from a tabulation of the state standards and guidelines posted on the website of the Batterer Intervention Services Coalition of Michigan (www .biscmi.org). The twelve states without standards posted there either do not have any (some states have guidelines and recommendations instead of standards) or had not submitted them to the coalition at the time of the tabulation. Forty-five states reportedly now have standards.

2. For instance, domestic violence workers in a western state called me, greatly concerned about risk assessment administered by the probation department. Cutoff scores on two instruments were being used to send men to a longer or shorter duration of batterer programming, with no input from domestic violence workers or consideration of the limits of the assessment. Even after three different trainings from domestic violence researchers, the practice continued with assertions that it was "evidence-based."

3. A review of the dozens of risk assessment studies with criminals in general raises a series of cautions and concerns about the conception and validation of the instruments and the way they are being used (Baird, 2009). The review, a report to the National Council on Crime and Delinquency, contends: "The justice field needs to step back and carefully review both the logic and the level of evidence supporting many current assessment practices" (p. 10). In particular, it questions the overuse of correlation coefficients of risk factors, analysis of correct classification (resulting in false positives and false negatives), and other measures of association in developing risk assessment because "they fail to convey how well a risk model can inform actual case decisions" (p. 11). In other words, the usefulness of a risk assessment can't be separated from how it can and will be used.

4. The use by police of risk assessment tools adds more immediate and reliable information based largely on direct observation. This sort of assessment can help police in their decision making about a case and their reporting on the case to the court. It gives

the court, probation officers, and social services a fuller picture of the risk, as well as some initial direction in responding to it. The main question is how willing are the police to take on the extra procedure, and how amendable are they to doing what they sometimes perceive as a social work task instead of law enforcement. Of course, police may perceive that doing risk assessment makes their job easier in the long run. For example, they may not have to return to a particular home as frequently because the violence was more comprehensively addressed in response to their risk assessment.

5. I have received several reports from domestic violence services around the country complaining of probation departments that interpret the LSI-R and a domestic violence assessment pretty much by the book. A combination of cutoff scores is used to send a man to one batterer program or another, and to set the number of required sessions. The batterer program staff and victims' advocates often have different observations and consequently varying recommendations in some cases. They feel that their training and experience enables them to offer additional insights that the instruments and the probation interpretations sometimes miss. The probation departments, however, feel that their evidence-based approach is sufficient and superior. They appear to miss some of the limitations of the instruments and the cautions that accompany them. Working out further collaborations for assessment interpretation and treatment recommendations is a warranted part of risk management. At a minimum, consulting with domestic violence services seems essential, and having women's services do the assessment and recommendations may be advantageous. The sense that the research evidence somehow endorses one instrument over another, or a pat set of interpretations based on cutoff scores, is unfounded.

6. "Repeated re-assault" refers to the cases in which a man physically struck his partner more than once during the follow-up period. Repeated re-assault accounted for the vast majority of those women who were physically injured in some way (from a bruise to hospitalization), and the men who were clearly unresponsive to intervention.

7. The prediction was also analyzed in terms of Receiver Operating Curves (ROC scores), which is an indication of the predictive strength of an instrument overall. The Area Under the Curve (AUC) considers both false positives and false negatives at various points of the scoring. The highest AUC was 0.83 (out of a possible 1.0) for a combination of risk factors and the women's perceptions. AUC for the DA and women's perceptions together was 0.73, and the DA alone was 0.64.

It must be emphasized that the instruments used in the study were merely simulations of the actual risk instruments. Our measures using the women's reports do not necessarily give the same scores as the actual instruments would, nor are all the instruments' items covered by our available data. Moreover, the SARA in particular relies on ratings by a professional rather than a response level reported by the woman, as used in our simulation. Interestingly, the ROC scores and sensitivity in our analysis are lower than but fairly similar to what was found with the actual instruments in other studies.

8. In our study, a substantial portion of the women's predictions still ended up as false negatives—that is, their partners re-assaulted them even though the women predicted

otherwise. These cases may be attributed in part to the very simplistic prediction we imposed on the women. They were simply asked over the phone, at the time of batterer program intake, to rate the likelihood of re-assault in the next few months, and also how safe they felt. However, De Becker (1997) talks of a process of denying one's intuitions, and other researchers have identified what they call an "optimistic bias" (Martin et al., 2000). Knowing more about these processes could help identify and correct mistaken predictions or misperceptions. In any case, caution is warranted about relying too heavily on women's perceptions and assessments alone.

9. Jones used the analytical technique of general estimating equations to compile the predictions for each of the three-month intervals over a fifteen-month period. This approach contrasts to the commonly used cumulative outcomes of any re-assault during an extended follow-up period. Unfortunately, several of the key time-varying factors, such as shelter contact and alcohol treatment, did not account for the nature and extent of the service or compliance with it—only contact with it. This may account for the factors' relatively weak improvement of the re-assault prediction.

10. There are three major approaches to identifying lethality that are also represented in research on domestic homicides: analysis of criminal justice data on homicides, or data collected about murder victims; in-depth case studies of imprisoned murderers or attempted murderers; and panel reviews of individual homicide cases. The first approach has focused particularly on the characteristics and circumstances associated with reported homicide cases, while the second has identified types of murderers or scenarios of murders. The third has exposed gaps or breakdowns in the criminal justice system whose repair would improve intervention and prevention.

11. Another approach to improving the management of homicide risk is the use of fatality review panels, which have been developed in several cities across the country—most notably in the DVERT program (Domestic Violence Enhanced Response Team) of Colorado Springs, Colorado (Watt, 2007; Websdale, 1999; J. Wilson & Websdale, 2006). These panels have been promoted by the National Domestic Violence Fatality Review Initiative, funded by the Department of Justice. The object of the panels is to identify the failures of intervention that contributed to a particular homicide and identify improvements that will reduce the number of such homicides in the future. Are there responses that the police, battered women's shelter, batterer program, courts, or hospital could have made that would have prevented the homicide under review?

A team of representatives from community agencies meet to discuss a recent homicide case in detail, draw from it procedures that need improvement, and develop a strategy for implementing improvements. As a recent qualitative study of a fatality review panel indicates, the review panels have problems of their own (Watt & Allen, 2008). There is a tendency for representatives to be defensive and avoid blame. But under the right conditions, review panels have been very useful in improving the response to potentially lethal cases. The reviews of single cases at a time, however, are less about developing risk assessments that can be generalized to a variety of cases, and more about identifying breakdowns in the intervention system and finding ways to fix them. It is really a means for enhancing a community's coordinated response.

12. The way in which risk is presented can have an effect on practitioners' response to a case. For instance, a series of studies in psychiatric hospitals shows that clinicians are more likely to hospitalize a violent patient when risk is presented in frequency format ("20 out of 100 patients") rather than probability ("20 percent likely") (Slovic, Monahan, & MacGregor, 2000).

13. For example, one of the research assistants in our multisite study analyzed 380 guided ratings by batterer program staff and found relatively weak predictions of re-assault overall (Gondolf & Wernik, 2009). The ratings consisted of ten items that reflect the behavioral criteria used by domestic violence workers in making judgments about treatment success. Analyses with both logistic regressions and ROC scores showed the sum of the clinician's ratings to be a significant predictor of especially severe re-assaults over a long follow-up period, as opposed to any re-assault in shorter or longer periods. But the association was very weak. Analyses of the individual items and the determinants of the ratings revealed "compliance with required attendance" and "techniques for avoiding abuse" to be the strongest predictors. Participant motivation, represented by these items, may underlie the ratings. The overall weak prediction, however, reinforces the limitations of program staff observations alone and the need to augment them with additional information.

14. See the Travis County Impact Supervision Initiative website (www.co.travis.tx.us/community_supervision/tcis_initiative.asp) for related articles and reports.

Chapter 6

1. A description of one example of this approach can be found at the website of the Allegheny County Coalition for Recovery, which works with developmentally disabled adults (www.coalitionforrecovery.org/index.html). We have been conducting an evaluation of a training program that intends to establish this sort of approach in case management in two rural counties in western Pennsylvania (Gondolf, 2011). Part of the motivation is to make the case management more efficient and less custodial. But a previous implementation of the training and approach in Pittsburgh also showed fewer hospitalizations and more independent living as a result.

2. The coordinated community response developed for St. Paul, Minnesota, outlined a similar set of components and what were essentially objectives: "The Blueprint uses interagency policies, protocols, case processing procedures, and information sharing to (a) maximize the ability of the state to gain a measure of control over a domestic violence offender; (b) use that control to intervene quickly when there are new acts of violence, intimidation or coercion; and (c) shift the burden of holding the offender accountable for violence or abuse from the *victim* to the *system*" (Pence & Eng, 2009, p. 7).

3. The program completion rate was a very high 75 percent, and the overall re-arrest

rate was 14.3 percent for completers and 34.6 percent for noncompleters over the follow-up period, which lasted approximately two and a half years.

4. The comparison of programs with different lengths in the multisite study has raised questions about the ideal length for batterer programs. The impact of program length has not been investigated in an experimental way—that is, by randomly assigning men to programs of different length. One study in New York City did compare the outcomes of men sent by the court's discretion to a twelve-week cognitive-behavioral therapeutic program with those sent to a twenty-six-week Duluth-type program ($N = 291$) (Cissner & Puffett, 2006). A little over a quarter of the men (28 percent) were sent to the shorter program, the rest to the longer one (72 percent), and the two groups' completion and re-arrest rates were compared. According to the researchers, "the results of this study indicate that program length and underlying program philosophy have little impact on participants' outcomes. Although defendants assigned to the longer, more rigorous program are somewhat less likely to have a new criminal contempt arrest, this finding did not reach significance" (p. 26).

These results left the researchers suspicious about the effectiveness of batterer programs in general. They acknowledge, however, that the study did not achieve experimental conditions. The participant characteristics differed across the two programs: for instance, the men referred to the longer programs tended to have less severe criminal histories and less severe current charges. It is also hard to know what contextual or system factors, such as the oversight and response by the courts, may have influenced the outcomes. Our multisite study suggests that difference in court oversight and response may contribute to the men's compliance and outcomes. The impact of program length in itself remains less clear, not only with regard to batterer programs but also to treatment in other fields (see, for example, Marshall & Serran, 2000). The advent of brief therapies and managed care, furthermore, have intensified the debate about the new idea that short may be better, in some cases.

5. I conducted a variety of tests controlling for the men's characteristics, and I made observations and conducted interviews in the community to identify other possible extraneous influences on the outcome, such as police practices, program staff changes, and employment level. The characteristics of the men before and after the implementation were equivalent, and I found little evidence of possible community influences.

6. The researchers continue with their reasons for focusing on the system as a whole and not its individual components: "The primary reason for this design is that individuals received various JOD interventions based on their needs and their particular circumstances, which makes comparisons with individuals who did not receive the same particular intervention inappropriate. In addition, considerable variation was found within intervention components provided to sample members. For example, in each site, offenders could be referred to one of several batterer intervention programs, which varied in content and duration. Moreover, victims received services based on their needs and interest in participation" (Visher, Harrell, & Yahner, 2008, p. 517).

7. Approximately 10 percent of the victims were male and 10 percent of the offenders were female, based on the determination at the court hearing of the primary offender. The subjects were interviewed first at two months following the court disposition and then nine months after that, covering the full eleven-month follow-up period. The results are presented for offenders and victims rather than for men and women. The offender outcomes, therefore, include those of a small percentage of females, and the victim outcomes include information from a small percentage of males.

8. One of the JOD researchers conducted one of the first experimental evaluations of batterer programs that produced a null set of findings (Harrell, 1991). Although this study had its own limitations and shortcomings, the researchers' negative assessment of the batterer programs in the JOD study may have been influenced by these previous results. See note 2 in chapter 2.

9. Only a quarter of the 2,265 identified batterer programs responded to an initial inquiry ($n = 543$). Approximately half of those programs were selected for the survey ($n = 260$). The response rate to the full survey was 75 percent for the selected batterer programs, but only about 50 percent for their accompanying courts. The number of programs actually answering the survey is therefore less than 200, or about 8 percent. Although the researchers argue that the respondents are representative of the initial 543 programs, it is difficult to make similar claims for the full population of programs across the country. As far as the questionnaire is concerned, it is not clear whether the response is representative of other staff members' perceptions or whether what is reported actually takes place. Many of the categorical answers—such as "often" and "sometimes"—are also open to interpretation.

10. The researchers of this study infer in their report that one of the main reasons for the weak implementation of accountability is the expectation of rehabilitation through the batterer programs (Labriola, Rempel, O'Sullivan, & Frank, 2007). They go on to argue that batterer programs "don't work," and that therefore the need for accountability to offset the failure is intensified. The JOD study and our multisite evaluation, as well as the studies of domestic violence councils, indicate a very different set of reasons for the weak implementation. Moreover, the researchers build on a tenuous "don't work" assumption that, as I discuss in chapter 3, is probably the result of some of the teams' bias against batterer programs (see the New York Model for Batterer Programs, retrieved May 23, 2011, from http://nymbp.org/principles.htm). I argue that the evidence suggests that rehabilitation and accountability interact: batterer programs work because of accountability.

11. The auditors first contacted representatives of the probation departments in all of the state's counties for data on arrests, batterer program referrals, attendance and completion, noncompliance probation revocations and other sanctions, and program monitoring, reviews, and approvals. Interestingly, several counties did not have the requested information available, even though it is apparently required or at least expected. Five counties were then selected as representative of the state's diversity in population, re-

gion, and income. The auditors established a random sample of 125 batterer program referrals from these counties (25 from each county) and obtained records on these men from the courts, programs, probation officers, and police departments. They also visited the probation departments to examine the documentation of program reviews.

12. The principal investigator and a research assistant compiled field notes of the observations, participation, debriefing interviews, and informal conversations (Gondolf, 2009a). We then separately summarized the main issues, challenges, and themes in the notes, and discussed and compared our summaries to help verify our conclusions. These conclusions were further clarified, focused, and validated through two advisory committee meetings. The committee was comprised of representatives from each of the collaborating agencies and three researchers from the mental health field specializing in the treatment of violent psychiatric patients.

13. In systems analysis, this tendency is referred to as homeostasis. Systems operate to sustain themselves and maintain equilibrium. To change a system, so the theory goes, homeostasis must be taken into account; the system as a whole may need to be modified and even restructured to accomplish a smaller sustainable change.

14. The concept of the blueprint differs from the one currently being applied to the violence prevention initiative for juvenile delinquency developed by the Center for the Study of Prevention of Violence at the University of Colorado (Mihalic, Irwin, Fagan, Ballard, & Elliott, 2004). The latter approach follows more of a technical assistance model that recommends evidence-based programming and monitors the implementation of, and facilitates fidelity to, the project design. There are certainly some elements that overlap with the St. Paul blueprint, but this blueprint is much more process-oriented and builds from the bottom up. It is an organic, problem-solving approach rather than a program implementation.

15. According to its authors, the St. Paul blueprint is anchored in six foundational principles: (1) adherence to an interagency approach and collective intervention goals; (2) building attention to the context and severity of abuse into each intervention; (3) recognition that most domestic violence is a patterned crime requiring continuing engagement with victims and offenders; (4) ensuring certain and swift (though not necessarily harsh) consequences for continued abuse; (5) using the power of the criminal justice system to send messages of help and accountability; and (6) acting in ways that reduce unintended consequences and the disparity of impacts on victims and offenders (Sadusky, Martinson, Lizdas, & McGee, 2010).

16. Other more specific changes under the blueprint include better communication across agencies and requiring offenders who are bailed out of jail to meet the next day with Project Remand, a nonprofit agency that provides pretrial services. Project Remand helps offenders review the conditions of their release, which often mandate no contact with victims. Previously, such conditions were reviewed just before offenders were released. According to advocates, this was poor timing because offenders were so eager to leave jail that they couldn't focus on the conditions.

Conclusion

1. A program director, reviewing some of the points in this book, raised a final overarching shortcoming. He asserted that the preoccupation with evidence-based practice, and evaluation research in general, are naïve considering the financial crisis impacting social services in general. The cutback in funding at all levels is not just hampering program development; it is undoing service programs and welfare supports. The poor, the working class, and people of color are being disproportionately affected. What may be most needed, therefore, is for programs to ban together and challenge the crippling cutbacks. Part of this means amassing more visible support of marginalized groups, and working jointly to stabilize program funding. The criminal justice system is ending up as the repository of too many social problems, with little chance for rehabilitation or restoration. Whether this is a pessimistic or a realistic view, there looms a potentially more imposing context than what is considered in this book. As this program director proposed, ultimately we may need a broader and more critical analysis of the political circumstances in which we find ourselves. And we shouldn't overlook such an analysis.

2. This book has virtually ignored another reason for practitioners' neglect of the research. Many are likely to be influenced by the critique of science and empirical research swirling through many university departments and among more activist-oriented service providers. The philosophy of science, postmodern thought, and critical theory all raise questions about the claims of objective truth in the research presented in this book. The posture of objectivity clouds the inevitable biases engendered by class, ethnicity, gender, political aims, and personal issues. "Objective and rigorous research" is ultimately a social construction in itself, based on its own ideology. Much of the debate surrounding the batterer program evaluations appear to bear this out, as do the political and economic forces driving the evidence-based practice movement. In a sense, the research I have reviewed is relative to "truths" found through other designs, methods, and observations.

This book, however, is confined to the parameters of evidence-based practice, since that at the moment has gained precedence in policy formation. As the critics would say, it is a hegemonic paradigm that essentially dominates and dismisses other ways of knowing. This postmodern view may contribute to what some researchers label as feminist opposition to their scientific findings. The perceived opposition is not merely ideological, but reinforced by some philosophical sensibilities that are grounded in academia. As I attempt to show, there is much more to the resistance, however. Specifically, there is evidence that supports the evolution of batterer programs as we know them, and weak evidence behind many of the alternatives being put forth.

References

Abramson, J. (2004). *Overdosed America: The broken promise of American medicine.* New York: Harper Collins.

Ackerman, R. (1993). *Silent sons.* New York: Simon and Schuster.

Adams, B. (2010, March 14). Taking a new look at domestic violence: Couples counseling and circles of peace show promise. *Salt Lake Tribune* (www.sltrib.com). Retrieved June 11, 2011, from http://archive.sltrib.com.

Adams, D. (1988). Treatment models of men who batter: A pro-feminist analysis. In K. Yllo & M. Bograd (Eds.), *Feminist perspectives on wife abuse* (pp. 176–199). New-bury Park, CA: Sage.

Adams, D. (2007). *Why do they kill? Men who murder their intimate partners.* Nashville, TN: Vanderbilt University Press.

Adams, D., & Cayouette, S. (2002). Emerge: A group education model for abusers. Chapter 4 in E. Aldarondo & F. Mederos (Eds.), *Programs for men who batter: Intervention and prevention strategies in a diverse society.* Kingston, NJ: Civic Research Institute.

Addis, M., Cardemil, E., Duncan, B., & Miller, S. (2006). Does manualization improve therapy outcomes? In J. Norcross, L. Beutler, & R. Levant (Eds.), *Evidence-based practices in mental health: Debate and dialogue on the fundamental questions* (pp. 131–160). Washington: American Psychological Association.

Aldarondo, E. (2002). Evaluating the efficacy of interventions with men who batter. Chapter 3 in E. Aldarondo & F. Mederos (Eds.), *Programs for men who batter: Intervention and prevention strategies in a diverse society.* Kingston, NJ: Civic Research Institute.

Aldarondo, E. (Ed.). (2007). *Advancing social justice through clinical practice.* New York: Routledge.

Aldarondo, E. (2010). Understanding the contributions of common interventions with men who batter to the reduction of re-assaults. *Juvenile and Family Court Journal,* 61 (4), 87–101.

Aldarondo, E., & Mederos, F. (Eds.). (2002). *Programs for men who batter: Intervention and prevention strategies in a diverse society.* Kingston, NJ: Civic Research Institute.

Aldenderfer, J. & Blashfield, K. (1984). *Cluster analysis.* Thousand Oaks, CA: Sage.

Alexander, P. (2007, July 14–17). *Stages of change and the group treatment of batterers.* Paper presented at the National Institute of Justice Conference, Arlington, VA.

Alexander, P., & Morris, E. (2008). Stages of change in batterers and their response to treatment. *Violence and Victims, 23,* 476–492.

Alexander, P., Morris, E., Tracy, A., & Frye, A. (2010). Stages of change and the group treatment of batterers: A randomized clinical trial. *Violence and Victims, 25,* 571–587.

Allen, N. (2005). A multi-level analysis of community coordinating councils. *American Journal of Community Psychology, 35,* 49–63.

Allen, N. (2006). An examination of the effectiveness of domestic violence coordinating councils. *Violence Against Women, 12,* 46–67.

Allen, N., Watt, K., & Hess, J. (2008). A qualitative study of the activities and outcomes of domestic violence coordinating councils. *American Journal of Community Psychology, 41,* 63–73.

Almeida, R., & Hudak, J. (2002). The cultural context model: Therapy with couples with domestic violence. Chapter 10 in E. Aldarondo & F. Mederos (Eds.), *Programs for men who batter: Intervention and prevention strategies in a diverse society.* Kingston, NJ: Civic Research Institute.

Anderson, C., & Stewart, S. (1983). *Mastering resistance: A practical guide to family therapy.* New York: Guilford.

Andrews, D., & Bonta, J. (1995). *LSI-R: The Level of Service Inventory—Revised.* Toronto: Multi-Health Systems.

Angell, M. (2004). *The truth about the drug companies: How they deceive us and what to do about it.* New York: Random House.

Angrist, J. (2006). Instrumental variables methods in experimental criminological research: What, why, and how? *Journal of Experimental Criminology, 1,* 23–44.

Angrist, J., Imbens, G., & Rubin, D. (1996). Identification of causal effects using instrumental variables. *Journal of the American Statistical Association, 91,* 444–455.

Apel, R., Bushway, S., Brame, R., Haviland, A., Nagin, D., & Paternoster, R. (2007). Unpacking the relationship between adolescent employment and antisocial behavior: A matched samples comparison. *Criminology, 45,* 67–97.

Apel, R., Bushway, S., Paternoster, R., Brame, R., & Sweeten, G. (2008). Using state child labor laws to identify the causal effect of youth employment on deviant behavior and academic achievement. *Journal of Quantitative Criminology, 24,* 337–362.

Archer, J. (2002). Sex differences in aggression between heterosexual partners: A meta-analytic review. *Aggression and Violent Behavior, 7,* 313–351.

Aronson, R. (Producer). (2005). *The soldier's heart* [Television broadcast]. Washington: Public Broadcasting Service. Retrieved June 8, 2011, from www.pbs.org/wgbh/pages/frontline/shows/heart/view/.

Atkinson, D., Fulrong, M., & Poston, W. (1986). Afro-American preferences for counselor characteristics. *Journal of Counseling Psychology, 33,* 326–330.

Augusta-Scott, T., & Dankwort, J. (2002). Partner abuse group intervention: Lessons from education and narrative therapy approaches. *Journal of Interpersonal Violence, 17,* 783–805.

Austin, J., & Dankwort, J. (1999). Standards for batterer programs. *Journal of Interpersonal Violence, 14,* 152–169.

Babcock, J., Canady, B., Graham, K., & Schart, L. (2007). The evolution of battering interventions: From the dark ages into the scientific age. In J. Hamel & T. Nicholls (Eds.), *Family therapy for domestic violence: A practitioner's guide to gender-inclusive research and treatment* (pp. 215–244). New York: Springer.

Babcock, J., Green, C., & Robie, C. (2004). Does batterers' treatment work? A meta-analytic review of domestic violence treatment outcome research. *Clinical Psychology Review, 23,* 1023–1053.

Babcock, J., Green, C., Webb, S., & Graham, K. (2004). A second failure to replicate the Gottman et al. (1995) typology of men who abuse intimate partners and possible reasons why. *Journal of Family Psychology, 18,* 396–400.

Babcock, J., Jacobson, N., Gottman, J., & Yerington, T. (2000). Attachment, emotional regulation, and the function of marital violence: Differences between secure, preoccupied, and dismissing violent and nonviolent husbands. *Journal of Family Violence, 15,* 391–409.

Babcock, J., & Steiner, R. (1999). The relationship between treatment, incarceration, and recidivism of battering: A program evaluation of Seattle's coordinated response to community response to domestic violence. *Journal of Family Psychology, 13,* 46–59.

Bachman, R. (2000). A comparison of annual incidence rates and contextual characteristics of intimate-partner violence against women from the National Crime Victimization Survey (NCVS) and the National Violence Against Women Survey (NVAWS). *Violence Against Women, 6,* 142–161.

Baird, C. (2009). *A question of evidence: A critique of risk assessment models used in the justice system.* Madison, WI: National Council on Crime and Delinquency. Retrieved May 21, 2011, from http://mw.nccd-crc.org/nccd/pubs/2009_a_question_evidence.pdf.

Bancroft, L. (2003). *Why does he do that? Inside the minds of angry and controlling men.* New York: Putnam.

Bancroft, L., & Silverman, J. (2002). *The batterer as parent: Addressing the impact of domestic violence on family dynamics.* Thousand Oaks, CA: Sage.

Bandura, A. (1973). *Aggression: A social learning analysis.* Englewood Cliffs, NJ: Prentice Hall.

Bartholomew, K., & Allison, C. (2006). An attachment perspective on abusive dynamics in intimate relationships. In M. Mikulincer & G. Goodman (Eds.), *Dynamics of romantic love: Attachment, caregiving, and sex* (pp. 102–127). New York: Guilford.

Baumeister, R. (2001, August). Violent pride. *Scientific American*, 96–101.

Baumeister, R., Bushman, B., & Campbell, W. (2000). Self-esteem, narcissism, and aggression: Does violence result from low self-esteem or from threatened egotism? *Current Directions in Psychological Science*, 9, 26–29.

Baumeister, R., Smart, L., & Boden, J. (1996). Relation of threatened egotism to violence and aggression: The dark side of high self-esteem. *Psychological Review*, 103, 5–33.

Bausell, R. (2007). *Snake oil science: The truth about complementary and alternative medicine*. New York: Oxford University Press.

Beaupre, S. (2006). *Domestic violence/intimate partner violence: Applying best practice guidelines*. Albany, NY: Access Continuing Education.

Belknap, J., & Melton, H. (2005). Are heterosexual men also victims of intimate partner abuse? Applied Research Forum, National Electronic Network on Violence Against Women. Retrieved June 10, 2011, from http://new.vawnet.org/Assoc_Files _VAWnet/AR_MaleVictims.pdf.

Bennett, L., & Piet, M. (1999). Standards for batterer intervention programs: In whose interest? *Violence Against Women*, 5, 6–24.

Bennett, L., Stoops, C., Call, C., & Flett, H. (2007). Program completion and re-arrest in a batterer intervention system. *Research on Social Work Practice*, 17, 42–54.

Berger, P., & Kellner, H. (1981). *Sociology reinterpreted: An essay on method and vocation*. New York: Anchor.

Berk, R. (2005). Randomized experiments as the bronze standard. *Journal of Experimental Criminology*, 1, 416–433.

Berk, R. (2007). Statistical inference and meta-analysis. *Journal of Experimental Criminology*, 3, 247–270.

Berkowitz, L. (1969). The frustration-aggression hypothesis revisited. In L. Berkowitz (Ed.), *Roots of aggression* (pp. 1–28). New York: Atherton.

Berkowitz, L. (1993). *Aggression: Its causes, consequences, and control*. New York: McGraw-Hill.

Berman, G. (2008). Learning from failure: A roundtable on criminal justice innovation. *Journal of Court Innovation*, 1, 97–122.

BISCMI [Batterer Intervention Services Coalition of Michigan]. (2008). *Other state's [sic] standards*. Okemos, MI: Author. Retrieved May 8, 2011, from http://biscmi .org/other_resources/state_standards.html.

BISCMI [Batterer Intervention Services Coalition of Michigan]. (2009, November 4–6). *Coordinated community responses: Are they effective? The reality, research, and results behind the Judicial Oversight Project*. 14th annual BISCMI conference, Battle Creek, MI. Retrieved June 10, 2011, from www.biscmi.org/jod/BISC-MI_2009 _National_Conference_Program.pdf.

Blake, W., & Darling, C. (1994). The dilemmas of the African American male. *Journal of Black Studies*, 24, 402–415.

Bledsoe, L., Bibhuti, S., & Barbee, A. (2006). Impact of coordinated response to intimate partner violence on offender accountability. *Journal of Aggression, Maltreatment & Trauma, 13*, 109–129.

Boba, R., & Lilley, D. (2009). Violence Against Women Act (VAWA) funding: A nationwide assessment of effects on rape and assault. *Violence Against Women, 15*, 168–185.

Bograd, M. (1984). Family system approaches to wife battering: A feminist critique. *American Journal of Psychiatry, 31*, 124–137.

Bograd, M., & Mederos, F. (1999). Battering and couples therapy: Universal screening and selection of treatment modality. *Journal of Marital and Family Therapy, 25*, 291–312.

Bolen, R. (2000). Validity of attachment theory. *Trauma, Violence, and Abuse, 1*, 128–153.

Boruch, R. (1997). *Randomized experiments for planning and evaluation.* Thousand Oaks, CA: Sage.

Boruch, R., Snyder, B., & DeMoya, D. (2000). The importance of randomized field trials. *Crime and Delinquency, 46*, 156–181.

Bouffard, J., & Muftic, L. (2007). An examination of the outcomes of various components of a coordinated community response to domestic violence by male offenders. *Journal of Family Violence, 22*, 353–366.

Bowen, E. (2011). An overview of partner violence risk assessment and the potential role of female victim risk appraisals. *Aggression and Violent Behavior, 16*, 214–226.

Bowen, E., Brown, L., & Gilchrist, E. (2002). Evaluating probation based offender programmes for domestic violence perpetrators: A pro-feminist approach. *Howard Journal of Criminal Justice, 41*, 221–236.

Bowker, L. (1983). *Beating wife beating.* Lexington, MA: Lexington.

Bowker, L. (Ed.). (1998). *Masculinities and violence.* Thousand Oaks, CA: Sage.

Bowlby, J. (1969). *Attachment* (2nd ed.). London: Hogarth.

Bowlby, J. (1988). *A secure base: Clinical applications of attachment theory.* New York: Routledge.

Brannen, S., & Rubin, A. (1996). Comparing the effectiveness of gender-specific and couples groups in a court-mandated spouse abuse treatment program. *Research on Social Work Practice, 6*, 405–424.

Briere, J., & Scott, C. (2006). *Principles of trauma therapy: A guide to symptoms, evaluation, and treatment.* Thousand Oaks, CA: Sage.

Briss, P., Zaza, S., Pappaioanou, M., Fielding, J., Wright-De Aguero, L., Truman, B., et al. (2000). Developing an evidence-based guide to community preventive services. *American Journal of Preventive Medicine, 18*, 35–44.

Brodeur, N., Rondeau, G., Brochu, S., Lindsay, J., & Phelps, J. (2008). Does the transtheoretical model predict attrition in domestic violence treatment programs? *Violence and Victims, 23*, 493–507.

Brown, B., Joe, G., & Thompson, P. (1985). Minority group status and treatment retention. *International Journal of the Addictions, 20*, 319–335.

Burke, B., Arkowitz, H., & Dunn, C. (2002). The efficacy of motivational interviewing. In W. Miller & S. Rollnick (Eds.), *Motivational interviewing: Preparing people for change* (pp. 217–250). New York: Guilford.

Burke, B., Arkowitz, H., & Menchola, M. (2003). The efficacy of motivational interviewing: A meta-analysis of controlled clinical trials. *Journal of Consulting & Clinical Psychology, 71*(5), 843–861.

Burke, K. (2010). Just what made drug courts successful? *New England Journal of Criminal and Civil Confinement, 36*, 39–58.

Burrowes, N., & Needs, A. (2009). Time to contemplate change? A framework for assessing readiness to change with offenders. *Aggression and Violent Behavior, 14*, 39–49.

Burton, R., Baldwin, S., Flynn, D., & Whitelaw, S. (2000). The "stages of change" model in health promotion: Science and ideology. *Critical Public Health, 10*, 55–70.

Butler, A., Chapman, J., Forman, E., & Beck, A. (2006). The empirical status of cognitive-behavioral therapy: A review of meta-analyses. *Clinical Psychology Review, 26*, 17–31.

Buttell, F., Muldoon, J., & Carney, M. (2005). An application of attachment theory to court-mandated batterers. *Journal of Family Violence, 20*, 211–217.

Buttell, F., & Pike, C. (2003). Investigating the differential effectiveness of a batterer treatment program on outcomes for African American and Caucasian batterers. *Research on Social Work Practice, 13*, 675–692.

BWJP [Battered Women's Justice Project]. (2008). Training opportunity: Audio conference on violence against women; Research/practitioner discourse. *Violence Against Women, 14*, 732–733.

Caesar, P., & Hamberger, L. (Eds.). (1989). *Treating men who batter: Theory, practice, and programs.* New York: Springer.

California State Auditor. (2006). *Batterer intervention programs: County probation departments, the courts and program compliance.* Sacramento, CA: Bureau of State Audits.

Campbell, J. (1995). Prediction of homicide of and by battered women. In J. Campbell (Ed.), *Assessing dangerousness: Violence by sexual offenders, batterers, and child abusers* (pp. 96–113). Thousand Oaks, CA: Sage.

Campbell, J. (2004). Helping women understand their risk in situations of intimate partner violence. *Journal of Interpersonal Violence, 19*, 1464–1477.

Campbell, J. (2005). Assessing dangerousness in domestic violence cases: History, challenges, and opportunities. *Criminology & Public Policy, 4*, 653–671.

Campbell, J. (2009, November 4–7). *A proposed system for generic and specific risk assessment for domestic violence perpetrators.* Paper presented at the annual meeting of the American Society of Criminology, Philadelphia.

Campbell, J., Dienemann, J., Kub, J., Wurmser, T., & Loy, E. (1999). Collaboration as partnership. *Violence Against Women, 5*, 1140–1157.

Campbell, J., Webster, D., Koziol-McLain, J., Block, C., & Campbell, D. (2003a). Assessing risk factors for intimate partner homicide. *National Institute of Justice Journal, no. 250*, 15–19.

Campbell, J., Webster, D., Koziol-McLain, J., Block, C., & Campbell, D. (2003b). Risk factors for femicide in abusive relationships: Results from a multi-site case control study. *American Journal of Public Health, 93*, 1089–1097.

Campbell, R., Damiani, C., & Menghra, S. (2004). *Enhancing responses to domestic violence: Promising practices from the Judicial Oversight Demonstration initiative.* New York: Vera Institute. Retrieved June 10, 2011, from www.vera.org/download?file=113/Enhancing%2Bresponses.pdf.

Campbell, R., & Wasco, S. (2000). Feminist approaches to social science: Epistemological and methodological tenets. *American Journal of Community Psychology, 28*, 773–791.

Capaldi, D., & Kim, H. (2007). Typological approaches to violence in couples: A critique and alternative conceptual approach. *Clinical Psychology Review, 27*, 253–265.

Carlin, K. (2001). Measuring success: Evaluating batterers intervention programs. Decatur, GA: Men Stopping Violence. Retrieved June 10, 2011, from www.men stoppingviolence.org.

Catalano, S. (2007). *Intimate partner violence in the United States* (NCJ 210675). Washington: Bureau of Justice Statistics. Retrieved June 10, 2011, from http://bjs .ojp.usdoj.gov/index.cfm?ty=pbdetail&iid=1000.

Catlett, B., Toews, M., & Walilko, V. (2010). Men's gendered constructions of intimate partner violence as predictors of court-mandated batterer treatment drop out. *American Journal of Community Psychology, 45*, 107–123.

Cattaneo, L., & Goodman, L. (2005). Risk factors for reabuse in intimate partner violence: A cross-disciplinary critical review. *Trauma, Violence, and Abuse, 6*, 141–175.

Cattaneo, L., & Goodman, L. (2009). New directions in risk assessment: An empowerment approach to risk management. *Family and Intimate Partner Violence Quarterly, 2*, 55–72.

Cattaneo, L., Stuewig, J., Goodman, L., Kaltman, S., & Dutton, M. (2007). Longitudinal helpseeking patterns among victims of intimate partner violence: The relationship between legal and extralegal services. *American Journal of Orthopsychiatry, 77*, 467–477.

Cellini, H. (2004). Child abuse, neglect, and delinquency: The neurological link. *Juvenile and Family Court Journal, 55*, 1–13.

Chafetz, M. (2005). *Big fat liars: How politicians, corporations, and the media use science and statistics to manipulate the public.* Nashville, TN: Nelson Current.

Choca, J., & Van Denburg, E. (1997). *Interpretative guide to the Millon Clinical Multiaxial Inventory* (2nd ed.). Washington: American Psychological Association.

Cissner, A., & Farole, D. (2009). *Avoiding failures of implementation: Lessons from process evaluation*. Washington: Bureau of Justice Assistance.

Cissner, A., & Puffett, N. (2006). *Do batterer program length or approach affect completion or re-arrest rates? A comparison of outcomes between defendants sentences to two batterer programs in Brooklyn*. New York: Center for Court Innovation.

Clatterbaugh, K. (1997). *Contemporary perspectives on masculinity: Men, women, and politics in modern society* (2nd ed.). Boulder, CO: Westview.

Clements, K., Holtzworth-Munroe, A., Gondolf, E., & Meehan, J. (2002, November 15–18). *Testing the Hotzworth-Munroe batterer typology among court-referred maritally violent men*. Paper presented at the annual meeting of the Association of the Advancement of Behavior Therapy, Reno, NV.

Cline, N. (2009, February, 10). E-mail message regarding JOD implementation to Juan Carlos, Family Violence Prevention Fund, San Francisco, CA.

Cohen, J. (1988). *Statistical power analysis for the behavioral sciences*. Hillsdale, NJ: Lawrence Erlbaum Associates.

Cohen, J. (1994). The earth is round (*p* > .05). *American Psychologist, 49*, 997–1003.

Cohen, P. (Producer). (2010). *Power and control: Domestic violence in America* [Television broadcast]. New York: Hillcrest Films. Retrieved June 6, 2011, from www.powerandcontrolfilm.com/the-topics/academics/linda-mills.

Coleman, H., Wampold, B., & Casalie, S. (1995). Ethnic minorities' rating of ethnically similar and European American counselors: A meta-analysis. *Journal of Counseling Psychology, 42*, 55–64.

Conrad, P. (2007). *The medicalization of society: On the transformation of human conditions into treatable disorders*. Baltimore, MD: Johns Hopkins University Press.

Cordray, D. (2000). Enhancing the scope of experimental inquiry in intervention studies. *Crime and Delinquency, 46*, 401–424.

Cornish, D., & Clarke, R. (1986). *The reasoning criminal: Rational choice perspectives on offending*. New York: Springer.

Corvo, K., Dutton, D., & Chen, W. (2008). Toward evidence-based practice with domestic violence perpetrators. *Journal of Aggression Maltreatment and Trauma, 16*, 111–130.

Coulter, M., & VandeWeerd, C. (2009). Reducing domestic violence and other criminal recidivism: Effectiveness of a multilevel batterer intervention program. *Violence and Victims, 24*, 139–152.

Craig, R. (1995). Interpersonal psychotherapy and MCMI-III-based assessment. In P. Retzlaff (Ed.), *Tactical psychotherapy of the personality disorders: An MCMI-III-based approach* (pp. 66-88). Boston: Allyn and Bacon.

Critical Components Project Team. (2008). *Keeping women safe: Eight critical components of an effective justice response to domestic violence*. Report submitted to the British Columbia Ministry of Public Safety. Retrieved May 22, 2011, from www.endingviolence.org/node/659.

Cross, J., Dickmann, E., Newman-Gonchar, R., & Fagan, J. (2009). Using mixed-method design and network analysis to measure development of interagency collaboration. *American Journal of Evaluation, 30*, 310–329.

Crowell, N., & Burgess, A. (1996). *Understanding violence against women.* Washington: National Academies Press.

Crowley, J. (2009). Fathers' rights groups, domestic violence and political countermobilization. *Social Forces, 88*, 723–756.

Crowley, R. (2001). *Program evaluation: A social change approach.* Decatur, GA: Men Stopping Violence. Retrieved June 7, 2011, from www.menstoppingviolence.org/WhatWeDo/Publish.php.

Daly, J., & Pelowski, S. (2000). Predictors of dropout among men who batter: A review of studies with implications for research and practice. *Violence and Victims, 15*, 137–160.

Davey, L., Day, A., & Howells, K. (2005). Anger, over-control and serious violent offending. *Aggression and Violent Behavior, 10*, 624–635.

Davies, J., Lyon, E., & Monti-Catania, D. (1998). *Safety planning with battered women: Complex lives/difficult choices.* Thousand Oaks, CA: Sage.

Davis, R., & Taylor, B. (1999). Does batterer treatment reduce violence? A synthesis of the literature. *Women and Criminal Justice, 10*, 69–93.

Davis, R., Taylor, B., & Maxwell, C. (2000). *Does batterer treatment reduce violence? A randomized experiment in Brooklyn* (Document No. 180772). Final report to the National Institute of Justice, Washington. Retrieved June 9, 2011, from www.ncjrs.gov/pdffiles1/nij/grants/180772.pdf.

De Becker, G. (1997). *The gift of fear: Survival signals that protect us from violence.* New York: Dell.

Debonnaire, T. (2009, May 12–15). *Working with BIPs for research readiness.* Workshop presented at "Bridging Perspectives: Intervening with Men Who Batter," Minneapolis, MN.

DeKeseredy, W. (2000). Current controversies in defining nonlethal violence against women in intimate heterosexual relationships: Empirical implications. *Violence Against Women, 6*, 705–727.

DeKeseredy, W., & Dragiewicz, M. (2007). Understanding the complexities of feminist perspectives on woman abuse: A commentary on Donald G. Dutton's *Rethinking Domestic Violence. Violence Against Women, 13*, 874–884.

DeKeseredy, W., & Schwartz, M. (2003). Backlash and whiplash: A critique of Canada's general social science survey on victimization. *Online Journal of Justice Studies, 1* (1). Retrieved June 9, 2011, from http://sisyphe.org/article.php3?id_article=1689.

Dewan, M., Steenbarger, B., & Greenberg, R. (2004). *The art and science of brief psychotherapies: A practitioner's guide.* Arlington VA: American Psychiatric Publishing.

Dia, D., Simmons, C., Oliver, M., & Cooper, R. (2009). Motivational interviewing for perpetrators of intimate partner violence. In P. Lehmann and C. Simmons (Eds.), Strengths-based batterer intervention: A new paradigm in ending family violence (pp. 87–111). New York: Springer.

Dobash, R., & Dobash, R. (2000). Evaluating criminal justice interventions for domestic violence. *Crime and Delinquency, 46*, 252–271.

Dobash, R., & Dobash, R. (2004). Women's violence to men in intimate relationships. *British Journal of Criminology, 44*, 324–349.

Dobash, R., Dobash, R., Cavanagh, K., & Medina-Ariza, J. (2007). Lethal and nonlethal violence against an intimate female partner: Comparing male murderers to nonlethal abusers. *Violence Against Women, 13*, 329–353.

Dossey, L. (1999). *Reinventing medicine: Beyond mind-body to a new era of healing.* New York: Harper Collins.

Dossey, L. (2008). Healing research: What we know and don't know. *Explore, 4*, 341–352.

Douglas, K., & Kropp, R. (2002). A prevention-based paradigm for violence risk assessment: Clinical and research application. *Criminal Justice and Behavior, 2*, 617–658.

Douglas, K., & Skeem, J. (2005). Violence risk assessment: Getting specific about being dynamic. *Psychology, Public Policy, and Law, 11*, 347–383.

Douglas, U., Bathrick, D., & Perry, P. (2008). Deconstructing male violence against women. *Violence Against Women, 14*, 247–261.

Dragiewicz, M. (2011). *Equality with a vengeance: Men's rights groups, battered women, and antifeminist backlash.* Boston: Northeastern University Press.

Dunford, F. (2000a). Determining program success: The importance of employing experimental research designs. *Crime and Delinquency, 46*, 425–434.

Dunford, F. (2000b). The San Diego Navy Experiment: An assessment of interventions for men who assault their wives. *Journal of Consulting and Clinical Psychology, 68*, 468–476.

Durlak, J., & Dupree, E. (2008). Implementation matters: A review of research on the influence of implementation on program outcomes and the factors affecting implementation. *American Journal of Community Psychology, 41*, 327–350.

Durlak, J., & Lipsey, M. (1991). A practitioner's guide to meta-analysis. *American Journal of Community Psychology, 19*, 291–332.

Dutton, D. (1998). *The abusive personality: Violence and control in intimate relationships.* New York: Guilford.

Dutton, D. (2007). *Rethinking domestic violence.* Vancouver: University of British Columbia Press.

Dutton, D. (2008). My back pages: Reflections on thirty years of domestic violence research. *Trauma Violence Abuse, 9*, 131–143.

Dutton, D. (2010). The gender paradigm and the architecture of antiscience. *Partner Abuse, 1*, 5–25.

Dutton, D., Bodnarchuk, M., Kropp, R., Hart, S., & Ogloff, J. (1997). Client personality disorders affecting wife assault post-treatment recidivism. *Violence and Victims, 12,* 37–50.

Dutton, D., & Corvo, K. (2006). Transforming a flawed policy: A call to revive psychology and science in domestic violence research and practice. *Aggression and Violent Behavior, 11,* 457–483.

Dutton, D., & Kropp, R. (2000). A review of domestic violence risk instruments. *Trauma, Violence & Abuse, 1,* 171–181.

Dutton, D., Saunders, K., Starzomski, A., & Bartholomew, K. (1994). Intimacy-anger and insecure attachment as precursors of abuse in intimate relationships. *Journal of Applied Social Psychology, 24,* 1367–1386.

Dutton, M., & Goodman, L. (2005). Coercion in intimate partner violence: Toward a new conceptualization. *Sex Roles, 52,* 743–756.

Eastman, N., & Campbell, C. (2006). Neuroscience and legal determination of criminal responsibility. *Nature Reviews Neuroscience, 7,* 311–318.

Eckhardt, C., Holtzworth-Munroe, A., Norlander, B., Sibley, A., & Cahill, M. (2008). Readiness to change, partner violence subtypes, and treatment outcomes among men in treatment for partner assault. *Violence and Victims, 23,* 446–475.

Eckhardt, C., Murphy, C., Black, D., & Suhr, L. (2006). Intervention programs for perpetrators of intimate partner violence: conclusions from a clinical research perspective. *Public Health Reports, 121,* 369–381.

Eckhardt, C., Samper, R., & Murphy, C. (2008). Anger disturbances among perpetrators of intimate partner violence: Clinical characteristics and outcomes of court-mandated treatment. *Journal of Interpersonal Violence, 23,* 1600–1617.

Edge, D., & Buchanan, C. (Producers). (2010). *The wounded platoon* [Television broadcast]. Washington: Public Broadcasting Service. Retrieved June 6, 2011, from http://video.pbs.org/video/1497566525.

Edleson, J. (2008). *Promising practices with men who batter.* Report submitted to the King County Domestic Violence Council, Seattle.

Edleson, J., & Bible, A. (2001). Collaborating for women's safety: Partnerships between research and practice. In C. Renzetti, J. Edleson, & R. Bergen (Eds.), *Sourcebook of violence against women* (pp. 73–95). Thousand Oaks, CA: Sage.

Edleson, J., & Tolman, R. (1992). *Intervention for men who batter: An ecological approach.* Thousand Oaks, CA: Sage.

Edleson, J., & Williams, O. (Eds.). (2007). *Parenting by men who batterer: New directions for assessment and intervention.* New York: Oxford University Press.

Elkin, I., Shea, M., & Watkins, J. (1989). The National Institute of Mental Health Treatment of Depression Collaborative Research Program: General effectiveness of treatments. *Archives of General Psychiatry, 46,* 971–982.

Elkins, D. (2009). *Humanistic psychology: A clinical manifesto.* Colorado Springs, CO: Universities of the Rockies Press.

Ellis, D., & DeKeseredy, W. (1996). *The wrong stuff: An introduction to the sociological study of deviance* (2nd ed.). Columbus, OH: Allyn and Bacon.

Engler-Carlson, M., & Stevens, M. (Eds.). (2006). *In the room with men: A casebook of therapeutic change.* Washington: American Psychological Association.

Erdur, O., Rude, S., & Baron, A. (2003). Symptom improvement and length of treatment in ethnically similar and dissimilar client-therapist pairings. *Journal of Counseling Psychology, 50,* 52–58.

Evidence-Based Medicine Working Group. (1992). Evidence-based medicine: A new approach to teaching the practice of medicine. *Journal of the American Medical Association, 268,* 2420–2425.

Ezzell, C. (2000, March). Brain terrain: Mapping the functions of various areas of the human brain is difficult—and controversial. *Scientific American, 282,* 22–24.

Fall, K., & Howard, S. (2004). *Alternatives to domestic violence: A homework manual for battering intervention groups* (2nd ed.). New York: Routledge.

Fals-Stewart, W., Kashdan, T., O'Farrell, T., & Bircher, G. (2002). Behavioral couples therapy for drug abusing patients: Effects on partner violence. *Journal of Substance Abuse Treatment, 22,* 87–96.

Faludi, S. (1999). *Stiffed: The betrayal of the American man.* New York: Morrow.

Fasteau, M. (1981). *The male machine.* New York: Delta.

Feder, L., & Boruch, R. (2000). The need for experiments in criminal justice settings. *Crime and Delinquency, 46,* 291–294.

Feder, L., & Dugan, L. (2002). A test of the efficacy of court-mandated counseling for domestic violence offenders. *Justice Quarterly, 19,* 343–376.

Feder, L., & Forde, D. (2000). *A test of the efficacy of court-mandated counseling for domestic violence offenders: The Broward experiment* (Document No. 184631). Final report submitted to the National Institute of Justice, Washington.

Feder, L., Jolin, A., & Feyerherm, W. (2000). Lessons from two randomized experiments in criminal justice settings. *Crime and Delinquency, 46,* 380–400.

Feder, L., & Wilson, D. (2005). A meta-analytic review of court-mandated batterer intervention programs: Can courts affect abusers' behavior? *Journal of Experimental Criminology, 1,* 239–262.

Ferrell, W. (1974). *The liberated man.* New York: Random House.

Fine, R. (1988). *Troubled men: The psychology, emotional conflicts, and therapy of men.* San Francisco: Jossey-Bass.

Fonagy, P. (1999). Male perpetrators of violence against women: An attachment theory perspective. *Journal of Applied Psychoanalytic Studies, 1,* 7–27.

Ford, D. (2003). Coercing victim participation in domestic violence prosecutions. *Journal of Interpersonal Violence, 18,* 669–685.

Ford, D., & Regoli, M. (1993). The criminal prosecution of wife assaulters. In N. Hilton (Ed.), *Legal responses to wife assault* (pp. 127–164). Newbury Park, CA: Sage.

Foster, E., Wiley-Exley, E., & Bickman, L. (2009).Old wine in new skins: The sensitivity of established findings to new methods. *Evaluation Review, 33,* 281–306.

Foster-Fishman, P., & Behrens, T. (2007). Systems change reborn: Rethinking our theories, methods, and efforts in human services reform and community-based change. *American Journal of Community Psychology, 39,* 191–196.

Frank, J., & Frank, J. (1993). *Persuasion and healing: A comparative study of psychotherapy* (3rd ed.). Baltimore, MD: Johns Hopkins University Press.

Franklin, A. (1999). Invisibility syndrome and racial identity development in psychotherapy and counseling African-American men. *Counseling Psychologist, 27,* 761–793.

Franklin, C., & Hopson, L. (2007). Facilitating the use of evidence-based practice in community organizations. *Journal of Social Work Education, 43,* 377–404.

Freire, P. (2000). *Pedagogy of the oppressed* (30th anniversary ed.). New York: Continuum.Fruzzetti, A. (2000). Dialectical behavior therapy for domestic violence: Rationale and procedures. *Cognitive and Behavioral Practice, 7,* 435–447.

Funkhouser, B., Garvin, D., Henderson, J., Hines, E., Kearney, S., Mackie, B., et al. (2009, November 4–6). *JODI county stories of lessons learned: Washtenaw Judicial Oversight Demonstration team.* Panel presentation at the 14th annual BISCMI conference, Battle Creek, MI.

Gamache, D., Edleson, J., & Schock, M. (1988). Coordinated police, judicial and social service response to woman battering: A multi-baseline evaluation across three communities. In G. Hotaling, D. Finkelhor, J. Kirkpatrick, & M. Straus (Eds.), *Coping with family violence: Research and policy perspectives* (pp. 193–209). Newbury Park, CA: Sage.

Garbarino, J. (1999). *Lost boys: Why our sons turn violent and how we can save them.* New York: Free Press.

Garfield, G. (1998). *A community involvement model: A response to violence against women in Central Harlem.* Unpublished report available from the African American Task Force on Violence Against Women of New York City, Harlem Legal Services, New York.

Garland, B., & Frankel, M. (Eds.). (2004). *Neuroscience and the law: Brain, mind, and the scales of justice.* New York: Dana.

Garner, J., & Maxwell, C. (2000). What are the lessons of the police arrest studies? *Journal of Aggression, Maltreatment & Trauma, 4,* 83–114.

Garner, J., & Maxwell, C. (2008). Coordinated community responses to intimate partner violence in the 20th and 21st centuries. *Criminology and Public Policy, 7,* 525–535.

Gartin, P. (1995). Dealing with design failures in randomized field experiments: Analytic issues regarding the evaluation of treatment effects. *Journal of Research in Crime and Delinquency, 32,* 425–445.

Geffner, R., & Mantooth, C. (2000). *Ending spouse/partner abuse: A psychoeducational approach for individuals and couples.* New York: Springer.

Gelles, R. (1983). An exchange/social control theory of domestic violence. In D. Finkelhor, R. Gelles, G. Hotaling, & M. Straus (Eds.), *The dark side of families: Current family violence research* (pp. 151–165). Thousand Oaks, CA: Sage.

Gelles, R., Elliott, D., Ford, D., Holtzworth-Munroe, A., & Gondolf, E. (2002, November 20–23). Domestic violence offenders: Research trends and new directions. Panel presentation at the annual meeting of the American Society of Criminology, Chicago.

Gelles, R., & Tolman, R. (1998). *The Kingston Screening Instrument for Domestic Violence (K-SID).* Unpublished risk instrument, University of Rhode Island, Providence.

Gendreau, P., Little, T. & Goggin, C. (1996). A meta-analysis of the predictors of adult offender recidivism: What works? *Criminology, 34,* 575–607.

Gilberg, J., NeVilles-Sorell, J., Olson, T., Rock, B., Sandman, B., Skye, B., et al. (2003). *Addressing domestic violence in Indian Country: Introductory manual.* Duluth, MN: Mending the Sacred Hoop Technical Assistance Project.

Gilgun, J. (2005). The four cornerstones of evidence-based practice in social work. *Research on Social Work Practice, 15,* 52–61.

Gilligan, C., Sanson-Fisher, R., & Shakeshaft, A. (2010). Appropriate research designs for evaluating community-level alcohol interventions: What next? *Alcohol & Alcoholism, 45,* 481–487.

Goldberg, C. (2005, August 8). Out of control anger: As many as 5 percent of people suffer from a disorder that can ruin their lives. *Boston Globe.* Retrieved June 21, 2010, from http//www.boston.com/news/globe/health_science/arm.

Goldkamp, J. (2008). Missing the target and missing the point: Successful random assignment but misleading results. *Journal of Experimental Criminology, 4,* 83–115.

Gondolf, E. (1985). *Men who batter: An integrated approach to stopping wife abuse.* Holmes Beach, FL: Learning Publications.

Gondolf, E. (1988). The effect of batterer counseling on shelter outcome. *Journal of Interpersonal Violence, 3,* 275–289.

Gondolf, E. (1998a). Service contact and delivery of a shelter outreach project. *Journal of Family Violence, 13,* 131–145.

Gondolf, E. (1998b). Victims of court-mandated batterers: Their victimization, helpseeking, and perceptions. *Violence Against Women, 4,* 659–676.

Gondolf, E. (1999a). Characteristics of court-mandated batterers in four cities: Diversity and dichotomies. *Violence Against Women, 5,* 1277–1293.

Gondolf, E. (1999b). A comparison of re-assault rates in four batterer programs: Do court referral, program length and services matter? *Journal of Interpersonal Violence, 14,* 41–61.

Gondolf, E. (1999c). MCMI results for batterer program participants in four cities: Less pathological than expected. *Journal of Family Violence, 14,* 1–17.

Gondolf, E. (2000a). How batterer program participants avoid re-assault. *Violence Against Women, 6,* 1204–1222.

Gondolf, E. (2000b). Human subject issues in batterer program evaluation. *Journal of Aggression, Maltreatment & Trauma, 4,* 273–297

Gondolf, E. (2000c). Mandatory court review and batterer program compliance. *Journal of Interpersonal Violence, 15,* 428–437.

Gondolf, E. (2000d). Reassault at 30 months after batterer program intake. *International Journal of Offender Therapy and Comparative Criminology, 44,* 111–128.

Gondolf, E. (2000e). *The way to change: A gender-based workbook for men who have abused their partners.* Holmes Beach, FL: Learning Publications.

Gondolf, E. (2001). Limitations of experimental evaluations of batterer programs. *Trauma, Violence, and Abuse, 2,* 79–88.

Gondolf, E. (2002a). *Batterer intervention systems: Issues, outcomes, and recommendations.* Thousand Oaks, CA: Sage.

Gondolf, E. (2002b). Service barriers for battered women with male partners in batterer programs. *Journal of Interpersonal Violence, 17,* 217–227.

Gondolf, E. (2004a). Evaluating batterer counseling programs: A difficult task showing some effects. *Aggression and Violent Behavior, 9,* 605–631.

Gondolf, E. (2004b). Regional and cultural utility of conventional batterer counseling. *Violence Against Women, 10,* 880–900.

Gondolf, E. (2005). *Culturally-focused batterer counseling for African-American men: A clinical trial of program effectiveness* (Document No. 210828). Final report submitted to the National Institute of Justice, Washington. Retrieved August 15, 2010, from www.ncjrs.gov/pdffiles1/nij/grants/210828.pdf.

Gondolf, E. (2007a). Culturally-focused batterer counseling for African American men: A clinical trial of re-assault and re-arrest outcomes. *Criminology and Public Policy, 6,* 341–366.

Gondolf, E. (2007b). Theoretical and research support for the Duluth Model: A reply to Dutton and Corvo. *Aggression and Violent Behavior, 12,* 644–657.

Gondolf, E. (2008a). Outcomes of case management for African American men in batterer counseling. *Journal of Family Violence, 23,* 173–181.

Gondolf, E. (2008b). Program completion in specialized batterer counseling for African-American men. *Journal of Interpersonal Violence, 23,* 94–116.

Gondolf, E. (2009a). Implementing mental health treatment for batterer program participants: Interagency breakdowns and underlying issues. *Violence Against Women, 15,* 638–655.

Gondolf, E. (2009b). Outcomes from referring batterer program participants to mental health treatment. *Journal of Family Violence, 24,* 577–588.

Gondolf, E. (2010). Lessons from a successful and failed random assignment testing batterer program innovations. *Journal of Experimental Criminology, 6,* 355–376.

Gondolf, E. (2011). *An evaluation of consumer-based, recovery-oriented case-management training for mental health workers.* Final report submitted to the Staunton Foundation, Pittsburgh.

Gondolf, E. (in press). Physical tactics of female partners against male batterer program participants. *Violence Against Women*.

Gondolf, E., & Beeman, A. (2003). Women's accounts of violence versus tactics-based outcome categories. *Violence Against Women, 9*, 278–302.

Gondolf, E., & Fisher, E. (1988). *Battered women as survivors: An alternative to learned helplessness*. Lexington, MA: Lexington.

Gondolf, E., & Heckert, A. (2003). Determinants of women's perceptions of risk in battering relationships. *Violence and Victims, 18*, 371–386.

Gondolf, E., Heckert, A., & Kimmel, C. (2002). Non-physical abuse among batterer program participants. *Journal of Family Violence, 17*, 293–315.

Gondolf, E., & Jones, A. (2001). The program effect of batterer programs in three cities. *Violence and Victims, 16*, 693–704.

Gondolf, E., & Wernik, H. (2009). Clinician ratings of batterer treatment behaviors. *Journal of Interpersonal Violence, 24*, 1792–1815.

Gondolf, E., & White, R. (2000). "Consumer" recommendations for batterer programs. *Violence Against Women, 6*, 196–215.

Gondolf, E., & White, R. (2001). Batterer program participants who repeatedly re-assault: Psychopathic tendencies and other disorders. *Journal of Interpersonal Violence, 16*, 361–380.

Gondolf, E., & Williams, O. (2001). Culturally-focused batterer counseling for African-American men. *Trauma, Violence, and Abuse, 4*, 283–295.

Gondolf, E., Yllo, K., & Campbell, J. (1997). Collaboration between researchers and advocates. In G. Kantor & J. Jasinski (Eds.), *Out of the darkness* (pp. 255–270). Thousand Oaks, CA: Sage.

Gordis, E. (1997, April). Patient-treatment matching—A commentary. *Alcohol Alert, 36*, 3.

Gormley, B. (2005). An adult attachment theoretical perspective of gender symmetry in intimate partner violence. *Sex Roles, 52*, 785–795.

Government Accountability Office. (2009). *Program evaluation: A variety of rigorous methods can help identify effective interventions*. Washington: Author. Retrieved May 8, 2011, from www.gao.gov/new.items/d1030.pdf.

Grapow, M., von Wattenwyl, R., Guller, U., Beyersdorf, F., & Zerkowski, H. (2006). Randomized controlled trials do not reflect reality: Real-world analyses are critical for treatment guidelines. *Journal of Thoracic and Cardiovascular Surgery, 132*, 5–7.

Griner, D, & Smith, T. (2006). Culturally adapted mental health intervention: A meta-analytic review. *Psychotherapy, 43*, 531–548.

Grisso, T., & Tomkins, A. (1996). Communicating violence risk assessments. *American Psychologist, 51*, 928–930.

Grove, W., & Meehl, P. (1996). Comparative efficiency of informal (subjective, impressionistic) and formal (mechanical, algorithmic) prediction procedures: The clinical-statistical controversy. *Psychology, Public Policy, and Law, 2*, 293–323.

Guba, E., & Lincoln, Y. (1989). *Fourth generation evaluation.* Thousand Oaks, CA; Sage.

Hagan, K., & Steinem, G. (1992). *Women respond to the men's movement.* San Francisco: Harper.

Hamberger, L. (1997). Cognitive-behavioral treatment for men who batter their partners. *Cognitive and Behavioral Practice, 4,* 147–169.

Hamberger, L. (2002). The men's group program: A community-based, cognitive-behavioral, pro-feminist intervention program. Chapter 7 in E. Aldarondo & F. Mederos (Eds.), *Programs for men who batter: Intervention and prevention strategies in a diverse society.* Kingston, NJ: Civic Research Institute.

Hamberger, L., & Lohr, J. (1997). An empirical classification of motivations for domestic violence. *Violence Against Women, 3,* 401–424.

Hamberger, L., Lohr, J., Bonge, D., & Tolin, D. (1996). A large sample empirical typology of male spouse abusers and its relationship to dimensions of abuse. *Violence and Victims, 11,* 277–292.

Hamberger, L., & Potente, T. (1994). Counseling heterosexual women arrested domestic violence: Implications for theory and practice. *Violence and Victims, 9,* 125–137.

Hamby, S. (2009). The gender debate about intimate partner violence: Solutions and dead ends. *Psychological Trauma, 1,* 24–34.

Hamel, J. (2005). *Gender inclusive treatment of intimate partner abuse: A comprehensive approach.* New York: Springer.

Hamel, J. (2010). Do we want to be politically correct, or do we want to reduce partner violence in our communities? *Partner Abuse, 1,* 82–91.

Hamel, J., & Nicholls, T. (Eds.) (2006). *Family interventions in domestic violence: A handbook of gender-inclusive theory and treatment.* New York: Springer.

Hampton, R., Carrillo, R., & Kim, J. (1998). Violence in communities of color. In R. Carillo & J. Tello (Eds.), *Family violence and men of color: Healing the wounded male spirit* (pp. 74–94). New York: Springer.

Hanson, K. (2005). Twenty-five years of progress in violence risk assessment. *Journal of Interpersonal Violence, 20,* 212–217.

Hanson, K., Bourgon, G., Helmus, L., & Hodgson, S. (2009). The principles of effective correctional treatment also apply to sexual offenders: A meta-analysis. *Criminal Justice and Behavior, 36,* 865–891.

Haque, Q. (2008, July 14–16). *Best practice in managing violence and related risks: Evidence-based implementation.* Workshop presented at the annual conference of the International Association of Forensic Mental Health Services, Vienna.

Harrell, A. (1991). *Evaluation of court-ordered treatment for domestic violence offenders.* Washington: Urban Institute.

Harrell, A., Visher, C., Newmark, L., & Yahner, J. (2009). *The Judicial Oversight Demonstration: Culminating report on the evaluation.* Washington: National Institute of Justice. Retrieved August 15, 2010, from www.ncjrs.gov/pdffiles1 /nij/224201.pdf.

Harris, P., Raymond, G., & Whittaker, T. (2004). The "effectiveness" of differential supervision. *Crime and Delinquency, 50*, 234–271.

Hart, B. (1989). *The Lethality Checklist.* Harrisburg, PA: Pennsylvania Coalition against Domestic Violence.

Hart, S. (2008, July 14–16). *The future of violence risk assessment and management: From prediction to prevention, from formula to formulation.* Keynote address at the annual conference of the International Association of Forensic Mental Health Services, Vienna.

Harway, M., & Hansen, M. (1993). Therapist perceptions of family violence. In M. Hansen & M. Harway (Eds.), *Battering and family therapy: A feminist perspective* (pp. 42–53). Thousand Oaks, CA: Sage.

Heckert, A., & Gondolf, E. (2000a). Assessing assault self-reports by batterer program participants and their partners. *Journal of Family Violence, 15*, 181–197.

Heckert, A., & Gondolf, E. (2000b). The effect of perceptions of sanctions on batterer program outcome. *Journal of Research in Crime and Delinquency, 37*, 369–391.

Heckert, A., & Gondolf, E. (2000c). Predictors of underreporting of male violence by batterer program participants and their partners. *Journal of Family Violence, 15*, 423–443.

Heckert, A., & Gondolf, E. (2004). Battered women's perceptions of risk versus risk factors and instruments in predicting repeat re-assault. *Journal of Interpersonal Violence, 19*, 778–800.

Heckert, A., & Gondolf, E. (2005). Do multiple outcomes and conditional factors improve prediction of domestic violence? *Violence and Victims, 20*, 3–24.

Heckman, J. (1997). Instrumental variables: A study of implicit behavioral assumptions underlying one widely used estimator for program evaluations. *Journal of Human Resources, 32*, 441–461.

Heckman, J., & Smith, J. (1995). Assessing the case for social experiments. *Journal of Economic Perspectives, 9*, 85–110.

Heilbrun, K. (1997). Prediction versus management models relevant to risk assessment: The importance of legal decision-making context. *Law and Human Behavior, 21*, 347–360.

Henderson, A., Bartholomew, K., & Dutton, D. (1997). He loves me, he loves me not: Attachment and separation resolution of abused women. *Journal of Family Violence, 12*, 169–191.

Henning, K., & Holdford, R. (2006). Minimization, denial, and victim blaming by batterers: How much does the truth matter? *Criminal Justice and Behavior, 33*, 110–130.

Hilton, N., & Harris, G. (2005). Predicting wife assault: A critical review and implications for policy and practice. *Trauma, Violence, and Abuse, 6*, 3–23.

Hilton, N., Harris, G., Rawson, K., & Beach, C. (2005). Communicating violence risk information to forensic decision makers. *Criminal Justice and Behavior, 32*, 97–116.

Hilton, N., Harris, G., Rice, M., Lang, C., & Cormier, C. (2004). A brief actuarial assessment for the prediction of wife assault recidivism: The ODARA. *Psychological Assessment, 16,* 267–275.

Hohmann, A., & Shear, M. (2002). Community-based intervention research: Coping with the "noise" of real life in study design. *American Journal of Psychiatry, 159,* 2–15.

Hollin, C. (2008). Evaluating offending behaviour programmes: Does only randomization glister? *Criminology and Criminal Justice, 8,* 89–106.

Holmes, D., Murray, S., Perron, A., & Rali, G. (2006). Deconstructing the evidence-based discourse in health sciences: Truth, power and fascism. *International Journal of Evidence Based Healthcare, 4,* 180–186.

Holtzworth-Munroe, A. (2005). Male versus female intimate partner violence: Putting controversial findings into context. *Journal of Marriage and Family, 67,* 1120–1125.

Holtzworth-Munroe, A., & Meehan, J. (2004). Typologies of men who are maritally violent: Scientific and clinical implications. *Journal of Interpersonal Violence, 19,* 1369–1389.

Holtzworth-Munroe, A., Meehan, J., Herron, K., Rehman, U., & Stuart, G. (2000). Testing the Holtzworth-Munroe and Stuart (1994) batterer typology. *Journal of Consulting and Clinical Psychology, 68,* 1000–1019.

Holtzworth-Munroe, A., Meehan, J., Herron, K., Rehman, U., & Stuart, G. (2003). Do subtypes of maritally violent men continue to differ over time? *Journal of Consulting and Clinical Psychology, 71,* 728–740.

Holtzworth-Munroe, A., & Stuart, G. (1994). Typologies of male batterers: Three subtypes and the differences among them. *Psychological Bulletin, 116,* 476–497.

Hoover, K., & Wallace T. (2008). *Studies in ethics, safety, and liability for engineers: Space shuttle Challenger.* Austin: University of Texas at Austin and the Texas Space Grant Consortium, National Aeronautics and Space Administration. Retrieved August 15, 2010, from www.tsgc.utexas.edu/archive/general/ethics/shuttle.html.

Hubbard, R., Marsden, M., Rachal, J., Harwood, H., Cavanaugh, E., & Ginzburg, H. (1989). *Drug abuse treatment: A national survey of effectiveness.* Chapel Hill: University of North Carolina Press.

Huey, S., & Polo, A. (2008). Evidence-based psychosocial treatments for ethnic minority youth: A review and meta-analysis. *Journal of Clinical Child and Adolescent Psychology, 37,* 262–301.

Huss, M., & Ralston, A. (2008). Do batterer subtypes actually matter? Treatment completion, treatment response, and recidivism across a batterer typology. *Criminal Justice and Behavior, 35,* 710–724.

Ip, E., Jones, A., Heckert, D., Zhang, Q, & Gondolf, E. (2010). Latent Markov model for analyzing temporal configuration for violence profiles and trajectories in a sample of batterers. *Sociological Methods and Research, 39,* 222–255.

Iyengar, R. (2007, August 7). The protection battered spouses don't need [Op ed]. *The New York Times.* Retrieved June 10, 2011, from www.nytimes.com.

Iyengar, R. (2009). Does the certainty of arrest reduce domestic violence? Evidence from mandatory and recommended arrest laws. *Journal of Public Economics*, *93*, 85–98.

Jackson, S., Feder, L., Forde, D., Davis, R., Maxwell, C., & Taylor, B. (2003). *Batterer intervention programs: Where do we go from here?* Washington: National Institute of Justice. Retrieved May 9, 2011, from www.ncjrs.gov/pdffiles1/nij/195079.pdf.

Jacobson, N., & Gottman, J. (1998). *When men batter women: New insights into ending abusive relationships.* New York: Simon and Schuster.

Jenkins, A. (1990). *Invitations to responsibility: The therapeutic engagement of men who are violent and abuse.* Adelaide, South Australia: Dulwich Centre.

Johnson, M. (2006). Conflict and control: Gender symmetry and asymmetry in domestic violence. *Violence Against Women*, *12*, 1003–1018.

Johnson, M. (2008). *A typology of domestic violence: Intimate terrorism, violent resistance, and situational couple violence.* Boston: Northeastern University Press.

Jones, A. (2000). The cost of batterer treatment: How much? Who pays? *Journal of Interpersonal Violence*, *15*, 566–586.

Jones, A. (2010, June 13). Letter responding to criticisms of instrumental variable analysis, to R. Davis, guest editor, *Journal of Experimental Criminology*.

Jones, A., D'Agostino, R., Gondolf, E., & Heckert, A. (2004). Assessing the effect of batterer program completion on re-assault using propensity scores. *Journal of Interpersonal Violence*, *19*, 1002–1021.

Jones, A., & Gondolf, E. (2001). Time-varying risk factors for re-assault by batterer program participants. *Journal of Family Violence*, *16*, 345–359.

Jones, A., & Gondolf, E. (2002). Assessing the effect of batterer program completion on re-assault: An instrumental variables analysis. *Journal of Quantitative Criminology*, *18*, 71–98.

Jones, A., Heckert, D., Gondolf, E., & Zhang, Q. (2010). Complex behavioral patterns and trajectories of domestic violence offenders. *Violence and Victims*, *25*, 3–17.

Jones, A., & Scharfstein, D. (2001). *Use of the odds ratio as a measure of effect size.* Unpublished manuscript, School of Medicine, Wake Forest University.

Jones, E. (1982). Psychotherapists' impressions of treatment outcome as a function of race. *Journal of Clinical Psychology*, *38*, 722–731.

Jordan, C. (2009). Advancing the study of violence against women: Evolving research agendas into science. *Violence Against Women*, *15*, 393–419.

Karno, M., & Longabaugh, R. (2004). What do we know? Process analysis and the search for a better understanding of Project MATCH's anger-by-treatment matching effect. *Journal of Studies on Alcohol*, *65*, 501–512.

Karno, M., & Longabaugh, R. (2007). Does matching matter? Examining matches and mismatches between patient attributes and therapy techniques in alcoholism treatment. *Addiction*, *102*, 587–596.

Kassinove, H., & Tafrate, R. (2002). *Anger management: The complete treatment guidebook for practitioners.* New York: Impact.

Katz, J. (1988). *Seductions of crime: The moral and sensual attractions in doing evil*. New York: Basic.

Katz, J. (2006). *The macho paradox: Why some men hurt women and how all men can help*. Naperville, IL: Sourcebooks.

Kazdin, A. (1994). Methodology, design, and evaluation in psychotherapy research. In A. Bergin & S. Garfield (Eds.), *Handbook of psychotherapy and behavior change* (pp. 19–71). Hoboken, NJ: Wiley.

Kelejian, H. (1971) Two-stage least squares and econometric models linear in the parameters but nonlinear in the endogenous variables. *Journal of the American Statistical Association, 66*, 373–374.

Kelly, J. (2007). The system concept and systemic change: Implications for community psychology. *American Journal of Community Psychology, 39*, 415–418.

Kesner, J., Julian, T., & McKenry, P. (1997). Application of attachment theory to male violence towards female intimates. *Journal of Family Violence, 12*, 211–228.

Kessler, R., Coccaro, E., Fava, M., Jaeger, S., Jin, R., & Walters, E. (2006). The prevalence and correlates of DSM-IV Intermittent Explosive Disorder in the National Comorbidity Survey replication. *Archives of General Psychiatry, 63*, 669–678.

Kilpatrick, D., Resick, P., & Williams, L. (2001). Fostering collaborations between violence against women researchers and practitioners. *Social Insight, 6*, 29–36.

Kim, J. (2008). Examining the effectiveness of solution-focused brief therapy: A meta-analysis. *Research on Social Work Practice, 18*, 107–116.

Kindlon, D., & Thompson, T. (2000). *Raising Cain: Protecting the emotional life of boys*. New York: Ballantine.

Kistenmacher, B., & Weiss, R. (2008). Motivational interviewing as a mechanism for change in men who batter: A randomized controlled trial. *Violence and Victims, 23*, 558–570.

Kivel, P. (1998). *Men's work: How to stop the violence that tears our lives apart* (2nd ed.). Center City, MN: Hazelden.

Klein, A. (2009, June). *Practical implications of current domestic violence research: For law enforcement, prosecutors and judges* (NIJ Special Report). Washington: National Institute of Justice. Retrieved May 5, 2010, from www.ncjrs.gov/pdffiles1/nij/225722 .pdf.

Klein, A., & Tobin, T. (2008). A longitudinal study of arrested batterers, 1995–2005. *Violence Against Women, 14*, 136–157.

Klevens, J., Baker, C., Shelley, G., & Ingram, E. (2008). Exploring the links between components of coordinated community responses and their impact on contact with intimate partner violence services. *Violence Against Women, 14*, 346–358.

Kluger, J. (2005, August 25). *Batterers intervention program study*. Memo to administrative judges and judges of the domestic violence and integrated domestic violence courts, State of New York, Unified Court System, Office of Court Administration, New York.

Koerner, B. (1999, April 4). It may be all the rage, but does it work? Some doubt anger-management class helps. *U.S. News & World Report, 126,* 44–45.

Kotulak, R. (2006, June 6). Anger attacks common and research tells why: Intermittent Explosive Disorder affects 1 in 20. *Chicago Tribune.* Retrieved June 9, 2011, from http://articles.chicagotribune.com.

Kraemer, J., Kazdin, A., Offord, D., Kessler, R., Jensen, P., & Kupfer, D. (1997). Coming to terms with the terms of risk. *Archives of General Psychiatry, 54,* 337–344.

Kreger, M., Brindis, C., Manuel, D., & Sassoubre, L. (2007). Lessons learned in systems change initiatives: Benchmarks and indicators. *American Journal of Community Psychology, 39,* 301–320.

Kristof, N. (2008, April 17). Divided they fall. *The New York Times.* Retrieved May 8, 2011, from www.nytimes.com.

Kropp, R. (2008). Intimate partner violence risk assessment and management. *Violence and Victims, 23,* 202–220.

Kropp, R. (2009, November 4–5). *Recent data and emerging issues in generic versus specific risk assessment with domestic violence perpetrators.* Paper presented at the annual meeting of the American Society of Criminology, Philadelphia.

Kropp, R., & Hart, S. (2000). The Spousal Assault Risk Assessment (SARA) guide: Reliability and validity in adult male offenders. *Law and Human Behavior, 24,* 101–118.

Kropp, R., Hart, S., & Belfrage, H. (2005). *The Brief Spousal Assault Form for the Evaluation of Risk (B-SAFER).* Vancouver: Proactive Resolutions.

Kropp, R., Hart, S., Webster, C., & Eaves, D. (1999). *Spousal Assault Risk Assessment guide (SARA).* Toronto: Multi-Health Systems.

Krucoff, M., Crater, S., Gallup, D., Blankenship, J., Cuffe, M., Guarneri, M., et al. (2005). Music, imagery, touch, and prayer as adjuncts to interventional cardiac care: The Monitoring and Actualization of Noetic Training (MANTRA) II randomized study. *Lancet, 366,* 211–217.

Labriola, M. (2005, November 17). *Testing the impacts of court monitoring and batterer intervention programs.* Slides presented at the annual meeting of the American Society for Criminology, Toronto.

Labriola, M., Rempel, M., & Davis, R. (2005). *Testing the effectiveness of batterer programs and judicial monitoring: Results from a randomized trial at the Bronx Misdemeanor Domestic Violence Court.* Final report submitted to National Institute of Justice, Washington. Retrieved June 9, 2011, from www.courtinnovation.org/sites/default/files/battererprogramseffectiveness.pdf.

Labriola, M., Rempel, M., & Davis, R. (2008). Do batterer programs reduce recidivism? Results from a randomized trial in the Bronx. *Justice Quarterly, 25,* 252–282

Labriola, M., Rempel, M., O'Sullivan, C., & Frank, P. (2007). *Court responses to batterer program non-compliance: A national perspective.* New York: Center for Court Innovation. Retrieved May 7, 2011, from http://courtinnovation.org/_uploads/documents/Court_Responses_March2007.pdf.

Landenberger, N., & Lipsey, M. (2005). The positive effects of cognitive-behavioral programs for offenders: A meta-analysis of factors associated with effective treatment. *Journal of Experimental Criminology, 1,* 451–476.

Lang, A. (1983). The addictive personality: A viable construct. In P. Levison, D. Gerstein, & D. Maloff (Eds.), *Commonalities in substance abuse and habitual behavior* (pp. 157–235). Lexington, MA: Lexington.

Langford, D. (1996). Predicting unpredictability: A model of women's processes predicting battering men's violence. *Scholarly Inquiry for Nursing Practice, 10,* 371–385.

Larance, L. (2006). Serving women who use force in their intimate heterosexual relationships: An extended view. *Violence Against Women, 12,* 622–640.

Lasker, R., & Weiss, E. (2003). Broadening participation in community problem solving: A multidisciplinary model to support collaborative practice and research. *Journal of Urban Health, 80,* 14–47.

Lawrence, R. (2006, April 11). Faith-based medicine [Op ed]. *The New York Times.*

Lee, M., Sebold, J., & Uken, A. (2003). *Solution-focused treatment of domestic violence offenders: Accountability for change.* New York: Oxford University Press.

Lehmann, P., & Simmons, C. (2009). *Strengths-based batterer intervention: A new paradigm in ending family violence.* New York: Springer.

Lehrner, A., & Allen, N. (2009). *Still a movement after all these years? Current tensions in the domestic violence movement. Violence Against Women, 15,* 656–677.

Leichsenring, F., & Leibing, E. (2003). The effectiveness of psychodynamic therapy and cognitive behavior therapy in the treatment of personality disorders: A meta-analysis. *American Journal of Psychiatry, 160,* 1223–1232.

Levant, R., & Pollack, W. (1995). *A new psychology of men.* New York: Basic.

Levesque, D., Driskell, M., & Prochaska, J. (2008). Acceptability of a stage-matched expert system intervention for domestic violence offenders. *Violence and Victims, 23,* 432–445.

Levitt, D., & Miles, T. (2006). Economic contributions to the understanding of crime. *Annual Review of Law and Social Science, 2,* 147–164.

Levy, T., & Orlans, M. (1998). *Attachment, trauma, and healing: Understanding and treating attachment disorder in children and families.* University Park, IL: Child Welfare League of America.

Lightman, D. (2008, September 15). Wall Street crisis is culmination of 28 years of deregulation. *McClatchy.* Retrieved August 22, 2011, from www.mcclatchydc .com/2008/09/15/52559/wall-street-crisis-is-culmination.html.

Lipsky, M. (1983). *Street-level bureaucracy: Dilemmas of the individual in public services.* New York: Russell Sage.

Lipsey, M., Chapman, G., & Landenberger, N. (2001). Cognitive-behavioral programs for offenders. *Annals of the American Academy of Political and Social Science, 578,* 144–157.

Litwack, T. (2001). Actuarial versus clinical assessments of dangerousness. *Psychology, Public Policy, and Law, 7*, 409–443.

Logan, S. (1990*). Social work practice with black families: A culturally specific perspective*. New York: Longman.

Longabaugh, R. (2003). What happened to patient-treatment matching? *Brown University Digest of Addiction Theory and Application, 22* (11), 8.

Loughran, T., & Mulvey, E. (2010). Estimating treatment effects: Matching quantification to the question. In A. Piquero & D. Weisburd (Eds.), *Handbook of Quantitative Criminology* (pp. 163–181). New York: Springer.

Loza, W., & Loza-Fanous, A. (1999a). Anger and prediction of violent and nonviolent offender's recidivism. *Journal of Interpersonal Violence, 14*, 1014–1029.

Loza, W., & Loza-Fanous, A. (1999b). The fallacy of reducing rape and violent recidivism by treating anger. *International Journal of Offender Therapy and Comparative Criminology, 43*, 492–502.

Luborsky, L., Rosenthal, R., & Diguer, L. (2002). The dodo bird verdict is alive and well—mostly. *Clinical Psychology Science and Practice, 9*, 2–12.

Luellen, J., Shadish, W., & Clark, M. (2005). Propensity scores: An introduction and experimental test. *Evaluation Review, 29*, 530–558.

Lundahl, B., & Burke, B. (2009). The effectiveness and applicability of motivational interviewing: A practice-friendly review of four meta-analyses. *Journal of Clinical Psychology, 65*, 1232–1245.

Lundahl, B., Kunz, C., Brownell, C., Tollefson, D., & Burke, B. (2010). A meta-analysis of motivational interviewing: Twenty-five years of empirical studies. *Research on Social Work Practice, 20*, 137–160.

Mackenzie, D. (2006). *What works in corrections: Reducing the criminal activities of offenders and delinquents*. New York: Cambridge University Press.

MacLeod, D., Pi, R., Smith, D., & Rose-Goodwin, L. (2008). *Batterer intervention systems in California: An evaluation*. San Francisco: Administrative Office of the Courts. Retrieved June, 10, 2011, from www.courtinfo.ca.gov/reference/documents/batterer-report.pdf.

Macrae, C., & Bodenhausen G. (2001). Social cognition: Categorical person perception. *British Journal of Psychology, 92*, 239–255.

Maiuro, R., & Eberle, J. (2008). State standards for domestic violence perpetrators treatment: Current status, trends and recommendations. *Violence and Victims, 23*, 133–155.

Maiuro, R., Hagar, T., Lin, H., & Olson, N. (2001). Are current state standards for domestic violence perpetrator treatment adequately informed by research? *Journal of Aggression, Maltreatment, and Trauma, 5*, 21–44.

Manjoo, F. (2008). *True enough: Learning to live in a post-fact society*. Hoboken, NJ: Wiley.

Mann, C. (1990, August). Meta-analysis in the breech. *Science, 249*, 476–480.

Marlatt, A. (2002). *Harm reduction: Pragmatic strategies for managing high-risk behaviors*. New York: Guilford.

Marshall, W., Anderson, D., & Fernandez, Y. (1999). *Cognitive-behavioral treatment of sexual offenders*. London: Wiley.

Marshall, W., & Burton, D. (2010). The importance of group processes in offender treatment. *Aggression and Violent Behavior, 15*, 141–149.

Marshall, W., & McGuire, J. (2003). Effect sizes in the treatment of sexual offenders. *International Journal of Offender Therapy and Comparative Criminology, 47*, 653–663.

Marshall, W., & Pithers, W. (1994). A reconsideration of treatment outcome with sex offenders. *Criminal Justice and Behavior, 21*, 10–28.

Marshall, W., & Serran, G. (2000). Improving the effectiveness of sexual offender treatment. *Trauma, Violence, and Abuse, 1*, 203–222.

Martin, A., Berenson, K., Griffing, S., Sage, R., Madry, L., Bingham, L., et al. (2000). The process of leaving an abusive relationship: The role of risk assessments and decision-certainty. *Journal of Family Violence, 15*, 109–121.

Martinson, R. (1974). What works? Questions and answers about prison reform. *The Public Interest, 35*, 22–54.

Maruna, S. (2001). *Making good: How ex-convicts reform and rebuild their lives*. Washington: American Psychological Association.

Maruna, S. (2006). Desistance. In E. McLaughlin & J. Muncie (Eds.), *The Sage dictionary of criminology* (2nd ed., pp. 120–123). Thousand Oaks, CA: Sage.

Mauricio, A., Tein, J., & Lopez, F. (2007). Borderline and antisocial personality scores as mediators between attachment and intimate partner violence. *Violence and Victims, 22*, 139–157.

Mayseless, O. (1991). Adult attachment patterns and courtship violence. *Family Relations, 40*, 21–28.

McCartney, K., & Rosenthal, R. (2000). Effect size, practical importance, and social policy for children. *Child Development, 71*, 173–181.

McCollum, E., & Stith, S. (2008). Couples treatment for interpersonal violence: A review of outcome research literature and current clinical practices. *Violence and Victims, 23*, 187–201.

McCrystal, P., & Wilson, G. (2009). Research training and professional social work education: Developing research-minded practice. *Social Work Education, 28*, 856–872.

McGuire, J. (2006). General offending behavior programs: Concept, theory, and practice. In C. Hollin & E. Palmer (Eds.), *Offending behavior programs: Development, application, and controversies* (pp. 69–111). Chichester, England: John Wiley and Sons.

McNeely, R., & Robinson-Simpson, G. (1987). The truth about domestic violence: A falsely framed issue. *Social Work, 32*, 485–490.

McNeill, F. (2006). A desistance paradigm for offender management. *Criminology and Criminal Justice, 6,* 39–62.

Mears, D. (2003). Research and interventions to reduce domestic violence revictimization. *Trauma, Violence, and Abuse, 4,* 127–147.

Mederos, F. (2002). Changing our visions of intervention: The evolution of programs for physically abusive men. Chapter 1 in E. Aldarondo & F. Mederos (Eds.), *Programs for men who batter: Intervention and prevention strategies in a diverse society.* Kingston, NJ: Civic Research Institute.

Meehan, J., Holtzworth-Munroe, A., & Herron, K. (2001). Maritally violent men's heart rate reactivity to marital interactions: A failure to replicate the Gottman et al. (1995) typology. *Journal of family Psychology, 15,* 394–408.Messner, M. (1997). *Politics of masculinities: Men in movements.* Thousand Oaks, CA; Sage.

Mihalic, S., Irwin, K., Fagan, A., Ballard, D., & Elliott, D. (2004, July). Successful program implementation: Lessons from blueprints. *Juvenile Justice Bulletin,* 1–11. Retrieved August 22, 2010, from www.ncjrs.gov/pdffiles1/ojjdp/204273.pdf.

Miller, S., & Meloy, M. (2006). Women's use of force: Voices of women arrested for domestic violence. *Violence Against Women, 12,* 89–115.

Miller, W., & Rollnick, S. (2002). *Motivational interviewing: Preparing people for change* (2nd ed.). New York: Guilford.

Millon, T. (1994). *Millon Clinical Multiaxial Inventory-III.* Minneapolis: National Computer Systems.

Mills, L. (2006). *Insult to injury: Rethinking our responses to intimate abuse.* Princeton, NJ: Princeton University Press.

Mills, L. (2009). *Violent partners: A breakthrough plan for ending the cycle of abuse.* New York: Basic.

Milne, D., Leck, C., & Choudhri, N. (2009) Collusion in clinical supervision: Literature review and case study in self-reflection. *Cognitive Behavior Therapist, 2,* 106–114.

Mitchell, I., & Beech, A. (2011). Towards a neurobiological model of offending. *Clinical Psychology Review, 31,* 872–882.

Moffitt, T., Caspi, A., Rutter, M., & Silva, P. (2001). *Sex differences in antisocial behavior.* Cambridge: Cambridge University Press.

Monahan, J., & Steadman, H. (1996).Violent storms and violent people: How meteorology can inform risk communication in mental health law. *American Psychologist, 51,* 931–938.

Morrison, S., Lindquist, C., Hawkins, S., O'Neil, J., Nesius, J., & Mathew, A. (2003). *Evidence-based review of batterer intervention and prevention programs.* Final report to the Centers for Disease Control and Prevention, Atlanta.

Mulholland, C. (2005). *Men and addiction.* Netdoctor. Retrieved June 6, 2011 from www.netdoctor.co.uk/menshealth/facts/addiction.htm.

Mullen, E., Bledsoe, S., & Bellamy, J. (2008). Implementing evidence-based social work practice. *Research on Social Work Practice, 18,* 325–338.

Mulvey, E., & Lidz, C. (1995). Conditional prediction: A model for research on dangerousness to others in a new era. *International Journal of Law and Psychiatry, 18*, 129–143.

Mulvey, E., Steinberg, L., Piquero, A., Besana, M., Fagan, J., Schubert, C., et al. (2010). Trajectories of desistance and continuity in antisocial behavior following court adjudication among serious adolescent offenders. *Development and Psychopathology, 22*, 453–475.

Muno, N. (2008, April 5). Domestic politics. *National Journal,* 32–37.

Murphy, C., & Eckhardt, C. (2005). *Treating the abusive partner: An individualized cognitive-behavioral approach.* New York: Guilford.

Murphy, C., & Maiuro, R. (2008). Understanding and facilitating the change process in perpetrators and victims of intimate partner violence: Summary and commentary. *Violence and Victims, 23*, 525–536.

Murphy, C., & Maiuro, R. (Eds.) (2009). *Motivational interviewing and stages of change in intimate partner violence.* New York: Springer.

Murphy, C., Meyer, S., & O'Leary, D. (1994). Dependency characteristics of partner assaultive men. *Journal of Abnormal Psychology, 103*, 729–735.

Murphy, C., Musser, P., & Maton, K. (1998). Coordinated community intervention for domestic abusers: Intervention system involvement and criminal recidivism. *Journal of Family Violence, 13*, 263–284.

Murphy, C., & Ting, L. (2010). Interventions for perpetrators of intimate partner violence: A review of efficacy research and recent trends. *Partner Abuse, 1*, 26–44.

Murphy, D. (2008). The effects of ethnic match and length of treatment on anger and aggression in male batterers. *Dissertation Abstracts International, Section A: Humanities and Social Sciences, 68* (11), 4871.

Musser, P., Semiatin, J., Taft, C., & Murphy, C. (2008). Motivational interviewing as a pregroup intervention for partner-violent men. *Violence and Victims, 23*, 539–557.

Nakken, C. (1996). *The addictive personality: Understanding the addictive process and compulsive behavior.* Center City, MN: Hazelden.

Nathan, P., Stuart, S., & Dolan, S. (2000). Research on psychotherapy efficacy and effectiveness: Between Scylla and Charybdis? *Psychological Bulletin, 126*, 964–981.

Neidig, P. (1985). Domestic conflict containment: A spouse abuse treatment program. *Social Casework, 66*, 195–204.

Nelson, L. (1999). National conference summary: Assembling the pieces; An African-American perspective on community and family violence. *Newsletter of the National Institute on Domestic Violence in the African American Community, 1* (2), 1–3.

Newman, C. (1994). Understanding client resistance: Methods for enhancing motivation to change. *Cognitive and Behavioral Practice, 1*, 47–69.

Nisbet, R., & Cohen, D. (1996). *Culture of honor: The psychology of violence in the South.* Boulder, CO: Westview.

Nitsch, L., & Garvin, D. (2009, May 12–15). *Same research, different perspective: Talking to referral sources and community partners program about efficacy.* Workshop presented at "Bridging Perspectives: Intervening with Men who Batter," Minneapolis, MN.

Norcross, J., Beutler, L., & Levant, R. (Eds.). (2006). *Evidence-based practices in mental health: Debate and dialogue on the fundamental questions.* Washington: American Psychological Association.

Norlander, B., & Eckhardt, C. (2005). Anger, hostility, and male perpetrators of intimate partner violence: A meta-analytic review. *Clinical Psychology Review, 25,* 119–152.

O'Leary, K., Heyman, R., & Neidig, P. (2002). Treatment of wife abuse: A comparison of gender-specific and conjoint approaches. *Behavior Therapy, 30,* 475–505.

Oliver, W. (1994). *The violent social world of African-American men.* New York: Lexington.

Ostrowsky, M. (2010). Are violent people more likely to have low self-esteem or high self-esteem? *Aggression and Violent Behavior, 15,* 69–75.

Palmer, S., Brown, R., & Barrera, M. (1992). Group treatment program for abusive husbands. *American Journal of Orthopsychiatry, 62,* 276–283.

Paymar, M. (2000). *Violent no more: Helping men end domestic abuse* (2nd ed.). Alameda, CA: Hunter House.

Pearson, F., Lipton, D., Cleland, C., & Yee, D. (2002). The effects of behavioral/cognitive-behavioral programs on recidivism. *Crime and Delinquency, 4,* 476–496.

Peele, S. (1998). *The meaning of addiction: An unconventional view.* New York: Jossey-Bass.

Pence, E. (1989). Batterer programs: Shifting from community collusion to community confrontation. In P. Caesar & L. Hamberger (Eds.), *Treating men who batter: Theory, practice, and programs.* New York: Springer.

Pence, E. (2002). The Duluth Domestic Abuse Intervention Project. Chapter 6 in E. Aldarondo & F. Mederos (Eds.), *Programs for men who batter: Intervention and prevention strategies in a diverse society.* Kingston, NJ: Civic Research Institute.

Pence, E., & Eng, D. (2009). *The blueprint for safety: An interagency response to domestic violence crimes.* St. Paul, MN: Praxis International. Retrieved June 10, 2011, from www.praxisinternational.org/blueprintforsafety.aspx.

Pence, E., & Lizdas, K. (1998). *The Duluth safety and accountability audit: A guide to assessing institutional responses to domestic violence.* Duluth, MN: Minnesota Program Development.

Pence, E., & McDonnell, C. (1999). Developing policies and protocols. In E. Pence & M. Shepard (Eds.), *Coordinated community response to domestic violence: Lessons from Duluth and beyond* (pp. 41–64). Thousand Oaks, CA: Sage.

Pence, E., & Paymar, M. (1993). *Education groups for men who batter: The Duluth model.* New York: Springer.

Pence, E., & Paymar, M. (2003). *Creating a process of change for men who batter: The Duluth curriculum*. Duluth, MN: Minnesota Program Development.

Pence, E., & Shepard, M. (1999). Developing a coordinated community response. In M. Shepard & E. Pence (Eds.), *Coordinating community responses to domestic violence: Lessons from Duluth and beyond* (pp. 3–25). Thousand Oaks, CA: Sage.

Perilla, J., & Perez, F. (2002). A program for immigrant Latino men who batter within the context of a comprehensive family intervention. Chapter 11 in E. Aldarondo & F. Mederos (Eds.), *Programs for men who batter: Intervention and prevention strategies in a diverse society*. Kingston, NJ: Civic Research Institute.

Perry, J. (2004). Review: Psychodynamic therapy and cognitive-behavioral therapy are effective in the treatment of personality disorders. *Evidence-Based Mental Health, 7*, 16.

Persons, J., & Silberschatz, G. (1998). Are results of randomized controlled trials useful to psychotherapists? *Journal of Consulting & Clinical Psychology, 66*, 126–136.

Peterson, R. (2008). Reducing intimate partner violence: Moving beyond criminal justice interventions. *Criminology and Public Policy, 7*, 537–545.

Pettit, L., & Smith, R. (2002). The AMEND model. Chapter 8 in E. Aldarondo & F. Mederos (Eds.), *Programs for men who batter: Intervention and prevention strategies in a diverse society*. Kingston, NJ: Civic Research Institute.

Pheifer, P. (2010, April 18). A voice for abuse victims. *Star Tribune*. Retrieved May 10, 2010, from www.startribune.com/lifestyle/family/91279944.html.

Piquero, A., Brame, R., Fagan, J., & Moffitt, T. (2006). Assessing the offending activity of criminal domestic violence suspects: Offense specialization, escalation, and de-esclation evidence from the spouse assault replication program. *Public Health Reports, 121*, 409–418.

Piquero, A., Fagan, J., Mulvey, E., Steinberg, L., & Ogden, C. (2005). Longitudinal offending trajectories among serious, youthful offenders. *Journal of Criminal Law and Criminology, 96*, 267–298.

Polaschek, D., Wilson, N., Townsend, M., & Daley, L. (2005). Cognitive-behavioral rehabilitation for high-risk violent offenders: An outcome evaluation of the violence prevention unit. *Journal of Interpersonal Violence, 20*, 1611–1627.

Pollack, W. (1998). *Real boys: Rescuing our sons from the myths of boyhood*. New York: Random House.

Pollack, W., & Cushman, A. (2001). *Real boys workbook*. New York: Villard.

Pollio, D. (2006). The art of evidence-based practice. *Research on Social Work Practice, 16*, 224–232.

Post, L., Klevens, J., Maxwell, C., Shelley, G., & Ingram, E. (2010). An examination of whether coordinated community responses affect intimate partner violence. *Journal of Interpersonal Violence, 25*, 75–93.

Postmus, J., Severson, M., Berry, M., & Yoo, J. (2009). Women's experiences of violence and seeking help. *Violence Against Women, 15*, 852–868.

Potter, H. (2007). Reaction essay: The need for a multi-faceted response to intimate partner abuse perpetrated by African-Americans. *Criminology and Public Policy, 6,* 367–376.

Price, B., & Rosenbaum, A. (2009). Batterer intervention programs: A report from the field. *Violence and Victims, 24,* 757–769.

Prochaska, J. (1984). *Systems of psychotherapy: A transtheoretical approach.* Homewood, IL: Dow Jones-Irwin.

Prochaska, J., & DiClemente, C. (1985). Common processes of change in smoking, weight control, and psychological distress. In S. Shiffman & T. Wills (Eds.), *Coping and substance use: A conceptual framework* (pp. 345–363). New York: Academic.

Project MATCH Research Group (1997). Matching alcoholism treatments to client heterogeneity: Project MATCH posttreatment drinking outcome. *Journal of Studies on Alcohol, 58,* 7–29.

Puffett, N., & Gavin, C. (2004). *Predictors of program outcome and recidivism at the Bronx Misdemeanor Domestic Violence Court.* New York: Center for Court Innovation.

Quinsey, V., Harris, G., Rice, G., & Cormier, C., (1998). *Violent offenders: Appraising and managing risk.* Washington: American Psychological Association.

Raab, S. (2000, March). Men explode. *Esquire, 134,* 244–248.

Ramey, H., & Grubb, S. (2009). Modernism, postmodernism and evidence-based practice. *Contemporary Family Therapy, 31,* 75–86.

Rapp, R., Otto, A., Lane, D., Redko, C., McGatha, S., & Carlson, R. (2008). Improving linkage with substance abuse treatment using brief case management and motivational interviewing. *Drug and Alcohol Dependence, 94,* 172–182.

Rasheed, J., & Rasheed, M. (Eds.). (1999). *Social work practice with African-American men: The invisible presence.* Thousand Oaks, CA: Sage.

Reed, G., & Eisman, E. (2006). Uses and misuses of evidence: Managed care, treatment guidelines, and outcome measurement in professional practice. In C. Goodheart, A., Kazdin, & R. Sternberg (Eds.), *Evidence-based psychotherapy: Where practice and research meet* (pp. 13–35). Washington: American Psychological Association.

Reiss, A., & Roth, J. (1993). *Understanding and preventing violence.* Washington: National Academies Press.

Richetin, J., & Richardson, D. (2008). Automatic processes and individual differences in aggressive behavior. *Aggression and Violent Behavior, 13,* 423–430.

Riggs, D., Caulfield, M., & Street, A. (2000). Risk for domestic violence: Factors associated with perpetration and victimization. *Journal of Clinical Psychology, 56,* 1289–1316.

Risk and Needs Assessment. (1997). *Domestic Violence Inventory (DVI): An inventory of scientific findings.* Phoenix, AZ: Author.

Rivett, M., & Rees, A. (2004). Dancing on razor's edge: Systemic group work with batterers. *Journal of Family Therapy, 26,* 142–162.

Roehl, J., & Guertin, K. (2000). Intimate partner violence: The current use of risk assessments in sentencing offenders. *Justice System Journal, 21,* 171–197.

Roehl, J., O'Sullivan, C., Webster, D., & Campbell, J. (2005). *Intimate partner violence risk assessment validation study: The RAVE study* (Document No. 209732). Washington: National Institute of Justice. Retrieved June 9, 2011, from www.ncjrs .gov/pdffiles1/nij/grants/209732.pdf.

Rogers, C. (1992). The necessary and sufficient conditions of therapeutic personality change. *Journal of Consulting and Clinical Psychology, 60,* 827–832.

Rogers Commission (1986). *Report of the presidential commission on the space shuttle Challenger accident.* Washington: Office of the President of the United States. Retrieved June 10, 2011, from http://history.nasa.gov/rogersrep/genindex.htm.

Rogers, R. (2000). The uncritical acceptance of risk assessment in forensic practice. *Law and Human Behavior, 24,* 595–605.

Rollnick, S., Miller, R., & Butler, C. (2008). *Motivational interviewing in health care: Helping patients change behavior.* New York: Guilford.

Rooney, R. (2009). *Strategies for working with involuntary clients* (2nd ed.). New York: Columbia University Press.

Rose, C. (Producer). (2009, October 29). *The great mysteries of the human brain* [Television broadcast]. New York: Charlie Rose, Inc. Retrieved June 7, 2011, from www.charlierose.com/view/interview/10694.

Rosenbaum, P., & Rubin, D. (1983). The central role of the propensity score in observational studies for causal effects. *Biometrika, 70,* 41–55.

Rosenheck, R., Fontana, A., & Cottrol, C. (1995). Effect of clinician-veteran racial pairing in the treatment of posttraumatic stress disorder. *American Journal of Psychiatry, 152,* 555–563.

Roussos, S., & Fawcett, S. (2000). A review of collaborative partnerships as a strategy for improving community health. *Annual Review of Public Health, 21,* 369–402.

Russel, M. (1995). *Confronting abusive beliefs: Group treatment for abusive men.* Thousand Oaks, CA: Sage.

Sadusky, J., Martinson, R., Lizdas, K., & McGee, C. (2010). The Praxis safety and accountability audit: Practicing a "sociology for people." *Violence Against Women, 16,* 1031–1044.

Saketopoulou, A. (1999). The therapeutic alliance in psychodynamic psychotherapy: Theoretical conceptions and research findings. *Psychotherapy, 36,* 329–342.

Salazar, L., Emshoff, J., Baker, C., & Crowley, T. (2007). Examining the behavior of a system: An outcome evaluation of a coordinated community response to domestic violence. *Journal of Family Violence, 22,* 631–641.

Saltzman, L. (2004). Definitional and methodological issues related to trans-national research on intimate partner violence. *Violence Against Women, 10,* 812–830.

Sampson, R. (2008). Moving to inequality: Neighborhood effects and experiments meet social structure. *American Journal of Sociology, 114,* 189–231.

Sarre, R. (2001). Beyond "what works?" A 25-year jubilee retrospective of Robert Martinson. *Australian and New Zealand Journal of Criminology, 34*, 38–46.

Satel, S., & Forster, G. (1999). *Multicultural mental health: Does your skin color matter more than your mind?* Washington: Center for Equal Opportunity.

Saunders, D. (1988). Other "truths" about domestic violence: A reply to McNeely and Robinson-Simpson. *Social Work, 33*, 179–183.

Saunders, D. (1996). Feminist cognitive-behavioral and process psychodynamic treatments for men who batter: Interaction of traits and treatment models. *Violence and Victims, 11*, 393–414.

Saunders, D. (2002). Are physical assaults by wives and girlfriends a major social problem? A review of the literature. *Violence Against Women, 8*, 1424–1448.

Saunders, D. (2004). The place of a typology of men who are "maritally" violent within a nested ecological model: A response to Holtzworth-Munroe and Meehan. *Journal of Interpersonal Violence, 19*, 1390–1395.

Saunders, D. (2008). Group interventions for men who batter: A summary of program descriptions and research. *Violence and Victims, 23*, 156–172.

Schechter, S. (1982). *Women and male violence: The visions and struggles of the battered women's movement.* Boston: South End.

Schorr, L. (1997). *Common purpose: Strengthening families and neighborhoods to rebuild America.* New York: Doubleday.

Schorr, L. (2009, August 20). To judge what will best help society's neediest, let's use a broad array of evaluation techniques. *The Chronicle of Philanthropy.* Retrieved August 22, 2011, from http://philanthropy.com/article/To-Judge-What-Will-Best -Hel/57351/.

Schumacher, J., Feldbau-Kohn, S., Slep, A., & Heyman, R. (2001). Risk factors for male-to-female partner physical abuse. *Aggression and Violent Behavior, 6*, 281–352.

Schwartz, M. (2000). Methodological issues in the use of survey data for measuring and characterizing violence against women. *Violence Against Women, 6*, 815–838.

Schwartz, M., & Nogrady, C. (1996). Fraternity membership, rape myths, and sexual aggression on a college campus. *Violence Against Women, 2*, 148–162.

Scott, K., & Wolfe, D. (2003). Readiness to change as a predictor of outcome in batterer treatment. *Journal of Consulting and Clinical Psychology, 71*, 879–889.

Serran, G., & Firestone, P. (2004). Intimate partner homicide: A review of the male proprietariness and the self-defense theories. *Aggression and Violent Behavior, 9*, 1–15.

Shepard, M., & Pence, E. (Eds.). (1999). *Coordinating community responses to domestic violence: Lessons from Duluth and beyond.* Thousand Oaks, CA: Sage.

Sherman, L. (1992). *Policing domestic violence: Experiments and dilemmas.* New York: Free Press.

Sherman, L. (2009). Evidence and liberty: The promise of experimental criminology. *Criminology and Criminal Justice, 9*, 5–28.

Shin, S., Chow, C., Camacho-Gonsalves, T., Levy, R., Allen, I, & Leff, H. (2005). A meta-analytic review of racial-ethnic matching for African American and Caucasian American clients and clinicians. *Journal of Counseling Psychology, 52,* 45–56.

Shlonsky, A. & Gibbs, L. (2004). Will the real evidence-based practice please stand up? Teaching the process of evidence-based practice to the helping professions. *Brief Treatment and Crisis Intervention, 4,* 137–153.

Shwartz, M., Baker, G., Mulvey, K., & Plough, A. (1997). Improving publicly funded substance abuse treatment: The value of case management. *American Journal of Public Health, 87,* 1659–1664.

Siegal, H., Li, L., & Rapp, R. (2002). Case management as a therapeutic enhancement: Impact on post-treatment criminality. *Journal of Addictive Diseases, 21,* 37–46.

Sinclair, H. (1989). *Manalive accountable programs for violent men.* San Rafael, CA: Manalive Training Programs for Men.

Sinclair, H. (2002). A community activist response to intimate partner violence. Chapter 5 in E. Aldarondo & F. Mederos (Eds.), *Programs for men who batter: Intervention and prevention strategies in a diverse society.* Kingston, NJ: Civic Research Institute.

Singer, T., Darling, A., Jackson, J., & Gondolf, E. (1988). Continued debate: The truth about domestic violence [Letters to the editor]. *Social Work, 33,* 189–191.

Skeem, J. (2008, July 14–16). *Treating psychopathic individuals: A hopeless pursuit?* Keynote address presented at the annual conference of the International Association of Forensic Mental Health Services, Vienna.

Skeem, J., Monahan, J., & Mulvey, E. (2002). Psychopathy, treatment involvement, and subsequent violence among civil psychiatric patients. *Law and Human Behavior, 26,* 577–603.

Skeem, J., Plaschek, D., & Manchak, S. (2009). Rehabilitation of high risk offenders. In J. Skeem, K. Douglas, & S. Lilienfeld (Eds.), *Psychological science in the courtroom: Consensus and controversies* (pp. 358–386). New York: Guilford.

Slovic, P., Monahan, J., & MacGregor, D. (2000). Violence risk assessment and risk communication: The effects of using actual cases, providing instruction, and employing probability versus frequency formats. *Law and Human Behavior, 24,* 271–29.

Smedslund, G., Dalsbø, T., Steiro, A., Winsvold, A., & Clench-Aas, J. (2007). Cognitive behavioural therapy for men who physically abuse their female partner. *Cochrane Database of Systematic Reviews,* Issue 3, Article No. CD006048. Retrieved May 10, 2011, from www.cochranelibrary.com.

Smyth, K. (2010, January 11). Focusing on what works: Federal fund's approach makes a misstep. *The Chronicle of Philanthropy.* Retrieved May 8, 2011, from http://philanthropy.com/article/Focusing-on-What-Works-/63600/.

Smyth, K., Goodman, L., & Glenn, K. (2006). The full-frame approach: A new response to marginalized women left behind by specialized services. *American Journal of Orthopsychiatry, 76,* 489–502.

Smyth, K., & Schorr, L. (2009). *A lot to lose: A call to rethink what constitutes "evidence" in finding social interventions that work.* Cambridge, MA: Harvard University. Retrieved June 10, 2011, from www.hks.harvard.edu.

Sonkin, D. (1986). Clairvoyance vs. common sense: Therapists' duty to warn and protect. *Violence and Victims, 1,* 7–22.

Sonkin, D., & Durphy, M. (1997). *Learning to live without violence: A handbook for men.* Volcano, CA: Volcano.

Sonkin, D., & Dutton, D. (2003). Treating assaultive men from an attachment perspective. *Journal of Aggression, Maltreatment & Trauma, 7,* 105–133.

Spohn, C. (2008). Introduction to coordinated community response to intimate partner violence. *Criminology and Public Policy, 7,* 489–493.

Sprow, M. (2009, May–June). The probation experiment: Travis County department utilizes evidence-based best practices to reduce recidivism. *County 21,* 24–28. Retrieved May 20, 2011, from www.county.org/resources/library/county_mag/county/213/3.html.

Staiger, D., & Stock, J. (1997). Instrumental variables regression with weak instruments. *Econometrica, 65,* 557–586.

Stark, E. (2007). *Coercive control: How men entrap women in personal life.* New York: Oxford University Press.

Steinman, M. (1990). Lowering recidivism among men who batter women. *Journal of Police Science and Administration, 7,* 124–132.

Steinman, M. (1991). Coordinated criminal justice interventions and recidivism among batterers. In M. Steinman (Ed.), *Woman battering: Policy responses* (pp. 221–236). Cincinnati, OH: Anderson.

Stith, S., Rosen, K., McCollum, E., & Thomsen, C. (2004). Treating intimate partner violence within intact couple relationships: Outcomes of multi-couple versus individual couple therapy. *Journal of Marriage and the Family Therapy, 30,* 305–318.

Stosny, S. (1995). *Treating attachment abuse: A compassion approach.* New York: Springer.

Straus, M. (1979). Measuring intrafamily conflict and violence: The Conflict Tactics Scales. *Journal of Marriage and the Family, 41,* 75–88.

Straus, M. (1999). The controversy over domestic violence by women: A methodological, theoretical and sociology of science analysis. In X. Arriaga & S. Oskamp (Eds.), *Violence in intimate relationships* (pp. 17–44). Thousand Oaks, CA: Sage.

Straus, M. (2004). Prevalence of violence against dating partners by male and female university students. *Violence Against Women, 10,* 790–811.

Straus, M. (2010). Thirty years of denying the evidence on gender symmetry in partner violence: Implications for prevention and treatment. *Partner Abuse, 1,* 332–362.

Straus, M., Gelles, R., & Steinmetz, S. (1980). *Behind closed doors: Violence in the American family*. New York: Doubleday.

Stuart, E., & Campbell, J. (1989). Assessment of patterns of dangerousness with battered women. *Issues in Mental Health Nursing, 10*, 245–260.

Stuart, R. (2005). Treatment for partner abuse: Time for a paradigm shift. *Professional Psychology, 36*, 254–263.

Sue, S. (1998). In search of cultural competence in psychotherapy and counseling. *American Psychologist, 53*, 440–448.

Sue, S. (2003). In defense of cultural competency in psychotherapy and treatment. *American Psychologist, 58*, 964–970.

Sue, S., Chun, C., & Gee, K. (1995). Ethnic minority intervention and treatment research. In J. Aponte, R. Rivers, & J. Wohl (Eds.), *Psychological interventions and cultural diversity* (pp. 266–282). Boston: Allyn and Bacon.

Sue, S., Fujino, D., Hu, L., Takeuchi, D., & Zane, N. (1991). Community mental health services for ethnic minority groups: A test of the cultural responsiveness hypothesis. *Journal of Counseling Psychology, 59*, 533–540.

Sue, S., Zane, N., Hall, G., & Berger, L. (2009). The case for cultural competency in psychotherapeutic interventions. *Annual Review of Psychology, 60*, 525–548.

Sue, S., Zane, N., Levant, R., Silverstein, L., Brown, L., & Olkin, R. (2006). How well do both evidence-based practices and treatment as usual satisfactorily address the various dimensions of diversity? In J. Norcross, L. Beutler, & R. Levant (Eds.), *Evidence-based practices in mental health: Debate and dialogue on the fundamental questions* (pp. 329–374). Washington: American Psychological Association.

Sue, S., Zane, N., & Young, K. (1994). Research on psychotherapy with culturally diverse populations. In A. Bergin & S. Garfield (Eds.), *Handbook of psychotherapy and behavior change* (pp. 783–817). Hoboken, NJ: Wiley.

Sutton, S. (2001). Back to the drawing board? A review of applications of the transtheoretical model to substance use. *Addiction, 96*, 175–187.

Swan, S., &. Snow, D. (2006). The development of a theory of women's use of violence in intimate relationships. *Violence Against Women, 12*, 1026–1045.

Taft, C., Murphy, C., King, D., Musser, P., & DeDeyn, J. (2003). Process and treatment adherence factors in group cognitive-behavioral therapy for partner violent men. *Journal of Consulting and Clinical Psychology, 71*, 812–820.

Taft, C., Murphy, C., Musser, P., & Remington, N. (2004). Personality, interpersonal, and motivational predictors of the working alliance in group cognitive-behavioral therapy for partner violent men. *Journal of Consulting and Clinical Psychology, 72*, 349–354.

Thorn, G., & Sarata, B. (1998). Psychotherapy with African-American men: What we know and what we need to know. *Journal of Multicultural Counseling and Development, 26*, 240–254.

Thorne-Finch, R. (1992). *Ending the silence: The origins and treatment of male violence against women.* Toronto: University of Toronto Press.

Thyer, B. (2004). What is evidence-based practice? *Brief Treatment and Crisis Intervention, 4,* 167–176.

Tift, L. (1993). *Battering of women: The failure of intervention and the case for prevention.* Boulder, CO: Westview.

Tjaden, P., & Thoennes, N. (2000). *Full report of the prevalence, incidence and consequences of violence against women: Findings from the National Violence Against Women Survey* (NCJ 183781). Washington: National Institute of Justice. Retrieved June, 10, 2010, from www.ncjrs.gov/pdffiles1/nij/183781.pdf.

Tolman, R., & Bhosley, G. (1990). A comparison of two types of pregroup preparation for men who batter. *Journal of Social Service Research, 13,* 33–43.

Tolman, R., & Weisz, A. (1995). Coordinated community intervention for domestic violence: The effects of arrest and prosecution on recidivism of woman abuse perpetrators. *Crime and Delinquency, 4,* 481–495.

Trone, T (1999). *Calculating intimate danger: MOSAIC and the emerging practice of risk assessment.* New York: Vera Institute of Justice.

Turgeon, C. (2008). Bridging theory and practice: A roundtable on court responses to domestic violence. *Journal of Court Innovation, 1,* 345–370.

Turk, E., & Salovey, P. (Eds.). (1988). *Reasoning inference and judgment in clinical psychology.* New York: Free Press.

Vaillant, G. (1995). *The natural history of alcoholism revisited.* Cambridge: Harvard University Press.

Vijayendra, R., & Woolcock, M. (2003). Integrating qualitative and quantitative approaches in program evaluation. In F. Bourguignon & L. Pereira da Silva, (Eds.), *The impact of economic policies on poverty and income distribution: Evaluation techniques and tools* (pp. 165–189). Washington: World Bank and Oxford University Press.

Visher, C., Harrell, A., & Yahner, J. (2008). Reducing intimate partner violence: An evaluation of a comprehensive justice system–community collaboration. *Criminology and Public Policy, 7,* 495–523.

Visher, C., Newmark, L., & Harrell, A. (2006). *Final report on the evaluation of the Judicial Oversight Demonstration: Vol. 2. Findings and lessons on implementation.* Washington: Urban Institute.

Visher, C., Newmark, L., & Harrell, A. (2008). *The evaluation of the Judicial Oversight Demonstration: Findings and lessons on implementation.* Washington: National Institute of Justice. Retrieved May 10, 2011, from www.ojp.usdoj.gov/nij/pubs-sum/219077.htm.

Wahlund, K., & Kristiansson, M. (2009). Aggression, psychopathy, and brain imaging: Review and future recommendations. *International Journal of Law and Psychiatry, 32,* 266–271.

Walker, J., & Bright, J. (2009). False inflated self-esteem and violence: A systematic review and cognitive model. *Journal of Forensic Psychiatry and Psychology, 20,* 1–32.

Walker, L. (1979). *The battered woman.* New York: Harper and Row.

Walker, L. (1989). Psychology and violence against women. *American Psychologist, 44,* 695–702.

Waltz, J. (2003). Dialectical behavior therapy in the treatment of abusive behavior. *Journal of Aggression, Maltreatment, and Trauma, 7,* 75–104.

Watt, K. (2007). Understanding risk factors for intimate partner femicide: The role of domestic violence fatality review teams. In A. Baldry & F. Winkel (Eds.), *Intimate partner violence prevention and intervention: The risk assessment and management approach* (pp. 45-60). New York: Nova Science.

Watt, K., & Allen, N. (2008, July). *Domestic violence fatality review teams and the promotion of systems change.* Paper presented at the annual meeting of the International Association of Forensic Mental Health Services, Vienna.

Websdale, N. (1999). Domestic violence fatality reviews: From a culture of blame to a culture of safety. *Juvenile and Family Court Journal, 50* (2), 61–74.

Websdale, N. (2010). *Familicidal hearts: The emotional styles of 211 killers.* New York: Oxford University Press.

Weiner, M. (1990). *Human services management: Analyses and applications* (2nd ed.). Belmont, CA: Wadsworth.

Weinrach, S., & Thomas, K. (1997). Diversity-sensitive counseling today: A postmodern clash of values. *Journal of Counseling and Development, 76,* 115–122.

Weisburd, D., Lum, C., & Yang, S. (2003). When can we conclude that treatments or programs "don't work"? *Annals of the American Academy of Political and Social Science, 587,* 31–48.

Weisz, A., Tolman, R., & Saunders, D. (2000). Assessing the risk of severe domestic violence: The importance of survivors' predictions. *Journal of Interpersonal Violence, 15,* 75–90.

Wells, R., Ward, A., Feinberg, M., & Alexander, J. (2008). What motivates people to participate more in community-based coalitions? *American Journal of Community Psychology, 42,* 94–104.

West, M., & George, C. (1999). Abuse and violence in intimate adult relationships: New perspectives from attachment theory. *Attachment and Human Development, 1,* 137–156.

Westen, D., Stirman, S., & DeRubeis, R. (2006). Are research patients and clinical trials representative of clinical practice? In J. Norcross, L. Beutler, & R. Levant (Eds.), *Evidence-based practices in mental health: Debate and dialogue on the fundamental questions* (pp. 161–189). Washington: American Psychological Association.

Wexler, D. (2006). *STOP domestic violence: Innovative skills, techniques, options, and plans for better relationships; Group leader's manual.* New York: Norton.

Wexler, D. (2009). *Men in therapy: New approaches for effective treatment.* New York: Norton.

Wexler, D. (2010). The secret world of men: Shame-o-phobia. *Psychotherapy Networker, 34* (3), 20–25.

White, R., & Gondolf, E. (2000). Implications of personality profiles for batterer treatment: Support for the gender-based, cognitive-behavioral approach. *Journal of Interpersonal Violence, 15*, 467–488.

Wierzbicki, M., & Pekarik, G. (1993). A meta-analysis of psychotherapy dropout. *Professional Psychology, 24*, 190–195.

Williams, K., & Houghton, A. (2004). Assessing the risk of domestic violence re-offending: A validation study. *Law and Human Behavior, 28*, 437–455.

Williams, L. (2004). Researcher-advocate collaborations to end violence against women. *Journal of Interpersonal Violence, 19*, 1350–1357.

Williams, O. (1994). Group work with African-American men who batter: Toward more ethnically-sensitive practice. *Journal of Comparative Family Studies, 25*, 91–103.

Williams, O. (1995). Treatment for African-American men who batter. *CURA Reporter: Bulletin of the Center for Urban and Regional Affairs, 25*(3), 12–16.

Williams, O. (1998). Healing and confronting the African American male who batters. In R. Carrillo & J. Tello (Eds.), *Family violence and men of color: Healing the wounded male spirit* (pp. 74–94). New York: Springer.

Williams, O. (1999). Working in groups with African-American men who batter. In L. Davis (Ed.), *Working with African-American men: A guide to practice* (pp. 229–242). Thousand Oaks, CA: Sage.

Williams, O., & Becker, L. (1994). Domestic partner abuse treatment programs and cultural competence: The results of a national study. *Violence and Victims, 8*, 287–296.

Williams, O., & Donnelly, D. (1997). *Batterer counseling curriculum for African American men: Facilitators manual.* Unpublished manual available from the Institute on Domestic Violence in the African American Community, Minneapolis.

Wilson, D., Bouffard, L., & MacKenzie, D. (2005). A quantitative review of structured group-oriented, cognitive-behavioral programs for offenders. *Criminal Justice and Behavior, 32*, 172–204.

Wilson, D., Mitchell, O., & MacKenzie, D. (2006). A systematic review of drug court effects on recidivism. *Journal of Experimental Criminology, 2*, 459–487.

Wilson, J., & Websdale, N. (2006). Domestic violence fatality review teams: An interprofessional model to reduce deaths. *Journal of Interprofessional Care, 20*, 535–544.

Wilson, M., & Daley, M. (1996). Male sexual proprietariness and violence against wives. *Current Directions in Psychological Science, 5*, 2–7.

Wisniewski, S., Rush, J., Nierenberg, A., Gaynes, B., Warden, D., Luther, J., et al. (2009). Can Phase II trial results of antidepressant medications be generalized to clinical practice? A STAR*D report. *American Journal of Psychiatry, 166*, 599–607.

Woolcock, M. (2009). *Towards a plurality of methods in project evaluation: A contextualized approach to understanding impact trajectories and efficacy* (BWPI Working Paper 73). Manchester, UK: Brooks World Poverty Institute, University of Manchester. Retrieved August 22, 2010, from www.bwpi.manchester.ac.uk/resources/Working-Papers/bwpi-wp-7309.pdf.

Worden, A. (2000). *Violence against women: Synthesis of research for judges* (Document No. 199911). Report submitted to the National Institute of Justice, Washington. Retrieved May 9, 2011, from www.ncjrs.gov/pdffiles1/nij/grants/199911.pdf.

Xiong, C. (2010, April 1). St. Paul has new blueprint for tackling domestic abuse. *Star Tribune.* Retrieved December 12, 2010, from www.startribune.com.

Yeung, B. (2010, May–June). New conditions of probation. *Miller-McCune,* 28–31. Retrieved June 9, 2011, from www.miller-mccune.com/legal-affairs/new-conditions-of-probation-11435/.

Zaza, S., Wright-DeAguero, L., Briss, P., Truman, B., Hopkins, D., Hennessy, M., et al. (2000). Data collection instrument and procedure for systematic reviews in the "Guide to Community Preventive Services." *American Journal of Preventive Medicine, 18,* 44–74.

Zeki, S., & Goodenough, O. (Eds.). (2006). *Law and the brain.* New York: Oxford University Press.

Zorza, J. (2011). The new domestic violence typologies: An accurate reconceptualization or another trivialization? *Family and Intimate Partner Quarterly, 3,* 225–236.

Index

to, 152–60, 163; future of, 136–38; implications of, 162–64; and motivational interviewing, 141–47, 162–63; and new psychology, 128–31; overview, 127–28; popularity vs. research results, 164–66; research evidence on, 132–33; and specialized treatment, 134–36; typologies of, 5, 131–38, 237

Cattaneo, Lauren, 185

Center for Court Innovation, 46, 72, 219

Centers for Disease Control and Prevention (CDC), 63, 211, 229

Challenger explosion, 199–200

change: capacity to, 115; readiness to (*see* readiness to change); stages of, 138–41, 237

childhood trauma, 96, 100–101, 108

children and domestic violence, 27

chronically violent men, 6, 48. *See also* high-risk men

clinical psychology, 123, 233

clinical trials, 32, 39

Cochrane Collaboration, 63, 114

code of honor, 107

coerced treatment, 2

coercion of women, 75, 184–86

cognitive-behavioral treatment: and accountability, 75; advantages of, 111–13; application to violence, 105–6; and attachment theory, 96–97, 98–99; continued wide use of, 108–9; vs. couples counseling, 149; criticism of, 108–9; defined, 23, 106; Duluth Batterer Program, 113–22; vs. new psychology, 91–95; vs. psychodynamic treatment, 85–87, 124–26; research findings, 109–11

cognitive restructuring, 106

cognitive schema, 105

cognitive transformation, 74

Cohen, Dov, 107–8

Cohen, Jacob, 63

collaboration between researchers and practitioners, 34, 241

colorblind approaches, 153

combat veterans, 91, 240

communicating risk, 184

community-accountability model, 73

community impact study, 211–12

community organizing, 117

compassion workshops, 86, 97

competing interests in evidence-based practice, 41–42

competition among programs, 28–29

Complementary and Alternative Medicine Specialized Research Center, 32–33

compliance, 9, 28, 53–55, 60, 104, 138, 143, 146–47, 213

compliance monitoring, 65, 69, 197, 206–8, 222–23, 229, 231, 237–38

Conflict Tactics Scale, 22–23, 49, 75, 79

confrontation, 119–20

consciousness-raising programs, 86

consequences, 15, 24–25, 35, 38, 48, 117, 173, 177, 192, 214, 220. *See also* accountability; sanctions for noncompliance

constellation of abuse, 23

context: impact on experimental designs, 55; impact on experimental designs and evaluation, 54–57; impact on subject selection, 40–41; importance of, 38–41; research findings vs. real world, 35–43

control, men's need for, 21, 105–6, 115

coordinated community response: accountability and safety audits, 226–28; approaches to, 186–91; beginnings of, 204–5; big-picture approach, 233–34; building of, 223–28; California evaluation study, 207–8; challenges of, 228–34; Chicago multisite study, 206–7; community impact study, 211–12; conclusions, 238; contextual considerations, 55–57; and domestic violence councils, 224–26; emerging systems, 203–4; implementation problems, 230–31; Judicial Oversight Demonstration project, 212–18; and multilevel treatment, 187–88; multisite intervention systems evaluation, 208–11; need and desire for, 228–29; neglected

dropping out: among minority races, 152; and batterer intervention, 70; and batterer typology, 132–34; California audit of probation departments, 220; and motivational interviewing, 142; and new psychology, 92–93, 104, 125; and risk assessment, 170, 180, 196; and stages of change, 162. *See also* noncompliance

drug-court model, 55, 104, 210

Duluth Batterer Program, 113–22; and anger treatment, 120–21; and attachment theory, 96; cognitive-behavioral treatment approach of, 85–86; and community organizing, 117; conclusions, 236; and confrontation, 119–20; and coordinated community response, 234; criticism of, 118; dialogical format, 115–16; fundamental concepts of, 114–16; gender debate on, 118–19; and masculine paradox, 89; and motivational interviewing, 141, 144–45; and new psychology, 94; overview, 113–14; Power and Control Wheel, 114–15; and shame, 119–20; supportive research on, 121–22; systems approach to program evaluations, 57; women-centered focus of, 116–17

Duluth Power and Control Wheel, 114–15, 187

Dutton, Donald, 19, 92, 96–97, 99

Dutton, Mary Ann, 75

DVI (Domestic Violence Inventory), 157, 176

DV-MOSAIC, 179

DVSI (Domestic Violence Screening Inventory), 172, 179

dysphoric/borderline batterers, 131, 161

dysphoric tendencies, 48

Eckhardt, Chris, 134

Edleson, Jeffrey, 78, 205

effectiveness of batterer programs. *See* batterer programs, effectiveness of

effect sizes, 61–64

Emerge, 86, 89, 93, 234

empathic dialogue, 141–47

empowerment, victim, 149, 184–85, 193

endogenous variables, 65

entitlement, 16, 89–90, 117, 122

Equality Wheel, 115

equations, 65

error terms, 65

ethics, 26, 35, 190, 200

ethnicity. *See* culturally oriented approaches; *specific ethnicities*

evidence-based answers on batterer programs, 124–26

evidence-based claims, 46–47

evidence-based practice: bias, effect of, 42–43; and categorization of batterers, 164; competing interests in, 41–42; conclusions, 235–36; and couples counseling, 148; future directions of, 239; implicit hierarchy in, 33–34; integrating research and practice, 43–45; medical, 40–41, 43–44; misuses of, 33–35; neglect of other knowledge, 34–35; new criteria for supporting, 31–33; overview, 4; political influences in, 39–40; practitioner perspective, 37–38, 43–44; program circumstances, 38–39; program context, 38–41; research findings vs. real-world context, 35–43; structural integration in, 44–45; subject selection, impact of context on, 40–41; translating research into practice, 35–37

evolutionary view of batterer programs, 20

excuses, 24, 111, 146, 162

exogenous variables, 65, 67

experimental evaluations, 50–61

external validity, 38

"family conflict" in domestic violence (faction), 42

family counseling, 49

family-only batterers, 131, 134, 136

family violence, 76, 149, 156, 215

fathers, absent and overbearing, 89

fathers' rights groups, 42

fear of intimacy, 89

jail: cost-effectiveness of, 80, 233; as court-imposed sanction, 2, 7, 219–20; and culturally oriented approaches, 163; effectiveness of, 15, 48; and evidence-based practice, 239; and JOD project, 214, 216; and LSI-R, 177; and multisite evaluation of intervention systems, 208, 210; overcrowding of, 114; and probation case management, 188; and risk assessment, 171, 173; as safety measure, 117; and systems management, 224

JOD (Judicial Oversight Demonstration) project, 57, 80, 212–18, 223, 230
Johnson, Michael, 118, 136
Jones, Allison Snow, 68, 180
judgment-based practice, 37–38
judicial oversight, 9, 54, 204, 210–11, 213
Judicial Oversight Demonstration (JOD) project, 57, 80, 212–18, 223, 230
"just say 'no'" campaign, 73

Kellner, Hansfield, 33
Kesner, John, 98
Kingston Screening Instrument for Domestic Violence (K-SID), 176
Kistenmacher, Barbara, 143
Kropp, Randall, 172, 184

Latessa, Edward, 112
Latinos, 15, 19, 128, 152
legal decision making, 103
Lethality Checklist, 3–4, 176
Level of Service Inventory—Revised (LSI-R), 176–77
Loza, Wagdy, 120
Loza-Fanous, Amel, 120

macro responses to social problems, 73
male culture, 106–8
male socialization, 106–8
Manalive, 86
manhood, 106–8
Manjoo, Farhad, 42–43
manuals of procedures, 36, 86

marginalized women, 201
marital rape, 27
Martinson, Robert, 74
Maryland batterer program, 140
Maryland evaluation study, 205
masculine paradox, 89–91
masculinity, psychology of, 89–91
MATCH, 135–36
Maton, Kenneth, 205
Maxwell, Chris, 215
MCMI (Millon Clinical Multiaxial Inventory), 99, 103, 110, 132, 134
Mederos, Fernando, 19–20, 151
medical evidence-based practice, 40–41
medical treatment of domestic violence, 102–3
medications, clinical trials for, 39
Meehan, Jeffrey, 131–32, 137
men as victims, 91, 93, 106, 163
Mending the Sacred Hoop, 122
Menergy, 93
men's movement, 89
Men Stopping Violence, 73, 86, 234
mental health issues: and attachment, 98; and compliance, 104; and coordinated community response, 6; as cop-out, 111; and Duluth Batterer Program, 114, 121; and evidence-based practice, 31, 35–36, 43; as focus of batterer programs, 17, 19–22, 49; multilevel treatment of, 187; and multisite evaluation of intervention systems, 208; and new psychology, 124; screening for, 94
mental health treatment, 47, 59–61, 104, 126, 154–55, 208, 220–24, 231
meta-analysis, 61–64, 66
Mickelson, Phil, 91
Millon Clinical Multiaxial Inventory. See MCMI (Millon Clinical Multiaxial Inventory)
Minneapolis police study, 36, 41
Minnesota study, 205
minority batterers, 15, 19, 61, 128, 152–60, 237
mismatching of counselors, 155
misogyny, 21

MOSAIC, 176, 179
mothers, overbearing, 90
motivational counseling, 191
motivational enhancement therapy, 142
motivational interviewing, 141–47, 162–63
Mulholland, Ciaran, 100
multifactor view of treatment, 92
multilevel treatment, 187–88
multisite intervention systems evaluation, 208–11
multisite studies, 56–57
murder, 107, 181–83
Murphy, Chris, 77, 143, 205
Muskie School of Public Service, University of Southern Maine, 80
Musser, Peter, 205
mutual combat, 22–23

narcissistic tendencies, 48, 90, 95, 110, 113, 119, 122, 147, 162
narrative therapy programs, 86
National Academy of Sciences, 50, 101
National Aeronautics and Space Administration (NASA), 200
National Family Violence Survey, 22, 36
National Institute of Justice (NIJ), 52, 54, 79, 212, 218, 242
National Institute on Alcohol Abuse and Alcoholism, 135
national survey of court actions, 219
National Survey of Family Violence, 76
Native Americans, 122, 152
neuroscience, 100–105
New Jersey program, 151–52
new psychology of batterers, 5–6, 87–88, 91–95, 122–26, 128–31
NIJ. See National Institute of Justice (NIJ)
Nisbet, Richard, 107–8
"no drop" prosecution policies, 224
noncompliance, 24–25, 60, 117, 186, 194, 209–10, 222, 228, 230–31. See also dropping out; sanctions for noncompliance
nondominant cultures. See minority batterers

Obama, Barack, 32
old psychology, 89
"one size fits all" approach, 16, 109, 127
"one size fits most" approach, 6, 121–22, 127, 165
Ontario Domestic Assault Risk Assessment (ODARA), 172, 176
open-ended interviews, 56
open probation, 23–24
overbearing fathers, 89
overbearing mothers, 90
overcontrolled murderers, 183
overhaul view of batterer programs, 19–20
overrides of random assignments, 67
overspecialization of services, 201

paradigm shifts, 94
parenting skills, 240
past violence, 120, 133, 161, 177
patient-treatment matching, 134–36
patriarchal structure of society, 34, 89–90
PCL (Psychopathy Check List), 177
Peele, Staunton, 100–105
Pence, Ellen, 114–15, 117, 122, 227
personality disorders, 96, 110
Peterson, Richard, 214–15
Pittsburgh evaluation study, 69, 104, 157–59, 165, 208–10, 223–24
political correctness, 155, 239
political influences, 8, 39–40, 42, 123, 200, 226
Portland, Oregon experiment, 58
positive thinking, 108
positivists, 34, 41–42, 72–73, 77–78
possessiveness, 183
power, men's need for, 21, 105–6
Power and Control Wheel, 114–15, 187
practice standards for risk assessment, 184
practitioner-led evaluations, 81
practitioners' perspective, 37–38, 43–44
practitioners' response to research, 78–81
Praxis International, 227
precontemplation scale, 141
prevention vs. intervention, 72–73, 240

privilege, 89–90, 92, 115, 117

probation, as alternative to "don't work" programs, 47–50

probation case management, 188–89

probation departments, California audit of, 219–20

pro-feminist programs, 85

professional discretion, 183–84

professionalization, 26, 123

program evaluations, 61–64

Project MATCH, 135–36

propensity score analysis, 65–66, 71–72

proprietariness, 183

psychodynamic treatment, 85–89, 96–98, 110–12, 124–26, 128–31, 134–36, 158, 160–61, 236–37

psychology of masculinity, 89–91

Psychopathy Check List (PCL), 177

punishment vs. therapy, 2, 25–26

pure science, 42

quality control, 28, 111, 118, 240

quasi-experimental studies, 211–18, 229

race. See culturally oriented approaches; specific races

Racial Identity Attitude Scale, 158

Ramey, Heather, 36, 43

randomized clinical trials, 32, 67

rape, 27, 89

rapport, 25, 142, 164–65, 178, 190

rational choice theory, 22, 105

RAVE (Risk Assessment Validation Experiment), 179

Reaching Out About Depression (ROAD), 201

readiness tests, 139

readiness to change, 5, 48, 138–40, 143–46, 164

re-arrest, 99, 132, 134, 140, 152, 157–58, 187–88, 206–7, 211, 230

re-assault, 69–70, 133–35, 150, 157–58, 172–73, 179–80, 185, 192, 206, 209–10

recidivism: and anger management, 120;

and batterer typology, 132; and coordinated community response, 204, 229; and couples counseling, 149; and domestic violence councils, 233; and judicial intervention, 215; in meta-analysis studies, 62; and probation case management, 189; and program completion, 207; and risk assessment, 172, 185, 192, 196; and "what works" approach, 74–75

referrals to batterer programs, 31

regression analysis, 185

rehabilitation, 13, 25, 74–75, 101, 121, 123, 239

researcher-practitioner collaboration, 34, 241

research findings: interpretation of, 43; vs. real-world context, 35–43; translating into practice, 35–37

resistance to treatment, 104, 112, 141, 143, 147, 162, 222

resources, shortage of, 29–31

Respect Agency, UK, 81

retaliation, 27, 147, 169, 174, 177, 224

risk assessment, 169–97; actuarial instruments for, 175–76; administrative challenges, 177–78; by battered women, 184–86; coordinated community response to, 186–91; and domestic homicide, 181–83; emergence of, 171–73; implications for batterer programs, 194–97; improving, 193–94; instruments for and approaches to, 175–85; and multilevel treatment, 187–88; need for, 191–92; overview, 169–70; practical concerns about, 173–75; and probation case management, 188–89; as process, 183–86; and professional discretion, 183–84; research on, 178–81; and risk management, 189–91; and structured judgment, 175–76; wise use of, 191–97; women's safety and, 3–4, 24. See also high-risk men

Risk Assessment Validation Experiment (RAVE), 179

risk management, 184, 189–91, 194. See also risk assessment

ROAD (Reaching Out About Depression), 201

safety concerns, 20; and cognitive-behavioral treatment, 112–13; and couples counseling, 151; feminist views on, 20–22; as guideposts to treatment, 23–24; and scarcity of resources, 29–30
safety planning, 190–91
Salazar, Laura, 205
sanctions for noncompliance, 2–3, 15, 38, 55–57, 146–47, 203, 213–14, 219–20, 231, 241. *See also* noncompliance
San Diego Navy Experiment, 51, 67, 148, 150
SARA (Spouse Abuse Risk Assessment), 172, 176, 186, 195
Saunders, Dan, 76, 78, 135
Schock, Michael, 205
Schorr, Lisabeth, 202, 229
science, pure vs. applied, 42
Scott, Katreena, 140
selection bias, 66, 68
Service, Training, Officers, and Prosecution (STOP), 204, 224
service delivery, 26–27
severely violent men, 109, 132, 170, 180, 183. *See also* high-risk men
sexism, 127
sexual abuse, 240
sexuality, 27
shame, 119–20, 183
shelters, women's, 198–99
situational couples violence, 76
skill-building programs, 86
Smedslund, Geir, 63
Smith, Jeffrey, 66
Smyth, Katya Fels, 202, 229
social change, 26–27
socialization model of behavior, 21–22
social learning theory, 21–22, 89
social workers, 123
solution-oriented programs, 86
Sonkin, Dan, 97
specialized treatment, 134–36, 201

special populations, 36
Spouse Abuse Risk Assessment (SARA), 172, 176, 186, 195
stage-based counseling, 169, 191
standards of care, 27–29, 31, 45, 240
standards of practice for risk assessment, 184
Stark, Evan, 75
State-Trait Anger Expression Inventory, 120
statistical modeling, 65–71
Stith, Sandra, 151
STOP (Service, Training, Officers, and Prosecution), 204, 224
Stosny, Steve, 97
St. Paul Blueprint for Safety, 227–28, 232
street-level bureaucracy, 227
strengths-based programs, 86
structural integration, 44–45
structured professional judgment, 175–76, 192
structured ratings, 192
Stuart, Ellen, 185
subject-inclusion criteria, 40–41
supervision, intensified, 74–75
swift and certain response, 210–11, 217, 224
systematic reviews of evaluation research, 72–78
system audits, 57
system management, 223–24
systems approaches, 198–204; to complex problems, 199–200; coordinated community response examples, 201–3; emergence and evaluation of, 203–4; failures with battered women, 198–99; and high-risk men, 238
systems coordinators, 222–23

tactics of batterers, 75–76
tailored treatments. *See* specialized treatment
target hardening, 191
terrorism prevention, 39
Texas court study, 140, 231
Ting, Laura, 77, 143